INTRODUCING CRITICISM
IN THE 21st CENTURY

WITHDRAWN

INTRODUCING CRITICISM IN THE 21st CENTURY

Second edition

Edited by Julian Wolfreys

EDINBURGH
University Press

Edinburgh University Press Ltd
The Tun – Holyrood Road
12(2f) Jackson's Entry
Edinburgh EH8 8PJ

www.euppublishing.com

First published as *Introducing Criticism at the 21st Century* by Edinburgh University Press in 2002.

Typeset in 10/12.5pt Sabon by
Servis Filmsetting Ltd, Stockport, Cheshire,
and printed and bound in Great Britain by
CPI Group (UK) Ltd, Croydon CR0 4YY

A CIP record for this book is available from the British Library

ISBN 978 0 7486 9529 4 (paperback)
ISBN 978 0 7486 9530 0 (webready PDF)
ISBN 978 0 7486 9531 7 (epub)

CONTENTS

Space, Place and Memory

INTRODUCTION: DEVELOPMENTS, DEBATES, DEPARTURES, DIFFERENCES, DIRECTIONS

Julian Wolfreys

INTRODUCTION? WHAT INTRODUCTION?

When the present volume was first published, at the beginning of the present century, the question of critical voices and areas of interest understood as belonging to this century appeared somewhat presumptive. Thus it seemed to me necessary to frame the work at hand, to suspend it before it got underway with a little caution and some reflexive interrogation, thus:

Any volume announcing itself as 'introducing criticism at the twenty-first century', whether directly or indirectly, immediately falls foul of its own, perhaps hubristic, project. After all, in the most basic sense the century in question can hardly be said in purely chronological terms to have got underway, let alone be near its conclusion (there might be philosophical arguments otherwise, but I cannot address those here, as interesting as these might be). The implications of a volume such as this would appear, therefore, to generate certain questions: Can the shape of criticism to come be predicted? Who would be so foolhardy? Does not the act of prediction suppose the eventual arrival of a particular form? Will there be criticism, either as such, or as we know it? Will there be universities and institutions of higher education in one hundred years' time? If there are, will there still be Departments of English and Cultural Studies or, more generally, studies in what we call the humanities? As much as such questions might sound like idle sophistry, there are very real concerns behind them. Even a cursory knowledge of the history of the development of literary studies, studies having to do with vernacular rather than 'classical' literature, will indicate a life of just over one hundred years, with cultural studies being much younger.

Though it is now 2015, it remains the case that the century is still 'young'. Indeed, a decade and a half in, it would still appear an entirely valid exercise to ask what critical discourses are currently in vogue, which seem to have an immediate or recent pertinence, which critical interests have been maintained and are still going strong. Equally, there might be a case for a volume that explores which critical approaches no longer curry favour in institutions of higher education, perhaps, to phrase this somewhat baldly, since the introduction in the UK of student fees. That would be a very different volume, and one not a little polemical at that, as polemical as it is urgently needed. But then, even polemic has a limited shelf life, while business as usual is maintained in one manner or another. For some departments, schools, or 'teams', history seems over in that an avowedly historicist, contextualist and sociological approach is dominant. In others, there is still a return to what are taken to be 'first' principles of critical thinking, where critical thinking is defined with reference to a certain Francophone interruption in literary studies some time in the late 1950s and early 1960s.

It has to be remarked, then, from the outset or, if at all possible, slightly earlier, that *Introducing Criticism at the 21st Century* still does not endeavour to be predictive. The present collection of essays does not attempt any form of proleptic gesture, even if the title has shifted a little, to *Introducing Criticism in the 21st Century*, in this, the second edition of the volume. In fact, the reverse is the case, each of the essays here being in some measure, if not retrospective exactly (they are not in any straightforward sense surveys of 'where we are', or 'how we got to be here'), then *interruptive*: the various chapters of the present volume situate themselves within current aspects of critical discourse, gathering the discourses which come to inform the positions and interests under discussion as so many incisions or, to think this another way, intensities – instants of a provisional gathering of flows and forces. At the same time, each of the essays presents to the reader an introduction that prepares the way for a 'new' critical thinking: not a thought that has never been had so much as a new way of approaching the matter of thinking critically, of introducing new perspectives, and so making new perceptions from within particular conventions of critical discourse. Each essay addresses the fluidity of various 'states of criticism' at the beginning of the century, taking into account how the different, yet occasionally overlapping critical discourses have come to assume their present identities. At the same time, however, of the fourteen essays presented here, not one is content simply to offer a disinterested survey. These are not, to use the language of speech-act theorists, extended constative utterances. Having something of the performative about them, they not only traverse their respective fields, they also transform. And more than this, they not only engage in discrete ways with the particular critical 'lines of flight' that come to inform their own singular articulations, they also overflow any arbitrarily imposed boundaries of a particular field of interest, in many cases touching upon, implicitly or otherwise, more directly addressing concerns and issues raised by other essays in this volume.

INTRODUCING INTRODUCTIONS

Consider the following definitions of 'introduction', taken from the *Oxford English Dictionary*:

1. a. The action of introducing; a leading or bringing in; a bringing into use or practice, bringing in in speech or writing, insertion, etc.
   b. Something introduced; a practice or thing newly brought in, etc.
   c. An inference. *Obs. rare.*
2. The action or process of leading to or preparing the way for something; that which leads on to some result; a preliminary or initiatory step or stage. *Obs.*
3. Initiation in the knowledge of a subject; instruction in rudiments, elementary teaching. *Obs.*
4. That which leads to the knowledge or understanding of something,
   a. In early use, that which initiates in a subject, a first lesson; in *pl.*, rudiments, elements (*obs.*).
   b. A preliminary explanation prefixed to or included in a book or other writing; the part of a book which leads up to the subject treated, or explains the author's design or purpose. Also, the corresponding part of a speech, lecture, etc.
   c. A text-book or treatise intended as a manual for beginners, or explaining the elementary principles of a subject.
   d. A course of study preliminary and preparatory to some special study; matter introductory to the special study of some subject, e.g. of a book or document of the Bible.
5. a. The action of introducing or making known personally; *esp.* the formal presentation of one person to another, or of persons to each other, with communication of names, titles, etc.
   c. The process of becoming acquainted, or that makes one acquainted, with a thing.
6. *Mus.* A preparatory passage or movement at the beginning of a piece of music.

There is, clearly, more than one 'introduction'. Each introduces 'introduction' differently. Every definition differs from every other in that, introducing nothing so much as its own orientation to introduction, it shifts the reader's perception concerning the nature of introduction conventionally understood. One is oriented in thought to a different thinking on the subject of introduction. We appear to have a family of introductions, allowing for the moment the figure of the family as the appropriate collective noun for introductions, while still allowing for the fact that difference, as much as any resemblance, is vital in the production of any identity or meaning. Each shares elements in common, while some are more familiar than others; certain of these definitions alert us to a fall into disuse. In what ways do these determinations of the notion of introduction and the introductory apply to *Introducing Criticism in the 21st Century*? In what manner, if at all, are they 'appropriate'? Can they be appropriated, is it proper to do so? Or is it improper to assume that an 'introduction' can ever truly be so, whether in some propaedeutic or apodictic fashion?

There are six principal definitions for introduction, and, in each of these, further subdivisions for the purpose of determination. Introduction is introduced, but never simply for the first time. There is something excessive at work in the very idea of the introductory, so much so in fact that the dictionary feels the need to keep reintroducing it, as though it somehow knew that the very work of introduction will always and in some fashion overflow its own boundaries, that it will disseminate itself in excess of the very contours assumed for the so-called concept that goes by the name of introduction. Introduction exceeds its parameters in the very act of speaking of itself. Despite the desire to remain constant in its constative constitution – there's that speech-act theory creeping in again – there appears to be some kind of disruptive performative at work here. Every time introduction is introduced, something different, some sign of difference incommensurable with or irreducible to the confines of the introductory, takes place in the very gesture of preamble or overture. This, I would contend, is precisely what takes place, again and again, in each of the chapters presented here. Each chapter is supposedly 'introductory' in its own right, and yet each disrupts the introductory in its critical interventions, its epistemological interests. In doing so, the propaedeutic function of the 'introduction' is left in ruins.

Or, rather, say that criticism which is transformative does not so much point out, desire or attempt to bring about the ruination of any pedagogical work grounded in the belief of preliminary work, often, in the case of criticism, having to do with methods or theories which, once learnt, can then be put into practice; instead, the kind of criticism envisioned in this volume makes it possible to understand how the imperative towards knowing the fundamentals that is implied in both the general conceptualization of 'introduction' and in the specific institutional drive to separate the introductory from the supposedly more 'advanced' work is always, in its very processes, already in ruins. Like the phenomenon which becomes available to our view through a consideration of the nature of multiple definitions concerning 'introduction', *Introducing Criticism in the 21st Century* stresses the impossibility of any simple introduction; it keeps 'introducing' and, in doing so, keeps on exceeding introduction, recognizing as it does that the notion of introduction is fallacious, to the extent that no entry onto a subject can ever be *for the first time*. No beginning gesture ever takes place which does not imply or otherwise orientate itself with regard to other forms of knowledge. Even a 'rudimentary teaching' operates through the possibility of relation and orientation, the principle being that something new can be shown only because the 'new' can be explained with reference to something not new. Every introduction fails, therefore, inasmuch as it is impossible to state first principles, and this failure is the sign not so much of what is lacking as it is of that excess within the introductory of which I have already spoken.

Some critics, these days happily very few, remain suspicious of so-called theoretical approaches to literature. It hardly needs saying though that there is no act of reading that is not, in some manner, informed by ideas, thoughts, concepts. The bad reader is always theoretical inasmuch as she is not reading per se but is looking for signs to confirm the object of a search and affirm in turn her own identity. But good reading takes place or has the possibility of taking place regardless of the epistemological or interdisciplinary framework within which it orients itself, and from within which it gets underway. All good reading should be critical; not suspicious of its subject, but engaged and responsible. No reading can ever truly be called such unless it manifests both an openness to that which is to be read and a respect for the singularity of that other. At the same time, it has to be said that, coming to terms with openness and obligation, reading also has to recognize its own role as being defined through continual reorientation and readjustment of its procedures, without allowing those procedures to ossify into protocols, mere programmed excuses for limiting the act of reading, or, worse still, not reading at all and avoiding reading in the name of methodology, ideology or institutionalized demand. In the end, as the chapters in this collection demonstrate, all criticism comes down to reading. But that 'in the end' is no ending at all, only the endless demand placed on reading. There can be no introduction to reading, but all reading can do is to reintroduce itself to the ways in which reading must take place, if it is to take place at all. If *Introducing Criticism in the 21st Century* can be said to introduce anything at all (and even now, at the end of this intro-duction, I remain uncertain as to what to think about this), it is to introduce the ends of criticism as the beginning – again – of reading. If this, perhaps, somewhat utopian hope of, desire for, a reading-to-come was significant at the beginning of the twenty-first century, it remains as important, if not more so, now. Good reading is an activism. It does not look on idly, but engages and participates in the world, and in the myriad texts that are the only access for the human subject to whatever it is we think we mean when we talk of 'world'.

THE POETICS AND POLITICS OF IDENTITY

THE WRITINGS OF INTIMACY: THEORIES OF AFFECT, EMOTION AND RELATIONALITY

Jennifer Cooke

Literature has long had intimate registers: the self-disclosures of autobiography, the personal nature of letters and diaries, the longings of love poetry and the mourning of elegies are all established elements of the literary canon. Our intimate relations have been repeatedly dramatized in fictions, plays and poetry, and, as society has become more frank about its sexual intimacies, so too has literature. The shifts which took place in twentieth-century Anglo-American and European discourses about sexuality and our intimate states have stemmed from factors including Sigmund Freud's psychoanalytic writings, which treated sexuality and desire as central to subjectivity; the rise of feminism, with its open discussions of marital unhappiness and new relational possibilities; the gradual relaxing of obscenity laws; the invention of the contraceptive pill; and the changes of laws banning homosexuality. The theoretical and critical discourses of feminism and queer theory were – and still remain – important for bringing discussions of intimacy to the fore, but as the twentieth century turned into the twenty-first, a new body of thinking which has sought to examine our affects and our emotions has come to take a central role in the discussion of intimacy. In the following, I will outline this new theoretical domain and discuss how it has shifted discussions of emotions from the simply private to the complexly social and public realms. I will take the specific example of shame, before examining how our intimate relationalities have become a key feature of twenty-first-century thinking on intimacy. Finally, I will end by bringing this discussion back to thinking about the literary dimension of such intimate writing.

THE 'AFFECTIVE TURN'

Beginning in the 1990s, the new 'affective turn' or 'turn to affect', as it has been alternately named, marked a fresh direction in theory and criticism, one which has been taken up across various disciplines, including by those in English departments. The affective turn is generally perceived to have occurred as a reaction to a previous collection of theories, including structuralism and the theories of poststructuralism and deconstruction which followed it; these three, along with the philosophical ideas of Bertrand Russell and Ludwig Wittgenstein, are often grouped under the moniker 'the linguistic turn'. All brushstroke terms, like these 'turns' intending to capture the paradigm shifts of theory, risk being reductive and potentially misleading: to group deconstruction under the linguistic turn, for instance, is to ignore how Jacques Derrida saw his deconstructive project as a challenge to the linguistic turn inaugurated by structuralism (Derrida quoted in Royle 2003: 62). With similar imprecision, the 'turn to affect' is used by some rather more expansively than others: certain theorists utilize a narrow definition of affect while others include theories of emotion under this umbrella too. Nevertheless, there are distinct differences in focus of the theories falling under the linguistic and the affective turns; speaking very broadly, the first focuses upon language and its organizing tropes, while the latter concerns our sensations, our bodily and emotional responses and reactions.[1] If the linguistic turn was dominated by discussions of the signifier, the affective turn attunes itself to the human sensorium, a move away from thinking about how language constructs the world around us towards what Constantina Papoulias and Felicity Callard call 'a desire to address intimate aspects of life through attending to an enfleshed understanding of action and thought' (2010: 34). In pursuit of this, critics are writing about intimate states and feelings as varied as happiness, shame, optimism, fear, anxiety, anger and disgust.[2] In some cases, the arguments seek to improve our cultural and social understanding by showing that a particular emotion or affect is not as immediately legible as might have been thought; for instance, that shame is not always negative or that our happiness can have a complicated dependence upon conforming to the restricting norms of how others define it for us. In other cases, theorists are examining how our feelings interact with and in some cases shape politics, law and justice.[3]

For those participating in the new affective turn, discussions over definitional differences have been lively, particularly when it comes to establishing what is being referred to by the terms 'affect' and 'emotion', since they are sometimes rigorously differentiated and then, at other points, used almost synonymously. Affect, a designation which has come primarily from psychology and science, is mostly understood to be a pre-cognitive, non-linguistic bodily sensation, such as an unspecified 'edgy' feeling, or a stimulus reaction, like the unconscious flickering of our eyes when a stranger enters the room.[4] In their introduction to *The Affect Theory Reader*, Melissa Gregg and Gregory J.

Seigworth provide the following as one of the first among their multiple explanations of affect: it is

> the name we give to those forces – visceral forces beneath, alongside or generally *other than* conscious knowing, vital forces beyond emotion – that can serve to drive us toward movement, toward thought and extension, that can likewise suspend us (as if in neutral) across a barely registering accretion of force-relations or that can leave us overwhelmed by the world's apparent intractability. (2010: 1)

If this makes clear that affect is a bodily sensation distinct from conscious recognitions of emotion and yet powerful enough to influence human mood and behaviour, it is also rather enigmatic and indistinct, despite its poetic resonance and rhetorical sophistication. This is because, as Clare Hemmings's more succinct definition helps us see, 'affect broadly refers to states of being, rather than to their manifestation or interpretation as emotions', and for these states we have a less stable vocabulary than we do for the emotions precisely because a state of being is not always clear and can be experienced before we recognize it or interpret it (2005: 551). Often, as Gregg and Seigworth's definition underlines in their insistence that affect is 'beneath, alongside, or generally *other than* conscious thinking', we will not be in a position to specify exactly what affect it *is*, which makes it difficult for theory to write about too.

In contrast, emotions are frequently defined as the conscious labelling of our sensations or feelings whereby we might make sense of the aforementioned edginess in the context of an upcoming examination and so interpret it as a symptom of anxiety or we might interpret the incipient excitement we experience when in the company of a particular person as love. The emotions are clearer, or so we might initially suppose. Yet, love is hardly a precise designation, as the ancient Greeks very well knew.[5] Author and theorist Hélène Cixous encapsulates the contradictions of this most prized, though often troublesome, of our emotions when she writes 'in love not all is love' (1991: 40). If, as Hemmings suggests, our emotions are 'interpretations' of affect, then there may not be a single, identifiable emotion we could confidently label 'love' or, indeed, 'anxiety'. Moreover, there is often a muddling of emotion and affect within the same discourse or they are studied in conjunction: in Gregg and Seigworth's list of the main academic fields engaged with affect theory, for instance, they feature 'critical discourses of the emotions (and histories of the emotions)' (2010: 8).[6] What these crossovers of theories of emotion and affect point to is actually a remarkably rich potential for research: it is clear, as this work continues apace across many disciplines, that the language we have to talk about how we feel is inadequate. The term 'affect' often seems to slip into the gap where the complexity and mutability of our emotional terrains and states of being remain undisclosed or only partially captured by the names we give to them. Thus, while there have been notable critiques of the way researchers from the humanities have adopted the term 'affect' from psychology and neuroscience without always fully understanding the context of the research it comes from and without using the term as precisely as those discourses do, the fact that the entry of a new term into critical discourse has excited such an efflorescence of interest and theorizing points to the need to expand our current explanations of the cultural importance of feelings, emotions and affects to our subjectivity and our sociality.[7]

Rather than dissecting the debates over terminology, another route for understanding the work within the affective turn is to map its multiple lineages, producing an understanding of the kinds of discourses which have led researchers to value this new theoretical development. As Ann Cvetkovich summarizes,

> significant among these are feminism and queer studies, where the gendering of emotion as feminine, affective responses to popular genres, and the close connections between the social construction of sexuality and the social construction of emotion (as part of histories of subjectivity and intimacy) have long been intellectual concerns. (Staiger, Cvetkovich and Reynolds 2010: 5)

She goes on to add to this list the work that has been done on trauma and cultural memory; the legacies of psychoanalysis, especially in adding to the 'appreciation for the complexities of psychic life'; and a 'renewed interest in phenomenology and the everyday experience of sensation and embodiment as ways of tracking this intersection of the social and the psychic' (Staiger, Cvetkovich and Reynolds 2010: 5). All these discourses, despite their diversity, are concerned with making sense of, tracking and theorizing our intimate experiences of others and of ourselves. One of the advantages of determining the intellectual origins of affect studies and those currently researching it is to avoid the tendency for one theoretical 'turn' to be positioned as though it completely and irrevocably overturns an earlier theoretical paradigm, thereby insinuating that the former is outdated, lacking or has failed. We saw at the start of this section that the affective turn is often perceived as the replacement for the linguistic turn, yet, as Hemmings has argued, there can be a tendency for advocates of a new theoretical domain to exaggerate the extent to which it overcomes, overturns or solves the problems produced by other, earlier theories (2005: 548–67). There are always continuities as well as ruptures in contiguous theoretical enquiries: as this book demonstrates, at any one time there are a range of theories jostling side by side, with overlapping dimensions. The moniker 'affective turn', then, has the benefit of showing a broad shift in critical focus towards analyzing how thought and action are embodied but it is less helpful in manifesting how these new priorities have been shaped by their predecessors. Thus, it is to one of these that we will now turn.

THE SOCIAL DIMENSION OF FEELINGS

If commonly our emotions and feelings have been understood as personal, intimate and private, they are now being reassessed as social, potentially paradigmatic, and a route to better understanding how we orientate ourselves in or towards the world. One of the key antecedents to the 'affective turn' was published in 1977, when the cultural Marxist Raymond Williams argued for attention to what he called 'structures of feeling' (1977: 128). Williams was seeking a route to understand how the social is constituted in lived realities in order to supplement a Marxist discourse which had, he claimed, focused on the social as simply structured by sets of worldviews, ideologies and class outlooks in such a way that they appeared fixed and implied that they had therefore finished evolving. He explained how, instead, attending to structures of feeling would consider 'meanings and values as they are actively lived and felt' by people in their everyday lives. This would entail examining 'characteristic elements of impulse, restraint, and tone; specifically affective elements of consciousness and relationships: not feelings against thought, but thought as felt and feeling as thought: practical consciousness of a present kind in a living and inter-relating continuity' (1977: 132). Here, the insistence that thinking and feeling are not to be opposed to one another – as they so often are in the colloquial dichotomy of the head versus the heart – but instead to be thought together is a characteristic which will be emphasized repeatedly, nearly twenty years later, by those working on affect. Literary critics such as Eve Kosofsky Sedgwick have argued that attention to the affects offers us ways to circumvent the continuation of dualistic thinking (Sedgwick and Frank 1995: 1–2; Sedgwick 2003: 1). Not all the writing that has recently gone on in the field of theorizing feelings has been in literature or literary theory by any means: much has been written about the emotions in cultural studies, history, the social sciences and neuroscience. However, in this early essay Williams reserves a special place for literature and the arts in articulating the 'first indications that a new structure [of feeling] is forming' because they are able to express – although they do not always do so – 'new semantic figures', new ways of understanding the social world (1977: 133).

A 'structure of feeling', as Williams meant it, is not quite the same as the focus on specific emotions and affects that has come to typify recent work. Nevertheless, as Lauren Berlant points out at the start of her book on the paradox of how optimism can staple us to unflourishing lives, several contemporary theorists are working with what she calls a 'refraction' of his concept in averring that 'affective atmospheres are shared, not solitary' (2011: 15). How might an affective atmosphere be shared? Berlant offers one answer to this in her description of what she calls 'an intimate public sphere' (2008: viii). This seemingly oxymoronic formulation is defined as a 'space of mediation in which the personal is refracted through the general'; in other words, it is a way of explaining how we find connections between what we think of as our personal feelings and how those are represented back to us in, and influenced by, public cultural formats such as television, magazines, films and literature (2008: viii). In Berlant's book *The Female Complaint*, she examines the intimate public sphere of 'women's culture', in which there is a prevalent view that 'women marked by femininity already have something in common and are in need of a conversation that feels intimate, revelatory, and a relief even when mediated by commodities' (2008: ix). This can be seen in the numerous cultural products aimed at women: soap operas, chat shows, romantic comedies and chick lit, alongside a range of consumer products which are positioned as an essential part of feminine life. For Berlant, this affective sphere of women's culture amounts to 'a way of experiencing one's own story as part of something social' (2008: x), so that even if that social experience does not fully or even partially reflect your own individual experience you still feel you can 'relate to it', in that woolly yet ubiquitous term. This attention to the way social and intimate spheres are mediated by consumer and popular culture for women in the United States is a central element of Berlant's work across many of her books, where she explores their socio-economic and historical context. Berlant insists that 'an intimate public is an achievement': it gives the people who identify with it a sense of belonging which they may not have had, and it generates discussion (2008: viii). Yet, of course, this intimate public sphere of women's culture is cut across by products aimed at women as consumers and thus is not a neutral space or necessarily an unmitigated public good. Nor should we be too quick to valorize positions simply because they are under-girded by our emotions: Berlant's work on the power of sentimentality in US culture is wary of the position that 'people ought to be legitimated because they have feelings' (2008: 2). While our emotions give us information about ourselves and the world, bringing us into realms of affective identification with others, attention to this can all too easily resolve into recommendations for adjustments to life rather than for political change. Buy a self-help book, go on a spa weekend, do some yoga or use shopping as therapy: the mainstream advice from the intimate public of women's culture tells us to try to survive our lives, Berlant's work highlights, rather than encouraging us to demand different socio-economic living conditions and more just political systems.

Other theorists, such as Teresa Brennan, give accounts of affective atmospheres within interpersonal interactions, exploring how feelings get caught up from one person and transmitted to another. For Brennan, 'the transmission of affect, whether it is grief, anxiety, or anger, is social or psychological in origin' (2004: 1). She discusses how affects are 'energetic', being projected outwards so that the person is relieved, or introjected so that one person internalizes the 'affective burden' of another. These are two-way processes: I project my anger outwards, which someone else introjects, making them feel angry too or perhaps just depressed. As Brennan articulates it, for this model 'there is no secure distinction between the "individual" and the "environment"' (2004: 6): we are not singular entities moving through the world with personal emotions that emerge from within us and affect only our own state of mind and mood; we are social, relational beings who are affected – whether we recognize it or not – by the states of others around us and who in turn affect those people too.[8]

Theorist Sara Ahmed agrees that our emotions are relational: they exist, she argues, through 'sociality' (2004: 10). Ahmed rejects the usual understanding of emotion as something that begins within the subject and travels out towards the world – she calls this the 'inside out' model (2004: 9). But she similarly dismantles the less prevalent model of the emotions as coming to us from without, which has been common in theories trying to understand crowd behaviour. In these critiques, we can see Ahmed's difference from the contagion model put forward by Brennan. Instead, she counters that emotions 'are not simply something "I" or "we" have. Rather, it is through emotions, or how we respond to objects and others, that surfaces or boundaries are made: the "I" and the "we" are shaped by, and even take the shape of, contact with others' (2004: 10). The example of an engagement ring is helpful here: while as an object it is culturally supposed to represent happiness, the emotions it actually evokes depend upon the context of the person who feels towards it. Are you the feminist who sees their friend's marriage as a betrayal of her politics? The parent relieved by their daughter's acquiescence to their expectations? Or the anxious lover, full of expectations for how this woman will become a wife? Ahmed's account is attuned to the sticky complications of emotions and how they become attached to certain objects, ideas and other people; she sees them as a 'form of cultural politics or world making' (2004: 12). Crucially, for Berlant and Ahmed understanding emotions and affects is about understanding how the present is constituted, a present which is personally, politically and socially complex, often messy and inevitably contradictory, and which unfolds unevenly. Neither of them is invested in seeing the political world as separate from the personal. Ahmed closes *The Cultural Politics of Emotions* by writing of the self and the world not as opposed or separate entities but as contiguous and mutually shaped contexts:

> The objects of emotion slide and stick and they join the intimate histories of bodies, with the public domain of justice and injustice. Justice is not simply a feeling. And feelings are not always just. But justice involves feelings, which move across the surfaces of the world, creating ripples in the intimate contours of our lives. Where we go, with these feelings, is an open question. (2004: 202)

This appears at once hopeful and circumspect. Berlant, too, writes with the hope for 'new idioms of the political, and of belonging itself' but with the caveat that even in the midst of our desires and demands for change, 'it is awkward and it is threatening to detach from what is already not working' (2011: 262, 263).[9] If we return to the engagement ring and the future marriage it ties the couple into, we can see how Berlant's statement expresses a 'stuckness' in which many find themselves caught.

SHAME: A TELLING EMOTIONAL EXAMPLE

If theorists are drawn to the emotions and affects because they are an intrinsic dimension of human sociality, it is nevertheless the case that some feelings have attracted rather more interest than others. Shame has been particularly popular, and with good reason: it is an intimate feeling which, despite our deepest desires to keep it secret, can write itself blushingly across our faces. Much work on shame has been inspired by the resurgence of interest led by Eve Kosofsky Sedgwick and her PhD student at the time, Adam Frank, into the largely forgotten theories of 1950s psychologist Silvan Tomkins. Sedgwick and Frank together edited a collection of Tomkins's work, entitling it *Shame and Her Sisters*. Published in 1995, this text presents Tomkins's affect theory as the promising redress to the tiredness Sedgwick and Frank claimed bedevilled contemporary theory in the mid-1990s. Tomkins's work was adopted with alacrity, with especial attention given to his insight that we are ashamed by ourselves, someone else, or a situation only when we have interest in them. One such study which declared itself productively fascinated by shame's less unpleasant contours was Elspeth Probyn's *Blush: Faces of Shame*. Probyn hopefully declares that 'shame is positive' (2005: xvi) because, 'through feeling shame, the body inaugurates an alternative way of being in the world. Shame, as the body's reflection on itself, may reorder the composition of the habitus [habitual ways of being], which in turn may allow for quite different choices' (2005: 56). We can see here an instructive tension in how Tomkins's work has been adopted. For Tomkins, the 'affect system provides the primary motives of human beings' (Sedgwick and Frank 1995: 36). As infants, we are subject to affects but do not as yet know what to do about them. One example given is an upset baby, crying because it has wind: it knows neither why it cries nor what to do to relieve its bodily discomfort. Later it learns how to biologically relieve itself and, even later, how to exert some control over the 'appearance and disappearance of his affect responses', but, Tomkins maintains, 'most humans never attain great precision of control over their affects' (Sedgwick and Frank 1995: 38). Probyn's discussion of shame has a much more plastic sense of this feeling than Tomkins's account: shame for her is more reflective and open to change. This testifies to the aforementioned difficulty that theorists have in distinguishing affects from emotions and also to the desire, typified in Probyn's account, to position our feelings as crucial tools in achieving social and political change.

Shame is a moral emotion, indexed to social visibility. Behaviours and actions I might happily perform in my own home without shame, even with pleasure, I may well be mortified by doing in public, for instance. Shame's incredible power lies in wanting to avoid feeling it. A lack of shame can be read as a deeply disturbing betrayal of the social bond or a symptom of social or psychological sickness: the figure of the serial killer exerts such fascination over society precisely because he (*sic*) is generally thought to feel no shame or remorse.[10] Shame can cause us to self-censor or, more unpleasantly, it can be used to influence the behaviour of others, either by threatening them with shame in order to keep them from certain behaviours or punishing them with shame, a fact which has not been lost on governments and lawmakers. In 2008 in the UK, for instance, people completing community service orders handed down by the courts were forced by decree of the Justice Secretary Jack Straw to wear high visibility vests with the words 'Community Payback' emblazoned across them so that people could distinguish them from regular council workers.[11] Philosopher Martha Nussbaum would not endorse this policy: she claims that shame, along with disgust, 'provide bad guidance for law in a society committed to equal respect among persons' and that to use shame in punishment and lawmaking 'seems tantamount to inviting people to discriminate and stigmatize' (2004: 337). This is because both disgust and shame 'have an intimate connection to social hierarchy and to a public culture that expresses the belief that people are unequal in worth' (2004: 340).

These examples underline Jacqueline Rose's point: 'shaming someone can be a political project' (2003: 2). Unsurprisingly, then, the refusal to feel ashamed can also be a moral decision and, in turn, becomes political, a sign of defiance or liberation. Celebrations like Gay Pride are a deliberate, public refutation of the traditional social and sexual shame heterosexual culture has historically attempted to extract from those who did not adhere to its conventions. Here, the desire of one group to make another feel ashamed is transmuted by the refusal of that shame into a political, public and social act of affirmation. However, Gay Pride is in fact constituted by the homophobia it seeks to combat; thus, while it is a response to an attempt to shame, its very existence is still within the economy of shame and its refusal. The concept of shame as potentially transformative and not always negative has therefore been important for queer theorists (Cvetkovich 2003: 47). Most studies of shame highlight how it is close to other feelings: interest, in the case of Tomkins, Sedgwick, Frank and Probyn, who point out that to feel shame we have to care in the first place; disgust in the case of Nussbaum; and love, particularly queer loves which 'depart from the scripts of normative existence' in the case of Ahmed, who claims there is an 'intimacy of shame and love' whereby 'shame both confirms and negates the love that sticks us together' (2004: 107). Even if not everyone agrees as to the utility of shame, it is a feeling that rarely comes alone and is able to tell us stories of how we are orientated in the world and to the society we live in, the communities we traverse, as well as those we care about.

SEX, RELATIONALITY AND THINKING BEYOND HETERONORMATIVITY

As we have seen with shame, certain social groups can be made to feel ashamed of their sexual orientation or their sexual preferences, especially if their practices do not align with what mainstream society deems normal. Sexuality is a key area where norms exert considerable pressure: typically, the pressure to be in a relationship, to love the right person, to marry, and to start a family. Yet, the traditional institutions of heterosexual intimacy are not proving to be all that durable in the contemporary, Western world: more marriages end in divorce than ever before; fewer people are choosing to marry; adultery is, as ever, rife. Sociologists point to fairly recent changes in the twentieth century – increased financial freedom and employment opportunities for women; a greater concentration upon equality in relationships; higher expectations of 'close' emotional bonds and communication between lovers – as factors which have altered the traditional institution of marriage and the heterosexual couple partnership, making them more difficult to maintain.[12] As feminists have been arguing for years, the structural inequalities of patriarchy and the gendered division of domestic labour sustained the institution of marriage for a long time, although to the detriment of opportunities for women. Such conditions are not generally considered acceptable to twenty-first-century women in the Western world, nor, often, to the partners they choose. Nevertheless, heteronormativity, where the assumption is that to be normal is to be heterosexual, monogamous and hoping to one day raise a family, remains strongly inscribed within Anglo-American laws, social practices and religions, as well as being reflected in our cultural objects. The problem with heteronormativity is that it tends to be invisible to people until or unless they fall outside one of its strictures and feel the force of being different to the norm. For this, the responsibility for explanation is usually laid at the feet of the person who is different. Straight people are not expected to confront their parents with the fact of their heterosexuality; those in conventional coupledom do not have to awkwardly explain their singleness or their polyamory in response to 'bring your partner' party invitations; a woman and a man staying in a hotel room together will attract no unusual stares if they walk into the lobby holding hands. To not be part of heteronormativity is to be made to feel different, perverse, at odds with others and socially liminal; such an experience understandably shapes a person's subjectivity and sense of self as well as their views on society. Heteronormativity makes a good many people – even some straight, heterosexual people – feel deeply uncomfortable about themselves and the society they live in.[13]

Analyzing and critiquing heteronormativity, its institutions and the cultural changes these are currently undergoing has thus been a key part of the research into intimacy over the past few decades.[14] Equally important in thinking about sex and sexuality has been the rise of queer theory which, following on from identity politics and alongside feminism, has explored the potential in new relational configurations, different sexual behaviours and lifestyles, and the way these have shaped alternative types of subjectivity. The differential binary of male/female obviously does not hold in the same way if a relationship is lesbian or gay, especially if those sexual orientations are refusing to reproduce the same kind of binary behaviours and stereotypes. This illuminates the constructed nature of heteronormativity in the first place and secondly opens up the possibility of challenging, reinscribing, reinventing or jettisoning stereo-types of gendered behaviour. Rosemary Hennessey provides a useful summary of how queer theory deliberately sidesteps essentialism when it comes to think-ing about gender and sexuality, seeing, instead of rigid positions and polarities based on sexual orientation, a potential fluidity that comes from the instability of desire and which might be beneficial for envisioning social change:

> Queer theory distances itself from lesbian and gay identity politics because it sees any identity as internally divided and therefore not an apt or effective rallying point for change. 'Queer' is a mark of the instability of identity. It makes visible the ways that heterosexuality functions as a normative power regime and highlights the arbitrariness of the neat dis-tinctions it enforces (between masculine and feminine, straight and gay, for example) in how sexuality and gender – and for some queer theorists race, too – come to be known. (2013: 135)

As Leo Bersani points out, our objects of attraction are culturally informed: whether gay or straight, 'we still have to learn to desire particular men and women, and not to desire others' (1995: 64). In fact, for Bersani the problem with intimacy cuts across sexual orientations because 'violence and avidity for power [are] inherent in all intimate negotiations between human beings' (1995: 108). Our sexual intimacies, then, are important sites not simply for pleasure or partnership but also for the confrontation with more negative facets of human sociality. In an unusually frank exchange between two queer theorists whose work leads them to be interested in similar things in different ways, Berlant writes to her interlocutor, Lee Edelman, 'In sex, in politics, in theory – in any infrastructure that we can call intimate or invested with the activity of living – we cannot banish the strangeness in ourselves or of anything in the world' (Berlant and Edelman 2013: 116). In this account, sex is not just something we do in bed: it is an encounter with the difference of someone else but also with the fact that we are not fully transparent to ourselves, let alone to others. In other words, our intimacies are composed of miscommunica-tion, misunderstanding, failure and difficulty as much as they might be scenes of self-expression and affirmation, pleasure and companionship. This is why theorists are continuing to write about how our intimacies are sites for think-ing about epistemology, the formation or dissolution of certainties about our identities, and relational change, as well as places where we simply engage in social or biological practices.

TELLING INTIMATE TALES

I want to close this chapter by shifting my account back towards the point I opened with: the intimate genres of literature.[15] An intriguing feature of the work on emotions, affect and relationality is an increasing use of the personal story, the anecdote, as a key contributor to the elaboration of theorization. We can return briefly to shame to find a compelling example: we all have a story about a time we felt ashamed, even if we would rather not tell it. This is borne out by Probyn's book, which opens every chapter bar one with an anecdote drawn from her life and features stories of shame throughout, mainly, but not only, her own. This is presented as a methodological decision: 'the emphasis on narrative', she claims, 'is important when you are dealing with new ideas and new ways of being' (2005: xv). Thus she writes 'in a spirit of experimentation' in order to 'talk about shame in more productive ways' (2005: xv). It is also surely a pedagogic enactment of hope: Probyn's disclosure of her own shame is done with the desire that such accounts perform the transformation of shame into a less negative state towards which the book aims (2005: xvi). Probyn is not alone in drawing upon her own stories while writing on feelings: the editors of *The Affect Theory Reader* choose to end their introduction with a section wherein each of them tells the story of their first encounter with affect theory (Seigworth and Gregg 2010: 19–25). Nussbaum begins her book *Hiding from Humanity: Disgust, Shame and the Law* by telling the tales of four short court cases to illustrate the wider story of how 'appeals to emotion are prominent in the law' (2004: 21). Like Probyn, Ahmed defends her inclusion of 'stories which might seem personal, and even about "[her] feelings"' in *The Cultural Politics of Emotion* as a conscious strategy: she names this a 'contact writing' whereby she does not 'simply interweave the personal and the public, the individual and the social, but show the ways in which they take shape through each other, or even how they shape each other' (2004: 14). This language of contact emerges again in anthropologist Kathleen Stewart's extraordinary ethnographic experiment, *Ordinary Affects*, which proceeds by presenting short, everyday scenes, wherein 'each scene begins anew the approach to the ordinary from an angle set off by the scene's affects' (2007: 5). The book works, weaving its poetic intensities of writing, by slowing down each scene to examine, to feel, the unfurling of the present moment and the attachments within it: she is trying, Stewart says, 'to create a contact zone for analysis' (2007: 5). Reading *Ordinary Affects* feels temporarily like inhabiting someone else's sensorium: not too strange since it is filled with ordinary encounters I too might or do have, yet nevertheless surprising in where the emphasis falls.

These examples have their precedents in the psychoanalytic case study, the feminist assertion of the personal as political, and the continuing trend for those engaged in the study of society's exclusions to have often also experienced them. Sedgwick's (2000) use of a series of dialogues with her therapist in 'A Dialogue on Love' testifies to this lineage, as does Judith Jack Halberstam's recent book on gender and the end of the 'normal', which opens with the scene of her partner's children asking, 'Are you a boy or a girl?' (2012: xvii). Lynne Pearce deems this a 'rhetorical innovation' in terms of feminist theorizing, although she notes how often these stories are told within arguments that still employ the traditional techniques of argumentation, such as deductive reasoning and refutation (2013: 17, 119). In other words, this is an addition rather than a substitution to existing practices. Nevertheless, while not exactly new, the tendency in writing on the emotions, affects and relationality to tell stories of the self effectively lodges the literary at the heart of the theoretical, producing writings both on and of intimacy.

QUESTIONS FOR FURTHER CONSIDERATION

1. This essay opens with a list of intimate genres of literary writing. Can you think of some further categories not listed here and why they are intimate?
2. Happiness commonly appears to be a straightforward emotion, yet theorists have shown how it is entangled in social expectations – what other people want for my happiness may be in tension with what I want. Can you consider how other emotions that appear to be straightforward might not be and why?
3. This chapter uses Sara Ahmed's example of the engagement ring as a cultural object which shows how it is our context which determines our reactions to this object and the one who wears/offers it. Can you think of another example of a culturally important object that reveals how our context and circumstances shape our reactions to others?
4. Shame shows itself on the body, as a blush. Which other emotions similarly show us how the mind and body work in tandem?
5. Can you think of examples of other laws and social regulations which rely on shame to enforce them?
6. List some of the laws and social practices which encourage heteronormativity. What kinds of reaction do you think someone who is not heteronormative would have to these?

BIBLIOGRAPHY

Ahmed, Sara (2004) *The Cultural Politics of Emotion*, New York: Routledge.
Ahmed, Sara (2010) *The Promise of Happiness*, Durham NC: Duke University Press.
Berlant, Lauren, ed. (2000) *Intimacy*, Chicago: University of Chicago Press.
Berlant, Lauren (2008) *The Female Complaint: The Unfinished Business of Sentimentality in American Culture*, Durham NC: Duke University Press.
Berlant, Lauren (2011) *Cruel Optimism*, Durham NC: Duke University Press.
Berlant, Lauren and Lee Edelman (2013) *Sex, or the Unbearable*, Durham NC: Duke University Press.
Bersani, Leo (1995) *Homos*, Cambridge MA: Harvard University Press.
Brennan, Teresa (2004) *The Transmission of Affect*, Ithaca and London: Cornell University Press.
Cixous, Hélène (1991) *The Book of Promethea*, trans. Betsy Wing, Lincoln NE: University of Nebraska Press.
Cooke, Jennifer (2013) 'Making a Scene: Towards an Anatomy of Contemporary Literary Intimacies', in Jennifer Cooke, ed. *Scenes of Intimacy: Reading, Writing and Theorizing Contemporary Literature*, London and New York: Bloomsbury Academic.
Cvetkovich, Ann (2003) *An Archive of Feelings: Trauma, Sexuality, and Lesbian Public Cultures*, Durham NC: Duke University Press.
Deleuze, Gilles and Félix Guattari (1987) *A Thousand Plateaus*, trans. Brian Massumi, Minneapolis: University of Minnesota Press.

Fisher, Philip (2002) *The Vehement Passions*, Princeton: Princeton University Press.

Giddens, Anthony (1992) *The Transformation of Intimacy: Sexuality, Love and Eroticism in Modern Societies*, Cambridge: Polity.

Halberstam, Judith Jack (2012) *Gaga Feminism: Sex, Gender, and the End of Normal*, Boston: Beacon Press.

'Happiness' (2007–8) *New Formations* 63.

'Happiness' (2009) *World Picture* 3 at <http://www.worldpicturejournal.com/WP_3/TOC.html> (accessed 9 September 2014).

Hemmings, Clare (2005) 'Invoking Affect: Cultural Theory and the Ontological Turn', *Cultural Studies* 19:5, pp. 548–67.

Hennessy, Rosemary (2013) 'The Material of Sex', in Donald Hall et al., eds., *The Routledge Queer Studies Reader*, London and New York: Routledge.

Illouz, Eva (2012) *Why Love Hurts: A Sociological Explanation*, Cambridge: Polity.

Kipnis, Laura (2000) 'Adultery', in Lauren Berlant, ed., *Intimacy*, Chicago: University of Chicago Press.

Lewis, Paul (2008) 'Straw Launches High Visibility Community Punishment', *Guardian*, 2 December, at <http://www.theguardian.com/politics/2008/dec/02/community-payback-orange-vests-slough?guni=Article:in%20body%20link> (accessed 15 November 2013).

Leys, Ruth (2011) 'The Turn to Affect: A Critique', *Critical Inquiry* 37, pp. 434–72.

Massumi, Brian (2002) *Parables for the Virtual: Movement, Affect, Sensation*, Durham NC: Duke University Press.

Miller, William Ian (1997) *The Anatomy of Disgust*, Cambridge MA: Harvard University Press.

Munt, Sally R. (2007) *Queer Attachments: The Cultural Politics of Shame*, Aldershot: Ashgate.

Ngai, Sianne (2005) *Ugly Feelings*, Cambridge MA: Harvard University Press.

Nussbaum, Martha C. (2001) *Upheavals of Thought: The Intelligence of Emotions*, Cambridge: Cambridge University Press.

Nussbaum, Martha C. (2004) *Hiding from Humanity: Disgust, Shame, and the Law*, Princeton: Princeton University Press.

Nussbaum, Martha C. (2013) *Political Emotions: Why Love Matters for Justice*, Cambridge MA and London: The Belknap Press.

Papoulias, Constantina and Felicity Callard (2010) 'Biology's Gift: Interrogating the Turn to Affect', *Body and Society* 16:1, pp. 29–56.

Pearce, Lynne (2013) *The Rhetorics of Feminism: Contemporary Cultural Theory and the Popular Press*, London and New York: Routledge.

Probyn, Elspeth (2005) *Blush: The Many Faces of Shame*, Minneapolis: University of Minnesota Press.

Rose, Jacqueline (2003) *On Not Being Able to Sleep: Psychoanalysis and the Modern World*, London: Vintage Press.

Royle, Nicholas (2003) *Jacques Derrida*, London and New York: Routledge.

Sedgwick, Eve Kosofsky (2000), 'A Dialogue on Love', in Lauren Berlant, ed., *Intimacy*, Chicago: University of Chicago Press.

Sedgwick, Eve Kosofsky (2003) *Touching Feeling: Affect, Pedagogy, Performativity*, Durham NC: Duke University Press.

Sedgwick, Eve Kosofsky and Adam Frank, eds. (1995) *Shame and Its Sisters: A Silvan Tomkins Reader*, Durham NC: Duke University Press.

Seigworth, Gregory J. and Melissa Gregg (2010) 'An Inventory of Shimmers', in Gregory J. Seigworth and Melissa Gregg, eds., *The Affect Theory Reader*, Durham NC: Duke University Press.

Seltzer, Mark (1998) *Serial Killers: Death and Life in America's Wound Culture*, New York and London: Routledge.

Staiger, Janet, Ann Cvetkovich and Ann Reynolds, eds. (2010) *Political Emotions: New Agendas in Communication*, London and New York: Routledge.

Stewart, Kathleen (2007) *Ordinary Affects*, Durham NC: Duke University Press.

Vogler, Candace (2000) 'Sex and Talk', in Lauren Berlant, ed., *Intimacy*, Chicago: University of Chicago Press.

Warner, Michael (2000) *The Trouble with Normal: Sex, Politics and the Ethics of Queer Life*, Cambridge MA: Harvard University Press.

Weeks, Jeffrey (1985) *Sexuality and Its Discontents: Meaning, Myths and Modern Sexualities*, London and New York: Routledge.

Williams, Raymond (1977) *Marxism and Literature*, Oxford: Oxford University Press.

NOTES

1. Probably the most well-known account of the shift I am tracking here comes in the opening pages of the essay 'Shame in the Cybernetic Fold: Reading Silvan Tomkins' by Eve Kosofsky Sedgwick and Adam Frank. This was their introductory essay to an edited collection of Tomkins's writing on affect, a publication often seen as a good marking point for the beginning of the rise of interest in affect studies. In the opening page of their essay, they state as one of the 'things theory knows today', that 'language is assumed to offer the most productive, if not the only possible, models for understanding representation' (1995: 1).

2. See, for example: Ahmed 2004, 2010; the special issue of *World Picture* 3 on 'Happiness' (2009); the special issue of *New Formations* 63 on 'Happiness' (2007–8); Sedgwick and Frank 1995; Probyn 2005; Munt 2007; Berlant 2011; Ngai 2005; Fisher 2002; Miller 1997; Nussbaum 2001.

3. See, for instance: Nussbaum 2013; Staiger, Cvetkovich and Reynolds 2010; Fisher 2002; Ahmed 2004.

4. The three main theorists who are probably the most influential in terms of affect are: Silvan Tomkins, whose work was revived by Sedgwick and Frank (1995); Gilles Deleuze and Félix Guattari (1987), including Deleuze's work on Spinoza; and Brian Massumi (2002), including his work on Deleuze and Guattari. The 'flickering eyes' example I take from Sara Ahmed, who in fact criticizes the over-emphasis on separating affect from emotion, arguing that they frequently 'slide into each other' and are context dependent. See Ahmed 2010: 230–1, fn. 1.

5. The Greeks distinguished four main loves: *agápē* (spiritual, selfless love), *érōs* (sensual love), *philia* (friendship) and *storgē* (familial affection).

6. For instance, Elspeth Probyn positions her book as an investigation of shame as an affect, but writes of her reaction to first viewing the red flat-top Australian rock as a 'cloudburst of emotion' composed of a range of nameable and unnameable feelings and several physiological reactions. See Probyn 2005: 45.

7. See: Hemmings 2005: 548–67; Leys 2011: 434–72; Papoulias and Callard 2010: 29–56.

8. Brennan's approach, as it unfolds over *The Transmission of Affect*, takes a rather different direction to others in the field of affect studies because of its commitment to working with psychoanalytic and religious conceptions and categories. Brennan, like many others, wants to maintain a clear distinction between feelings (which she defines as 'sensory states produced by thought') and affects ('which are thoughtless'), although her ability to maintain this distinction in her discussions is uneven (2004: 116).

9. The latter quote is the closing clause of the book.

10. Mark Seltzer discusses how the contemporary figure of the serial killer is one emptied out of identity; instead, the serial killer internalizes the psychiatric and scientific 'type' he is supposed to be, entirely constructing his sense of self out of the sense that his type of self can be constructed. This bypassing of individuality

also acts as a disavowal of social differentiation and agency over self-formation. See 'The Profile of the Serial Killer', in Seltzer 1998: 125–58.

11. Notably, and tellingly, Straw claimed that the vests were *not* intended to shame the wearers but to demonstrate to the public that 'justice was being done'. Yet for the punishment to be visible in this way is clearly not unrelated to how the wearers may be induced or, perhaps more importantly, be expected to feel ashamed. The journalist reporting on this policy certainly frames it as emotionally punitive. See Lewis 2008.

12. See Giddens 1992; Illouz 2012; Berlant 2000, especially the essays 'Adultery' by Laura Kipnis (9–47) and 'Sex and Talk' by Candace Vogler (48–85). These thinkers track changes in different manners, some more conservatively than others, some more hopefully.

13. It is easy to see how society's heteronormativity might be able to make a lesbian family feel uncomfortable. But it is also capable of making people like single mothers, childless forty-somethings and divorcees feel like failures or as though they need to explain themselves and their circumstances.

14. See, for instance, Warner 2000 and Weeks 1985.

15. For more on literary intimacy, see my 'Making a Scene: Towards an Anatomy of Contemporary Literary Intimacies', in Cooke 2013: 3–21.

GENDER AND TRANSGENDER CRITICISM

Sarah Gamble

In their introduction to the book *Genders*, David Glover and Cora Kaplan make the observation that: '*gender* is a much contested concept, as slippery as it is indispensable, but a site of unease rather than agreement' (2000: ix). As a neologism founded upon an already disputed term, 'transgender' is thus doubly problematic. Describing the word's etymology, Jay Prosser observes that 'transgender' has both a specific and a general function, describing an individual who 'crosse[s] the line of gender but not of sex', as well as functioning as a container term, one that refers not only to transgenderists but to those subjects from whom it was originally invented to distinguish transgenderists: transsexuals and drag queens, transvestites and cross-dressers, along with butches and intersexuals and any subject who 'trans-es' sex or gender boundaries (1998: 176).

Furthermore, it is difficult to define with any exactitude the ground covered by either term, since both tend to elide into theoretical territories identified by other names. It could be argued that it is only relatively recently that gender and transgender theory have emerged as categories in their own rights, having been developed via debates taking place within, for example, feminist theory, queer theory, masculinity theory, postcolonial theory, philosophy, and gay and lesbian studies. Both words also 'double up' in another way, too, for they are as much political as they are theoretical, interacting with the material world that exists beyond the intellectual realm of the academy. Thus they are descriptive of movements within politics and sociology as well as ideas to do with culture and representation.

One of the founding thinkers concerning gender was the psychoanalyst

Robert Stoller, who in 1968 published *Sex and Gender: On the Development of Masculinity and Femininity*, in which he drew a distinction between sex and gender which has proved invaluable to subsequent theorists. Regarding gender as 'culturally determined' (Stoller 1968: ix), he argued that an individual's gender identity may not necessarily correspond to their primary biological sexual characteristics:

> one can speak of the male sex or the female sex, but one can also talk about masculinity and femininity and not necessarily be implying anything about anatomy or physiology. Thus, while sex and gender seem to common sense to be practically synonymous, and in everyday life to be inextricably bound together, one purpose of this study will be to confirm the fact that the two realms (sex and gender) are not at all inevitably bound in anything like a one-to-one relationship, but each may go in its quite independent way. (1968: xiii)

From this perspective, gender can be viewed as a *behaviour*, a learned or conditioned response to a society's view of how 'men' and 'women' should act. The motivation behind much of the twentieth-century feminist movement stems from such a view: the belief that, while men's and women's biological difference is an inescapable fact, inequalities between them stem from culturally generated biases concerning the gendered categories of 'masculinity' and 'femininity'. The idea that gender is culturally constructed was invaluable to feminists of the second wave, such as Kate Millett, who in *Sexual Politics* (1970) drew on Stoller's work in order to argue that women's oppression is rooted in social conceptions of 'femininity'. Gayle Rubin's 1975 essay, 'The Traffic in Women: Notes on the "Political Economy" of Sex', made a very similar point. Rubin defines what she terms the 'sex/gender system' as 'the set of arrangements by which a society transforms biological sexuality into products of human activity' (Humm 1992: 257).

By the late 1980s such feminist arguments were coming under attack from theorists steeped in postmodernist theory, for whom the assumption that all woman are impressed within a cross-cultural gender system appeared dangerously simplistic. In 'The Technology of Gender', published in 1987, Teresa de Lauretis claims that 'the notion of gender as sexual difference' has 'now become a limitation, something of a liability to feminist thought' In its insistence on placing 'male' and 'female' in opposition, the feminist definition of gender 'keeps feminist thinking bound to the terms of Western patriarchy itself, contained within the frame of a conceptual opposition' (1987: 1). In order to escape from this restrictive dialectic, which does not enable differences between 'women' as a category to be articulated, 'we need a notion of gender that is not so bound up with sexual difference as to be virtually coterminous with it' (1987: 2). For de Lauretis, the answer lies in approaching gender as a *representation*, 'a symbolic system or system of meanings, that correlates sex to cultural contents according to social values and hierarchies' (1987: 5), and investigating how the gendered subject is produced through a variety of discourses and technologies. As a film theorist, her primary concern is with cinema, which functions as a 'technology of gender' (1987: 13) in the way in which it constructs sexualized images of women through a range of techniques (camera angles, lighting and so on), and codes (the positioning of the viewing subject in relation to the image viewed). The consequence of such an anatomization of gender as a system is that it will enable the feminist theorist to occupy – however briefly – a space *outside* the gender system in an 'ongoing effort to create new spaces of discourse, to rewrite cultural narratives, and to define the terms of another perspective – a view from "elsewhere"' (1987: 25). Such a perspective, however, is always contingent, in a permanent process of oscillation within and without gender ideologies: what de Lauretis terms 'a movement between the (represented) discursive space of the positions made available by hegemonic discourses and the space-off, the elsewhere, of these discourses' (1987: 26).

De Lauretis's argument abandons simplistic sex/gender distinctions in order to argue for gender as a complex discursive construction. But Judith Butler, whose 1990 book *Gender Trouble* has exercised an enormous influence upon modern gender theory, goes even further. Like de Lauretis, Butler takes issue with feminist conceptions of gender, which, she says, 'have assumed that there is some existing identity, understood through the category of women, who not only initiates feminist interests and goals within discourse, but constitutes the subject for whom political representation is pursued' (1990: 1). While de Lauretis retains an adherence to the notion of subjectivity which is implicated in a process of 'continuous engagement in social reality' (1987: 18), Butler is concerned with a more radical deconstruction of the subject. Her argument proceeds from the assumption that a universal concept of 'woman' is a signifier that has become divorced from humanist conceptions of subjectivity, and thus 'is no longer understood in stable or abiding terms' (1990: 1) – it is 'a troublesome term, a site of contest, a cause for anxiety' (1990: 3).

For Butler, the distinction between sex and gender is one way in which simplistic notions of 'woman' are troubled, for 'the unity of the subject is thus already potentially contested by the distinction that permits of gender as a multiple interpretation of sex' (1990: 6). Following the path of her own logic to the extreme, she proceeds to argue that:

> If gender is the cultural meanings that the sexed boy assumes, then a gender cannot be said to follow from a sex in any one way. Taken to its logical limit, the sex/gender distinction suggests a radical discontinuity between sexed bodies and culturally constructed genders. Assuming for the moment the stability of binary sex, it does not follow that the construction of 'men' will accrue exclusively to the bodies of males or that 'women' will interpret only female bodies. Further, even if the sexes appear to be unproblematically binary in their morphology and

constitution (which will become a question), there is no reason to assume that genders ought to remain as two. The presumption of a binary gender system implicitly retains the belief in a mimetic relation of gender to sex whereby gender mirrors sex or is otherwise restricted by it. When the constructed status of gender is theorized as radically independent of sex, gender itself becomes a free-floating artifice, with the consequence that *man* and *masculine* might just as easily signify a female body as a male one, and *woman* and *feminine* a male body as easily as a female one.

This radical splitting of the gendered subject poses yet another set of problems. Can we refer to a 'given' sex or a 'given' gender without first inquiring into how sex and/or gender is given, through what means? And what is 'sex' anyway? Is it natural, anatomical, chromosomal, or hormonal, and how is a feminist critic to assess the scientific discourses which purport to establish such 'facts' for us? . . . If the immutable character of sex is contested, perhaps this construct called 'sex' was as culturally constructed as gender; indeed, perhaps it was always already gender, with the consequence that the distinction between sex and gender turns out to be no distinction at all. (1990: 6–7)

This statement constitutes a radical leap beyond the sphere of debate established by de Lauretis, for what Butler effectively does in this passage is to turn the 'sex versus gender' argument on its head. Not only does she point out the radical consequences of cutting gender free from sex, the signifier from the body being signified, she also begins to interrogate the very means by which the concept of 'sex' itself is produced. In this context, 'sex' has as little to do with biology as gender: 'gender ought not to be conceived merely as the cultural inscription of meaning on a pregiven sex . . . gender must also designate the very apparatus of production whereby the sexes themselves are established' (1990: 7).

The implications of this argument are far-reaching, since it comes to affect the very concept of identity. As Butler asks, 'how do the regulatory practices that govern gender also govern culturally intelligible notions of identity?' (1990: 16–17). The subject is not granted *a priori* existence in Butler's argument, but is the constant process of being constituted and maintained through a network of discourses: it is always, to use her words, a 'fictive production' (1990: 24).

In this sense, *gender* is not a noun, but neither is it a set of free-floating attributes, for we have seen that the substantive effect of gender is performatively produced and compelled by the regulatory practices of gender coherence. Hence, within the inherited discourse of the metaphysics of substance, gender proves to be performative – that is, constituting the identity it is purported to be. In this sense, gender is always a doing, though not a doing by a subject who might be said to preexist the deed. (1990: 24–5)

Although this process is rendered invisible within the context of the cultural 'norm' of heterosexuality, subversive sexual practices and bodily performances call it into question by threatening to establish identities outside of the confines of the masculine/feminine paradigm. In *Gender Trouble*, Butler looks at practices such as cross-dressing and drag, arguing that, in their parodic imitation of gender norms, they highlight the performativity which is an essential element of *all* gendered behaviour.

> As much as drag creates a unified picture of 'woman' (what its critics often oppose), it also reveals the distinctness of those aspects of gendered experience which are falsely naturalized as a unity through the regulatory fiction of heterosexual coherence. *In imitating gender, drag implicitly reveals the imitative structure of gender itself – as well as its contingency.* (1990: 137)

If no appeal can be made to a 'true' or 'authentic' identity based on gender or on sex, heterosexual binarism gives way to an infinite range of gendered identities and practices: and it is from this line of reasoning that transgender theory springs.

It has already been noted that gender theorists such as Judith Butler seek to destabilize universal notions of 'woman': an endeavour that argues against centuries of certainty concerning the meaning of that term. 'Transgender', on the other hand, is a word that has no history, and no basis in a stable epistemology – it is, axiomatically, a volatile and much-disputed term. As transsexual Riki Anne Wilchins says, the meaning of 'transgender' is fluid and subject to constant qualification:

> *Transgender* began its life as a name for those folks who identified neither as crossdressers nor as transsexuals – primarily people who changed their gender but not their genitals . . .
> The term gradually mutated to include any genderqueers who didn't actually change their genitals: crossdressers, transgenders, stone butches, hermaphrodites and drag people. Finally, tossing in the towel on the noun-list approach, people began using it to refer to transsexuals as well, which was fine with some transsexuals, but made others feel they were being erased. (1997: 15–16)

In her book *Gender Outlaw*, Kate Bornstein displays a similar struggle with definition, arguing for the use of 'transgendered' as a collective noun capable of encompassing the infinite variety of subversive gender identities in order to bind them together into a cohesive site upon which to base a politics of activism.

> So let's claim the word 'transgendered' so as to be more inclusive. Let's let it mean 'transgressively gendered'. Then, we have a group of people who break the rules, codes, and shackles of gender. Then we have a

healthy-size contingent! It's the transgendered who need to embrace the lesbians and gays, because it's the transgendered who are in fact the more inclusive category. (1994: 234–5)

Many texts in transgender studies do not make use of the term at all, as evinced by Sandy Stone's seminal essay 'The *Empire* Strikes Back: a Posttranssexual Manifesto', published in 1992. This essay outlines the key features of this area of theory, arguing that, for transsexuals themselves, the transsexed body does not necessarily represent the potential for gender subversion envisaged by theorists such as Butler. Instead, Stone asserts that transsexuals, who desire surgical intervention in order to literally become a member of the opposite gender, have very stereotyped ideas concerning gender identity. 'Sex and gender', she argues, 'are quite separate issues, but transsexuals commonly blur the distinction by confusing the performative character of gender with the physical "fact" of sex, referring to their perceptions of their situation as being in the "wrong" body' (1992: 281–2). In fact, the medical discourse surrounding gender reassignment surgery demands that no differentiation be made between gender and sex, since 'candidates for surgery were evaluated on the basis of their *performance* in the gender of choice. The criteria constituted a fully acculturated, consensual definition of gender' (1992: 291). This is reflected in the narratives of sex change found in transsexual autobiographies, in which 'the authors . . . reinforce a binary, oppositional mode of gender identification. They go from being unambiguous men, albeit unhappy men, to unambiguous women. There is no territory between' (1992: 286).

Stone's essay is an appeal to the transsexual community to formulate different stories of gender identity, instead of colluding with medical discourses that entrap them within the male/female binarism. She portrays the transsexual body as a 'battlefield . . . a hotly contested site of cultural inscription, a meaning machine for the production of ideal type' (1992: 294), and argues for the necessity of a counter-discourse that would originate from within transsexualism itself. Such a refusal to be reabsorbed into society's views of what constitutes 'normal' or 'natural' gender would result, according to Stone, in the construction of a historical narrative of transsexualism which would throw into high relief the constructedness of *all* gender identities:

> In the transsexual as text we may find the potential to map the refigured body onto conventional gender discourse and thereby disrupt it, to take advantage of the dissonances created by such a juxtaposition to fragment and reconstitute the elements of gender in new and unexpected geometries. (1992: 296)

Transsexuals must, therefore, resist the imperative to 'pass', creating identities for themselves which correspond absolutely to dominant ideological expectations concerning gender. Instead, they should seek for ways to represent 'the intertextual possibilities of the transsexual body' (1992: 297), grounding their histories in the gaps and interstices between gender categories. Stone ends her essay by imagining the implications of such an act. In articulating their difference and variety, Stone envisages a situation in which

> the disruptions of the old patterns of desire that the multiple dissonances of the transsexual body imply produce not an irreducible alterity but a myriad of alterities, whose unanticipated juxtapositions hold what Donna Haraway has called the promises of monsters – physicalities of constantly shifting figure and ground that exceed the frame of any possible representation. (1992: 299)

Stone's mention of Donna Haraway in the extract quoted above indicates the importance of her work as an intertext for Stone's essay. Indeed, Stone's choice of title – 'The *Empire* Strikes Back: A Posttransexual Manifesto' – itself constitutes a linguistic gesture towards Haraway's influential piece 'A Cyborg Manifesto: Science Technology and Socialist-Feminism in the Late Twentieth Century', originally published in *Socialist Review* in 1985. Although Haraway is not a transgender theorist *per se*, and does not write from a position within the transgender community, Stone's referencing of Haraway indicates the usefulness of many of her ideas to the ongoing task of formulating a transgendered discourse.

The figure that occupies a particularly iconic position in Haraway's argument in this essay is the cyborg, which she describes as 'a hybrid of machine and organism, a creature of social reality as well as a creature of fiction' (1991: 149). Although the cyborg is an imaginary creation drawn from science fiction, for Haraway it functions as a potent symbol of the contradictions encountered by female subjects in a twentieth-century technocracy, in which they are aligned with a 'natural' condition which is increasingly being called into question by the expansion of industrial capitalism. Although Haraway's concern is with women, as Stone discerns, her statements concerning the cyborg translate neatly into a transgender context. For a start, Haraway is emphatic in her claim that 'the cyborg is a creature in a post-gender world; it has no truck with bisexuality, pre-oedipal symbiosis, unalienated labour, or other seductions to organic wholeness through a final appropriation of all the powers of the parts into a higher unity' (1991: 150). The cyborg, therefore, like the transgendered subject, disrupts gender boundaries purely by the fact of its existence. Because its genesis lies outside the boundaries of gender, it has no myth of origin, and thus no history: it 'would not recognise the Garden of Eden' (1991: 151). Instead, the body of the cyborg springs from a complex of alliances formed between technology, capitalism and science, just as does the surgically transformed transgendered body in Stone's analysis. But although both the cyborg and the transgendered individual are generated from within such materialistic practices, they also call them into question through the very fact of their hybridity. As Haraway says:

A cyborg world might be about lived social and bodily realities in which people are not afraid of their joint kinship with animals and machines, not afraid of permanently partial identities and contradictory stand-points. The political struggle is to see from both perspectives at once because each reveals both dominations and possibilities unimaginable from the other vantage point. Single vision produces worse illusions than double vision or many-headed monsters. Cyborg unities are monstrous and illegitimate; in our present circumstances, we could hardly hope for more potent myths of resistance and recoupling. (1991: 154)

Compare this with Judith Butler's assertion in *Gender Trouble* that 'the very notion of "the person" is called into question by the cultural emergence of those "incoherent" or "discontinuous" gendered beings who appear to be persons but who fail to conform to the gendered norms of cultural intelligibility by which persons are defined' (1990: 17). Both cyborgs and the transgendered subject are figures who disrupt determinist ideologies and standpoints, breaching categories and signalling new, often contradictory, possibilities for alliances across boundaries. Moreover, both call the concept of subjectivity itself into question, for neither can be codified or contained within discourses that appeal to essentialist conceptions of what constitutes the 'natural'. The cyborg, says Haraway, 'is a kind of disassembled and reassembled, postmodern collective and personal self', and a cyborg politics would fore-ground the belief that 'the body . . . can be dispersed and interfaced in nearly infinite, polymorphous ways' (1991: 163). Indeed, by the end of her essay, Haraway – while still ostensibly addressing a feminist audience – certainly gestures towards the possibility of the cyborg functioning as a transgendered symbol:

Our bodies, ourselves; bodies are maps of power and identity. Cyborgs are no exception. A cyborg body is not innocent; it was not born in a garden; it does not seek unitary identity and so generate antagonistic dualisms without end (or until the world ends); it takes irony for granted. One is too few, and two is only one possibility . . . Cyborgs might con-sider more seriously the partial, fluid, sometimes aspect of sex and sexual embodiment. Gender might not be global identity after all, even if it has profound historical breadth and depth. (1991: 180)

In her wish to cut the transgendered body loose from essentialist myths of origin, and her assertion that its 'emergent polyvocalities of lived experience' (Stone 1992: 293) will lay stress on gender identity as something attained rather than inborn, Sandy Stone develops the possibilities Haraway's cyborg presents to transgender theory. Moreover, Stone does not merely extend the content of Haraway's argument: importantly, she also appropriates its rhe-torical tone. The first section of 'A Cyborg Manifesto', subheaded 'An *Ironic* Dream of a Common Language for Women in the Integrated Circuit' (1991:

149, italics mine) signals the importance of irony as a key tactic in Haraway's debate:

> Irony is about contradictions that do not resolve into larger wholes, even dialectically, about the tension of holding incompatible things together because both or all are necessary and true. Irony is about humour and serious play. It is also a rhetorical strategy and a political method. (1991: 149)

It can be argued that irony also forms the dominant mode of representation within many transgendered narratives which, like Sandy Stone's, tend to mingle the personal with the political, and lived experience with theory. Stone's essay draws attention to the importance of autobiography in transgender writing, texts which conventionally chart the process of surgical gender reassignment. The first fully autobiographical work by a transsexual, *I Changed My Sex!*, was published by Hedy Jo Star in the mid-1950s, and it has been followed by many other transgender accounts, including *A Personal Biography* by Christine Jorgensen (1967) and *Conundrum: An Extraordinary Narrative of Transsexualism* by the journalist Jan Morris (1974).

The autobiographical mode, however, gave way in the 1990s to a new form of transgender writing which has clearly been influenced by the rise of gender theory, but which also retrains, albeit in an ironic form, much of the autobiographical drive towards self-disclosure. In 'The *Empire* Strikes Back', Stone comments that 'many transsexuals keep something they call by the argot term "O.T.F.": The Obligatory Transsexual File. This usually contains newspaper articles and bits of forbidden diary entries about "inappropriate" gender behaviour' (1992: 285), and this notion of a transgendered identity assembled, postmodern style, out of fragments collated from a variety of sources, becomes a concept central to theoretical writing produced by transgendered individuals themselves.

One of the prominent texts in this area is *Gender Outlaw: On Men, Women and the Rest of Us* by the male-to-female transsexual Kate Bornstein. The critic Jay Prosser has observed that this text constitutes 'our first "postmodern" transsexual (thus posttranssexual) autobiography' which 'fragments continuous and connective narrative into deliberately disjointed vignettes. Bornstein doesn't so much narrativize her transsexual life as (a performance artist) she performs it, acting out – without integrating into a singular stable gender identity – its parts' (1998: 174). Bornstein herself claims the book is an attempt to develop 'a transgendered style' which is 'based on collage. You know – a little bit from here, a little bit from there? Sort of a cut-and-paste thing' (1994: 3). The typography of her text emphasizes this, its mosaic of different typefaces and layouts visually echoing Bornstein's vacillation between personal disclosure and theorizing. At the heart of it all is a serious debate about identity, both personal and collective. But as far as Bornstein is concerned, as a heterosexual man transformed into a lesbian woman, gender identity is a polymorphous, infinitely mutable, concept:

> I love the idea of being without an identity, it gives me a lot of room to play around; but it makes me dizzy, having nowhere to hang my hat. When I get too tired of not having an identity, I take one on: it doesn't really matter what identity I take on, as long as it's recognizable. I can be a writer, a lover, a confidante, a femme, a top, or a woman. (1994: 39)

Bornstein is a true posttranssexual in the sense of Stone's use of the word, in that she argues against the transsexual desire for gender conformity, for the attainment of 'true' masculinity or femininity. While she clearly believes in the necessity of the acquisition of a gender identity, which, she says, 'answers the question "who am I?"' (1994: 24), that identity is neither innate nor fixed:

> What **does** a man feel like?
> What does a woman feel like?
> Do **you** feel 'like a man?'
> Do you feel 'like a woman?'
> I'd really like to know that from people. (1994: 24)

Instead, she argues for a fluid conception of gender, which 'is the refusal to remain one gender or another. Gender fluidity is the ability to freely and knowingly become one or many of a limitless number of genders, for any length of time, at any rate of change' (1994: 52). To this end, Bornstein proposes the concept of the 'third'; 'the concept of the outlaw, who subscribes to a dynamic of change, outside any given dichotomy' (1994: 97).

Bornstein's approach, if not quite her upbeat tone, is echoed in a text published three years later: *Read My Lips: Sexual Subversion and the End of Gender* by Riki Anne Wilchins. Like Bornstein's, Wilchins' book is mixture of theorization (Michel Foucault and Judith Butler are amongst the references cited) and personal exploration, presented in an assemblage of styles and typography. Wilchins, like Bornstein a male-to-female transsexual, similarly argues against the sex/gender distinction:

> Gender is not what culture creates out of my body's sex; rather, sex is what culture makes when it genders my body. The cultural system of gender looks at my body, creates a narrative of binary difference, and says, 'Honest, it was here when I arrived. It's all Mother Nature's doing.' The story of a natural sex that justifies gender evaporates, and we see sex standing revealed as an effect of gender, not its cause. Sex, the bodily feature most completely in-the-raw, turns out to be thoroughly cooked, and our comforting distinction between sex and gender collapses. We are left staring once again at the Perpetual Motion Machine of gender as it spins endlessly on and on, creating difference at every turn. (1997: 51)

However, the tone of the extract cited above is an indicator that Wilchins regards the creation of a 'third space' as a rather more problematic project than does Bornstein. As she says, 'Perhaps sex is not a noun at all. Perhaps it is really a verb, a cultural imperative – as in "Sex yourself!" – in the face of which none of us has a choice' (1997: 57). Whereas Bornstein portrays the transgendered as totemic shaman figures who, in the exhibition of their own wondrously ambiguous bodies, open the way to new conceptualizations of gender, Wilchins envisages an escape from the constrictions of the sex/gender system as a more complicated and tortuous process. In her analysis, a transgendered identity is defined much more by reference to separation from others, and what links are established between transgendered subjects are both tenuous and provisional:

> Loneliness, and the inability to find partners, is one of the best-kept secrets in the transcommunity. It's something many of us carry around like a private shame, a secret wound we hide from view. This is because we are convinced the isolation only confirms our deepest fears – that we are somehow deficient. It should remind us, once again, that the personal is political.
>
> The gender system, which marks many kinds of bodies as either non-erotic or erotically problematic, is at work in the most intimate spaces of our lives. We fall off the grid of erotic intelligibility which sections the body into known, recognizable parts. Transbodies are the cracks in the gender sidewalk. When we find partners, they must be willing to negotiate the ambiguity of the terrain. (1997: 120)

Wilchins's reiteration of the feminist slogan 'the personal is political' is significant here. *Gender Outlaw* ends with a monologue entitled 'The Seven Year Itch', which concludes with a vision of the transsexual subject sloughing off a succession of identities in order to become 'the one the dictionary has trouble naming':

> Get your last looks now, 'cause I'm changing already
> And by the time the next seven years have come and gone
> I'm gonna be new all over again. (Bornstein 1994: 238)

Bornstein's concern here is with cultural classification, metamorphosis and performance: in contrast, *Read My Lips* concludes with a 'selected chronology' of significant events in the history of transsexual activism. In these very different conclusions are foregrounded both the differences and similarities between Bornstein and Wilchins. Bornstein is a performer, her text grounded in the *acting out* of a transgendered identity that does not seek to reconcile its disparate parts into a unified whole, and which lays far more stress on the 'personal' side of 'the personal is political' equation. Wilchins's intentions are more explicitly political, as one would expect from one of the founders of the activist organizations Transsexual Menace and GenderPAC, a conclusion backed up by her claim that 'everything I've been saying has an explicit political agenda to it: I am absolutely trying to use language and knowledge to subvert certain ideas about bodies, gender and desire' (1997: 194).

In her text, Wilchins seems torn between the desire to formulate some kind of cohesive identity for trans people – arguing, for example, that 'if you're engaged in an activist struggle, you'd better look very closely at the identity you're choosing to mobilize around' (1997: 186) – and an awareness that it is both impossible and inadvisable to do so. Her vision of 'a third force, another kind of politics', which is not grounded in an appeal to a unified identity, is distinctly reminiscent of Bornstein's concept of the 'third space'.

> Will a movement without identities be messy? Yes, as messy and multi-layered as we actually are. Won't a political movement lacking a unified subject have contradictions and discord? Of course. But as Judith Butler suggested, maybe it's time to stop sacrificing the complexity of our lives at the altar of unified identity, to acknowledge our contradictions and take political action with all of them intact. Unity is a product of encouraging diversity, not of reinforcing its absence.
>
> Our contradictions and differences are more than political obstacles: they are reminders of our boundlessness, that no label or movement can ever hope to encompass all we are or hope to be. And that diversity is our strength in the face of the familiar, tyrannical Western project to impose the monolithic, all-enveloping truths that marginalized, suppressed, and erased us in the first place. (Wilchins 1997: 199)

The contradictions within Wilchins's argument – with which she is very consciously struggling throughout her text – are indicative of both the problems and the possibilities presented by the attempt to formulate a transgender identity. After all, 'transgender' itself is an amorphous term, and any body of theory has to define the kind of 'body' from which it arises: a difficult task, given the multiplicity of different possibilities and permutations which arise from the overturning of dualistic conceptions of gender. The view that the 'contradictions and differences' of transgendered identity are envisaged at once as 'political obstacles' and as utopian 'reminders of our boundlessness' may be a neat paradox, but it's unclear exactly how – in spite of Wilchins's assertion that 'a unified national movement to end gender-based oppression is right before us' (1997: 200) – such a conundrum can be resolved.

It is this that many feminists see as an insurmountable problem to an acceptance of a transgender politics: in particular, an essentialist feminism associated primarily with the second wave which is concerned with establishing a firm definition of 'woman' on which to base an activist politics. From such a standpoint, 'gender' does not unproblematically slide into 'transgender'. On the contrary, from such a perspective any ideology which blurs gender boundaries is profoundly threatening. Therefore it is perhaps not surprising that one of the common themes linking all three of the transgender texts discussed here is the voicing of the authors' concern regarding their relationship with feminism. Standy Stone's reference to 'Empire' in 'The *Empire* Strikes Back' is to

Janice G. Raymond's contentious work *The Transsexual Empire: The Making of the She-Male*, which not only exemplifies the hard-line feminist reaction to transgenderism, but also included a personal attack upon Stone herself. Raymond's book was originally published in 1979, and is forthright in its condemnation of male-to-female transsexuals who wish to identify themselves with feminism. Raymond argues that 'the transsexually constructed lesbian-feminist may have renounced femininity but not masculinity and masculinist behaviour (despite deceptive appearances)' (1994: 101). In other words, once a man, always man, regardless of surgery or any sense of identity that asserts the contrary: instead, 'the transsexually constructed lesbian-feminist is the man who indeed gets to be "the man" in an exclusive women's club to which he would otherwise have no access' (1994: 111).

A revised edition of *The Transsexual Empire* published in 1994 demonstrated Raymond standing by the opinions she had first asserted fifteen years before. In a new introduction, she reiterates her view that transsexualism is 'largely a male phenomenon'; 'the invention of men initially developed for men' (1994: xiii, xiv). In seeking to transform themselves through surgery, male-to-female transsexuals merely perpetuate the patriarchal assumption that women's bodies can be owned and controlled. Raymond has little patience with postmodernist theories regarding gender performativity, arguing that, far from revealing gender as being acted out upon the body, surgically constructed transsexuals 'are not simply acting, nor are they text, or genre . . . They purport to be the real thing' (1994: xxiii). Moreover, transgenderism is condemned for 'encourag[ing] a *style rather than a politics of resistance*, in which an expressive individualism has taken the place of collective political challenges to power . . . men and women mixing and matching but not moving beyond both' (1994: xxxiv–xxxv).

Nor is Raymond alone in her opinion that the transsexual identification with feminism is problematic. Giving the lie to Sandy Stone's assertion that *The Transsexual Empire* represented 'a specific moment in feminist analysis' (1992: 283), in 1999 Germaine Greer published *The Whole Woman* in which, in a chapter provocatively entitled 'Pantomime Dames', she attacks the transsexual phenomenon in terms which echo Raymond's. She regards transsexualism as symbolizing an insidious attempt to infiltrate the feminist movement, appropriating it from within. Her conclusion is that, when the transsexual 'forces his [*sic*] way into the few private spaces women may enjoy and shouts down their objections, and bombards the women who will not accept him with threats and hate mail, he does as rapists have always done' (Greer 1999: 74). Two years before the publication of *The Transsexual Empire*, Greer had publicly opposed the appointment of a transsexual woman to the staff of Newnham College, Cambridge, which is all-female; and she remains adamantly opposed to male-to-female transsexuals. The unshakeability of her views is evidenced by a column she wrote for the *Guardian* in 2009, in which she stated that:

nowadays we are all likely to meet people who think they are women, have women's names, and feminine clothes and lots of eyeshadow, who seem to us to be some kind of ghastly parody, though it isn't polite to say so. We pretend that all the people passing for female really are. Other delusions may be challenged, but not a man's delusion that he is female. (Greer 2009)

One of the most common narrative tropes of transgender narratives, therefore, is the experience of exclusion from feminist – particularly lesbian-feminist – networks. Consequently, Bornstein comes to the conclusion that

any revolution in deconstructing gender should look for no support among communities of people whose identities depend on the existence of . . . [a] bi-polar gender system. This would include, but most certainly is not limited to, the fundamentalist right wing, purists in the lesbian and gay male communities who believe in the ultimate goal of assimilation into the dominant culture, and some cultural and radical feminists. (1994: 132)

Riki Anne Wilchins relates the story of attempting to infiltrate the Michigan Womyn's Music Festival, which had instituted 'a policy of "womyn-born womyn only"' (1997: 109). Although this episode ends in victory, with the women attending the festival voicing support for the transgender cause, Wilchins nevertheless gives bitter voice to an extended policy of exclusion on the part of the lesbian-feminist movement:

I knew the name for what I was, and I knew I belonged with other lesbians. But the women's community greeted us less like prodigal sisters returned to the fold than like the unchanged kitty litter. Following a decade of fruitless efforts to claim my place in the lesbian movement and sick of being harassed at parties, in bars, and in groups, I left for good. (1997: 111)

Although some trans women do now attend the Michigan Womyn's Music Festival, their presence continues to be contentious. In 2013, following the launch of an online petition calling for artists to boycott the festival, the organisers released a statement that denies excluding male-to-female transsexuals:

We have said that this space, for this week, is intended to be for womyn who were born female, raised as girls and who continue to identify as womyn. This is an intention for the spirit of our gathering, rather than the focus of the festival. It is not a policy, or a ban on anyone. We do not 'restrict festival attendance to cisgendered womyn, prohibiting trans women' as was recently claimed in several Advocate articles. We do not and will not question anyone's gender. Rather, we trust the greater queer community to respect this intention, leaving the onus on each individual to choose whether or how to respect it. (Vogel 2014)

However supportive this statement may at first sound, its support for trans women is enunciated somewhat equivocally. Its phrasing is hardly an open invitation, since it implies that those not 'born female' must each individually reflect on whether they have the right to claim a place within this 'womyn'-only space. Thus, it echoes the wavering between isolation and collectivism which is a common characteristic of transgendered texts themselves, which struggle to construct a cohesive identity outside the common frame of reference provided by heterosexuality.

It could be argued that the transgender or genderqueer subject has become a far more common – and perhaps commonly accepted – figure in contemporary culture, with the result that we are more accommodating to transsexual experience, and understanding of the complexity of the term itself. The American reality competition *Ru Paul's Drag Race* (2009–present), which in its search for 'America's next drag superstar' actively debates issues around transsexuality and transgender, has become a TV phenomenon. The British artist and potter Grayson Perry accepted the prestigious Turner Prize in 2003 in the persona of his female alter ego Claire, and delivered the Radio 4 Reith lectures in 2013 wearing a series of outrageous and eye-catching outfits and full makeup. Also in 2013, DC Comics announced that a transgender character was to be introduced in its *Batgirl* series. However, the extent to which the current popularity of transsexual, transgendered and other ambiguously gendered subjects has led to the inclusion of transsexual voices within the cultural mainstream is debatable. In 2014, Sheila Jeffreys published *Gender Hurts: A Feminist Analysis of the Politics of Transgenderism*, which reiterates the view that transgender individuals have no place within feminism in its argument that 'there is nothing progressive about men's fantasies of being women, quite the reverse' (2014: 9). Patricia Elliot observes in the introduction to her book *Debates in Transgender, Queer and Feminist Theory*, published in 2010, 'Although much has changed since the early 1990s, the transsexual body remains a battlefield; only the kinds of battles taking place on it have diversified' (2010, 3), and Riki Wilchins's introduction to a new edition of *Read My Lips* published in 2013 reinforces this sense that, while transsexuals may be everywhere, the struggle for definition and acceptance remains:

> Since the maturing of gay rights, the emergence of a small but significant population of genderqueers is slowly revealing how the gender system regulates and maintains itself. While we have always had drag queens, these individuals cannot be so easily written off as entertainment for those lucky enough to inhabit normative genders. As such, they are a serious affront to the gender system. They demonstrate alternatives to the binary. The anger and confusion they arouse show gender regulation at work. The discrimination they inspire provides an object lesson in the steep costs for difference and defiance. They show that boxes are not so real after all. (Wilchins 2013: 12)

NOTES TOWARDS A READING OF ANGELA CARTER'S
THE PASSION OF NEW EVE

The Passion of New Eve was published in 1977, hence predating the advent of the gender and transgender theories outlined above. As many critics have by now observed, however, it is extraordinarily amenable to readings which draw on such theories, since the narrating subject is him/herself transgendered, relating a story of metamorphosis from male to female achieved through surgical intervention. Evelyn begins his narrative as male, but, caught up in a futuristic civil war in America, he is kidnapped by a militant feminist group and surgically transformed into New Eve, 'a perfect specimen of woman-hood' (Carter 1982: 68). The rest of the novel centres on Eve's adventures in a post-apocalyptic world, in which she experiences the difference of life as a woman. 'The technological Eve in person' (Carter 1982: 146), she can also, of course, be regarded as a literal incarnation of Donna Haraway's cyborg.

Writing in 1994, Heather Johnson observes that *The Passion of New Eve* 'seems to pre-empt, by nearly two decades, recent developments in the discipline of gender studies such as the intersection of theory and transsexual autobiography in the work of Stone, Kate Bornstein and others' (1997: 167); a point echoed more recently by Claire Westall, who similarly notes that Carter's *oeuvre* in general 'substantially preceded transgender studies and interest in transsexual and transvestite figures as potentially disruptive, as established by Sandy Stone (1991), Marjorie Garber (1992) and the canonical writings of Judith Butler (1990, 1993, and 2004)' (Westall 2012: 131). *The Passion of New Eve* thus represents a fascinating conundrum for contemporary readers who approach it well versed in queer and transgender theories that had not been yet been explored when the novel was written, a fact that motivated Joseph Bristow and Trev Lynn Broughton's claim that *The Passion of New Eve* places Carter 'in the vanguard of transgender theory' (Bristow and Broughton 1997: 18). However, what they term the 'Butlerification' of Carter's fiction (1997: 19) has been taken up by Joanne Trevenna in order to argue that critics are perhaps too quick to read *The Passion of New Eve* through reference to Butler's work. Instead, Trevenna asserts that the strong association between Carter and Butler that has become virtually *de rigour* in Carter criticism runs the risk of obscuring other interpretations. In particular, Carter's interest in the constructedness of gender identity may have more in common with the views of Simone de Beauvoir, whose most famous assertion – 'one is not born, but rather becomes, a woman' (Trevenna 2002: 268) – is played out in dramatic fashion through the life-story of Eve/lyn.

Although Angela Carter herself never cited transsexual autobiography as a referent for this text, *The Passion of New Eve* nonetheless follows a trajectory which is reminiscent of such narratives, reproducing the split consciousness which Jay Prosser regards as a foundational characteristic of autobiographical texts written by transsexuals: 'the split between the "I" of the *bios* and the "I" of the *graph*, the past self written and the present self writing, [which] is heightened by the story of sex change' (1998: 102). Read in such a context, Eve/lyn's narration in *The Passion of New Eve* is itself revealed as transgendered, for although the narrative voice with which the novel begins is apparently gendered male, it is refracted through the female consciousness of Eve, who is telling her story in retrospect.

While *The Passion of New Eve* may employ, whether knowingly or not, many of the tropes and conventions of transsexual autobiography, it does not, ultimately, sustain them. In 'The *Empire* Strikes Back', Sandy Stone – as has already been described – is critical of the way in which such narratives record the male subject's attainment of an unambiguous, essentialist femininity, '"woman" as male fetish . . . replicating a socially enforced role' (1992: 285). Carter's novel is crucially different, in that it is based around a character who makes the transition from male to female *unwillingly*. Therefore, whereas the narratives described by Stone and others relate the experience of transition from the 'wrong' body to the 'right' one, Carter's evokes a subject who in the wake of enforced surgery is left struggling with the very sense of bodily estrangement the transsexual has left behind:

> when I looked in the mirror, I saw Eve; I did not see myself. I saw a young woman who, though she was I, I could in no way acknowledge as myself, for this one was only a lyrical abstraction of femininity to me, a tinted arrangement of curved lines. (Carter 1982: 74)

Such a dislocation between the gendered subject and the gendered body opens the novels out to interpretations based upon Judith Butler's conception of the performativity of gender. Indeed, Eve/lyn's dilemma can be read as a literalization of Butler's point that 'the inner truth of gender is a fabrication and . . . a true gender is a fantasy instituted and inscribed on the surface of bodies' (1990: 136). The transformation of Eve/lyn's body may make her biologically female, but that is not enough – the attainment of 'true' femininity also demands the conscious acquisition of a whole range of behaviours. This experience, however, leads her to the belief that all feminine behaviour is essentially performative: 'although I was a woman, I was also passing for a woman, but then, many women born spend their whole lives in just such imitations' (Carter 1982: 101).

There is another figure in *The Passion of New Eve*, however, who can be read as reinforcing the notion that gender identity is constructed rather than natural. Embedded in the narrative of an 'enforced' transsexual is the tragic story of an 'authentic' transsexual, Tristessa de St Ange. Denied the opportunity to 'match his function to his form', Tristessa instead becomes 'the greatest female impersonator of his generation' (Carter 1982: 173, 144) by transforming him/herself into a Hollywood movie star and an icon of femininity which is all the more powerful for its artificiality:

He had made himself the shrine of his own desires, had made of himself the only woman he could have loved! If a woman is indeed beautiful only in so far as she incarnates most completely the secret aspirations of man, no wonder Tristessa had been able to become the most beautiful woman in the world, an unbegotten woman who made no concessions to humanity.

Tristessa, the sensuous fabrication of the flea pits. How could a real woman ever have been so much a woman as you? (Carter 1982: 128–9)

The ironic tone in which that question is posed again recalls Stone's critique of transsexual depictions of women. Although undeniably tragic, Tristessa is not in many ways meant to be regarded sympathetically, for in her screen roles she perpetuates an image of femininity that defines it through repeated references to passivity and suffering – as Eve/lyn observes, 'how much he must have loved and hated women, to let Tristessa be so beautiful and make her suffer so!' (Carter 1982: 144). Carter's depiction of Tristessa here is distinctly reminiscent of a rather tart comment made in her 1975 essay 'The Wound in the Face', in which she ponders the significance of 'the transvestite influence' on 1970s fashion for women:

Is it that the physical image of women took such a battering in the 1960s that when femininity did, for want of anything better, return, the only people we could go to to find out what it had looked like were the dedicated male impersonators who had kept the concept alive in the sequinned gowns, their spike heeled shoes and their peony lipsticks? Probably. 'The feminine character, and the idea of femininity on which it is modelled, are products of a masculine society,' says Theodor Adorno. Clearly a female impersonator knows more about his idea of the character he is mimicking than I do, because it is his own invention, *and has nothing to do with me*. (1997: 110, emphasis added)

Indeed, *The Passion of New Eve* can be read as a satire upon transsexuality which retraces some of the same ideas as those evoked by essentialist feminists such as Janice Raymond and Germaine Greer – that transsexualism perpetuates a male conception of what femininity is. Eve/lyn later learns that Tristessa was refused surgery by the radical feminist Mother because 'she was struck by the awfully ineradicable quality of his maleness' (Carter 1982: 173). That idea can only be taken so far, however, for Carter's other target in this novel is essentialist feminism itself. Mother performs surgery upon her own body, not to change her gender, but to align herself more firmly with mythic feminine archetypes: she is 'the hand-carved figurehead of her own, self-constructed theology' (Carter 1982: 60). But in the final analysis Mother is not meant to be taken any more seriously than Tristessa for, like Tristessa, Mother's transformation is a performance which is ultimately incapable of being sustained. By the end of the novel Mother has deteriorated into a mad old drunk singing on a Californian beach, having failed in her attempt to convert the world into a place where her mythic symbolism will have meaning and power.

Stone, Bornstein and Wilchins all envisage an ideology that has escaped the prison-house of gender dualism – be it a 'third space' (Bornstein), a 'third force' (Wilchins) or 'a myriad of alterities' (Stone). *The Passion of New Eve* can be approached as a novel that encourages a supportive reading of such theories. It critiques dualistic conceptions of gender by presenting its reader with grotesque parodies of extreme masculinity and femininity, while at the same time centring its narrative in a voice which encompasses the experience of both. When Eve/lyn – once a man and now a woman – and Tristessa – the man who has lived his entire life as a woman – have sex in the middle of the desert, it is portrayed as an act which so confounds customary ways of conceptualizing gender that the system founders in confusion:

> Masculine and feminine are correlatives which involve one another. I am sure of that – the quality and its negation are locked in necessity. But what the nature of masculine and feminine might be, whether they involve male and female, if they have anything to do with Tristessa's so long neglected apparatus or my own factory fresh incision and engine-turned breasts, that I do not know. Though I have been both man and woman, still I do not know the answer to these questions. Still they bewilder me. (Carter 1982: 149–50)

At the novel's conclusion Eve/lyn, who may or may not be pregnant with Tristessa's child, sails off into an unknown and unimaginable (hence unrepresentable) future. Such an inconclusive conclusion is indicative of the difficulties involved in challenging dominant ideologies of gender which shape our patterns of thought at the deepest level. As Sandy Stone says of the attempt to formulate a position from which a transsexual discourse could be enunciated:

> For a transsexual, *as a transsexual,* to generate a true, effective and representational counterdiscourse is to speak from outside the boundaries of gender, beyond the constructed oppositional nodes which have been predefined as the only positions from which discourse is possible. How, then, can the transsexual speak? If the transsexual were to speak, what would s/he say? (1992: 295)

It is significant that Carter's chosen mode here is science fiction, while Stone makes extensive use of science fiction references in her essay (after all, 'The *Empire* Strikes Back' is not only a sideswipe at Raymond, but also echoes the title of George Lucas's cinematic science fiction epic). For both Carter and Stone, the individual who is no longer bound within gender dualisms is a cyborg subject, their half-natural, half-technological origins placing them in the futuristic realm of the posthuman. From this perspective, the transgendered subject represents the culmination of all our thinking about gender, and becomes the symbol of future, as yet half-imagined, possibilities.

QUESTIONS FOR FURTHER CONSIDERATION

1. In *The Second Sex* (1949), Simone de Beauvoir asserts that 'One is not born, but rather becomes, a woman.' Debate the relevance of this statement to contemporary gender theory.
2. If gender is a 'fiction', then how does one account for the body?
3. Is feminism necessarily dependent upon the maintenance of a stable definition of 'woman'?
4. How does gender identity affect narrative identity in *The Passion of New Eve*?
5. Does Eve/lyn symbolize emancipation from the confines of gender, does s/he simply move from one side of the gender binary to the other?
6. Do you read the ending of *The Passion of New Eve* as utopian, or as evasive?

BIBLIOGRAPHY

Bornstein, Kate (1994) *Gender Outlaw: On Men, Women and the Rest of Us*, London and New York: Routledge.

Bornstein, Kate (1997) *My Gender Workbook: How to Become a Real Man, a Real Woman, the Real You, or Something Else Entirely*, London: Routledge.

Bornstein, Kate (2013) *My New Gender Workbook: A Step-By-Step Guide to Achieving World Peace through Gender Anarchy and Sex Positivity*, London: Routledge.

Bristow, Joseph and Trev Lynn Broughton (1997) 'Introduction', in *The Infernal Desires of Angela Carter: Fiction, Femininity, Feminism*, Harlow: Addison Wesley Longman.

Butler, Judith (1990) *Gender Trouble: Feminism and the Subversion of Identity*, London: Routledge.

Butler, Judith (1993) *Bodies That Matter: On the Discursive Limits of 'Sex'*, London: Routledge.

Butler, Judith (2004) *Undoing Gender*, London: Routledge.

Califia, Pat (1997) *Sex Changes: The Politics of Transgenderism*, San Francisco: Cleis Press.

Carter, Angela (1982) *The Passion of New Eve*, London: Virago Press.

Carter, Angela (1997) 'The Wound in the Face', in *Shaking A Leg: Collected Journalism and Writings*, London: Vintage.

Cixous, Hélène (1986) 'Sorties', in Hélène Cixous and Catherine Clément, *The Newly-Born Woman*, Manchester: Manchester University Press.

Cromwell, Jason (1999) *Transmen and Ftms: Identities, Bodies, Genders and Sexualities*, Chicago: University of Illinois Press.

Devor, Holly (1989) *Gender Blending: Confronting the Limits of Duality*, Bloomington: Indiana University Press.

Elliot, Patricia (2010) *Debates in Transgender, Queer and Feminist Theory*, Farnham: Ashgate.

Fausto-Sterling, Anne (1989) *Sexing the Body: Gender Politics and the Construction of Sexuality*, New York: Basic Books.

Feinberg, Leslie (1977) *Transgender Warriors: Making History from Joan of Arc to Dennis Rodman*, Boston MA: Beacon Press.

Feinberg, Leslie (1993) *Stone Butch Blues*, Ithaca NY: Firebrand Books.

Foucault, Michel (1990) *The History of Sexuality Volume I: An Introduction*, London: Penguin Books.

Glover, David and Cora Kaplan, eds. (2000) *Genders*, London: Routledge.

Greer, Germaine (1999) *The Whole Woman*, London: Doubleday.

Greer, Germaine (2009) 'Caster Semenya Sex Row: What Makes a Woman?', *Guardian*, 20 August, at <http://www.theguardian.com/sport/2009/aug/20/ger maine-greer-caster-semenya> (accessed 28 June 2014).

Halberstam, Judith (2005) *In a Queer Time and Place: Transgender Bodies, Subcultural Lives*, New York: New York University.

Halberstam, Judith (2012) *Female Masculinity*, Durham NC: Duke University Press.

Haraway, Donna J. (1991) 'A Cyborg Manifesto: Science, Technology, and Socialist-Feminism in the Late Twentieth Century', in *Simians, Cyborgs and Women: The Reinvention of Nature*, London: Free Association Books.

Hayes, Cressida J. (2003) 'Feminist Solidarity after Queer Theory', *Signs* 28:4, pp. 1093–120.

Humm, Maggie (1992) *Modern Feminisms: Political, Literary, Cultural*, New York: Columbia University Press.

Jeffreys, Sheila (2014) *Gender Hurts: A Feminist Analysis of the Politics of Transgenderism*, London: Routledge.

Johnson, Heather L. (1997) 'Unexpected Geometries: Transgressive Symbolism and the Transsexual Subject in Angela Carter's *The Passion of New Eve*', in Joseph Bristow and Trev Lynn Broughton, eds., *The Infernal Desires of Angela Carter: Fiction, Femininity, Feminism*, Harlow: Addison Wesley Longman.

Lauretis, Teresa de (1987) *Technologies of Gender: Essays on Theory, Film, and Fiction*, London: Macmillan.

More, Kate and Stephen Whittle, eds. (1999) *Reclaiming Genders: Transsexual Grammars at the Fin de Siècle*, London: Cassell.

Prosser, Jay (1998) *Second Skins: The Body Narratives of Transsexuality*, New York: Columbia University Press.

Raymond, Janice (1994) *The Transsexual Empire: The Making of the She-Male*, New York: Teachers College Press.

Riviere, Joan (1986) 'Womanliness as a Masquerade', in Victor Burgin, James Donald and Cora Kaplan, eds., *Formations of Fantasy*, London: Methuen.

Rubin, Gayle (1975) 'The Traffic in Women: Notes on the "Political Economy" of Sex', in Rayna R. Reites, ed., *Toward an Anthropology of Women*, New York: Monthly Review Press.

Sedgwick, Eve Kosofsky (1992) *The Epistemology of the Closet*, Berkeley: University of California Press.

Sedgwick, Eve Kosofsky and Andrew Parker, eds. (1994) *Performance and Performativity*, London: Routledge.

Stoller, Robert J. (1968) *Sex and Gender: On the Development of Masculinity and Femininity*, London: Hogarth Press.

Stone, Sandy (1992) 'The *Empire* Strikes Back: A Posttranssexual Manifesto', in Julia Epstein and Kristina Straub, eds., *Body Guards: The Cultural Politics of Gender Ambiguity*, London: Routledge.

Stryker, Susan and Stephen Whittle, eds. (2006) *The Transgender Studies Reader*, London: Routledge.

Stryker, Susan and Aren Z. Aisura, eds. (2013) *The Transgender Studies Reader 2*, London: Routledge.

Trevenna, Joanne (2002) 'Gender as Performance: Questioning the "Butlerification" of Angela Carter's Fiction', *Journal of Gender Studies* 11:3, pp. 267–76.

Tripp, Anna, ed. (2000) *Gender*, Basingstoke: Palgrave Press.

Vogel, Lisa (2014) Letter from Michigan Womyn's Music Festival, 9 May, at <http://www.michfest.com/lettertothecommunity050914.htm> (accessed 28 June 2014).

Westall, Claire (2012) '"His almost vanished voice": Gendering and Transgendering Bodily Signification and the Voice in Angela Carter's *The Passion of New Eve*', in

Rina Kim and Claire Westall, eds., *Cross-Gendered Literary Voices*, Basingstoke: Palgrave Macmillan.

Wilchins, Riki Anne (1997) *Read My Lips: Sexual Subversion and the End of Gender*, Ithaca NY: Firebrand Books.

Wilchins, Riki Anne (2004) *Queer Theory, Gender Theory: An Instant Primer*, New York: Alyson Publications.

Wilchins, Riki (2013, new edn.) *Read My Lips: Sexual Subversion and the End of Gender*, Riverdale NY: Magnus Books.

LOVE AND THE OTHER:
THE EXAMPLE OF GIORGIO AGAMBEN

Julian Wolfreys

There has been much talk concerning the Other in criticism – and the other also, with just a little 'o'. This has concerned the concept of otherness, regarding gender, ethnicity, sexual identity and orientation, the human and animal (supposing we might separate them, or know what the distinction is), questions of materiality and ontology, and so on, and so on. (You'll forgive me if I don't switch between little and large 'o/O's. This in itself would make interminable the various discussions here, and lead me and my reader, you, the other, astray. I will remain with the 'other' in mind. Yet, as discussions of ethics and memory work highlight, there is a much more singular, not to say intimate relationship between a 'self' and an 'other', not to mention the scenario – I won't call it a 'fact' – wherein, the self is the other, for the other, an other self already. I am other to the other I acknowledge, to each and every other. And my otherness – or alterity, to employ an alternative critical term – is, moreover, never the same for each and every other, to whom, for whom I am an other. The intimate apprehension of which I speak has to do with love, a topic, hardly a concept, which has been given short shrift by philosophers, and only slightly more attention by literary critics, save that it speaks to, or exemplifies, they believe, those allegedly more pressing questions of gender, sexual orientation, etc. In this chapter therefore, I wish to consider love as love, if this is possible, in relation to the idea of the other, and as a way of introducing the work of Giorgio Agamben, one of the twenty-first century's most significant philosophers.

'Seeing something simply in its being-thus – irreparable, but not for that reason necessary; thus, but not for that reason contingent – is love' (Agamben 1993c: 25). Thus, Giorgio Agamben, in a statement that equates the unveiling of love's nakedness and violence. I, the subject, I find myself, *in* love, as a result of this transgression of the other. I see the other's being in its most naked state and am struck, violated by this, and by that for which there is no reparation, to which no repair or correction can be effected. It is as if one of those 'Love is . . .' cartoons by Stefano Casali, with the two plump, nude, child-like figures had suddenly erupted from within, displaying something much darker, much more disquieting, leaving no-one untouched or clothed. (Or perhaps that moment in *Shrek*, when Princess Fiona suddenly morphs into, thereby revealing, her inner ogre.)

Love is perhaps the most profound and fundamental, and yet least obvious of transgressions. I shall illustrate this proposition by examining its ubiquitous traces, as these are found everywhere in the text of Giorgio Agamben. From the outset though, we should neither confuse nor conflate 'love' with either desire or any erotism, as I shall go on to explain. Separating what is already other than these clinical and quasi-classical terms, love must be maintained as other to them. Simply put, love as other is unavailable to definition or determination. It arrives as a singular and unexpected, unpredictable event of the other, which both touches and traverses me. Thus, love, as this 'experience of the other' is irreducible to any systematic or symptomatic mapping. As the double genitives – event of the other, experience of the other – attest, love, apprehended in this phantom motion and traversal is both my experience of the other and the other's experience *in me*. The other, in my indirect yet intimate apprehension of it, is thus transgressive in the most fundamental manner. For it crosses the limits of my being, my psyche. It enters and translates me. It awakens an alterity that was already mine but of which I had little awareness until after the event of transgression. Love is thus that which opens the subject to indirect apperception. Crossing the limits of a supposedly secure identity, the temporal event that is the experience of being touched by love transmutates selfhood in its traversal; it transforms in a loving transgression from within the space of the self, of being itself. This is what we come to read in Agamben's text. But additionally, it is also what we see take place in the writing of that text, as I shall show.

Neither synonymous with the other nor supplementary to any notion of the other, love remains in Agamben as that for which we will have to account in a language that, though indirect, must keep itself separate from the philosopher's economy. More than merely 'found', as if it were encountered, scattered like the wind-blown detritus of hastily ripped apart love letters, love places itself in one's way. The subject in reading is interrupted by love, as if it arrived to call the reader, to become the beloved, 'in the spirit of a pseudo-Platonic letter' (Agamben 1993a: 3). It appears momentarily, here and there, disposing of its traces, in between one subject and another, or as the visible manifestation for the reader, the 'illumination' of and for a subject otherwise remaining unrepresentable. Hardly a subject at all, except in the example of one essay, 'The Passion of Facticity', which perversely and ingeniously speaks to the trace of love precisely at those places where it is found only *in absentia*, love remains, nonetheless – and as a trope, a *topos*, a *souvenir*.

– Of what?

Of that which is never present, no longer present, nor available to presence. A *souvenir* is kept as a memory trace, it can cause one to reflect and so cause the other to appear, however indirectly. Love in the text of Agamben is therefore the souvenir of the other, as well as the sign under which the face to face with the other might be possible, however unlikely. Love's trace remains in the place of, thereby giving place to the other.

– Why *love*?

Without getting ahead of ourselves, it is to be observed that love is the necessary pre-condition of knowledge. In his commentary on the apparent absence of love in Martin Heidegger's *Being and Time*, a lack or silence that has troubled a number of commentators since that volume first appeared, Giorgio Agamben observes that, as far as one can discern, for Heidegger, love 'conditions precisely the possibility of knowledge and the access of truth' (Agamben 1999: 186). It not only conditions the possibility of knowledge. In disturbing the time of reading with the demand for a different temporality, it opens a space in the search for truth, and in doing so interrupts the subject as the displaced phantom for the other; and specifically, the Other, as my title has it, *in* love.

– To my knowledge, Agamben never uses the term 'Other'. Is it the best term to use if you're going to speak of Agamben? After all, Agamben has striven to keep a distance between himself and the work of Derrida or, by extension, Levinas, apropos any thinking of the matter of an 'ethics of the other'.

– It is, I think, precisely because neither the 'other' nor the 'Other' appear, nor do they become distinctly visible in Agamben's text, that I take the work of alterity to be all the more persistent, particularly if we note, as I plan to, and as I have already signalled, the frequency of love. Beyond the obvious distance of Agamben from various philosophers of alterity, if I can put it like that, the very absence of the other signals itself and so demands consideration. What is also striking about such an absence – and this is no more than speculation, the projection of a fiction – is that beyond the immediate distance that Agamben wishes to maintain from the discourse of alterity, there might be, perhaps, a question of refusing an encounter with psychoanalysis. Philosophy denies psychoanalysis, for psychoanalysis would insist on the other of philosophy, for which the philosopher – and in this term I wish to signal specifically Agamben *contra* both Derrida's psychoanalyzing of the philosophical corpus and Levinas's return to a theological Other – cannot countenance alterity, an alterity that haunts philosophy as surely as does literature. Whilst one cannot give more space to that consideration here, given love's frequency, it would be perverse, if not to discuss otherness, the other, alterity, then at least to acknowledge its phantom presence, the breath of its passage, through the affirmation of its absence in the text of Agamben. The perversion arises because love *is not philosophical. It remains – and as such is unavailable to philosophy, its institutions, its practice, its discourses.* Love is the hauntological sign that plays on the ontological imperative in the philosophical corpus. If love arrives as a trace, interrupting repeatedly any reading, then love must arrive from somewhere – or even some*one*, some *other*. Arrival, interruption, disruption, transmission: all of these are impossible without an other location or location of an other, however occluded or impossible to situate such an imaginary or phantasmatic locus might be. That Agamben does not play down the play of love, that he turns and returns to it, that it returns insistently to him, suggests at least the possibility of the impossible, that is to say an unfigurable alterity within his discourse, that which is so wholly and completely other, that it remains as the unnameable in the text of Agamben and for Agamben.

To insist on this point, it may be also that the question has to be why Agamben avoids the term. In this avoidance (if it is one), there is an echo of infrequency, which Agamben notes concerning the paucity of references to love in Heidegger, and which therefore should give us pause, as I have remarked. Is Agamben's silence – how can we tell if it is a silence? Is silence the same as avoidance? Or does silence admit to an unbearable proximity for Agamben? – itself structural, and is this structure, at once strategic and necessary, informed by the haunting force of Heidegger? But beyond the question of avoidance (and we should not rush to assume this is simply the case, if it is at all), there is also another question concerning the possible relationship to be read between Agamben and any Derridean or Levinasian project having to do with that 'ethics of the other' to which you allude. I am not at all sure I can answer these questions. What I would say, though, is that perhaps – imagine this fiction if you will – love is the name of the other; love names that which cannot be named, and so it is that naming directly must be avoided, if the wholly other is to remain the secret love of Agamben's text. This is, of course, only an hypothesis. But bear with me, and listen to the title, once more.

You might hear in this title, in passing, what I take to be at the heart of all love's motivations, its numerous *stimmung* – all those otherwise untranslatable intonations, moods, emotive states, and even opinions – as these are recorded and move across, thereby *inspir*ing the text of Agamben. Whether Agamben writes of troubadour poetry, Auschwitz, a radical reformulation of historicity, or the condition of the sovereign state, the innumerable *stimmung* and their pulse is felt. Even where it is not mentioned or paused over, Agamben's writing nonetheless finds its endless motivation, its rhythmic turns, in love. Agamben's is, we might say, a text *in love*, and as such expresses and stages the text that is *in love*, acting out in its patterns and pulses the endless desire of a face to face with the other that haunts Agamben's writing. It is out of love, love of, for the other that Agamben moves after love, proceeds in the wake of love across multiple spaces, differing discourses, and several centuries, in order to begin to 'measure the revolutionary and novel character of a conception of love that despite changes during the passing of seven centuries, is still, with all of its ambiguities and contradictions, substantially ours' (1993b: 23). The persistent *stimmung* and *souvenirs* of love repeat and transform knowledge for Agamben, and so by the dynamics and tempi of the amorous phantasm the reader encounters, coming face to face with, the unspeakable other in the motions of the text.

– Then it might be said that such movements and e-motions leave deposited across the surface of Agamben's writing the whisper of a phantom breath (*phantasikon pneuma*), as if the merest scent were all that were left in the place one finds oneself. It is as if one recognises that, the other having departed ahead of one, this leaves the subject with the realisation that one is always after the other, one is always *after* love. One trails belatedly in the wake of the other. And this belated reflection, the untimely apprehension of finding oneself traversed and transgressed by the other, is what causes Agamben to identify what takes place between one face and another, in the face to face, and in the face of the other, singularly the other *in* love.

– Indeed. For it is not only that the other is in love with the self, as Agamben's coyly lyrical text reveals, hesitantly and in sudden, momentary unveilings. It is not a question of there being simply some 'external body' (1993b: 23). It is also that there, *there* half-concealed and half-revealed is the other, *in* love, in what is signalled in the name of love. The other who, or which, is in love, might be that other with whom I find myself face to face, facing up to the fact that love takes place, if at all, *between*. But this is not all. Indeed, it is nothing more than mere semblance, merely mimetic resemblance – and therefore not *vraisemblance* – of what remains unavailable to direct perception. This alterity in 'love' . . .

– and also 'in love', for does this 'condition of being' not name an alterity for and of the self, an otherness, which takes one out of oneself, in a 'self-showing' to the subject, to the other of the subject and the subject of the other? Is not this idiom, 'in love' the most transparent and enigmatic of ex-pressions, e-motions, articulating revelation and encryption of the self-transgressing and the self-transgressed?

. . . this name for nothing as such, is, fundamentally and originarily, that which is at the fathomless heart of the revelation of the self to itself in the self-showing of its being; and therefore in the reflexive transcendence of Being, as this is given to one, by the other.

In this chapter therefore, in having placed myself face to face with what has already fled, and so setting out on an endless quest after Agamben in order to come face to face with that which love gives to Agamben throughout his text, we come to find ourselves, together, in the proximity of a line or two from Giorgio Agamben's essay, 'The Face', the concluding essay from the second part of *Means without End: Notes on Politics* (2000: 91–100). In pursuing the tropic and topical work of love in the text of Agamben, we find ourselves in the midst of a clearing. For Agamben's text in its loving engagement constitutes the most sustained, transparent and yet, simultaneously, opaque of commentaries indebted to the phenomenological tradition. And this will lead, as I shall have occasion to argue in conclusion to this essay, with the most profound call for a reorientation, to the question of temporality in any hegemonic model of historicity, which currently and in recent decades has informed, not to say dominated, academic, critical, political and philosophical discourses.

Agamben's remarks on love, through which various historical others come face to face with love, attuning themselves singularly in relation to that which takes place in the space between one face and another, constitute a history or, perhaps, genealogy of what he calls in *Stanzas* the 'phantasmatic character of the process of love' in its 'heroic-demonic' dimension. It is this, according to Agamben, that drives Being's very historicity (1993b: 121, 120). Thus, love in the text of Agamben brings us face to face with the very grounds of history itself. This very orientation – of, and *towards*, the face to face – thus serves to remark that which is called in *The Coming Community* 'the multiple common place . . . the place of the neighbor that each person inevitably receives' (1993c: 25). Without the reorientation and opening to the common place there can be no reading of the historical nor an apprehension of the necessary deconstruction of the historical in the name of that which is to come, and hence the weak messianic hope of a radical and revolutionary reorientation of Being towards its other. This 'common place', which both takes and gives place, is, argues Agamben, 'nothing but the coming to itself of each singularity'. This, moreover, is an otherwise 'unrepresentable space', an 'empty place where each can move freely, . . . where spatial proximity borders on opportune time'. This space or place, in which transgression is the free radical condition of the making or taking-place of shared space wherein one comes to singularity through the subject's reception of the neighbour, the lover, the other, is, according to Agamben that which is 'designates', if not 'the very place of love', then 'love as the experience of taking-place in whatever singularity' (1993c: 25).

Such statements or observations on the part of the author concerning love remark it as a 'topic' (never quite a concept and perhaps more properly the taking-place that a word stages, a phantasm or 'spacing') . . .

– and as you have noted, they turn up and are treated throughout Agamben's *oeuvre*; not least throughout *Stanzas* and with less immediate intensity in *The Coming Community*, but additionally such reflections are to be read through the space of a carefully demarcated paragraph in *Idea of Prose*, and in that small but telling essay concerning the apparent absence or, at least, marked paucity of love in Martin Heidegger's *Being and Time* (Agamben 1995: 61; 1999: 185–204).

– Once we have been interrupted by love, it is always a matter of turning back, of reflecting and reorientation. Whatever the subject, ostensibly, where love arrives as the sign of the experience of a certain singularity, such singularity announces the other *in* love, as my title has it. But to continue, this re-encounter, this revenant experience, is not only an abstract reflection. It informs the most immediate and materially grounded experiences of one's subjectivity. Here is Agamben, speaking of the encounter with another's face and the taking place that goes by the strange name of love. 'I look someone in the eyes', confesses Agamben. To which gesture, which gaze, there is returned the, momentarily, equivocal response: 'either these eyes are cast down . . . or they look back at me' (2000: 93). Agamben maintains the equivocation, and with that the maintenance of an opening in the glimpse of another before meaning is given, relation established, in hypothesizing that, on the one hand, 'they can look at me shamelessly . . . Or, they can look at me with a chaste impudence and *without reserve, thereby letting love and the word happen in the emptiness of our gazes*' (2000: 93, emphasis added).

Something takes place here in the blink of an eye. I am witness to, and the subject of, a transgression, literally a movement across the boundaries of self-hood. What occurs however is not in one direction, solely, and, moreover, is irreducible to, resists alignment with, any thinking of desire or any erotics. The 'endless joy of erotic experience' of which Agamben speaks in *Stanzas* has nothing to do with love as such, its experience or passage. For such joy would belong to a recuperative and aggrandizing economics of the self-same. Such joy is the place where I can tell myself I master and so silence the breath of the other, where I engage in the ineluctability of the narcissistic loop, trapped always on playback. However, love opens one beyond this; there is a mutual experience of the other within the same, from either side. It happens – and I experience this happening, as it happens to me; I am not outside this experience that I observe – before I can articulate fully what has taken place, before I can name the experience or surround its nakedness and intimacy with the armature of an epistemology. There is in the experience the transgressive arrival of *phainesthai* before *epistasthai*. In this, love arrives, in coming (*venire*) it surfaces within my consciousness, from beneath (*sou-venir*). And this is perceived, as Agamben argues Heidegger perceived throughout the composition of *Being and Time*, 'precisely because the mode of Being of an opening [which is given in the gaze and its circuitous reciprocation] . . . is more original than all knowledge (and takes place, according to Scheler and Augustine, in love)' (1999: 187). More original than all knowledge, in this touch of the other, then, an originary interpellation befalls the subject, calling to him or her, in which call or interruption *there* is the instauration of the phantasmic memory, a memory all the more spectral for having never been mine. The situation of opening in love as the singular condition of that originary coming to pass prior to knowledge is not to be ignored. The open return of the gaze, doubled and displaced, haunted in its very opening, once apprehended in this manner forces on one the recognition that 'love can no longer be conceived as it is commonly represented, that is, as a relation between . . . two subjects. It must, instead', Agamben continues in his reading of Heideggerian Being, 'find its place and proper articulation in the Being-already-in-the-world that characterizes Dasein's transcendence' (1999: 187). Being is given, and gives place to the other *in* love, the other *in love,* an other which traverses the one and the other, leaving neither separate or untouched. The very idea of relation as stable is undone.

The question of love is then, when truly considered, irreducible to the stasis of representation, specifically that of a relation between beings. Rather, as its unveiling through the passage between gazes makes manifest, the appearance or *apparitioning* of love has a temporal and spatial dimension, consisting in its showing of itself (*phainesthai*). Such 'self-showing' or *seeming,* as Heidegger has it '[*Scheinen*]' (1996: 25) is at the same time revealed and yet remains veiled in the semblance or *phainomenon* of an other, materialized in the *eidolon,* in which, a correspondence having been sent and received, self and other remain themselves and yet other also, without correspondence, without relation. Love is what has been 'let happen', in Agamben's phrase, whereby the reciprocity of the gaze, in opening the self to other, shows the self to itself as the other self-showing, in that self-showing of seeming *and* illumination, appearance as casting or shedding light. 'Let happen' marks the *factical* element in the phenomenology of love that Agamben is tracing, in which gesture he follows Heidegger, bringing to light that which remains for Heidegger the secret motivation in *Being and Time.*

– Love is not natural; it does not spring from out of nowhere, but is of the order of a making.

– No, from this perspective, love is the most unnatural experience. Uncanny in its intimacy, it is made. Love is therefore what comes to be crafted, not engendered through the touch that is shared between two souls, revealed and yet remaining invisible in the reciprocity, and touch, of the gaze, of eye touching upon eye. Love, as Agamben observes in a commentary on Heidegger's Augustinian heritage, 'is not natural', for in 'Latin, *facticius* is opposed to *nativus*' (1999: 189). And furthermore, there is no relation as such, much less anything that one can represent as being fixed in place in this giving-place that allows or lets love happen as a factical making. For the gazes are mutually, sympathetically, empty, it should be noted, as they fall into, enfolding, one another. Falling in love, as the commonplace has it is, in effect, far from common, for it causes to be made known, given out to the self that shows itself in the registration of the appearance of the other in the singular encounter with and experience of the other's gaze, a fleeting apprehension of Being as fallen. Love is just the memory of the originary fallenness of Being, of one finding oneself in the world. Love is uncanny to the extent that it is the memory trace, the encrypted mnemotechnic of the very condition of Being in its facticity, its historicity.

– Yet, all takes place between, or there is nothing. At the same time however, it is not only love that the gazes let happen. It is also, before knowledge, the word. To phrase this another way, and in order to move on from this in following Agamben, after Heidegger: it is not a question of articulating a phenomenology of love – although this preliminary project may well be what one finds scattered in intermittent traces across Agamben's publications, through little occasions or experiences, what might be termed surges – but rather that love *is* phenomenological. If it can be seen, if it can be understood in its revelation as the semblance of that which the other lets happen, then this is as a phenomenology, a *phainomenon* and a *logos*. (Heidegger first observes the intertwining of *phainomenon* and *logos* in the expression 'phenomenology' in Part II, §7 of *Being and Time* [1962: 24].) Love is just this correspondence and mutual coinage: the intimate touch between the *phainomenon, the phainesthai*, and the *logos*, the word or communication that carries in it the phantom, phantasm or revenant of Being.

– I begin to see in this a missed encounter. It occurs that Agamben has found himself, repeatedly, face to face with Heidegger, but never directly. A séance takes place. What is more, in the name of love and as a result of the gaze that is staged everywhere, this encounter has resulted in those numerous frequencies that score Agamben's text with their commentaries on love, in the midst of so many different and singular critical discussions. Whether these are focused on politics, philosophy, poetics, or human identity, there is always a turn on the part of the philosopher, who finds in his turn the return of love, *there* as the secret that, unveiled everywhere, leaves its traces on the text. And all the while, this remains without apparent system or order in the work of Agamben.

This is, for Agamben, the idea of love, which comes down to the following experience:

> To live in intimacy with a stranger, not in order to draw him closer, or to make him known, but rather to keep him strange, remote: unapparent – so unapparent that *his name contains him entirely*. And, even in discomfort, *to be nothing else*, day after day, *than the ever open place, the unwaning light* in which that one being, that thing remains forever *exposed and sealed off*. (1995: 61; emphases added)

To live with someone implies a practice, a knowledge, a familiarity and understanding. However, Agamben maintains the unfamiliarity, the strangeness of intimacy in order to articulate all the more powerfully the 'idea' of love. Such an idea opens, once more, a space, a taking and giving place, which in its staging or manifestation estranges, makes unquiet or unhomely the phantom effects of love. The other, reduced to a name, resides within that sign, that *logos* as supplement to the self, always exposed by, *in*, the phenomenological light of Being. The coming *logos* that love offers to countersign, itself being traced by the countersignature of the other, this is the only passage, the sole transgressive translation of an otherwise inexpressible existence, 'pure Being ... which is simply ineffable', unless expressed, and thereby translated from potentiality to actuality, as the singular inscription of the self. In this formula, and in the 'process of acquiring knowledge', *love* is the signature, logos, or '"letter of which you are the meaning"' (Agamben 1999: 247).

The experience of love perhaps, then, serves to open expression of, and to, the otherwise, the wholly other and the ineffable that is inscribed in the sign of love, a palimpsest and imprimatur of the opening of alterity. It gives place therefore to the naming of this experience, however indirectly, whereby the *logos* provides the semblance of what remains hidden, invisible, or 'sealed off'; of what is made, of what takes place and has place, as 'the very taking place of language in the unspeakable experience of the Voice' (Agamben 1991: 66). Such places, such *topoi*, wherein love is unveiled in its facticity are also *lieux de mémoire*, sites of memory as I have sought to establish. What comes back therefore in the illumination that arrives to the gaze in its being returned is love, once more, as *revenant*, as *souvenir*, the ghostly memory made from the touch between the eyes of an other. But this memory is unlike any other memory. For, as I have already implied, it is a memory that has never been my own, or, indeed, anyone's. This is the disquiet of the scenario given above. To live in intimacy with one who returns one's gaze, but to whom one remains as a stranger – here is a forceful dislocation in the affirmation of love. In this manner the self is opened, and uncovers as it discovers in itself an abyss, a radical alterity *in love*. The return of the gaze affords a taking place and a staging of place opening what is between us for the memory of the other – and what is more, the other in love. My eyes 'find' what was already *exposed and sealed off*, as do the eyes of the other in looking into mine. Thus, as Agamben argues apropos the Provençal troubadours, love (*Amors*), in being the name given by the poets to the 'experience of the poetic word', from which the word, *logos*, emerges, thereby giving place not to 'psychological or biographical events that are successively expressed in words, names rather the attempt to *live the topos itself, the event of language as a fundamental amorous and poetic experience*' (1991: 68). *Logos* then as memory of *topos*, in which place the revenant or *phainesthai* has seemed to appear, letting love happen.

– Which suggests a temporal, if not historical dimension, a dimension to the encounter with each and every other, always already haunted by the untimely reminder and remainder that love announces?

– Yes, yes; but, it has to be said, this temporal condition is why Agamben is so insistent on demanding a face to face with Heidegger, particularly apropos that which haunts Heidegger's major work, the trace of love, by which Being is marked, and remarks, 'the descent of actuality toward manifestation' (1999: 247). That manifestation or apparition is, there can be no doubt, the sign of the other, *in love*. It designates not the 'factual situation' of the relation between beings. Rather it signifies what Heidegger terms 'the "character of Being" (*Seinscharakter*) and "e-motion" proper to life', which is for Agamben a 'kind of prehistory of the analytic of Dasein and the self-transcendence of Being-in-the-world' (1999: 190–1). [A brief digression: Agamben passes over in silence that phrase translated as 'character of Being'. Yet, the translation only alludes somewhat weakly to what is in the Heideggerian portmanteau, which is that Being is a 'character' not simply in the sense of personality, but also, as an inscription, a letter, or manifestation of the meaning of Being.] Such signification, Agamben has us understand, is fundamental to the falling, the 'thrownness' of Dasein, a '"movement [as Heidegger describes it] that produces itself and that, nevertheless does not produce itself, producing the emptiness in which it moves; for its emptiness is the possibility of movement"' (Heidegger, quoted in Agamben 1999: 191). Here, we see – do we not? – in this remarkable expression of Heidegger's precisely the opening, the spacing and the movement, e-motion, which informs, bearing up in itself, the illumination that *love* offers in the text of Agamben, as it situates itself, again and again, at the very heart of Being in the face of the other. And that it is a movement, e-motion directed towards a falling *ex-stasis*, is itself indicative of the temporality at stake in *being-in-love*, which affirms in its singular experience Dasein's self-transcendence.

One could therefore say, in response to Agamben's prompt, that if 'the structure of Dasein is marked by a kind of original fetishism' (1999: 196) (Agamben is at pains to point out the shared etymological heritage between facticity and fetishism), as he claims, then this fetish is to be found precisely in the *eidolon*, the phantasmic image of the beloved haunting my imagination, in the face of the otherwise ineffable alterity which lies at the radically depthless depths of *love*. The other arrives in the guise of love to interrupt me in the midst of my everyday existence, in which I reside inauthentically in a condition of having forgotten the condition of Being. It thus calls to mind the authenticity of Being, and so reminds us that, though forgotten, love, the *sou-venir* is 'always already present ... and traverse[s] our Being from the beginning' (1999: 198). Along with hate therefore, love is, for Heidegger, as it is for Agamben, a 'fundamental' guise or manner, 'through which Dasein experiences ... the opening and retreat of the being that it is and must be'. In love, Agamben continues, the being 'establishes himself more deeply in that into which he is thrown, appropriating his very facticity' (1999: 199). The subject, opened to memory by the revenance of love, finds himself traversed, transgressed by the temporal e-motion of the other, *in love*. Love is thus the experience of an impossible face to face, and is transgressive precisely because in Being, as Agamben claims, 'the *passion of Facticity* in which man bears ... nonbeing and darkness', love exceeds mere narcissistic dialectical strife at the cost of the beloved, to become through its singular experience 'the passion and exposition of facticity itself and ... the irreducible impropriety of beings' (1999: 204). The most authentic experience for Agamben in that it is the only possibility of the taking place of the face-to-face (which is the gift, the giving place of the other *in* love), love sheds light on, illuminating the lover and the beloved *'in their concealment, in an eternal facticity beyond Being'* (1999: 204, emphasis original). Love is neither mine, nor yours; it is not proper, neither is it a property. Love is made and so makes us in its name. That 'eternal' facticity to which Agamben addresses himself, and which he seeks to outface in almost every text, thereby bringing its invisible persistence to light, bespeaks in secret the memory beneath the surface of my consciousness, traversing that border, transgressing the limits of consciousness. Always already there, the facticity of love, the only authentic souvenir of Being, promises to return, revenant source of illumination that it is.

– But hadn't you remarked how being-in-love was marked not only by a temporality but also an experience of historicity, of the historicity of beings, which offered to rewrite conventional discourses of historicity?

– Yes, it remains for me to address this. So, permit me to recall here that love is the 'experience of taking place in a whatever singularity'. Thus, the experience of love is 'invariably accompanied by a certain experience of time, which is implicit in it, [and] conditions it' (Agamben 1993c: 25). While Agamben is speaking of the implication of time within any conception of history, the perception of the singular experience of love as similarly temporal opens to us the brief sketch towards a different reading of history that Agamben enables. Singularity, understood properly, can only be perceived through the possibility that whatever singularity we address is, fundamentally, and in principle endlessly iterable. If love is neither yours nor mine but is made, then there is the temporal condition by which making occurs, repeatedly, yet with a difference. Every time is singular, and therefore other. Yet, every time that love returns it is disturbed by its familiar unfamiliarity, by that untimely return, despite the fundamental forgetting that informs Being. Love undoes from within as anachronic ghost that model or modality of history defined by Agamben as the 'vulgar representation of time as a precise and homogeneous continuum' (1993a: 91). Love therefore admits – confesses and gives entrance to – its own uncanny condition, in that it enlightens us, thereby illuminating, 'the basis of the radical "otherness" of time, and of its "destructive" character' (1993a: 93) with regard to history conceived as undifferentiated continuum. A 'destructive' character, love as *logos* scores through the unbroken line of history, rupturing its calm surface, thereby haunting and insuring 'Western man's incapacity to master time and his consequent obsession with gaining it and passing it' (1993a: 93).

Such incapacity is doubtless caught up with the possessiveness of desire, with the desire to possess, to make property what is improper. It is also the repeated reminder that one is always after that by which one is obsessed, and which, on the one hand, one can never catch up with, while on the other, one is always placed in a belated relation, the one to, or let us say in the wake of, the other.

– One is never on time, then.

– And for a very good reason, time being, like love, always untimely. Hence, as Agamben recollects, the 'Augustinian anxiety *in the face* of time's fleeting essence'; for time's movement, like love we feel, is ' "the thing existing which is not when it is, and is when it is not: A half-glimpsed becoming" ' (1993a: 98, emphasis added). We are back with the gaze, this time from that coy, lidded location of the other, in its provisional response. The other, half-glimpsed, looks us in the face and we are called, interrupted, displaced from the untransgressed continuity of our inauthentic historical Being. Half-glimpsed – and yet, 'for everyone there is an immediate and available experience on which a new concept of time could be founded' (1993a: 104).

In conclusion then, turning to a doubled past – on the one hand to Aristotle and on the other to the Provençal troubadours, to whom Agamben returns and turns his face on other occasions – the philosopher places a hope in the *souvenir*, that which is to come as revenant transgression, the heterogeneity of pleasure; heterogeneous in that, as pleasure, it is irreducible to and 'outside any measurable duration' (1993a: 104). It transgresses duration's boundaries, and with that any finite determinability. In history, yet outside its flow, we experience, in the blink of an eye, that which we later remember, and which befalls, and so transgresses us, 'the full, discontinuous, finite and complete time of pleasure' (1993a: 104). Pleasure, everywhere and nowhere as such, always transgressing being as temporal experience beyond, without measurable time. It is this, Agamben demands, which we must 'set against the empty, continuous and infinite time of vulgar historicism . . . [and the] chronological time of pseudo-history' (1993a: 105). The other in love transgresses me, and makes this possibility an actuality, every time *there* is love in some other place, and yet simultaneously touching me, traversing and haunting me; and every time, also, that the other is apprehended as *being-in-love*.

QUESTIONS FOR FURTHER CONSIDERATION

1. Is it possible to define love in general terms?
2. In what ways do writers represent love? What are the formal aspects of such representation?
3. Is love separable from sexuality in literary representation?
4. What is the relationship between love and the idea of singularity?
5. To what extent does love define the self?

BIBLIOGRAPHY

Agamben, Giorgio (1991) *Language and Death: The Place of Death*, trans. Karen E. Pinkus, with Michael Hardt, Minneapolis: University of Minnesota Press.

Agamben, Giorgio (1993a) *Infancy and History: Essays on the Destruction of Experience*, trans. Liz Heron, London: Verso.

Agamben, Giorgio (1993b) *Stanzas: Word and Phantasm in Western Culture*, trans. Ronald L. Martinez, Minneapolis: University of Minnesota Press.

Agamben, Giorgio (1993c) *The Coming Community*, trans. Michael Hardt, Minneapolis: University of Minnesota Press.

Agamben, Giorgio (1995) *Idea of Prose*, trans. Michael Sullivan and Sam Whitsitt, Albany: State University of New York Press.

Agamben, Giorgio (1999) *Potentialities: Collected Essays in Philosophy*, ed., trans., and int., Daniel Heller-Roazen, Stanford: Stanford University Press.

Agamben, Giorgio (2000) *Means without End: Notes on Politics*, trans. Vincenzo Binetti and Cesare Casarino, Minneapolis: University of Minnesota Press.

Heidegger, Martin (1962) *Being and Time*, trans. John Macquarrie and Edward Robinson, New York: Harper & Row.

CRITICAL VOICES, ETHICAL QUESTIONS

CRITICAL COMPANIONS: DERRIDA, HARAWAY AND OTHER ANIMALS

Lynn Turner

The 'question of animality' is not one question among others . . . it also represents the limit upon which all the great questions are formed and determined, . . . all the concepts that attempt to delimit what is 'proper to man,' the essence and future of humanity, ethics, politics, law, 'human rights,' 'crimes against humanity,' 'genocide,' etc.

Jacques Derrida (2004: 62–3)

They are here. We are there. Prick up your ears. This chapter reckons with the way that critical voices in the twenty-first century are engaged with the animal question. Without the inordinate amount of space due to the burgeoning field now naming animals as its focus, I will cut a path particular to the shattering frames of thought exposed by Jacques Derrida and Donna Haraway. I choose this path for several reasons. One is that both thinkers make available entirely different modes of enquiry or types of question than did the discourse of 'animal rights' of Peter Singer (1995 [1975]) and Tom Regan (2004 [1983]), important as that has been and continues to be in making a difference to animals' lives. In so doing, both Derrida and Haraway have massively reshaped contemporary critical thought such that the animal question cannot be set aside under the ruse of a specific lobby. The shift from rights to ethics that Derrida and Haraway enable is at the heart of this chapter. While they stem from different disciplinary training – philosophy and biology respectively – as non-dialectical thinkers with their ears to the ground, alert to the myriad non-human species with whom we are obliged to share space, grounds, and conditions of possibility, they are, in Haraway's parlance, good to 'think with'.

Working with the notion of 'critical companions' I draw out the crises of companionship on which both thinkers insist. '*We are, constitutively, companion species*', Haraway underscores, even as many of our companions face extinction at an ever escalating rate indexing the emergency in our everyday (2003: 2, original emphasis). Without assimilating Derrida and Haraway to each other, I frame their work as a critical companionship through the commensal practices of the meal. Rather than the primal scene of the ritual transformation of nature into culture – the raw into the cooked – in the name of a transcendent human subject, the meal becomes a complex environment where, as Haraway puts it, 'all of the actors are not human and all of the humans are not "us," however defined' (2008b: 159). This is not strictly a question of 'who comes after the subject?', to use the title of the journal issue that prompted Derrida to charge the frame of the 'who' as that which cleanly maintains the subject in opposition to an effaced 'what' (Derrida 1995: 272).[1] Rather, through the ethics of encounters with others that cannot not include non-human others, it dismantles 'the fictions of *either* being subjects *or* objects' (Haraway 2008b: 158, emphasis added). In his own critical insistence on a posthumanism that ceases to centre upon the subject and that moves away from the discourse of rights that again supposes a subject as bearer of such rights, Cary Wolfe provocatively translates Derrida's investment as '*what* comes after the subject' (2008: 110, emphasis added).

The way in which renewed attention to the work of Derrida revises the critical understanding of deconstruction as a consequence of the publication of *The Animal That Therefore I Am* is pertinent for the tenor of this volume.[2] Wolfe is a major figure in this renewal, both through making available the first English translation of Derrida's 'And Say the Animal Responded' (2003) in his important collection *Zoontologies*, and in terms of showing how the deconstructive ethics of infinite hospitality ranges beyond the subject of rights in his equally influential *Animal Rites* and *What is Posthumanism?* (Wolfe 2003, 2010).[3] Scholars such as Susan Fraiman find this redescription of the critical work of animal studies one that also happens to substantially bypass work by ecofeminists to effect a kind of masculinization of the field through both the politics of citation and by eschewing 'feminine' sentimentality (Fraiman 2012). Regarding the latter she serves notice on Wolfe's oft-cited tenet that the reworked ethics of critical animal studies '*has nothing to do with whether you like animals*' (Wolfe 2003: 7, emphasis added, quoted in Fraiman 2012: 102). For this reader, Wolfe's clause is lodged in the strategy of getting the widest audience possible politically engaged with non-human others. Indeed Haraway herself – one whose admission of sentimental attachment is well known – is 'rankle[d] when folks assume that deep-in-the-flesh relationship [with animals] isn't driving a good bit of what's going on in [Wolfe's] work'.[4]

Framing this chapter through Derrida and Haraway in some sense addresses the question of citation, not least since Haraway's most recent book, *When Species Meet*, does name Derrida, while his scant acknowledgement of less anthropocentric work in contemporary scientific endeavour is the poorer for lack of any reciprocal engagement with Haraway (see Haraway 2008a: 19–26). Giving emphasis to the theoretical work of deconstruction is not to dodge the question of the animal but rather to recall the matter of the text as a wider condition than the specific instance of 'language', human or otherwise. In recalling this matter, the field in which we are engaged changes shape; who – or what – we are addressing or addressed by becomes unsettled. Though many have sought to correct a 'linguisticistic' misreading of the remit of deconstruction, it has doggedly persisted. The generalized frame of 'writing' expounded in Derrida's early landmark *Of Grammatology* already implicated 'the entire field of the living', as he reminds us in the 'Violence Against Animals' interview with Elizabeth Roudinesco (Derrida 2004: 63).[5] Yet this implication has been resisted. As recently as 2013, Rosi Braidotti remarked that her 'great respect for deconstruction' is marred by 'some impatience with its linguistic frame of reference' (2013: 30). Even Haraway, in her enthusiasm for the philosophical urgency regarding animals that Derrida's work has marshalled, criticizes what she regards as his failure to examine 'the practices of communication outside the writing technologies he did know how to talk about' when faced with a certain little cat, one morning, in his bathroom (2008a: 21).

FOR STARTERS: WE ARE ~~NOT~~ ALONE

L'Animal Autobiographique, the themed colloquium in Derrida's honour at Cerisy-la-Salle held in 1997, convened a prestigious philosophical audience: other speakers included, among others: Mireille Calle-Gruber, Laurent Milesi, Jean-Luc Nancy and Nicholas Royle. Derrida made it as plain as possible that his long address was not simply an update on his research that year but was intimately directed at them, saying: 'For everything I am about to confide to you no doubt comes back to asking you to *respond* to me, you, to me concerning what it is to *respond*. If you can' (2008a: 8, emphasis original). The resulting posthumously published book, *The Animal That Therefore I Am* (including the titular essay, first published in English in 2002, as well as 'And Say the Animal Responded' first published in 2003), has provided inspiration for a wide range of thinkers. These works have energized those already working in animal studies as well as those newly awoken to the root and branch revision of the humanities – and the sciences – that the animal question provokes, some already engaged with deconstruction, others only tangentially. Some of the earliest engagements express surprise at the domestic scene that Derrida, now famously, narrates regarding the little cat regarding him outside of the automaticity of reaction (see Baker 2000: 185).[6] Some recognize the strategic political value in the gravitas lent to the cause by 'a great French philosopher' (Adams 2010: 5). Some demonstrate that Derrida was always thinking about animals (see Lawlor 2007).

In Derrida's questioning as to whether his audience could respond, quoted above, the short, blunt, second sentence casts doubt on human exceptionalism, even there in the refined environment of a colloquium and even here as I relay the question to the reader of this volume. However it does so in a particular manner, in line with the deconstructive 'method' of reverse and displace at work in this text. I freeze 'method' in scare-quotes to index Derrida's resistance to formulating a classical method as such. The latter, in aiming for an ordered regularity and ideality untouched by that to which it is merely applied, would blunt his hope for particularity, for the this-ness of *this* text, *this* question. It would close off the possibility of welcoming the other without qualification. In the closing paragraphs of 'Signature Event Context', Derrida comes closest to what we might better call a process than a method when he advocates the double gesture, writing: 'Deconstruction . . . must, by means of a double gesture, a double science, a double writing, practice an *overturning* of the classical opposition *and* a general *displacement* of the system' (1982: 329, emphasis original).

The classical opposition at stake in *The Animal That Therefore I Am* is that between response and reaction, it underwrites but also propels the performative division of the one who calls himself 'man' from the one he calls 'the animal' (Derrida 2008a: 30–2). Neatly severed in this way, our Cartesian legacy continues to present the human as the one who is able to respond while the animal can merely react (Descartes 2008: 47–8). Vouched for by a philosophical pedigree, the cant of this division nevertheless surfaces in every class introducing the question of the animal when students initially and commonsensically 'respond' by saying 'But surely animals *can't* . . .'. In refuting any one of the abilities classically attributed to man – to speak, to lie, to laugh, to grieve, to give, to point, to dress, to die – in such a way, I mean to draw ironic attention to the automaticity of their response. The cleavage is all the more ludicrous, as Derrida points out, by the supposed catch-all name of 'the animal', incorporating everything from cockroaches to squid to eagles to horses. It is not his purpose or frame to simply re-measure species such that each would be allotted its own, proper, domain, thus producing a new identity politics of due representation.

However, it is worth remarking here that current scientific research increasingly features discoveries regarding the intelligence of particular animals – especially the great apes, elephants and cetaceans, all shown to be able to recognize themselves in a mirror, all characterized by complex brains with spindle cells.[7] Alone, this would dislodge Descartes' faith in the segregation of 'the animal'. Such research supports campaigns such as the Great Ape Project or the recent discussion of non-human personhood for cetaceans by the Indian government.[8] Both award basic protections modelled on 'human rights' – such as the rights not to be imprisoned, not to be tortured and not to be killed – for particular species based on relative intelligence. Scholars such as Wolfe have endorsed gains such as these for their strategic value in ending animal suffering, while rightly pointing to their provisionality and to their inadequacy for thinking through the 'ethics of *the question of the human as well as the non-*

human animal' (Wolfe 2003: 192, emphasis original). In the interview 'Violence Against Animals' Derrida voices sympathy towards campaigns for animal rights, but raises concerns regarding both the maintenance of the Cartesian subject of 'rights' – that offers no critical revision of either 'the subject' or of 'rights' – and its basis in an implicitly eugenic taxonomy (this framing of the limitations of 'animal rights' is in relation to the work of Peter Singer and Paola Cavalieri, at the prompt of Derrida's interlocutor, Roudinesco) (Derrida 2004: 64–8). In her lucid *Critical Animal Studies: An Introduction*, Dawne McCance explicitly sets out the ways in which Singer's utilitarian animal advocacy repeats the speciesism of which he is critical when he refers to 'defective [human] infants' as a single category that may be judged and found wanting in comparison to particular animals (echoing the erasures performed by 'the animal') (2013: 29). There is a greater radicality to Derrida's double gesture. For him, it is not a matter of re-ordering species such that more gain recognition for the capacity to respond. This would only duplicate the problem of bypassing any examination of the supposed autonomy of the responding subject and maintain a eugenic hierarchy that pre-approves those 'most like us'. Nor is it a matter of holding at bay the automaticity of reaction. Rather the 'displacement of the system' is at work when Derrida asks his illustrious audience whether they are *able* to respond. After Derrida, the conditions of response have changed: it is no longer a capacity possessed by an autonomous subject. Without dissolving differences into biological continuism, our fantasy of autonomy is nevertheless disseminated through what he names a 'limitrophic' relation with others. That is to say, the limits between species are sites of cultivation, sites of growth and of complication, dramatically revising how we understand difference (see Derrida 2008a: 29–30).[9] As Derrida remarks, this 'is co-implication itself' (2004: 66). We are not untouched by others – including animal others! – we are not alone. This does not mean, however, that we know or even perceive the company that we keep.

The question of ability again comes to the fore, albeit in a transfigured sense, when Derrida insists on the importance of Jeremy Bentham's question 'can they suffer?' rather than 'can they think?' as a means of re-orienting our relation to non-human others (2008a: 28). Counter-intuitively, this does not immediately, or primarily, operate as a call to empathy. For Derrida it is the *ability to suffer* that both modifies 'ability' which is now 'no longer a power', and also places vulnerability and mortality as that which we all have in common. It gives 'the most radical means of thinking the finitude that we share with animals' (2008a: 28). It is in light of this deconstruction of the opposition of ability and privation that Wolfe proposes an ingenious new theoretical compatibility between animal studies and disability studies (see Wolfe 2008). Rather than continue Singer's calculus of rights and the relativism of 'mental capacity' or measurable ability to suffer (minus Derrida's transformation of 'ability'), Wolfe disarms the framework of rights that would disenfranchise 'defectives'. He does this not through following familiar lines of thinking in disability studies which might simply invert disability into a new kind of ability, but through appealing to Derrida's shared 'non-power at the heart of power' (2008a: 28). Diminishing power or ability in this way also displaces the dialectical pattern that habitually understands humans as initially weak and requiring a long maturity yet destined to subsequently grasp or overcome the world in technological mastery (in distinction to the counter-myth situating animals as always and already in perfect adaptation to their environment and hence having 'no need to sublate it to better serve their own ends). In so doing, this displacement profoundly undermines the conceptual succession from nature towards history.

Following 'the animal' through the pages of *The Animal That Therefore I Am* is a readerly exercise worth taking literally. The French play on the coincidence of 'I am' and 'I follow' has generated much commentary that expands upon Derrida's dislodging of presence as affirmed by Descartes' well known 'I think therefore I am'.[10] Yet so entrenched is the conceptual hierarchy of man versus animal that readers can mistake the problem that is under review for the future that Derrida himself affirms. 'The animal' named in the very title, dogging the subject's every move, does not address any given animal in particular but marks the *concept* that the linked fiction, 'man', organizes in support of the metaphysical edifice indexed in my opening epigraph.

Like the scene with the little cat in the bathroom that doubles the quotidian with the philosophical such that they uncannily share ground rather than remain barred to each other (as David Wood [2004: 133] suggests), a supplementary opposition follows that of response and reaction. This is the layered sense of nudity that veers between both Derrida's banal situation before his cat and the metaphysical figure of Truth as unveiling.[11] Out of the seeming obviousness of clothing as distinctively human – even as a primary distinctively human technology motivated by the dialectical overcoming of weakness – versus the seeming obviousness of the absence of clothing as such on other species authorized by their perfect adaptation to nature, a nature that is categorically ahistorical, Derrida refashions the stakes. 'Clothing' becomes a particular instance of a wider condition. This wider condition is that of hiding (Derrida 2008a: 61). We none of us step into the naked truth of presence. Our hiding is always addressed to the other. Thus, when Derrida writes 'The animal, therefore, is not naked because it is naked. There is no nudity "in nature"', he indicts our terrible *conceptual* heritage that blights thought even today (2008a: 5). And when he begins, in the biblical evocation of the opening sentence 'In the beginning, I would like to trust myself to words that, *were it possible*, would be naked', we gather that he does not affirm any condition of original nudity (2008a: 1, emphasis added).

In the more improvisational style of the second essay in *The Animal That Therefore I Am*, 'But as for me, who am I?' Derrida muses at length on his dream of animals dreaming and adjusts his own phrasing and framing. He shifts from condemning the foreclosure in the question 'Does the animal dream?' – foreclosed by the opposition the animal versus the human, reaction versus response – to imagining, as if he 'were dreaming . . . in all innocence, of *an animal* that doesn't intend harm to *the animal*' (2008a: 62–4, emphasis added). Derrida's phrasing here is subtle. *If* he were innocent he would rule out any harm through the cut of the homogenizing concept 'the animal'. Derrida, we know, is one who assiduously refrains from endorsing any absolutes: he would not affirm 'friendship' as such for example, since it would make a claim upon the reliability of the concept, but rather advocate a revised version of Aristotle's 'most friendship possible', from which the ability to calculate any formula for this outcome has been removed (Derrida 1997: 8). The sheer difficulty of devising a formula that would erase every trace of violence is brought into focus through his earlier consideration of sacrifice in the interview with Jean-Luc Nancy '"Eating Well" or the Calculation of the Subject' (Derrida 1995). There, Derrida voices a strong critique of our common failure to 'sacrifice sacrifice' such that there is implicitly a space left open for a 'non-criminal putting to death' typically directed as those we call animal. Yet in his implicit use of the psychoanalysis of Nicolas Abraham and Maria Torok and thus a metonymic complication of eating and identification, Derrida frames symbolic anthropophagy as the contaminant, situating ingestion and violence as what Haraway might name 'messmates'. Indeed the linked notions that violence can never be excluded from eating and that in so eating, one never does so alone, marks a contact zone of broad agreement between Derrida and Haraway.

AND FOR THE MAIN: THE ASSAULT COURSE

No one agreed. Everyone made worlds grow from their figure of the meal.

Donna Haraway (2008a: 293)

In 2003, to a hungry audience scenting the broader zeitgeist of the 'animal turn', Haraway's *Companion Species Manifesto* named 'dog writing to be a branch of feminist theory, or the other way around' (2003: 3). For her established readers this came as no surprise, since a section of *Primate Visions* from 1989 had already dared to name and explore primatology as a genre of feminist theory.[12] Companionship was already in a critical state: both crucial and in crisis. With her custom irony, Haraway had narrated at length the consequences of a commission inviting her to write the definition for the term 'gender' in a dictionary of Marxism (to be issued in six languages!).[13] There she was not only compelled to point out the awkward insertion of a term that could make no sense within a system of thought that naturalized sex through a division of labour, but also exposed the contingent association of the 'sex/gender' distinction influential in Anglo-American feminism, rather than, say, 'race/gender', through digging into the diverging translations of her given word: 'Geschlecht'. Coincidentally, while Haraway was asking awkward questions regarding the consolidation of the term 'gender' as the cultural successor to an imagined ground of 'sex', Derrida too was unearthing room for manoeuvre in several essays on this generative term 'Geschlecht',[14] similarly finding 'sex', 'race', 'species', 'genus', 'stock', 'family', 'generation' or 'genealogy' or 'community' within the term before Heidegger entrenched it within the terrain of 'humankind' as such (Derrida 2008b: 28). Leaving 'gender' behind – in the 'post-gender' gestures of Haraway's celebrated 'Cyborg Manifesto' – did not point to a disengagement from, or the completion of, the task of feminism, far from it.[15] Rather it indexed the non-dialectical character of her thought and refusal to persist in thinking of nature or sex as the inert ground from which culture or history or gender would spring. Moreover, it indexed her manifesto claim for 'pleasure in the confusion of boundaries', itself a wilfully provocative step away from the abject revulsion that psychoanalysis maintains and the clean grasp of the concept that speculative thought endorses (Haraway 1991: 150).

In her most recent work Haraway returns to companionship to flesh out its constitutive quality. Not only are we always already in relation with others – whether we know or acknowledge this or not – but relation, for Haraway is the minimal unit: 'Beings do not preexist their relatings' (2003: 6). Relating, in this light, does not fall prone to the erasure of the body that the psychoanalytic embrace of the signifier endorses. This remains the case even if such relations challenge the limits of our perception. While her most well-known storied analyses concern companion animals such as dogs shifted away from the instrumentalizing exceptional discourse of the pet, Haraway is clear that the wider term 'companion species' incorporates a host of organisms whose companionship may well be troubling, excessive or downright unwelcome. Anna Tsing has compellingly demonstrated, in light of Haraway's work, that we inhabit a long-term and conflicted companionship with fungi, from yeast to *Candida* to the imperial imprint of *Serpula lacrymans* (dry rot), as the British military inadvertently disseminated its spores from the Himalayas to wherever their wooden vessels – and subsequently wooden railway ties – landed (Tsing 2012: 141–54). A tropology of ingestion comes to figure prominently in Haraway's meditations upon companionship. She reminds readers in the opening pages of *When Species Meet* that the Latin roots of 'companion' immediately expose us to the ethics of a shared meal, '*cum panis*' or 'with bread' (2008a: 17). Towards the end of this extensive book Haraway recalls two specific meals: both cause consternation amongst the colleagues for whom these meals were or would have been prepared. She finds this consternation not to be an obstacle that must be surmounted or overcome, but rather a condition for what she names 'nourishing indigestion' as the 'necessary physiological state for eating well together' (2008a: 300). Haraway's explicit nod to Derrida's ethics of infinite hospitality affirms her seeming oxymoron not as a concept but as a process that does not result in a new ground, that is to say, it again affirms Haraway's thought as non-dialectical. Haraway's stance here is all the more remarkable in this context since the meals that she proffers continue to invoke heated arguments regarding who or what we eat (see, for example, Giraud 2013).

The first invitation to dine that Haraway recalls takes place on the day of her interview in 1980, in the Department of the History of Consciousness at the University of California. On that day, interest in the appointment of a new member of staff was singularly displaced by the news heralded by two of the department's then graduate students: they were about to attend a 'birth celebration' in the 'feminist, anarchist pagan cyberwitch mountains' replete with the consumption of the placenta (Haraway 2008a: 293). This is the meal referenced in my epigraph. Haraway recounts the story with characteristic generosity, refraining from judgement or the proposition of a better outcome, or applying an omniscient grid of intelligibility. Instead, and with an acuity directed at herself as well as others, she speaks to the ensuing critical negotiation regarding 'who could, should, must or must not, eat the placenta' (2008a: 293). We learn that the 'radical feminist vegan' present felt that *only* vegans should partake of the meal since it derived from life rather than the death of appropriated animals, and that others invoked ancient matriarchal placentophagy as inspiration for a 'return to nature' – to the disapproval of still others diagnosing a romantic primitivisation at work in such desires. However, we do not learn who actually ate this meal, whether anyone could not stomach it, or which improvised rules held sway. Haraway confirms only that it *was* eaten, cooked, with onions. In respect of this scene, Fraiman remarks, 'if everyone was once inside a placenta, now every guest, male and female, ha[d] placenta inside them' (2012: 114).[16] Though she does not dwell on the thought, it is clearly resonant with the totemic fantasy of consanguinity with the consumed totem (and all the more ironic since kinship in the time of totemism, according to Freud, was formed through the joining of literal and symbolic in the totem meal coincident with the imagined patriarchal origin of culture, rather than through birth and the transmission of genetic material) (Freud 2005: 141–2). Haraway finds her own ironic consanguinity in Santa Cruz among those who 'refuse[d] to assimilate to each other even as they drew nourishment from one another' (2008a: 294).

The second meal that Haraway sketches produces sufficient disagreement between colleagues that the menu for future departmental feasts was radically revised: the feral pig roast, to be killed and cooked by an environmentalist colleague who was also a hunter, was to be supplanted by packaged cuts of meat from a delicatessen. In sketching this scene, Haraway peoples it with the spectre of the invasive 'alien' pig as pest; the more sympathetic respect for the intelligent and emotional pig; the complex interplay between hunters and hunted; and the discrepancy between personally hunted and slaughtered meat versus industrially produced product.[17] That she narrates the conflict regarding whether this was permissible as insurmountable in that instance does not mean she affirms the decision not to repeat the confrontation with a whole roast pig as necessarily the correct one (indeed she refers to 'foreclosed cosmopolitics')

(2008a: 299). Neither meal produces a recipe for solving the question of how to eat well, even as both are world-forming. Haraway's affirmation that we must 'cohabit without a final peace' (2008a: 299) expresses a reciprocity with Derrida's ethics of eating well which similarly refuses to provide *the* answer, including that of vegetarianism, even as he repeats with emphasis the question *'how* for goodness sake should one *eat well?'* (echoing my discussion of method above) (Derrida 1995: 282, emphasis original).

Haraway, in particular, continues to draw fire from vegan critics, not least since her emphasis on what she re-terms 'killing well' engages in much more detail than Derrida with our daily connections with the deaths of non-human animal others (Haraway 2008a: 296). Derrida indicts the

> farming and regimentalisation at a demographic level unknown in the past, by means of genetic experimentation, the industrialization of what can be called the production for consumption of animal meat, artificial insemination on a massive scale, more and more audacious manipulation of the genome, the reduction of the animal not only to production and overactive reproduction (hormones, genetics, crossbreeding, cloning, etc.) of meat for consumption, but also of all sorts of other end products, and all of that in the service of a certain being and the putative human well-being of man. (2008a: 25)

Between this quotation and my opening epigraph it is clear just how fundamental the question of the animal is for Derrida. His emphasis on the impossibility of absolutely repealing the violence of 'eating the other' also registers on a psychoanalytic and thus unconscious plane that Haraway rarely invokes. Yet Haraway's in-depth engagement with the situated biological, physical, economic and relational particularities of numerous critters brings us to the vexatious minutiae in which our daily lives are thickly embedded, from stray dog adoption (the Save-a-Sato Foundation shipping strays from the streets of Puerto Rico to their 'forever homes' in the US), to the lives and deaths of chickens amid the avian flu outbreak of 2004, to laboratory experimentation on animals including the engineered production of patented animals such as 'OncoMouse' *for* cancer research (Haraway 2003: 89–97; 2008a: 265–74; 1997: 79–87). It also leads to the heightened rhetoric and challenge of her term 'killing well'. Haraway arrives at this phrasing in light of Derrida's critique of Levinasian ethics. Levinas's ethical command 'Thou shalt not kill' falls to the failure to 'sacrifice sacrifice' for Derrida, meaning that it implicitly refers to a human community and implies the 'non-criminal putting to death' of those positioned outside of its remit. Yet rather than replace it with a comprehensive 'Thou shalt not put to death the living in general' Derrida maintains an ethics of infinite hospitality with the injunction that one must eat well (such comprehensive ambition would both prove truly unwieldy should such entities as Ebola virus assume the claims of the living in general, and also block the insight of infinite hospitality which cannot decide in advance from whom or from what an ethical demand may arise) (Derrida 1995: 279). Haraway phrases it thus:

> The problem is to live responsibly within the multiplicitous necessity and labor of killing, so as to be in the open, in quest of the capacity to respond in relentless historical, nonteleological multispecies contingency. Perhaps the commandment should read, 'Thou shalt not make killable.' (2008a: 80, emphasis added)

She goes on to say that she 'do[es] not think we can nurture living until we get better at facing killing' (2008a: 81). In light of Haraway's 'quest' for – and not possession of – 'the capacity to respond', this does not equate to a general advocacy of slaughter or submission to the *status quo*, far from it. Rather she asks us to insistently risk our curiosity in asking after the networks of relations in which we dwell with other animals. After Haraway, we want to know what forces of global capital conspire when three quarters of the world's production of soy is destined not as an alternative protein for vegetarians but for animal feed (thus depleting the likelihood of animals being pasture raised) and is fast-tracking the monocultural destruction of environments, particularly in Latin America, in order to produce cheap meat for the West and increasingly for China; we ask how a natural and non-animal-based clothing such as cotton still contributes to the monocultural destruction of habitats and pesticidal decimation of insect life when not grown organically; we question whether the paper of the book in our hands was delivered through sustainable forestry practices, whether the energy used to power our computers is 'clean' or under what circumstances its components were assembled and by whom.[18] All these instances touch on our quotidian proximity to practices that kill, even if we refuse its most obvious evidence in the consumption of meat, and underline Haraway's plea that we learn to kill well.

In the previous section I drew attention to Wolfe's putting to work of deconstruction in his important revision of the relation between animal studies and disability studies. Quite how persuasively his contentious case study – that of Temple Grandin – supports his argument however, is a vexed matter. Anat Pick, in critical counterpoint to Wolfe, does not view Grandin's autobiography of autism as an opening to a new and non-anthropocentric conception of thought. Rather she sees it as an 'avowedly Cartesian story, which quickly turns into a tale of betrayal' when her experience of 'thinking in pictures' like – as Grandin claims – animals do, leads her to design 'better' abattoirs (Pick 2011: 66). Through organizing the path from holding pens to slaughter for cattle without what they may perceive as visual intimidation such as bright light (by altering the orientation of the slaughterhouse to the sun) and devising a circular route in mimicry of the ways that cattle move together (rather than the brutal instrumentation of the quickest progression from field to plate) amongst many other techniques, might it be said that Grandin's ambition is to kill well?[19] Returning to Derrida and Haraway's refusal to provide a masterplan regarding how exactly to eat or kill well is not to avoid saying yes or no to this question. Rather it leads us to ask wider questions excavating the contingencies of life and death in the slaughterhouse and reminds us that 'Beings do not preexist their relatings.' While such multinationals as McDonald's take pride in having consulted Grandin in order to better design their production of burgers, issues of sheer scale, environment depletion, quality and source of feed remain extremely deeply troubling.[20] Following Haraway, however, we would not fetishise the machine, the technology of killing (her famous 'cyborg' drew ironic distance from techno-fetishism). A model slaughterhouse cannot guarantee killing well. As Kelly Oliver points out, following Derrida and the notion of limitrophy as the cultivation of limits that grow, 'there is always the danger of trophe become trophy, of nourishment becoming a monument to status or victory' (2009: 127). This is effectively the accusation that Pick levels at Grandin: instead of entering into 'communion with other lives', Grandin's reflections on the restraining chute for kosher slaughter that she designed 'celebrate the body-made-docile by a feat of technology' (Pick 2011: 70). Grandin herself subsequently revises her views: 'At first I thought engineering could make all the improvements happen, but later in my career I learned that good engineering and design must be coupled with good management' (Grandin and Johnson 2010: 296). While that still emphasizes the application of a model, merely expanding it to management, it does step in the direction of the wider network at stake. Slaughterhouses, Haraway reminds us, are not filled only with non-human animals. Who is it that we imagine to people them? In an interview Haraway is quick to remind us that

> The overwhelming workforce now in animal agriculture are parolees, immigrants, and women of color, legal and illegal, and the attack on labor is deeply tied to the industrialization of animals and the production of cheap food. Cheap food has been an imperial strategy since before Rome.[21]

This is hardly limited to the United States. At the time of writing this chapter the Australian Agricultural Company has explicit plans to provide training and experience of work for inmates from a Darwin prison in an abattoir.[22] That is a long way from the negotiated meals Haraway affirms.

SOMETHING FOR AFTERS: TRAUMA TROUBLE

> It is time to theorize an 'unfamiliar' unconscious, a different primal scene, where everything does not stem from the dramas of identity and reproduction. Ties through blood – including blood recast in the coin of genes and information – have been bloody enough already. I believe there will be no racial or sexual peace, no livable nature, until we learn to produce humanity through something more and less than kinship.
>
> Donna Haraway (1997: 265)

The last section of this chapter closes imperfectly in light of a certain kind of repetition. Thus far repetition has been located through its Cartesian expulsion from human response and subsequent reframing via Derrida as a condition of all experience. The subtle work of the latter bears some reiteration in connection with psychoanalysis and specifically in terms of the sophisticated engagement with the animal question by John Mowitt. Known for his broad-ranging disciplinary acuity and innovation with particular regard to sonic experience, in his study on the whisper Mowitt remarks that 'animal studies has reached so intimately into the concept of the subject that its preoccupations have been made to resonate, as madness did half a century ago, in every corner of Western thought' (2011: 172). While acknowledging the impact of Derrida and Wolfe in demanding this shakedown of the subject, Mowitt frames the problem in this manner in light of Michel Foucault. He specifically invokes Foucault's history of the expulsion of those we call mad from the category claimed by the subject, that of reason, the implication being that the subject has similarly banished the animal.[23] For Mowitt, moving from the discourse analysis of Foucault to the psychoanalytic frame of trauma, what then comes to attention is the way in which the animal returns – traumatically, even *as* trauma as such – within the subject. However, in my reading, it is hard to shake off the risk of the containment of the radicality affirmed by both Derrida and Haraway, by the language of trauma studies in its conceptual attachment to the subject, the animal and to language as the privileged field of the signifier.

Sensitive to acoustic meters in excess of 'the voice', Mowitt works the difficult-to-grasp ground of the whisper as the means by which to catch wind of traumatic repetition. Whispering becomes this means through what it does rather than what it is (rather as if Foucault were listening in on a psychoanalytic session). For Mowitt, whispers channel the archaic pain of the domestication of animals and those humans who enjoin 'the capacity to heal with the capacity to train' (2011: 174). I phrase it in this way since across Mowitt's case studies, from the film named *The Horse Whisperer* to a hybrid television episode combining two series, *The Ghost Whisperer* and *The Dog Whisperer*, whispering both convenes non-human sounds *and* settles on the traumatic suffering of human subjects.[24] While the non-human whispers include a brief and highly suggestive reference to Pilgrim, the traumatized horse of the first example, 'telling . . . secrets to himself, or picking them up from the insects, the wind the thud of his own hooves', in explicit if fleeting reference to Derrida's recasting of autoaffection as constitutively open to the outside in *Voice and Phenomenon*, the question of trauma becomes increasingly aligned with human subjects . . . (Mowitt 2011: 178; see Derrida 2011). This tendency may well arise from the dominant conception of trauma as the site of the failure of words; traumatic experience is precisely unvoiced. Psychoanalysis spent its early years finding the means for hysterical patients to speak of rather than symptomatize their reminiscences, after all.

Reading Mowitt after Haraway however, I want to double back on elements from his field of enquiry that might retrieve other communicative processes from their psychoanalytic eclipse. For example, in name-checking Paul Patton's essay on competing models of power in the training of horses, Mowitt alights on the putting of 'linguistic knowledge back on the table' (2011: 172; see Patton 2003). Yet there are other ingredients also served up on this table. What strikes me as crucial in Patton's own rather Foucauldian exegesis is his invocation of Monty Roberts' method of 'horse whispering'. In distinction to methods of 'breaking' horses both widely used and as specifically used by Roberts' own brutal father (since, yes, there is a story of traumatized humans also shadowing this narrative) he aims for a non-violent method of 'starting' horses. Crucially, Roberts gleaned that horses were communicative participants in domestication and not simply its oppressed object. Moreover he learns this by, and develops his 'join-up' language on the basis of, observing herds of wild mustangs in which mares discipline errant young horses (Patton 2003: 89). Discipline in and as communication does not arrive when horses meet humans. Like writing for the Nambikwara, which did not commence with the contaminating arrival of Europe in the form of Claude Lévi-Strauss, discipline was already there.[25] While perhaps working through psychic processes in producing the figure of the father by means of a totemic animal, Roberts *also* opens a companionate relation between humans and horses that exceeds that familiar scene.[26]

Returning to Derrida, however, we can also return to the scene of psychoanalysis such that it need not legislate language, narrowly construed, as the privileged site for the working through of trauma. Thinking between the implicit recourse to Abraham and Torok in the 'Eating Well' interview and Derrida's explicit engagement with their work in his ostensible introduction to their book *The Wolf Man's Magic Word*, we can open the path to a non-linguistic eating well (Derrida 1986: xi–xlviii).[27] That is to say, while the interview displaces ethics as an encounter based on a 'face-to-face' meeting with the other that assumes a human community retaining the sacrifice or 'non-criminal putting to death' of the other named animal (1995: 282), the introduction consolidates Derrida's move beyond the mouth as the speaking telos of the subject. Within this telos as Abraham and Torok articulate it, the human mouth is haunted by the loss of the object, the breast, while the word steps in to fill 'the communion of empty mouths' (1994: 128). In shifting beyond the mouth as the privileged orifice functioning as the 'metonymy of introjection', Derrida implies the possibility of other identifications taking place at the 'edge of [all] the orifices (of orality, but also of the ear, the eye-and all the "senses" in general)' (1995: 282).

He thus opens the possibility of thinking of identification and even an unconscious that is not governed by language in its strict sense, and thus to the possibility of psychic lives in other animals. In 'Say the Animal Responded', the section of *The Animal That Therefore I Am* explicitly directed at the psychoanalysis of Jacques Lacan, Derrida restates the case of the trace as a wider category than the signifier and explicitly links this to animals:

the structure of the trace presupposes that *to trace* amounts to *erasing a trace* as much as to imprinting it, all sorts of sometimes ritual animal practices, for example, in burial and mourning, associate the experience of the trace with that of the erasure of the trace. (2008a: 135, emphasis original)

'Burial and mourning' both take us to the territory that 'the animal' is not supposed to traverse and return us to the question of traumatic experience. While Derrida acknowledges some progress with the animal question in Lacan, he also notes its repetition in the *Ecrits*, through Lacan's recruitment of the ability to erase one's tracks or lie as the defining proper of the human. Insisting on the vulnerability of all our traces of whatever kind, Derrida ironically reminds Lacan of the Unconscious and widens the latter so that again, a constitutive non-presence affects the living in general. In a peculiar way this thought returns us to the ability to suffer. In this case suffering as the condition of experience out of joint with itself, in other words as traumatic.

In calling for an 'unfamiliar unconscious' Haraway knowingly demands the unfamiliar: that which is not of 'the family', even as the logic of the uncanny yokes the familiar and unfamiliar together, as 'something which ought to have remained hidden but which has nevertheless come to light' (Freud 1997: 217). Neither out of the blue, nor anti-psychoanalytic *per se*, Thryza Nichols Goodeve names Haraway's call as indicative of her project at large. Always and already we are 'blindsided' in our relatings with others including non-human others (Haraway 2000: 124). Now is the time to theorize this community less exclusively and with the least pain possible.

QUESTIONS FOR FURTHER CONSIDERATION

1. What makes the 'question of the animal' more than a local issue of animal rights?
2. Can it be said the deconstruction is intrinsically concerned with animals? In what ways?
3. Is food simply about nutrition or does it go beyond the meeting of basic needs? In what ways?
4. What do you understand to be the similarities and differences between Derrida's and Haraway's approaches to animals?
5. Neither Derrida nor Haraway produce a rule or a law for deciding how to 'eat well' or 'kill well'. Why?
6. Who or what is a companion?

BIBLIOGRAPHY

Abraham, Nicolas and Maria Torok (1994) 'Mourning *or* Melancholia: Introjection *versus* Incorporation' [1972], in *The Shell and The Kernel*, trans. Nicholas T. Rand, Chicago: University of Chicago Press.
Adams, Carol (2010) 'Preface to the Twentieth Anniversary Edition', in *The Sexual Politics of Meat*, London: Continuum.

Baker, Steve (2000) *The Postmodern Animal*, London: Reaktion.

Braidotti, Rosi (2013) *The Posthuman*, Cambridge: Polity.

Derrida, Jacques (1976) *Of Grammatology*, trans. Gayatri Chakravorty Spivak, Baltimore: Johns Hopkins University Press.

Derrida, Jacques (1982) 'Signature Event Context', in *Margins of Philosophy*, trans. Alan Bass, Chicago: University of Chicago Press.

Derrida, Jacques (1986) 'Foreword: *Fors*: The Anglish Words of Nicolas Abraham and Maria Torok', in *The Wolf Man's Magic Word: A Cryptonomy*, trans. Nicholas Rand, Minneapolis: Minnesota University Press.

Derrida, Jacques (1995) '"Eating Well" or the Calculation of the Subject' [1988], trans. Peter Connor and Avital Ronell, in *Points . . . Interviews 1974–1994*, ed. Elizabeth Weber, Stanford: Stanford University Press.

Derrida, Jacques (1997) *Politics of Friendship*, trans. George Collins, London: Verso.

Derrida, Jacques (1999) 'L'Animal que donc Je suis', in Marie-Louise Mallet, ed., *L'Animal Autobiographique*, Paris: Des Femmes.

Derrida, Jacques (2003) 'And Say the Animal Responded', trans. David Wills, in Cary Wolfe, ed., *Zootologies: The Question of the Animal*, Minneapolis: Minnesota University Press.

Derrida, Jacques (2004) 'Violence Against Animals', in Derrida and Elizabeth Roudinesco, *For What Tomorrow . . .*, trans. Jeff Fort, Stanford: Stanford University Press.

Derrida, Jacques (2008a) *The Animal That Therefore I Am*, trans. David Wills, New York: Fordham University Press.

Derrida, Jacques (2008b) *Psyche: Inventions of the Other, Volume 2*, eds. Peggy Kamuf and Elizabeth Rottenberg, Stanford: Stanford University Press.

Derrida, Jacques (2009) *The Beast & The Sovereign, Volume 1*, trans. Geoffrey Bennington, Chicago: University of Chicago Press.

Derrida, Jacques (2011) *Voice and Phenomenon*, trans. Leonard Lawlor, Evanston: Northwestern University Press.

Descartes, René (2008) *A Discourse on the Method* [1637], trans. Ian Maclean, Oxford: Oxford University Press.

Fraiman, Susan (2012) 'Pussy Panic versus Liking Animals: Tracking Gender in Animal Studies', *Critical Inquiry* 39, pp. 89–115.

Freud, Sigmund (1997) 'The Uncanny' [1919], in *Writings on Art and Literature*, trans. James Strachey, Stanford: Stanford University Press.

Freud, Sigmund (2005) 'Totem and Taboo: Some Correspondences Between the Psychic Lives of Savages and Neurotics' [1915], in *On Murder, Mourning and Melancholia*, trans. Shaun Whiteside, London: Penguin.

Giraud, Eva (2013) 'Veganism as Affirmative Biopolitics: Moving Towards a Posthumanist Ethics?' *PhaenEx* 8:2, pp. 47–79.

Grandin, Temple and Catherine Johnson (2010), *Animals Make Us Human: Creating the Best Life for Animals*, Orlando: Houghton Mifflin Harcourt Publishing.

Haraway, Donna (1989) *Primate Visions: Gender, Race, and Nature in the World of Modern Science*, New York: Routledge.

Haraway, Donna (1991) *Simians, Cyborgs and Women: the Reinvention of Nature*, London: Free Association Books.

Haraway, Donna (1997) *Modest_Witness@Second_Millenium.FemaleMan© _Meets_OncoMouseTM*, New York and London: Routledge.

Haraway, Donna (2000) *How Like A Leaf*, New York and London: Routledge.

Haraway, Donna (2003) *The Companion Species Manifesto: Dogs, People and Significant Otherness*, Chicago: Prickly Paradigm Press.

Haraway, Donna (2008a) *When Species Meet*, Minneapolis: Minnesota University Press.

Haraway, Donna (2008b) 'Otherworldly Conversations: Terran Topics, Local Terms', in Stacy Alaimo and Susan Hekman, eds., *Material Feminisms*, Indianapolis: Indiana University Press.

Lawlor, Leonard (2007) *This Is Not Sufficient: An Essay on Animality and Human Nature in Derrida*, New York: Columbia University Press.

McCance, Dawne (2013) *Critical Animal Studies: An Introduction*, New York: State University of New York Press.

Mowitt, John (2011) 'Like a Whisper', *differences: a journal of feminist cultural studies* 22:2–3.

Oliver, Kelly (2009) *Animal Lessons: How They Teach Us to Be Human*, New York: Columbia University Press.

Patton, Paul (2003) 'Language, Power and the Training of Horses', in Cary Wolfe, ed., *Zootologies: The Question of the Animal*, Minneapolis: Minnesota University Press.

Pick, Anat (2011) *Creaturely Poetics: Animality and Vulnerability in Literature and Film*, New York: Columbia University Press.

Regan, Tom (2004 [1983]) *The Case for Animal Rights* (updated with a new Preface), Oakland: University of California Press.

Royle, Nicholas (2011) *Veering: A Theory of Literature*, Edinburgh: Edinburgh University Press.

Singer, Peter (1995 [1975]) *Animal Liberation: Second Edition*, London: Pimlico.

Shukin, Nicole (2009) *Animal Capital: Rendering Life in Biopolitical Times*, Minneapolis: Minnesota University Press.

Tsing, Anna (2012) 'Unruly Edges: Mushrooms as Companion Species', *Environmental Humanities* 1, pp. 141–54.

Turner, Lynn (2013) 'Insect Asides', in Turner, ed., *The Animal Question in Deconstruction*, Edinburgh: Edinburgh University Press.

Wolfe, Cary (2003) *Animal Rites: American Culture and the Discourse of Species*, Chicago: University of Chicago Press.

Wolfe, Cary (2008) 'Learning from Temple Grandin, or, Animal Studies, Disability Studies and Who Comes After the Subject', *New Formations*, 64.

Wolfe, Cary (2010) *What is Posthumanism?* Minneapolis: Minnesota University Press.

Wood, David (2004) 'Thinking with Cats', in Matthew Calarco and Peter Atterton, eds., *Animal Philosophy: Essential Readings in Continental Thought*, London: Continuum.

Ziarek, Eva Płonowska (1995) *The Rhetoric of Failure: Deconstruction of Skepticism, Reinvention of Modernism*, New York: State University of New York Press.

NOTES

1. 'Who Comes After the Subject?' was the title of the special issue of *Topoi* (7:2, 1988) for which Derrida's 'Eating Well' took place.
2. Derrida 2008a. The titular essay was first published in *Critical Inquiry* 28, 2002, pp. 369–418.
3. See also the influential *Posthumanities* series Wolfe edits for Minnesota University Press in which was published Haraway's *When Species Meet*.
4. Donna Haraway, interviewed by Jeffrey Williams, at http://theconversant. org/?p=2522 (accessed 10 September 2014).
5. For a good early-ish corrective to this misreading see Ziarek 1995.
6. Writing prior to any English translations, Baker cites the French original (Derrida 1999).
7. See for example, this report: http://news.discovery.com/animals/whales-dolphins/ dolphins-human-brain-120626.htm (accessed 10 September 2014).
8. For the Great Ape Project, see http://www.projetogap.org.br/en, and for cetacean

non-personhood see: http://www.dw.de/dolphins-gain-unprecedented-protection-in-india/a-16834519 (accessed 10 September 2014).

9. I discuss Derrida's invocation of limitrophy in texts as early as *Margins of Philosophy* in 'Insect Asides' (Turner 2013).

10. See the translator's note regarding 'Je suis' in Derrida 2008a: 162.

11. The notion of veering has been dramatically reimagined as 'not only human' in Nicholas Royle's recent *Veering: A Theory of Literature* (Royle 2011).

12. See Part Three, 'The Politics of Being Female: Primatology Is a Genre of Feminist Theory', in Haraway 1989: 279–382.

13. See '"Gender" for a Marxist Dictionary' (1987), in Haraway 1991: 127–48.

14. See '*Geschlecht* I: Sexual Difference, Ontological Difference' (1983) and 'Heidegger's Hand (*Geschlecht* II)' (1987) in Derrida 2008b: 7–26, 27–62.

15. 'A Cyborg Manifesto: Science, Technology, and Socialist-Feminism in the Late Twentieth Century' (1985), in Haraway 1991: 150.

16. Fraiman sketches Haraway's tale of placentophagy in relation to Carol Adams' vegan-feminist renunciation of meat.

17. She does not note whether anyone objected to the eating of a pig on grounds that it was not kosher.

18. See the World Wildlife Fund's report on Soy at: http://wwf.panda.org/what_we_do/footprint/agriculture/soy/soyreport (accessed 11 September 2014). For information on cotton production see: http://www.cottonedon.org (accessed 11 September 2014).

19. Temple Grandin's websites archive her publications and designs for 'humane slaughter': http://www.templegrandin.com; http://www.grandinlivestockhandling systems.com (accessed 11 September 2014). In contrast, the explicit instrumentation of early US slaughterhouse design as a Taylorist 'disassembly line' is chillingly detailed in perverse complicity with a proto-cinematic logic of animation in Shukin 2009.

20. The McDonald's website includes interviews with Canadian Moms called as witnesses to the safety of beef and welfare of cattle: they cite Grandin as one of the welfare experts ensuring humane slaughter: http://www.mcdonalds.ca/ca/en/food/all-access_moms/heres_the_beef.html (accessed 11 September 2014). The Canadian Coalition for Farm Animals posts a rather different interpretation of conditions on Canadian farms (from whence McDonald's states it sources all its beef): http://www.humanefood.ca/beefcattle.html (accessed 11 September 2014).

21. Donna Haraway, interviewed by Jeffrey Williams, at http://theconversant.org/?p=2522 (accessed 11 September 2014).

22. See this article on the Australian Broadcasting Corporation's website, first posted on 6 January 2014, 'Concerns Over Abattoir Work on NT Prisoners', at http://www.abc.net.au/news/2014-01-06/abattoir-prionsers-darwin/5186434 (accessed 11 September 2014).

23. Derrida discusses the conceptual and historical overlap between the asylum and the zoo in *The Beast & The Sovereign, Volume 1* (2009: 395–402).

24. *The Horse Whisperer* (dir. Robert Redford, US, Touchstone Pictures, 1998), *The Ghost Whisperer* (creator John Gray, Touchstone Television Productions, 2005–10) and *The Dog Whisperer* (MPH Entertainment Productions, 2004–14).

25. Derrida famously discusses Lévi-Strauss in this context in *Of Grammatology* (1976: 135–6).

26. Feminist scholars such as Kelly Oliver have remarked that Freud's *Totem and Taboo* glosses over both modes of kinship that predate the nuclear family as well as the scattered incoherent references to feminine fancies and maternal deities in the rush to render the father original, necessary and human. See Oliver 2009: 248–57.

27. I say 'ostensible' since it rather cryptically contains this transformation of their work.

ETHICAL CRITICISM AND THE PHILOSOPHICAL TURN

Kenneth Womack

Questions about ethics continue to exert a profound influence upon the direction of contemporary literary criticism. Yet, as Geoffrey Galt Harpham observes in *Shadows of Ethics: Criticism and the Just Society*, ethical criticism functions in the eyes of many literary scholars as an 'alien discourse' that challenges or undermines the theoretical project's capacity for promoting 'literature's immediacy, concreteness, vitality, and affective richness' (1999: ix). During the last two decades, ethical criticism's fusion with continental philosophy has produced a more theoretically rigorous form of literary critique that continues to elevate its status as a viable interpretive mechanism. In contrast with North American variations of the paradigm that find their origins in Kantian moral philosophy and troll dangerously close to the shoals of moral relativism, ethical criticism's European manifestations offer a more forceful analysis by emphasizing continental philosophy's various and ongoing accounts of alterity, otherness and phenomenology. While both schools of thought may hale from decidedly different venues of intellectual thought, ethical criticism's various manifestations demonstrate the theoretical project's larger interest in assessing the value systems that inform our textual interpretations.

In North America, ethical criticism finds its contemporary origins in the works of such scholars as Wayne C. Booth, Martha C. Nussbaum and J. Hillis Miller. Volumes such as Booth's *The Company We Keep: An Ethics of Fiction* and Nussbaum's *Love's Knowledge: Essays on Philosophy and Literature* demonstrate the interpretive power of ethical criticism, as well as the value of its critical machinery to scholarly investigations regarding the nature of literary character, the cultural landscapes of fiction, and the ethical motivations of satire – the narrative manoeuvre that Booth ascribes to our desire to 'make and remake ourselves' (1988: 14). Critics such as Booth and Nussbaum avoid the textual violence of censorship to advocate instead a form of criticism that explores the moral sensibilities that inform works of art. In *Love's Knowledge*, Nussbaum illustrates the nature of ethical criticism's recent emergence as a viable interpretive paradigm: 'Questions about justice, about well-being and social distribution, about moral realism and relativism, about the nature of rationality, about the concept of the person, about the emotions and desires, about the role of luck in human life – all these and others are debated from many sides with considerable excitement and even urgency', she writes (1990: 169–70). In its desire to examine the ethical nature of these artistic works, ethical criticism seeks to create a meaningful bond between the life of the narrative and the life of the reader. Although ethical criticism hardly functions as a conventional interpretive paradigm in the tradition of Marxist, Lacanian, or gender textual readings, it serves effectively nevertheless as a self-reflexive means for critics to explain the contradictory emotions and problematic moral stances that often mask complex and fully realized literary characters. Ethical criticism provides its practitioners, moreover, with the capacity to posit socially relevant interpretations by celebrating the Aristotelian qualities of living well and flourishing. In this way, ethical criticism evokes the particularly 'human character' of literature that Tobin Siebers extols the merits of in *The Ethics of Criticism* (1988).

Principal amongst continental philosophy's turn toward ethics are such thinkers as Emmanuel Levinas and Jacques Derrida. Levinas's moral philosophy highlights notions of responsibility, the concept of the gift, and a more universalized cognizance of otherness in the Western philosophical tradition. In addition to analyzing the nature of our relationships with others as well as ourselves, Levinas's ethical theories intersect a wide array of contemporary theoretical debates regarding feminist studies, pluralistic models of reading, and cultural criticism. As Jill Robbins observes in *Altered Reading: Levinas and Literature*, Levinasian ethics 'denotes the putting into question of the self by the infinitizing mode of the face of the other' (1999: xiii). In addition to demonstrating the notion of an 'unconditional ethical imperative', in the words of Simon Critchley, Derrida's conceptions of deconstructive reading provide us with a powerful mechanism for comprehending the ethical implications of philosophy, politics and democracy. In *The Ethics of Deconstruction: Derrida and Levinas*, Critchley contends that Derrida's ethical problematics can be valuably understood in terms of the philosopher's ongoing textual dialogue with Levinas. 'An ethical moment is essential to deconstructive reading', Critchley writes, and 'ethics is the goal, or horizon, towards which Derrida's work tends' (1999: 2).

In addition to examining the most significant strands of North American postulations of ethical criticism and continental philosophy's various forms of ethical critique, this chapter will offer an exemplary reading of the intersections between ethics and literature via interpretive sketches of George Eliot's *Silas Marner* and Spike Jonze's *Being John Malkovich*. Eliot's novel, for example, provides readers with a narrative that illustrates Levinasian notions of responsibility and the gift as Silas Marner, a friendless weaver, finds redemption through his love for the orphan Eppie rather than a treasured cache of gold. Jonze's *Being John Malkovich* examines a variety of metaphysical and existential questions, while also offering a useful forum for addressing Critchley's concept of an 'unconditional ethical imperative'. Jonze's film, with its powerful depiction of moral philosophy's phenomenological concept of a catapleptic impression, functions as a revelatory means for discussing the dimensions of ethics that mark its narrative, as well as our understanding of various aspects of *Being John Malkovich*'s larger ethical spaces.

ETHICAL CRITICISM IN NORTH AMERICA

In many ways, the recent revival of ethical criticism in North American intellectual circles finds its roots in the desire of literary theorists to re-examine our complicated relationships with literary texts. In one of the more forceful ethical critiques of literary theory, *The Ethics of Criticism*, Siebers identifies the crisis that confronts modern criticism – an interpretive dilemma that 'derives in part from an ethical reaction to the perceived violence of the critical act' (1988: 15). He further argues that an ethical approach to literary study requires critics to engage their subjects self-consciously with sustained attention to the potential consequences of their interpretive choices: 'The ethics of criticism involves critics in the process of making decisions and of studying how these choices affect the lives of fellow critics, writers, students, and readers as well as our ways of defining literature and human nature.' Siebers ascribes the aforementioned crisis in criticism to a linguistic paradox that inevitably problematizes critical practice. 'Modern literature has its own cast of characters', he writes. 'It speaks in a discourse largely concerned with issues of language, but behind its definitions of language lie ideals of human character' (1988: 10). Siebers argues that acknowledging the place of ethics in critical theory affords practitioners of the discipline with the autonomy to offer relevant conclusions about literary texts and their considerable social and ideological import. 'Literary criticism cannot endure without the freedom to make judgments', Siebers notes, 'and modern theory urgently needs to regain the capacity to decide' (1988: 41). The ability to render sound, moral interpretations, then, provides the foundation for an ethical criticism that fully engages the remarkably human nature of literary study. Such a reading methodology allows for the self-conscious reassessment of our evaluative procedures and their potential for the production of meaningful critiques. As Siebers concludes: 'To criticize ethically brings the critic into a special field of action: the field of human conduct and belief concerning the human' (1988: 1).

For many practitioners of ethical criticism, Louise M. Rosenblatt's *The*

Reader, the Text, the Poem: The Transactional Theory of the Literary Work supplies ethical critics with an interpretational matrix for explaining the motives of readers and their 'transactions' with literary texts. Rosenblatt identifies two different types of reading strategies – aesthetic reading, in which the reader devotes particular attention to what occurs *during* the actual reading event, and nonaesthetic reading, a reading strategy in which the reader focuses attention upon the traces of knowledge and data that will remain *after* the event. Rosenblatt designates the latter strategy as a kind of 'efferent' reading in which readers primarily interest themselves in what will be derived materially from the experience (1978: 23–5). Efferent readers reflect upon the verbal symbols in literature, 'what the symbols designate, what they may be contributing to the end result that [the reader] seeks – the information, the concepts, the guides to action, that will be left with [the reader] when the reading is over' (1978: 27). Booth argues that ethical criticism functions as a methodology for distinguishing the 'efferent freight' that results from this reading strategy (1988: 14). Rosenblatt describes the act of reading itself – whether aesthetic or nonaesthetic – as a transaction that derives from the peculiar array of experiences that define the reader's persona: 'Each reader brings to the transaction not only a specific past life and literary history, not only a repertory of internalized "codes", but also a very active present, with all its preoccupations, anxieties, questions, and aspirations', she writes (1978: 144). This recognition of the complexity of the reading transaction underscores the deep interconnections between readers and the human communities in which they live and seek personal fulfilment.

Rosenblatt argues that the transaction of reading involves 'laying bare the assumptions about human beings and society and the hierarchy of values that govern the world derived from the text' (1978: 149–50), a conclusion regarding the ethical value of art in the human community that John Gardner illuminates in his influential volume, *On Moral Fiction*. He argues that literary works should offer readers the opportunity for receiving knowledge from its pages, the possibility – rather than the didactic requirement – of emerging from a reading experience with a heightened sense of communal awareness. Gardner writes:

> We recognize art by its careful, thoroughly honest search for and analysis of values. It is not didactic because, instead of teaching by authority and force, it explores, open-mindedly, to learn what it should teach. It clarifies, like an experiment in a chemistry lab, and confirms. As a chemist's experiment tests the laws of nature and dramatically reveals the truth or falsity of scientific hypotheses, moral art tests values and rouses trustworthy feelings about the better and the worse in human action. (1978: 19)

The role of the ethical critic, then, involves the articulation of a given text's ability to convey notions of knowledge and universal good to its readers, whether through the auspices of allegory, satire, morality plays, haiku, or any other fictive means of representation. In Gardner's estimation, ethical critics can only accomplish this end through the fomentation of understanding in their readership. 'Knowledge may or may not lead to belief', he writes. But 'understanding always does, since to believe one understands a complex situation is to form at least a tentative theory of how one ought to behave in it' (1978: 139). Thus, ethical criticism examines the ways in which literary characters respond to the divergent forces they encounter in the fictional landscapes that they occupy. Their human behaviours and actions provide the interpretive basis for moral reflection and conclusion.

As Gardner notes in *On Moral Fiction*, however, practitioners of ethical criticism must invariably confront the spectre of censorship, a dangerous commodity rooted in the human tendency to instruct without regard for the plurality of competing value systems at work in both the theoretical realm of literary criticism and the larger world of humankind. 'Didacticism', he cautions, 'inevitably simplifies morality and thus misses it' (1978: 137). Similarly, critics must avoid the perils of attempting to establish models of behaviour and codified moral standards of acceptability, for such practices inevitably lead to the textual injustice of censorship. Gardner writes: 'I would not claim that even the worst bad art should be outlawed, since morality by compulsion is a fool's morality' (1978: 106). Despite his own admonitions to the contrary in *On Moral Fiction* – and because of the dearth of genuine scholarly wisdom inherent in his study of moral criticism – Gardner himself nevertheless trolls dangerously close to the shores of censorship when he speaks of carrying out 'art's proper work': art 'destroys only evil', he argues. 'If art destroys good, mistaking it for evil, then that art is false, an error; it requires denunciation' (1978: 15). Such a proposition inevitably leads to the establishment of singular standards of good and evil in the heterogeneous, pluralistic spheres of criticism and human reality. Can *ethical* critics, in good conscience, operate from superior positions of moral privilege and arrogant didacticism?

Understanding the place of moral philosophy in the latest incarnation of ethical criticism offers a means for exploring this dilemma. Bernard Williams's *Ethics and the Limits of Philosophy*, for instance, discusses the ways in which the tenets of moral philosophy provide a context for us 'to recreate ethical life' in the sceptical world of contemporary Western culture (1985: vii). In addition to examining the Johnsonian question of how to live, Williams devotes particular attention to assessing the role of the ethical critic. 'Given people who are in some general sense committed to thinking in ethical terms, how should they think?' he asks. 'Are their ethical thoughts sound?' (1985: 71). The issue of a valid ethical criticism itself poses a spurious philosophical quandary, for it requires the critic to define standards of moral correctness, or, as Williams concludes, to dispense with establishing them altogether. 'An ethical theory is a theoretical account of what ethical thought and practice are', he writes, which 'either implies a general test for the correctness of basic ethical beliefs and principles or else implies that there cannot be such a test' (1985: 72). Williams suggests that critics can only surmount this dilemma by interpreting a given set of events from an empathetic position, and, moreover, through their 'ability to arrive at shared ethical judgments' (1985: 97). In this way, ethical critics and moral philosophers alike engage in a form of ethical practice that allows for the reflexive process of critical contemplation, a self-conscious methodology for critically articulating the pluralistic nuances of that which constitutes a shared sense of moral correctness.

In addition to questioning the nature of our communal sense of ethical propriety, moral philosophers such as Williams attempt to account for the motives of those critics who dare to engage in the interpretation of human values. Such critics must assume the risks – whether or not they employ an equitable and pluralistic system of evaluation – of impinging upon the current direction of the philosophical conversation regarding human ethics. 'Critical reflection should seek for as much shared understanding as it can find on any issue, and use any ethical material that, in the context of the reflective discussion, makes some sense and commands some loyalty', Williams notes, although 'the only serious enterprise is living, and we have to live after the reflection' (1985: 117). For this reason, the principles of moral philosophy charge ethical critics with the maintenance of a sense of free intellectual discourse, in addition to obliging them to render sound moral conclusions. 'We should not try to seal determinate values into future society', he warns, for 'to try to transmit free inquiry and the reflective consciousness is to transmit something more than nothing, and something that demands some forms of life rather than others' (1985: 173).

Ethical criticism endeavours, as a matter of course, to communicate the meaning of this 'something' and its greater social relevance through the interpretation of literary works. In *The Company We Keep*, Booth offers an expansive account of ethical criticism and its potential for literary study, while also attempting to allay any fears that his heuristic rests upon dogmatic foundations. Booth affords particular attention to the range of hermeneutic functions that ethical criticism performs, as well as to its unfortunate lack of clarity as an interpretive paradigm:

> We can no longer pretend that ethical criticism is passé. It is practiced everywhere, often surreptitiously, often guiltily, and often badly, partly because it is the most difficult of all critical modes, but partly because we have so little serious talk about why it is important, what purposes it serves, and how it might be done well. (1988: 19)

Booth notes that ethical criticism's opponents often misread the paradigm's intent as didactic in nature. Instead, Booth argues, 'ethical criticism attempts to describe the encounters of a story-teller's ethos with that of the reader or listener. Ethical critics need not begin with the intent to evaluate, but their descriptions will always entail appraisals of the value of what is being described.' In this way, Booth supports a reflexive interpretational methodology, an ethical criticism that allows for the recognition of the interconnections between the reading experience and the life of the reader. Ethical criticism acknowledges, moreover, the powerful factors of language and ideology in its textual assessments. 'There are no neutral ethical terms', Booth writes, 'and a fully responsible ethical criticism will make explicit those appraisals that are implicit whenever a reader or listener reports on stories about human beings in action' (1988: 8–9).

Booth defines these instances of appraisal – these practical applications of ethical criticism – as acts of 'coduction', referential moments in which critics compare their reading experiences with the conclusions of others. Like Siebers, who argues that 'the heart of ethics is the desire for community' (1988: 202), Booth notes that the act of 'judgment requires a community' of trustworthy friends and colleagues (1988: 72). Coduction, in Booth's schema, valorizes the reflexive relationship that develops between texts and their readers, as well as the equally reflexive manner in which texts postulate meaning. 'The question of whether value is in the poem or in the reader is radically and permanently ambiguous, requiring two answers', Booth writes. 'Of course the value is not in there, *actually*, until it is actualized, by the reader. But of course it could not be actualized if it were not there, *in potential*, in the poem' (1988: 89). Booth also notes ethical criticism's pluralistic imperatives and their value to the understanding and operation of ideological paradigms. In his analysis of feminist criticism, for example, Booth discusses the ways in which 'the feminist challenge' derives from fundamental ethical dilemmas inherent in the construction of literary texts: 'Every literary work implies either that women can enter its imaginative world as equals or that they cannot – that instead they must, in reading, decide whether or not to enter a world in which men are a privileged center' (1988: 387). As Booth reveals, feminist criticism itself functions as type of ethical criticism, a means of literary interpretation that seeks to repair an abiding social injustice that, through its misogyny, problematizes the lives of the larger community of readers.

In *The Ethics of Reading: Kant, de Man, Eliot, Trollope, James, and Benjamin*, Miller posits an 'ethics of reading' that seeks to explain the reflexive process that occurs between the text and the reader, in addition to offering testimony to the ethical possibilities of poststructuralism, particularly deconstruction. Miller argues that the act of reading ethically transpires when 'an author turns back on himself, so to speak, turns back on a text he or she has written, re-reads it' (1987: 15). For Miller, such a process allows readers – the *de facto* authors of the texts that they appraise – to offer relevant conclusions about the moral properties of literary works and the ethical sensibilities of the readers' theoretical premises, whether they be deconstructive or otherwise. In *Versions of Pygmalion*, Miller proffers a similar argument regarding the 'ethics of narration' and the shifting, performative aspects of reading experiences. Miller derives the title of his volume from the story of Pygmalion in Book 10 of the *Metamorphoses* – a narrative in which something inanimate comes alive, just as reading ethically creates a vital, living relationship between the text and the reader. Miller devotes special attention to the ways in which reading defies stasis, as well as to the manner in which reading ethically, moreover, evolves during successive readings of a given text: 'Reading occurs in a certain spot to a certain person in a certain historical, personal, institutional, and political situation, but it always exceeds what was predictable from those circumstances', he observes. 'It makes something happen that is a deviation from its context, and what happens demands a new definition each time' (1990: 22). In his paradigm for the ethics of reading, Miller allows for the negative possibilities of reading, aspects that Booth, in his effort to celebrate ethical criticism and its myriad of affirmative outcomes, prefers to ignore: 'A theory of the ethics of reading that takes seriously the possibility that reading might lead to other morally good or valuable actions would also have to allow for the possibility that the reading even of a morally exemplary book might cause something morally deplorable to occur', Miller writes (1990: 21). In this manner, Miller postulates a valuable corollary to the reflexive properties of ethical criticism and the ways in which context and temporality possess the propensity to alter the quality of reading experiences.

Like Williams, Nussbaum advocates an ethical criticism with tenable foundations in moral philosophy, as well as an interpretive mechanism that functions as an impetus for sustaining moral discourse and social interconnection. In addition to her enthusiastic subscription to many of the arguments inherent in Booth's ontology for an ethical criticism, Nussbaum proffers a series of essays in *Love's Knowledge* that sharpen the ethical paradigm's focus through her discussion about the interrelations between philosophy and literature, as well as through her close, ethical readings of a diversity of writers, including Henry James, Proust, Ann Beattie and Samuel Beckett, among others. Drawing upon selected works by these figures, Nussbaum examines the ways in which style and content impinge upon ethical issues, while also deliberating about the manner in which the ethical interpretation of literary works offers readers a means for exploring the moral import of emotions and locating paths to self-knowledge. Nussbaum affords particular attention to the roles that stylistics, linguistics and structure play in articulating the moral essence of a given narrative. In Nussbaum's schema, the literary artist bears the responsibility for honourably positing narratives that allow readers the opportunity to discover their own paths to self-understanding and meaning, to formulate their own strategies for living well. Like Booth, Nussbaum equates the quality of life with the ethical dimensions of literature. 'The novel is itself a moral achievement', she writes, 'and the well-lived life is a work of literary art' (1990: 148).

In addition to advancing the ethical notion of community in her work, Nussbaum argues for the place of love as a subject in the evolving discourse of ethical criticism. 'The subject of romantic and erotic love is not often treated in works on moral philosophy', she admits (1990: 336). For this reason, Nussbaum differentiates between the Kantian notions of 'pathological' and 'practical' love in her analysis. Pathological love, she notes, signifies the often irrational emotions of romantic love in sharp contrast to the more enduring qualities of practical love, an emotion that Nussbaum defines as 'an attitude of concern that one can will oneself to have toward another human being, and which is, for that reason, a part of morality'. The moral dimensions of practical love, therefore, merit considerable attention as a methodology for understanding the many ways in which readers respond ethically to literary texts. Moreover, 'if one believes, in addition, that the realm of morality is of special and perhaps of supreme importance in human life . . . one will be likely, having once made that distinction, to ascribe high *human* worth to practical love' (1990: 336–7). In this way, the acknowledgement of practical love provides additional insight into human conceptions of living well and the manner in which literary texts depict love's capacity to produce personal fulfilment. Nussbaum also refines the communal aspects that mark the ethical paradigm. She extends the metaphor that ethical criticism forges a type of community between text and reader to allow for the possibility not only of living well as an individual, but also of living together well in a much larger sense of the word. 'A community is formed by author and readers', she writes. 'In this community separateness and qualitative difference are not neglected; the privacy and the imagining of each is nourished and encouraged. But at the same time it is stressed that living together is the object of our ethical interest' (1990: 48). In *Poetic Justice: The Literary Imagination and Public Life* (1995), Nussbaum advances this concept through her exploration of the value of ethical reading as a means for influencing political theory and public discourse: 'If we think of reading in this way, as combining one's own absorbed imagining with periods of more detached (and interactive) critical scrutiny, we can already begin to see why we might find in it an activity well suited to public reasoning in a democratic society' (1995: 9). By widening the scope of the ethical paradigm to account for a range of emotional states, as well as a variety of public and private modes of discourse, Nussbaum shares in the creation of an ethical criticism that provides for the relevant interpretation of the social, political, and cultural nuances of the human community.

Despite the publication in recent years of a number of volumes devoted to the humanistic study of literary works – a roster of monographs that includes Cora Diamond's *The Realistic Spirit: Wittgenstein, Philosophy, and the Mind*, Adam Zachary Newton's *Narrative Ethics*, and Kim L. Worthington's *Self as Narrative: Subjectivity and Community in Contemporary Fiction* – ethical criticism, particularly in its North American manifestations, must still successfully contend with several issues of historical and contemporary import in order to authenticate itself as a viable interpretive paradigm. Apart from continuing to underscore its usefulness to literary study, ethical criticism must effectively differentiate itself from the contemporary critical prejudice associated with the 'traditional humanism' previously associated with such figures as F. R. Leavis and Northrop Frye. Practitioners of ethical criticism are succeeding in this regard in a variety of ways, including their critical alliance with the ethical philosophy of Emmanuel Levinas and via the recent emergence of the law and literature movement. By also demonstrating its significant pedagogical value, as well as establishing itself as a meaningful component in the future of the theoretical project, the ethical paradigm may yet realize Booth's vision in *The Company We Keep* of a reading methodology that shuns theoretical dogma in favour of 'critical pluralism' and highlights the ethical interconnections between the lives of readers and their textual experiences (1988: 489).

ETHICAL CRITICISM AND CONTINENTAL PHILOSOPHY

In European critical circles, Levinas's fundamental ethical concepts function at the core of their advancement of an ethical criticism. Such philosophically vexed issues as obligation and responsibility, for instance, are perhaps most usefully considered via Levinas's conceptions of alterity, contemporary moral philosophy's *sine qua non* for understanding the nature of our innate responsibilities to our human others. In 'Is Ontology Fundamental?' Levinas discusses the ethical significance of other beings in relation to the needs and desires of ourselves. Our ethical obligations to others, Levinas reasons, find their origins in our inability to erase them via negation. Simply put, unless we succeed in negating others through violence, domination, or slavery, we must comprehend others as beings *par excellence* who become signified as 'faces', the Levinasian term that refers to the moral consciousness and particularity inherent in others. This 'primacy of ontology', in Levinas's words, demonstrates the nature of the collective interrelationships that human beings share with one another (1996: 10). In 'The Trace of the Other', Levinas argues that 'the relationship with the other puts me into question, empties me of myself' (1986: 350). More importantly for our purposes here, Levinas describes the concept of the face as 'the concrete figure for alterity' (quoted in Robbins 1999: 23). The notion of alterity itself – which Paul-Laurent Assoun characterizes as 'the primal scene of ethics' (1998: 96) – refers to our inherent responsibilities and obligations to the irreducible face of the other. These aspects of our human condition find their origins in the recognition of sameness that we find in others. This similarity of identity and human empathy establishes the foundation for our alterity – in short, the possibility of being 'altered' – and for the responsibilities and obligations that we afford to other beings.

In *Time and the Other*, Levinas identifies the absolute exteriority of alterity, as opposed to the binary, dialectic or reciprocal structure implied in the idea of the other. Hence, alterity implies a state of being apprehended, a state of infinite and absolute otherness. In 'Philosophy and the Idea of Infinity', Levinas writes that 'we can say that the alterity of the infinite is not cancelled, is not extinguished in the thought that thinks it. In thinking infinity the I from the first *thinks more than it thinks*. Infinity does not enter into the *idea* of infinity, is not grasped; this idea is not a concept', he continues. 'The infinite is radically, absolutely, other' (1987: 54). Alterity's boundless possibilities for registering otherness, for allowing us to comprehend the experiences of other beings, demonstrates its ethical imperatives. Its exteriority forces us to recognize an ethics of difference and of otherness. Such encounters with other beings oblige us, then, to incur the spheres of responsibility inherent in our alterity. When we perceive the face of the other, we can no longer, at least ethically, suspend responsibility for other beings. In such instances, Levinas writes in 'Meaning and Sense', 'the I loses its sovereign self-confidence, its identification, in which consciousness returns triumphantly to itself to rest on itself. Before the exigency of the Other (*Autrui*), the I is expelled from this rest and is not the already glorious consciousness of this exile. Any complacency', he adds, 'would destroy the straightforwardness of the ethical movement' (1996: 54).

Levinas's ethical thought – with its accent upon the moral necessity for establishing altered relationships amongst the human community – exerts a considerable influence upon the direction of European moral philosophy, as evidenced by Derrida's various forays into ethical theory. In his important essay, 'Donner la mort' – published as *The Gift of Death* in 1995 – Derrida examines the concepts of giving, faith and responsibility. As central components at the foundation of any genuinely altered relationship, these issues demonstrate what Derrida refers to as the 'very ordeal of the undecidable', which denotes the risk inherent in venturing into such relationships in the first place (1995: 5). The act of giving, for example, demands that the giver engage in altruistic behaviour that may not be appreciated or accepted by the recipient of his or her generosity; similarly, an act of faith obliges its participants to behold themselves to powers and belief systems beyond the boundaries of their selves. Perhaps even more interestingly, the concept of responsibility requires that the ethical agent assume responsibility for others who may or may not accept, respect or understand the agent's munificent behaviour. As Derrida posits in his essay, even the gift of death itself is problematized by divergent arenas of meaning. Sacrificing one's own life in the service of one's country depends upon the length and degree of human memory regarding the sacrificer's selfless act, an act that, intriguingly enough, may result in the 'gift' of death for one's enemy. Ironically, then, the sacrificial agent nobly exchanges his or her own life without recognizing the alterity – in a Levinasian sense – of a faceless enemy.

Ethical critics confront similarly problematic moral conundrums regarding our motivations for engaging in ethical behaviour. 'What is given – and this would also represent a kind of death', Derrida observes, 'is not some thing, but goodness itself, a giving goodness, the act of giving or the donation of the gift.' For Derrida, this is a 'goodness that must not only forget itself but whose source remains inaccessible to the donee' (1995: 41). In short, the giver must be able to engage in the act of giving for motives that spring from pure goodness. Any residual expectations would serve to undermine the original act of altruism on behalf of the giver. The gift of death presents even more vexing dilemmas for the giver bent on delivering an act of goodness. 'Death is very much that which nobody can undergo or confront in my place. My irreplace-ability is there conferred, delivered, "given", one can say, by death' (Derrida 1995: 41). The gift of death, then, necessarily encounters the discrepancy between individual and collective acts of goodness. Giving one's life ensures a personal level of responsibility for an act that might result in collective degrees of goodness. Hence, the giver may enjoy the effects of an altered relationship that the recipients of his or her gift may never fully comprehend, recognize, or even accept. Yet, as Derrida notes, it is only through these acts of giving – risky and potentially unknowable as they may be – that we create opportunities for glimpsing the face of our human others.

Luce Irigaray grapples with ethical issues of another sort in her classic work of literary criticism, *An Ethics of Sexual Difference*, in which she maintains that genuine notions of sexual difference between the masculine and the feminine – as well as between their highly contingent outlooks and perspec-tives – will only occur after the advent of an ethical revolution in which men no longer control the nature of discourse and speech acts. Only then, Irigaray writes, will everyone, male as well as female, have equal 'access to transcend-ence' (1993: 217). Irigaray's ethical theories of sexual difference find their origins in her postulation of an intersubjective relation in which males and females weigh their senses of self-love in relation to their capacities for reg-istering the otherness of their gendered counterparts. Irigaray argues that masculine versions of love of the self concern how men relate to themselves. According to Irigaray, males reveal their love of self in terms of their nostalgia for maternal love, a quest for finding God through their fathers, and sexual love. Conversely, Irigaray's feminized model of self-love involves a complex interrelationship between maternity, the socialized gratification of her male counterparts' love of self, and an inherent sense of altruism. Hence, Irigaray's sexual ethics of difference concerns the manner in which males and females see themselves in relation to the larger worlds in which they live. 'Whatever iden-tifications are possible', Irigaray remarks, 'one will never exactly occupy the place of the other – they are irreducible one to the other' (1993: 13). Irigaray asserts that a recognition of these fundamental distinctions points to signal ways in which males and females might form more fulfilling and evenly bal-anced relationships.

In *Ethics of Eros: Irigaray's Rewriting of the Philosophers*, Tina Chanter ascribes this most ethical of Irigaray's philosophical conclusions to the think-er's Hegelian observations about woman's place in the dialectic of nature and history. Ultimately, Irigaray's theories of sexual difference elevate the needs of the community over the individual. In Irigaray's schema, masculinized controls over speech acts and language must be unloosed in order to enrich the entire human community of males and females alike. Yet the rights of the individual remain sacrosanct in Irigaray's philosophy as well. 'The possibility of articulat-ing an ethic of sexual difference is bound up with the need to insist on recog-nizing the validity of the specific rights and duties of specific groups distinct from their identity as defined by the social whole', Chanter writes. 'Insofar as this project appeals to the importance of specifying multiple ways of existing in a society', she adds, 'it opens the way for an ethics that extends beyond sexual difference' (1995: 126). In *Beyond Accommodation: Ethical Feminism, Deconstruction, and the Law*, Drucilla Cornell explains Irigaray's philosophy in terms of its attention to the nature of females' various means of identifying themselves with the world. Cornell argues that women often live in states of 'dereliction' that force them to live as outcasts of sorts in their own social and familial environments. 'The politics of identification signify Woman and let her "speak",' Cornell asserts. 'But this battle takes place only within the shared framework based on a rejection of ego psychology' (1999: 75). Because masculine desires frequently mitigate female relations with themselves and others via language, Cornell argues, we are left with an 'uncapturable' feminine *jouissance*. This aporia exists at the core of Irigaray's ethics of sexual difference, an ethical system that seeks to explain the socialized interpersonal discrepancies that continue to problematize male-female relationships, as well as the ways in which women see themselves in relation to the world.

In recent years, Alain Badiou has emerged as one of France's most influential moral philosophers. Badiou's philosophical project can be usefully understood in terms of the two principal thrusts of his ethical theory regarding the nature of human interaction: 1) that the creation and approval of knowledge establishes, names and recognizes various forms of consolidated identity in the human community; 2) that some singular truths do persist within human discourse, despite contemporary philosophy's various challenges to the notion of universal truth. Perhaps even more significantly, Badiou argues for the abandonment of the ethics of otherness that has pervaded continental philosophy – and especially the work of such eminent thinkers as Levinas, Derrida and Irigaray, among others. In Badiou's ethical schema, genuine ethical issues emerge in specific situations and under sets of circumstances that exist without regard for the nature of a person's differentiation or otherness. For this reason, Badiou posits a theory of ethical deliberation in which a plurality of human beings considers the particularized events and situations that produce a given ethical dilemma. Through their act of deliberation, the participants would concoct a series of procedures germane to the circumstances of the issue at hand. In this manner, the deliberators would subsequently produce their own ethical norms and truths in order to respond to the contingencies inherent in the ethical dilemma of the moment. By relying upon a sustainable theory of ethical evaluation, Badiou's ethical philosophy elevates human interaction over otherness. In short, the needs of the community trump the desires of the individual.

Badiou devotes considerable attention to the identification of evil as a state of being that evidences itself in particular events and circumstances. In addition to differentiating evil from violence – which he defines as the means via which human beings persevere beyond (or beneath) good and evil – Badiou contends that evil is a subjective category of the self. 'Evil is the process of a simulacrum of truth', Badiou writes. 'And in its essence, under a name of its invention, it is terror directed at everyone' (2001: 77). According to Badiou, our recognition of evil is only made possible by the contrastive existence of goodness, which allows us, then, to perceive evil as a condition of human experience that evolves under a given set of circumstances. Hence, evil emerges through our encounters with goodness, a concept that, in itself, assists us in our communal goal of warding off evil. Because evil necessarily exists at the margins of goodness Badiou suggests that philosophers abandon any interest in elevating certain manifestations of evil – what contemporary moral philosophers refer to as 'radical evil', for example – over others. Evil assumes different types and various levels of scale in direct relationship to the nature of the circumstances under which it develops. Badiou argues that the horrors of Nazism and ethnic extermination, for instance, underscore 'both that which measures all the Evil our time is capable of, being itself beyond measure, and that to which we must compare everything (thus measuring it unceasingly) that we say is to be judged in terms of the manifest certainty of Evil. As the supreme negative example', Badiou adds, 'this crime is inimitable, but every crime is an imitation of it' (2001: 63). Simply put, evil exists, as with goodness, as one of the inalienable (albeit enduring and unfortunate) truths of human interaction.

In *Getting It Right: Language, Literature, and Ethics*, Geoffrey Galt Harpham examines ethical criticism's potential as an interdisciplinary means of interpretation. Perhaps more significantly, though, he usefully (and indeed, uniquely) merges the scholarship of continental philosophy – especially Levinasian philosophy – with North American conceptions of moral philosophy's role in the creation of an evaluative criticism. Ethical criticism should be 'considered a matrix, a hub from which the various discourses and disciplines fan out and at which they meet, crossing out of themselves to encounter each other', he writes. 'Ethics is perhaps best conceived as a 'conceptual base' – neither as organic drive nor as properly conceptual superstructure, but rather as a necessary, and necessarily impure and unsystematic, mediation between unconscious and instinctual life and its cognitive and cultural transformation' (1992: 17–18). Harpham supports this endeavour through his examinations of such 'ethical terms' as 'obligation', '*ought*', 'ethical duty' and 'ethicity'. Through their delineation, he seeks to establish meaningful interconnections between ethical criticism and other means of textual inquiry. Harpham argues that the issue of choice lies at the heart of obligation. 'One can – one must – choose which principle to be governed by', he observes. 'Ethics in general is a species of risk that affords no rigorous way to tell ethical reasons from other reasons, choices from obligations' (1992: 37). He further asserts that 'at the dead center of ethics lies the *ought*', or the ethical obligation. This notion of an *ought* – the moral obligations of an ethical person – reveals that person's 'commitments, values, character. To be ethical, an *ought* must not refer itself to threats or desires, coercion or self-ends' (1992: 18). Harpham defines 'ethical duty' as a form of critical reflection: 'One must always reflect', he writes. 'This is the law that ethical discourse virtually presumes as well as teaches' (1992: 42).

In Harpham's conception of an ethical terminology, 'ethicity' refers to the interpretive moment in ethical criticism: 'the most dramatic of narrative turnings, the climactic point just between the knitting and unravelling of the action, the fort and the da, the moment when the rising line of complication peaks, pauses, and begins its descent into the dénouement'. Addressing the narratological and characterological essences of this evaluative instance – what Harpham calls the 'macro-turn' – enables ethical critics, through their obligations to their own sets of values and commitments, to reflect upon and interpret the moral choices depicted in narratives (1992: 171). In many ways, this notion highlights the central attributes that undergird both European and North American manifestations of ethical criticism. Drawing upon Levinasian notions of alterity, scholars such as Harpham clearly represent the best of both philosophical worlds in which continental philosophy's interest in otherness tempers the North American academy's risky forays into moral relativism. Both scholarly worlds – different and confrontational as they may seem at times – ultimately recognize that it is our perceptions of the ethics of the texts themselves, and our experiences with them, that truly matter.

NOTES TOWARDS READINGS OF GEORGE ELIOT'S *SILAS MARNER* AND SPIKE JONZE'S *BEING JOHN MALKOVICH*

As a reading paradigm, ethical criticism offers a valuable lens for examining the manner in which literary characters experience moments of moral clarity and interpersonal change. Originally published in 1861, Eliot's *Silas Marner* illustrates a variety of ethical principles inherent in the evolving critical vocabulary of continental philosophy's postwar ethical turn. In many ways, the novel's protagonist enjoys an altered relationship not only with Eppie, the little orphan girl who punctures the self-imposed asceticism of his insular world, but with himself. Eliot's novel also affords us with a useful exemplar of the gift in a Derridean sense, particularly in terms of the aspects of responsibility and self-sacrifice that giving necessarily entails. Readers often celebrate *Silas Marner* because of its intriguing psychological interplay, as well as for its heart-warming conclusion. An ethical reading of the novel, though, allows us to consider the intra- and interpersonal predicaments that act as important precursors to *Silas Marner*'s moving denouement.

For Silas, enjoying a genuinely altered relationship with anyone – much less himself – would seem to test the bounds of probability. Afflicted by periodic, trance-like bouts of protracted catalepsis, Silas endures a lonely existence in which only the mounting guineas in his treasured iron pot inspire any real passion in him for living. Thunderstruck after experiencing the theft of his gold, Silas's psyche slowly erodes as he realizes the extent of his loss, artificial as it may be: 'He put his trembling hands to his head, and gave a wild ringing scream, the cry of desolation', Eliot writes (1996: 34). The shock of his new reality, with its contingent uncertainty and personal malaise, prepares Silas for the gift that he enjoys literally in the company of Eppie, the orphan who changes his life when she happens upon his cottage. Believing that 'the gold had turned into the child' (Eliot 1996: 103), Silas accepts the burden of the gift when he recognizes the responsibility involved in his act of altruism: 'Unlike the gold, which needed nothing, and must be worshipped in close-locked solitude', Eliot writes, 'Eppie was a creature of endless claims and ever-growing desires, seeking and loving sunshine, and living sounds, and living movements; making trial of everything, with trust in new joy, and stirring the human kindness in all eyes that looked on her' (1996: 105–6). Later, when her birth-father arrives on the scene and threatens to come between the girl and Silas, her loving surrogate, Eppie validates the power of the weaver's gift and the genuine extent of Silas's altered outlook upon the increasingly wide world that exists beyond his lonely cottage walls:

> 'We've been used to be happy together every day, and I can't think o' no happiness without him. And he says he'd nobody i' the world till I was sent to him, and he'd have nothing when I was gone. And he's took care of me and loved me from the first, and I'll cleave to him as long as he lives, and nobody shall ever come between him and me.' (Eliot 1996: 143)

In this manner, Eliot illustrates love's remarkable capacity for altering our perspectives and establishing genuine interpersonal transcendence. In his highly original film, *Being John Malkovich*, director Spike Jonze and screenwriter Charlie Kaufman examine another gift of sorts that affords them with a mechanism for investigating the manner in which literary and filmic stylistics contribute to the ethical impressions that often exist within a given narrative's textual recesses. As Nussbaum notes, an artist's sense of style – whether visual, literary, or otherwise – often functions as a means for rendering ethical judgments. In *Love's Knowledge*, Nussbaum argues that

> form and style are not incidental features. A view of life is *told*. The telling itself – the selection of genre, formal structures, sentences, vocabulary, of the whole manner of addressing the reader's sense of life – all of this expresses a sense of life and of value, a sense of what matters and what does not, of what learning and communicating are, of life's relations and connections. Life is never simply *presented* by a text; it is always *represented as* something. (1990: 5)

Jonze's ethics of style finds its origins in the film's clever plot device involving a mysterious portal that allows curiosity seekers the opportunity to venture into the mind of actor John Malkovich. For much of the film, a kind of absurdist comedy functions as Jonze's stylistic *métier* and as the prelude to the larger ethical implications that he will explore in the film's final, stunning reel.

The film itself devotes much of its initial energy to contending with what appears to be its singular narrative thrust, a gimmick of sorts in which people pay $200 for the opportunity to spend fifteen minutes inside Malkovich's brain before being expelled, rather amazingly, onto a grassy median near the New Jersey Turnpike. Orchestrated by dejected puppeteer Craig (John Cusack) in cahoots with his dowdy wife Lotte (Cameron Diaz) and his devious co-worker Maxine (Catherine Keener), the trio's scheme for exploiting the portal begins to unravel when their relationship devolves into a love triangle and they start asking questions about the origins of this freak of time and space that has altered their lives. At times, *Being John Malkovich* seems to be grappling with issues of celebrity, addiction and identity politics, yet the film's simultaneously evocative and disturbing final scene utterly changes everything that comes before it in the screenplay. In this way, *Being John Malkovich* both aspires to more substantial literary pretensions *and* takes on greater significance. Jonze and Kaufman accomplish this end by self-consciously staging a scene that allows their audience to experience a 'cataleptic impression' – a cognitive, philosophical phenomenon that, according to Nussbaum, 'has the power, just through its own felt quality, to drag us to assent, to convince us that things could not be otherwise. It is defined as a mark or impress upon the soul' (1990: 265). In the scene – a surreal, simplistic image of a young girl tranquilly swimming in a suburban pool that could be located, rather pointedly, anywhere – Jonze and Kaufman ask questions about the ethics of our desires and the often perplexing interrelationship between the desires of the self and the needs of the community. We become transfigured by the experience of viewing the scene, alarmed by the sinister possibilities that it entails, and cognizant, for the first time in the film's duration, that *Being John Malkovich* seeks to interrogate ethical issues that exist at the core of our very being.

ETHICAL CRITICISM: A POSTSCRIPT

As literary studies has continued to evolve in the twenty-first century, ethical criticism as an interpretive movement has been continually beset – and not surprisingly – by charges of moral relativism. Chief amongst the paradigm's detractors is Judge Richard A. Posner, who takes particular issue with ethical criticism's influential role in the law and literature movement. The crux of Posner's disagreement with ethical criticism lies in his contention that 'the aesthetic outlook *is* a moral outlook', that ethical critics in some way insist on separating moral and aesthetic levels of inquiry. Posner's defence of the 'aesthetic tradition' against ethical criticism rests upon three principal arguments: first, Posner writes that 'immersion in literature does not make us better citizens or people'; second, 'we should not be put off by morally offensive views encountered in literature even when the author seems to share them'; and finally, 'authors' moral qualities or opinions should not affect our valuations of their works' (1997: 2). Given his stature as a distinguished American jurist, Judge Posner has garnered considerable attention for his positions.

Yet Posner's assertion that literary immersion lacks the capacity for transforming readers into better citizens or people fails to problematize the efforts of ethical criticism on two levels: first, recent ethical criticism does not in fact seek to elevate literature as a force for moral socialization; and second, ethical critics do not champion literature as a means of moral guidance – as textbooks for living life effectively and with a moral imperative – but as a means, rather, for engaging in self-reflection via the terminology of moral philosophy. As it stands, Posner never attempts to grapple with the latter issue, the core of Booth's and Nussbaum's argument in favour of an ethical criticism. Instead, Posner challenges this subject through a series of non-sequitur attacks, including such moments when he argues that 'we should be skeptical about any claims that readers can extract from works of imaginative literature practical lessons for living' (1997: 10).

While Posner's arguments 'against ethical criticism' often seem contradictory and frequently out of touch with the contemporary nature of literary study, his essay nevertheless demonstrates that ethical criticism must still clarify and refine itself as a functioning interpretive methodology. In addition to allaying the fears of moral relativism inherent in Posner's critique, the ethical paradigm must also differentiate itself from the rigid humanism of earlier critics such as Leavis and Gardner. By underscoring ethical criticism's lack of hermeneutic clarity, Posner's 'Against Ethical Criticism' may prove to be a significant moment, rather ironically, in the paradigm's evolution as a means of literary critique. Rather than delivering a death-blow to ethical criticism as a humanist field of inquiry, Posner's essay reminds us that the ethical paradigm – with all of its contingent possibilities and theoretical promise – still needs to assert its associations with contemporary moral philosophy and clarify its viability as an interpretive methodology.

QUESTIONS FOR FURTHER CONSIDERATION

1. What are the principal differences between ethical criticism's incarnations in North America and Europe, respectively? What are each movement's fundamental similarities?
2. What historical issues might have led to the academy's general interest in ethical issues in the latter half of the twentieth century?
3. How has the ethical turn impacted the direction of literary criticism since the 1980s? Is there any evidence of an ethical renewal of sorts in the academy?
4. What are the principal strengths of ethical criticism as an interpretive paradigm? What seem to be its overall weaknesses as a form of literary critique?
5. Compare the ethical premises exhibited by such thinkers as Wayne C. Booth, Martha C. Nussbaum, Jacques Derrida and Luce Irigaray. How are they similar? How do they diverge from each other's views about ethics?

6. Drawing upon other novels and films in addition to the aforementioned works by George Eliot and Spike Jonze, how does a consideration for ethical issues alter your understanding of the ideological imperatives inherent in various literary and filmic texts?

BIBLIOGRAPHY

Assoun, Paul-Laurent (1998) 'The Subject and the Other in Levinas and Lacan', trans. Dianah Jackson and Denise Merkle, in Sarah Harasym, ed., *Levinas and Lacan: The Missed Encounter*, Albany: State University of New York Press.

Badiou, Alain (2001) *Ethics: An Essay on the Understanding of Evil*, trans. Peter Hallward, London: Verso.

Bernasconi, Robert and Simon Critchley, eds., (1991) *Re-Reading Levinas*, Bloomington: Indiana University Press.

Booth, Wayne C. (1988) *The Company We Keep: An Ethics of Fiction*, Berkeley: University of California Press.

Burke, Seán (1999) 'The Aesthetic, the Cognitive, and the Ethical: Criticism and Discursive Responsibility', in David Fuller and Patricia Waugh, eds., *The Arts and Sciences of Criticism*, Oxford: Oxford University Press.

Champagne, Roland (1998) *The Ethics of Reading According to Emmanuel Levinas*, Amsterdam: Rodopi.

Chanter, Tina (1995) *Ethics of Eros: Irigaray's Rewriting of the Philosophers*, London: Routledge.

Chow, Rey (1998) *Ethics After Idealism: Theory, Culture, Ethnicity, Reading*, Bloomington: Indiana University Press.

Cohen, Tom (1998) *Ideology and Inscription: 'Cultural Studies' after Benjamin, de Man, and Bakhtin*, Cambridge: Cambridge University Press.

Cornell, Drucilla (1999) *Beyond Accommodation: Ethical Feminism, Deconstruction, and the Law*, Lanham: Rowman and Littlefield.

Critchley, Simon (1997) *Very Little . . . Almost Nothing: Death, Philosophy, Literature*, London: Routledge.

Critchley, Simon (1999) *The Ethics of Deconstruction: Derrida and Levinas*. West Lafayette: Purdue University Press.

Derrida, Jacques (1995) *The Gift of Death*, trans. David Wills, Chicago: University of Chicago Press.

Derrida, Jacques (1997) '. . .and Pomegranates', trans. Samuel Weber, in Hent de Vries and Samuel Weber, eds., *Violence, Identity, and Self-Determination*, Stanford: Stanford University Press.

Eaglestone, Robert (1998) *Ethical Criticism: Reading After Levinas*, Edinburgh: Edinburgh University Press.

Eliot, George (1996) *Silas Marner* [1861], New York: Dover.

Gardner, John (1978) *On Moral Fiction*, New York: Basic.

Gibson, Andrew (1999) *Postmodernity, Ethics, and the Novel: From Leavis to Levinas*, London: Routledge.

Harpham, Geoffrey Galt (1992) *Getting It Right: Language, Literature, and Ethics*, Chicago: University of Chicago Press.

Harpham, Geoffrey Galt (1999) *Shadows of Ethics: Criticism and the Just Society*, Durham NC: Duke University Press.

Irigaray, Luce (1993) *An Ethics of Sexual Difference*, trans. Carolyn Burke and Gillian C. Gill, Ithaca: Cornell University Press.

Jonze, Spike, dir. (2000) *Being John Malkovich*, Gramercy Pictures.

Levinas, Emmanuel (1985) *Time and the Other*, trans. Richard Cohen, Pittsburgh: Duquesne University Press.

Levinas, Emmanuel (1986) 'The Trace of the Other', trans. Alphonso Lingis, in Mark

C. Taylor, ed., *Deconstruction in Context: Literature and Philosophy*, Chicago: University of Chicago Press.

Levinas, Emmanuel (1987), 'Philosophy and the Idea of Infinity', in *Collected Philosophical Papers*, trans. Alphonso Lingis, Dordrecht: Martinus Nijhoff.

Levinas, Emmanuel (1996) *Basic Philosophical Writings*, ed. Adriaan T. Peperzak, Simon Critchley and Robert Bernasconi, Bloomington: Indiana University Press.

Lyotard, Jean-François (1984) *The Postmodern Condition: A Report on Knowledge*, trans. Geoffrey Bennington and Brian Massumi, Minneapolis: University of Minnesota Press.

McGinn, Colin (1997) *Ethics, Evil, and Fiction*, Oxford: Clarendon.

Miller, J. Hillis (1987) *The Ethics of Reading: Kant, de Man, Eliot, Trollope, James, and Benjamin*, New York: Columbia University Press.

Miller, J. Hillis (1990) *Versions of Pygmalion*, Cambridge MA: Harvard University Press.

Newton, Adam Zachary (1995) *Narrative Ethics*, Cambridge MA: Harvard University Press.

Norris, Christopher (1994) *Truth and the Ethics of Criticism*, New York: St. Martin's.

Nussbaum, Martha C. (1990) *Love's Knowledge: Essays on Philosophy and Literature*, Oxford: Oxford University Press.

Nussbaum, Martha C. (1995) *Poetic Justice: The Literary Imagination and Public Life*, Boston: Beacon.

Parker, David (1994) *Ethics, Theory, and the Novel*, Cambridge: Cambridge University Press.

Posner, Richard A. (1997) 'Against Ethical Criticism', *Philosophy and Literature* 21, pp. 1–27.

Robbins, Jill (1999) *Altered Reading: Levinas and Literature*, Chicago: University of Chicago Press.

Rosenblatt, Louise M. (1978) *The Reader, the Text, the Poem: The Transactional Theory of the Literary Work*, Carbondale: Southern Illinois University Press.

Siebers, Tobin (1988) *The Ethics of Criticism*, Ithaca: Cornell University Press.

Walker, Margaret Urban (1998) *Moral Understandings: A Feminist Study in Ethics*, New York: Routledge.

Williams, Bernard (1985) *Ethics and the Limits of Philosophy*, Cambridge MA: Harvard University Press.

Worthington, Kim L. (1996) *Self as Narrative: Subjectivity and Community in Contemporary Fiction*, Oxford: Clarendon.

LEVINAS AND CRITICISM: ETHICS IN THE IMPOSSIBILITY OF CRITICISM

Frederick Young

It is true that Ethics, in Levinas's sense, is an Ethics without law and without concept, which maintains its non-violent purity only before being determined as concepts and laws. This is not an objection: let us not forget that Levinas does not seek to propose laws or moral rules, does not seek to determine *a* morality, but rather the essence of the ethical relation in general. But as this determination does not offer itself as a *theory* of Ethics, in question, then, is an Ethics of Ethics . . . A coherence which breaks down the coherence of the discourse against coherence – the infinite concept, hidden within the protest against the concept.

Jacques Derrida, 'Violence and Metaphysics'

Why write about a philosopher in an introduction to different approaches to the practice and theory of literary criticism? What can Emmanuel Levinas, whose ethical project goes not only against the grain of classical rhetoric, aesthetics and literary criticism, but also against the whole enterprise of philosophy itself, offer a student of criticism? In other words, what relevance does Levinas have for us? Levinas's contribution to continental philosophy is the revitalization of the question of ethics and, more importantly, the rethinking of ethics not as a branch of philosophy (or ontology[1]) but as something that is prior to and unworks philosophy's totalizing practice. Levinas's ethics radically differs from ethics or morality as understood as a discipline within philosophy. Whereas philosophy attempts to speak for the Other,[2] to give the Other voice and meaning to what it doesn't understand, to perform the violence of speaking for the Other, Levinas's project is to refigure ethics as an interruption of the very practice of philosophy.

What can his work tell us about the nature and project of literary criticism? Because of Levinas's particular view of ethics, he would regard literary criticism, understood as pre-set principles which could then be applied to a literary text, as functioning similarly to philosophy, which by means of imposing a methodology, or code, attempts to speak *for* the Other. In this way, both philosophy and literary criticism are a discourse of the Same, that which does not respect difference or the possibility of encountering the Other. In other words, literary criticism imposes meaning on a work of literature, just as philosophy imposes meaning on that which eludes it. In literary criticism and philosophy, the *example* functions as a mimetic or representational relation. This process only reflects its own meaning, and by attempting to speak for the other, only reflects itself – the mimetology of self-reflexivity. For Levinas, ethics is always a problem of relation, and, I will argue, of unworking any form of mimesis or representation.

For Levinas, the project of philosophy as a process of totalization must itself be interrupted, and he does this through a radical rethinking of the question of ethics, no longer understood as a branch of philosophy, as systematic or codifiable doctrine, that *ought* to be applied to specific experiences or situations, but rather as a performative operation that exceeds, or perhaps interrupts, philosophy's grip. In other words, ethics for Levinas is prior to philosophy (the history of metaphysics, of ontology) and, then, before any philosophy of ethics. Thus, Jacques Derrida calls it an 'Ethics of Ethics', an ethics that does not follow the rule of representation or the example. For instance, there can be no example of an ethical action applied to a specific situation since there is no prior code of ethics to fall back upon. That is, ethics is a matter of relation with the Other and therefore before meaning itself. This encounter with the Other (Autrui), what Levinas terms the 'face to face' is a performative relation prior to an ontological mediation; thus, in the 'face to face' encounter with the Other, no code of ethics is applicable. As Jill Robbins states in *Altered Reading*, 'For Levinas . . . ethics denotes not a set of moral precepts but a responsibility – at its most originary – that arises in the encounter with the face of another' (1999: 41). This 'encounter' with the 'face of another' is precisely what is at stake for Levinas.

This chapter attempts to shed light on some of Levinas's important concepts as well as some of his terminology. This is in no way meant to be a comprehensive commentary on Levinas's work. Rather, this chapter attempts to explore key concepts of his project relating to notions of performativity, ontology, art, rhetoric and deconstruction.[3] However, before addressing these crucial questions in greater detail, it is necessary to understand Levinas's ethical project and its relation to philosophy. At the risk of momentarily oversimplifying Levinas, he loosely shares a common thread with many twentieth-century continental philosophers, who, perhaps taking their cue from Nietzsche, unwork the very project of philosophy itself, which tries to speak for the other by imposing meaning on that which is foreign to it.[4]

In the section on ethics and ontology below I will explore what Levinas has in common with Heidegger as well as some of their crucial differences. Levinas's ethics shares with Heidegger's 'fundamental ontology' a need to work against philosophy, or metaphysics, to somehow get behind or before it. Although their respective projects differ greatly – and the fact that their own works changed throughout their lives is also of importance – the section on ethics and ontology will delve more deeply into Heidegger and Levinas. The section on saying and said will address how these two terms function for Levinas's project as a means of understanding how both the performative and constative operate. In the section on rhetoric and art, I will look at Levinas's views on both art and classical rhetoric against the project and possibility of ethics because, for Levinas, both art and rhetoric are involved with representation and the application of a set of rules. However, this is complicated when we consider his relationship with Maurice Blanchot and Jacques Derrida. I will also then complicate Levinas's views on art and rhetoric to explore how his definitions are informed by a Platonic inheritance and how Levinas's interruptive ethics are much closer to investigations of the 'literary' itself and an ethical performative. In this sense, Levinas's project, although certainly not identical, is similar to that of thinkers such as Philippe Lacoue-Labarthe, Maurice Blanchot, Jacques Derrida, Hélène Cixous and Paul de Man in that the representational or mimetic structures of philosophy, relation and method are brought into question.

RELATION: ETHICS AND ONTOLOGY

In order to understand Levinas's importance for a student of criticism, it is vital to understand his relationship to ontology. Ontology, the question of being, is both fundamental and foundational to philosophy. The various branches of philosophy, such as epistemology, ethics and aesthetics, are all predicated upon ontology. To really grasp what is at stake in Levinas's ethics and his challenge to philosophy, we have to consider Martin Heidegger's 'fundamental ontology' as articulated in *Being and Time*, in which he calls for the 'destruction' of ontology, beginning with Plato and culminating in Hegel. Heidegger radicalizes the problem of ontology and offers a critique of the Cartesian subject[5] by means of the 'equipmental structure', what Heidegger calls Dasein (literally 'being there'). Dasein is always already 'being-in-the-world'.[6] Hence, the experience of Dasein is prior to the subject/object duality of Descartes. Heidegger uses the word Dasein because he does not want to use the word 'subject', which falls into the notion of the subject/object split and is based upon an abstract notion of being, precisely what the tradition of philosophy embraces and what Heidegger seeks to avoid. For Heidegger, the history of philosophy is, in a sense, 'a history of a mistake' in which philosophers since Plato have misunderstood the question of the meaning of being by understanding it as an abstraction, an empty category which serves to classify knowledge. Heidegger attempts to 'get behind' philosophy, which he sees as ontological, and develop a 'transcendental fundamental ontology'. Thus Heidegger turns to the question of Dasein, being-in-the-world, which, for him, is prior to the object/subject split of Descartes. By means of articulating the structure of the world in which Dasein is being-in-the-world, Heidegger attempts to get out of traditional ontology and Cartesian duality.

While this is not the place to attempt to describe Heidegger's project, what concerns us is the problem that Heidegger's 'fundamental ontology'[7] presents for Levinas's ethics. Even though Heidegger tries to unwork a Cartesian relation by destroying Cartesian precepts, for Levinas, Heidegger still understands *relation* as being, and this is a problem because, for Levinas, he inadvertently falls back into ontology. Thus Heidegger's project with Dasein, while opening up a critique of Descartes and the history of philosophy, nonetheless reinscribes ontology because first and foremost the question of being, not of the Other, is Heidegger's main concern. As Critchley asserts in *The Ethics of Deconstruction*:

> Levinasian ethics bears a critical relation to the philosophical tradition. For Levinas, Western philosophy has most often been what he calls 'ontology', by which he means the attempt to comprehend the Being of what is, or beings (das Sein des Seienden) . . . the most recent example of which is Heidegger's fundamental ontology, in which the elaboration of the question of the meaning of Being presupposes *ab initio* a comprehension of Being. (Critchley 1999: 5)

We can begin to see what is at stake in how to think the problem of relation, of the Other, without a mediation of being. In *Totality and Infinity* Levinas states, '*Being and Time* has argued perhaps but one sole thesis: Being is inseparable from the comprehension of Being (which unfolds as time); Being is already an appeal to subjectivity' (1969: 45). As long as Heidegger continues to emphasize being, he cannot get away from the subject. Thus Heidegger's project falls short of the radical relation of Levinas's ethics because Heidegger, for Levinas, still has not eliminated being as a relation, and Dasein itself falls into a strange subjectivity. There is no direct 'face'-to-'face' relation for Heidegger; despite his invaluable critique of ontology, he still reduces the relation between Dasein and Dasein as mediated by the question and problematic of being. The problem Heidegger's 'fundamental ontology' presents is that the tradition of philosophy is based upon abstraction, and while Heidegger attempts to get beyond philosophy, he still remains within being, which for Levinas misses the ethical. In *Totality and Infinity* Levinas states the problem explicitly:

> The primacy of ontology for Heidegger does not rest on the truism: 'to know an existant it is necessary to have comprehended the Being of existents.' To affirm the priority of Being over existents is to already decide

the essence of philosophy; it is to subordinate the relation with someone, who is an existant (the ethical relation), to a relation with the Being of existents. (1969: 45)

Again, for Levinas, Heidegger 'affirms the priority of Being over existants' at the expense of an ethical relation between existants. In his commentary on Levinas, Adriaan Peperzak further emphasizes the crucial difference between Levinas and Heidegger:

> The supremacy of reason, by which the human subject, according to Plato, feels at home in understanding the world as a relation of ideas [forms], is replaced by another relation between Dasein and Being, but still Dasein stays shut up in its relation to the phosphorescent Anonymous enabling all beings to present themselves to it, without ever producing true alterity. The truth of Dasein is that the being which is 'always mine' is also a being for which its own being is the issue. (1993: 53–4)

In other words, Heidegger replaces Plato's relation of ideas (the Forms) with another, or different, relation of Dasein being-with another Dasein, or of Dasein's relation to being. We can see Dasein is based upon Heidegger's 'fundamental ontology', which replaces Plato's traditional ontology. For Heidegger, being-in-the-world, which Dasein is always already in, is prior to Plato's notion of ontology, which bases being upon an abstraction. By extension, Descartes' subject, for Heidegger, is predicated on Platonic ontology. However, while Heidegger clearly radicalizes the problem of being for philosophy, he nonetheless fixates on a nostalgia for being.

Heidegger becomes vital for Levinas because *Being and Time* was the first real attempt to challenge the sovereignty of the Cartesian subject. Levinas's ethical project undoes the notion of being and how all relation, albeit Cartesian or Heideggerian, relies on ontology. Levinas attempts to unwork the very notion of relation as ontology. He regards his ethics and the 'face to face' as prior to Heidegger's ontology and the description of how Dasein relates to another Dasein as *mitsein*. What is at stake for a student of literary criticism is to see how, for Levinas, literary criticism, so long as it functions as a method of application, would necessarily *be* part and parcel of an ontological practice. In other words, any relation between a literary method and an *object* of study, such as a film or work of literature, is mediated by ontology, or being. Thus, we can begin to see how for Levinas literary criticism is haunted by ontology. Levinas attempts a radical unworking of relation as being, which sets up the possibility of application; his ethics will involve an asymmetrical relation based on a performative ethics, which interrupts the mediation of relation based on being.

According to Levinas, however, ethics is not a branch of philosophy but rather the interruption of philosophy's attempt at totalization, to speak *for* the Other, or in relation to the Other as an *object* of study. Hence, ethics for

Levinas is prior to philosophy or ontology: 'The establishing of the primacy of the ethical ... a primacy upon which all other structures rest (and in particular all those which seem to put us primordially in contact with an impersonal sublimity, aesthetic or ontological), is one of the objectives of the present work' (Levinas, quoted in Robbins 1999: xxi). Carl Thomas Wall, in *Radical Passivity*, also states that 'Ethics is beyond experience. It is beyond the experience of a subject and that of Dasein' (1999: 38). Ethics is a relation, or perhaps really a non-relation, an excess of being that works against the relation of subject and object, which is central to philosophy, especially since Descartes and Hegel. Levinas's ethics cannot be codified; it is not a prescriptive set of maxims that one ought to live by. Rather, what's at stake is a matter of an asymmetrical and non-mimetic relation prior to ontology, in which one faces rather than speaks for the Other (Autrui), that can never be static or repeatable but is performative. The encounter with the Other interrupts the sovereignty of the subject/object relation of traditional ontology as well as *Befindlichkeit* (how Dasein always already finds itself in the world) of Dasein. It is a relation without relation, an excess, a performative operation that unworks the subject/ object split. As Critchley states, 'In the language of transcendental philosophy, the face is the condition of possibility for ethics. For Levinas, then, the ethical relation – and ethics is simply and entirely the event of this relation – is one in which I am related to the face of the Other ...' (1999: 5).

Thus, it is also crucial to understand how the notion of identity and the Same function not only for Western philosophy, but for any of its derivative disciplines. For philosophy, everything under investigation is reduced to the Same. In other words, or putting words in for the other, philosophy collapses the relation between the Same and the Other into the Same. The relation is absorbed into mediation. What is at stake is how the relation (un)works in Levinas. Levinas introduces the figure of the face as a means of understanding the ethical. As Robbins states, 'the face is a collusion between world and that which exceeds world' (1999: 58).

Levinas's project in *Totality and Infinity* explores the ethical significance of the face of the Other, unmediated by being, in order to avoid the violent appropriation of ontology, the violence of speaking for the Other. The face does not represent anything for Levinas. Rather, it is a performative, or as Wall expresses it in *Radical Passivity*, ethics is 'an operation' (1999: 35). For Levinas, 'The relationship with the other ... puts me into question, empties me of myself ... The I loses its sovereign coincidence with itself, its identification, in which consciousness returned triumphantly to itself ... The I is expelled from this rest' (1969: 350–3). Furthermore, as Robbins contends, 'For Levinas, ethics in the most general sense is the question of self-sufficiency, the interruption of self – described variously as an obligation, an imperative, an imposition, a responsibility – that arises in the encounter with the face of the other' (1999: 23).

According to Levinas, the face is a condition for the possibility of ethics (Critchley), an excess that cannot be contained or contextualized. In this sense, it is a performative; ethics opens up a relation (Robbins 1999: 5–7). 'I don't think the infinity of Autrui, I face it; speak to it' (Robbins 1999: 7). The relation to the other is not a relation in the sense of a mediation, even to call it a relation is tenuous; rather 'the other is . . . a surplus, radical asymmetry' (Robbins 1999: 4). As Levinas remarks of this relation:

> The relation between the Other and me, which dawns forth in his expression, issues neither in number or concept. The Other remains infinitely transcendent, infinitely foreign; his face in which epiphany is produced and which appeals to me breaks with the world that can be common to us, whose virtualities are inscribed in our *nature* and absolute difference. (1969: 194).

Levinas describes how the face resists sublation and containment:

> The face resists possession, resists my powers. In its epiphany, in expression, the sensible, still graspable, turns into total resistance to the grasp. This mutation can occur only by the opening of a new dimension. For the resistance to the grasp is not produced as an insurmountable resistance, like the hardness of the rock against which the effort of the hand comes to naught, like the remoteness of a star in the immensity of space. The expression the face introduces into the world does not defy the feebleness of my powers, but my ability for power. The face, still a thing among things, breaks through the form that nevertheless delimits it. This means concretely: the face speaks to me and thereby invites me to a relation incommensurate with a power exercised, be it enjoyment or knowledge. (1969: 197–8)

Significantly, although Levinas describes the face, it is not the face of a subject; it is important to realize that the face is not literal or empirical but rather interrupts the ontological relation. Precisely because it is not a subject, it interrupts the ontological grounding that constitutes subjectivity: 'The face is present in its refusal to be contained. In this sense it cannot be comprehended, that is encompassed. It is neither seen nor touched – for in visual or tactile sensation the identity of the I envelops the alterity of the object, which precisely becomes a context' (Levinas 1969: 194). But what is crucial for Levinas is that the face is not a sign nor a representation of a subject; it is not semiotic – rather, as Critchley states, 'its possibility is the condition of ethics'. As Robbins puts it, 'For Levinas, to decode the face in the manner of other signs would be to reduce it violently, to turn it – horribly – into a mask, that is, not just a surface but something petrified and immobile' (1999: 60). To 'petrify' the face would be to ontologize it.

Because the face cannot *be* contained, it radically interrupts an ontological 'context'. The Other should not be understood as an object or another subject, nor a dialectical negation, because both must assume an ontology. Rather, the Other (Autrui), for Levinas, radically breaks any relation mediated by being.

SAYING AND SAID

The crucial question here is how does Levinas's ethics perform the radical relation, or interruption, of ontology? To think about the difference between Levinas's 'face to face' and ontology is to think about the difference between the Saying and the Said. In the *Ethics of Deconstruction* Critchley states, 'Whereas *Totality and Infinity* writes about ethics, *Otherwise than Being* is the performative enactment of ethical writing' (1999: 8). Provisionally, we can note that Saying is performative, while the Said is constative. In other words, Saying is ethical while the Said is ontological. In his famous lectures, *How To Do Things With Words*, the Anglo-American philosopher of language J. L. Austin introduced the concept of performatives and constatives.[8] For Austin, a performative is, or rather, I should say, *does*, the following:

> When I say before the registrar or altar, &c., 'I do', I am not reporting on a marriage: I am indulging in it. What are we to call a sentence or utterance of this type? I propose to call it a performative sentence or a performative utterance, or for short, 'a performative'. The term 'performative' will be used in a variety of cognate ways and constructions, much as the term 'imperative' is. The name is derived, of course, from 'perform', the usual verb with the noun 'action': it indicates that the issuing of the utterance is the performing of an action – it is not normally thought of as just saying something. (Austin 1975: 7)

For Austin, a performative is not a statement of truth; it is not verifiable, but rather concerns solely the action. 'I do' speaks of the action of 'doing', not of whether that action is good or bad, true or false. In other words, the performative is not subject to the traditional representational conditions of truth.[9] In contrast to the performative, however, the constative can be verified. According to Austin, the constative, unlike the performative, is a statement of fact.

For Levinas, Saying or speech is the way to unwork the ontological reification of the subject to the Other: 'the Saying is the sheer radicality of human speaking, of the event of being in relation with the Other; it is the non-thematizable ethical residue ... of language that escapes comprehension, interrupts philosophy, and is the very enactment of the ethical movement from the Same [of ontology] to the Other' (Critchley 1999: 7). Thus, for Levinas, the Saying is a performative that cannot be reduced to a constative, to the calculative functions of truth and identity. The Saying is not descriptive. Levinas employs the term Said to describe the prepositional, or constative, function of philosophy/ontology. The Saying, unlike the Said, opens up an 'exposure to the other'.

The Saying opens up a relation[10] to the Other unmediated by being, the 'face to face'. In other words, the Saying is in excess of any mediation of being, nor can this performative *be* Said. The Said, in contrast, is constative and occurs when the Saying is reduced to meaning, wherein it is static, becomes codifiable and is brought back into philosophy, or the Same. Thus, 'the ethical movement from Same to Other' opens up a relation more primal and direct, always performative, which 'interrupts' the constative or ontological relation of philosophy. According to Levinas, the performativity of Saying exposes me to the Other, creating an opening to the Other that cannot be refused nor closed by philosophy. Critchley argues that

> The Saying is my exposure – corporeal, sensible – to the Other, my inability to refuse the Other's approach. It is a performative stating, proposing, or expressive position of myself facing the Other. It is a verbal or non-verbal ethical performance, whose essence cannot be caught in constative prepositions. It is a performative doing that cannot be reduced to a constative description. (1999: 7)

For Levinas, this performative operation of Saying occurs in the 'face to face', in which the Other is greeted without being reduced to the Same. It is important to understand that the 'face to face' is not just another figure in the history of Western philosophy such as the subject/object split or Dasein being-with another Dasein. As Robbins asserts, 'The face is always on the move' (1999: 48). It is a performative, which opens up the relation to the Other. As Robbins states, 'the face is performative and not personified. It does not represent an actual face, but rather opens up the ethical relation with the Other.' While, on the other hand, 'the Said', as Robbins continues, 'is the linguistic equivalent of the economy of the Same. The Saying and the Said is a correlative relation (exceeding correlation) that marks the difference between a constative speech, oriented toward its addressee, interlocutionary and ethical, and a speech oriented toward the referent, more like a speaking *about* than a speaking *to* the other' (1999: 144). Again, we can see that the Saying is a performative that does not speak *about* the Other, as philosophy does, but rather, the Saying speaks *to* the Other, an absolutely crucial distinction for Levinas.

That stated, how is the Saying not reduced or brought back to the Said? And yet, is it possible to maintain the distinction between the Saying and the Said? Have I *said* too much about Levinas's performativity? Is not the Saying at risk of falling back into the Said as the performative is described or reinscribed back into philosophy? In other words, does not the Saying once described become Said? Does not the performative, once understood, return to the Same, the Said, philosophy? As Critchley notes,

> Given that philosophy speaks the language of the Said – that is, it consists of propositions and statements – The methodological problem that haunts every page of *Otherwise Than Being* is the following: How is the Saying, my exposure to the Other, to be Said or given a philosophical exposition without utterly betraying this Saying? How can one write the otherwise than Being in the language of Being . . . ? (1999: 164)[11]

We can now see the importance of Saying as a performative for Levinas as well as how the Said as constative reifies the ontological relation that he attempts to unwork.

ON ART AND RHETORIC

Critical for students of criticism, Levinas views both aesthetics and classical rhetoric as antithetical to his ethical project. His conception of rhetoric and aesthetics goes back to the Platonic conception of art as a representation, or image, of a representation of truth, or being. For Levinas, art as an image, based on Plato's metaphor of the cave, is far removed from truth though still locked within ontological assumptions. Levinas regards rhetoric as a type of 'angling', or sophistry, designed to manipulate language and twist its meaning. In other words, rhetoric goes against the 'face to face' encounter with the Other and attempts to use language to convert the Other, which necessarily objectifies it. Therefore classical rhetoric, for Levinas, manipulates the Other and obfuscates the 'face to face' encounter. Hence, such conceptions of rhetoric and art would be incommensurable with Levinas's ethical project.

What appears problematic in Levinas's notion of art and rhetoric, however, is that he inherits this particular Platonic conception without applying the same critical rigour with which he otherwise is so careful to critique Plato and the ontological tradition of philosophy. In other words, both art and rhetoric are based on ontological presuppositions. Levinas's view and distrust of art and rhetoric has more to do with the question of ontology and how both art and rhetoric as branches of understanding miss the critical ethical relation. Levinas opposes an aesthetics that would represent, or speak for, the Other, as well as a rhetoric with a set of precepts deployed to manipulate the Other. In other words, art or rhetoric as a set of codes applied to a specific situation are no different, really, than morality or ethics as a branch of philosophy. Thus, any concept of art and rhetoric, as well as literary criticism, which applies meaning to art, is necessarily 'incommensurable' with Levinas's ethics. As Jill Robbins states in *Altered Reading*:

> Any approach to the question of the relationship of Levinas's philosophy to literature has also to deal with the incommensurability between Levinas's ethics and the discourse of literary criticism. Literary criticism, whether it is conceived as the determination of a work's meaning or as an analysis of its formal structures, would be derivative upon Levinas's more originary question of the ethical, part of what Heidegger calls a regional ontology. Hence Levinas's philosophy cannot function as an extrinsic approach to the literary work of art, that is, it cannot give rise to an application. (1999: xx)

We can see how literary criticism, by attempting to interpret meaning and analyse form, is already inscribed for Levinas as ontological. Any effort to attribute meaning or to apply a method to a work of art attempts to speak for the Other. What now begins to emerge is that, for Levinas, classical rhetoric as prescriptive obfuscates or, perhaps, abolishes the possibility of the ethical – in an act of ontological violence. According to Levinas, as a system of static devices classical rhetoric could only offer a modality of 'angling', or appropriation, that reduces the relation to a mediation of being. Therefore, both art and rhetoric cannot escape ontology because they are ontology.

Does this then mean that Levinas has no interest in aesthetics or rhetoric? That his ethics is incommensurate with any project of criticism and therefore of no use or aid to the student of criticism? In *Altered Readings*, Robbins suggests that what 'Levinas is really interested in is art in relation to ethics, interruption rather than ontology' (1999: 154). In other words, Levinas could only understand aesthetics and rhetoric as an ethical interruption, a performative, that unworks ontology. What becomes crucial, then, is to begin to think of art and rhetoric not as an ontological relation of the Same that would describe a constative condition, but rather as a performative that radically unworks and brings into question the ontology of relation. What is at stake for Levinas, I would argue, is the problem of how art and rhetoric are conceived traditionally as mimetic. Therefore, the task, in order to face the Other, is to interrupt mimesis.[12] In this sense, Levinas is quite interested in aesthetics and rhetoric but not as they are *conceived* in philosophy, rather as an 'interruption', as a performative that unworks the literary text as an *object* of study to which a method could apply or 'angle' meaning. What really is at stake for Levinas, and here he is quite close to Blanchot and Derrida,[13] is the very possibility of the literary, not as static but as something that, perhaps, unworks meaning.

NOTES TOWARDS A READING OF ANDREY TARKOVSKY'S THE SACRIFICE

The first thing to describe is the event, not your attitude to it.

The Sacrifice is a parable. The significant events it contains can be interpreted in more than one way.

Andrey Tarkovsky, *Sculpting in Time*

How is it possible to interpret a work of literature in light of Levinas's radicalization of ethics? Any attempt to *apply* a theory of Levinas to a work of literature, or film, risks reducing the ethical performative relation back into ontology, mimesis. Again, the question must be asked, what can Levinas offer a student of literary criticism, when literary criticism, as a domain of ontology, reduces the Other to the Same? In other words, any application of Levinas would fail before it began. The problem here is that of mimesis, of representation. Is it possible to approach a literary text without deploying a methodology, without representing Levinas?

In the last and infamous scene of Tarkovsky's *The Sacrifice*,[14] Alexander burns down his house, his books, and the map that was a gift from the postman, Otto.[15] Alexander, an intellectual, sacrifices his house after World

War III begins – it remains unclear as to whether or not the war is actually taking place or if Alexander has just imagined it. Our question is, how do we read this sacrifice? Is the sacrifice something intended to bring about harmony? Is it to bring about an exchange – to sacrifice oneself in order to save others? In other words, does the one who sacrifices expect something in return? If so, then it would fall into the economy of mimesis because it would require something from the Other – an exchange. The event of the sacrifice would be reduced to a constative, the Said. The agreement in advance of the sacrifice would explain (away) the event, would close off the 'face to face' with the Other. Vital to our concern with the sacrifice is the (im)possibility of an event, the event of sacrifice. In other words, if we look at the event of the sacrifice as a performative, then understanding the event, applying meaning to it, becomes impossible.

In *Sculpting in Time*, Tarkovsky conveys his idea of sacrifice:

> What moved me was the theme of the harmony which is born only of sacrifice, the twofold dependence of love . . . I am interested in the character who is capable of sacrificing himself and his way of life – regardless of whether that sacrifice is made in the name of spiritual values, or for the sake of someone else, or of his own salvation, or of all these things together. Such behavior precludes, by its very nature, all of those selfish interests that make up a 'normal' rationale for action; it refutes the laws of a materialistic worldview. It is often absurd and unpractical. And yet – or indeed for that very reason – the man who acts in this way brings about fundamental changes in people's lives and in the course of history. The space he lives in becomes a rare, distinctive point of contrast to the empirical concepts of our experience, an area where reality – I would say – is all the more strongly present. (1986: 217–18)

The question we have to ask is whether or not Alexander's sacrifice can be seen as harmonious. If the sacrifice is a gift in order to exchange oneself to prevent a greater disaster, such as the annihilation of the world, we must ask whether or not such an exchange is mimetic. Does a sacrifice, if understood as harmonious, really offer itself to the Other, or does it impose its own demands, in which case it would be the Said? I sacrifice myself in order that the Other accepts my demands. For Levinas, this form of sacrifice would obliterate the 'face to face' of the Other. Remember that the face to face makes no demands on the Other and interrupts any attempt to do so. Rather than opening up to the Other an unconditional gift, if such as thing is possible, sacrifice for the sake of harmony is mimetic – it is an exchange within the economy of the Same – the face is closed off from the self who sacrifices it*self*. The performative of the sacrifice is already inscribed as predetermined or stated by the self who sacrifices – this is ontological *par excellence*.

However, it is possible to read *The Sacrifice* against the grain of how Tarkovsky describes it in *Sculpting in Time*. I would argue that, rather than look at the event of the sacrifice as constative, as ontological, as Said, as speaking for the Other, it is vital to think of the sacrifice, the event itself, as a performative interruption impossible to determine and assign meaning to. The performative Saying exceeds any agreement, contract or exchange; it does not attempt to get an 'angle' on the Other. The event of the burning house, of Alexander running away from the ambulance drivers, all of this is only the affect of the interruption of the event, the sacrifice, which we cannot experience. Remember that experience remains part and parcel of ontology and the subject, the 'I'. A cue for this unsettling event, to the performative or asymmetrical relation of the sacrifice, comes in the final scene. Alexander's son, the 'little man', is lying under the Japanese tree that he and his father planted at the beginning of the film. The ambulance carrying Alexander passes by the boy, and it is uncanny that this does not affect him. Throughout the film, the boy had not spoken because of a throat operation that took place outside of the film. The boy looks up at the sky as the camera begins to pan up the tree, and breaks his silence: 'In the beginning was the Word . . . Why is that papa?' In *Sculpting in Time*, Tarkovsky sees addressing the father as perhaps Christian – as recalling Christ's sacrifice. Christ's sacrifice makes demands on the Other by calling on people to renounce their sins. Christ's sacrifice does not face the Other, but rather makes demands on the Other. But if we look at the sacrifice as performative, something that resists meaning, or exceeds or interrupts meaning, what Christ Said, then we can begin to see how the act of the sacrifice faces the Other without demand.

The 'little man's' constative statement, 'In the beginning was the Word', is out of place. It should have taken place before the disaster, the sacrifice, but rather is a strange affect displaced after the event; the beginning should precede the disaster. The boy's calmness, the uncanniness of his speech, indicates that something is out of joint. Any meaning or definitive explanation is off frame, outside of what is given. The constative grounding, or explanation of the meaning of the sacrifice, is displaced by the unknowable and undecidable, the performativity of the sacrifice. The sacrifice is not harmonious, or Said, but rather is performative, outside the demands of the self on the Other. Through performativity the sacrifice opens up the only possibility of the 'face to face' with the Other – there are no demands of the self in the (im)possibility of the disaster.[16] After the displaced constative, comes the boy's interrogative, 'Why is that papa?' Aside from the strangeness of the boy addressing his father by looking up at the sky just after his father passes by in the ambulance, the unanswered question itself fails to address the performativity of the event, of the sacrifice. The question, or what Heidegger calls the 'piety of the question',[17] comes after the displaced constative and cannot get to the performativity of the event because the question is ontological, it demands meaning, the Said. In other words, the sacrifice, read as performance, unworks the ontological basis of the question – thus, the sacrifice is an interruption, a Saying that opens up the 'face to face'. In this way the question can only address or explore the ontological nature and the essence of something knowable, of something that can be Said. The question never reaches the performativity of the event or sacrifice. In this sense, both the constative utterance and the question of the boy are displaced and cannot get at the event, the performativity of the sacrifice. In order to open up the 'face to face' with the Other, the sacrifice must unwork (interrupt) the demands of the self on the Other, the harmony of exchange.

ETHICS AND TEKHNE

In the previous sections we have spent a considerable amount of time looking at Levinas's ethics in relation to Heideggerian ontology, and also the question of art. This section addresses the so-called 'technological turn' in continental philosophy and the importance of *tekhne*. Of particular interest to students of criticism is that much of the technological turn in philosophy that has happened over the past ten years or so, and is becoming more available to English readers. It can easily be argued that the French philosopher Bernard Stiegler is the most important, if not the most focused, contemporary thinker on the idea of *tekhne*.[18] It is only over the past few years that his major works have become available in large part to readers of English. While it is not possible to explicate all of Stiegler's concepts on *tekhne* here, I would like to focus on his major concepts as they relate to Levinas's ethics: 1) The notion that 'the tool and human invent each other'. 2) His reading of the Ancient Greek phrase '*tekhne tou biou*', or 'the art of living'. 3) And finally Stiegler's increasing politicization in the light of his philosophical discoveries. This might open an encounter between the singular ethical act of Levinas and the possibility of an ethics of the political, or a meta-critique taking up Stiegler's increasing concern with digitalization, globalization and capitalism. However, before moving directly into an encounter between Levinas and Stiegler it will be useful to give some philosophical background for the Ancient Greek term *tekhne*.

It can be argued that Marx and Heidegger were both vital thinkers regarding technics. As Stiegler states: 'Envisioning the possibility of a tech-nology that would constitute a theory of *technics*, Marx outlined a new perspective. Engels invoked a dialectic between tool and hand that was to trouble the frontier between the organic and inorganic' (Stiegler 1998: 2). Stiegler implies a liminal zone between 'life' and 'matter' that technics seems to occupy. While the tool might be thought to be ontic, its movement with the hand produces a transformation of materiality (in the literal sense), as it opens technics to something more than just an object as it is in action.[19] In this way, Marx, it could be said, is the first to radicalize *tekhne* (as tool) by orientating the Greek concept towards practice and the attempt at a material transformation of the world.

However, Heidegger's[20] notion of *tekhne* has perhaps had the biggest influence on continental philosophy. In 'The Origin of the Work of Art' he traced *tekhne* back to the Greeks not only in its scientific determination as 'tool' but also more importantly as an 'event' (*Ereignis*) or 'making appear.' In this way *tekhne* is re-discovered as art. The brilliance of Heidegger's essay lies in its moving from an instrumental and scientific understanding of *tekhne* as technology or tool, to that of a work of art, or event – a truth of appearing and withdrawing more primal than calculative truth. Heidegger discovers within *tekhne* a truth (*Aletheia*) as an event or 'making appear' which goes beyond the instrumental and humanist notion of truth as calculation or representation. *Tekhne* has an equal force in Gilles Deleuze's philosophy, and throughout the work of Jacques Derrida, although there is not the space here to trace their insights.

In *Technics and Time, 1: The Fault of Epimetheus*, Stiegler makes the remarkable statement 'that the tool and human invent each other'. Two vital aspects are at play here. First, that the tool (*tekhne*) and the human being share an 'origin' of invention, and second, that the humanist chronology of a human being *prior to* a tool is challenged, as neither tool nor human can essentially be understood without the other. This temporality stalls chronological time. In other words, the human is defined alongside the tool, as each invents the other – a necessary fictive truth of an event without origin. They cannot *be* separated. The apparatus is woven in the human. And we can further state that intentionality 'lies' somewhere between or 'with' (*mit*) the human and the tool. This brings up interesting questions as to where thinking is located. The human? The tool? Or somewhere 'between?' It also sheds some light on Heidegger's infamous statement that 'buildings think'. As we have seen that Levinas's ethics are prior to Heidegger's fundamental ontology, it is also possible to imagine a non-relation of classical ontology that does not privilege the history of the *subjectum*. The fictive origin of human and tool opens up an ethical question as to the veracity of an ontological relation or traditional hierarchy of human and tool in that order. Here we might see an ethics 'in' this fictive move of human and tool, not as *mitsein*, but as co-inventors whose intentions or consciousness are not questions to be answered, but rather their co-existence is a relation of an ethical and incalculable event, of 'the art of living'.

The next aspect of Stiegler's work I would like to briefly address is his mediation of the Greek phrase, '*techne tou biou*',[21] or the 'art of living.' As we have already seen, *tekhne* not only contains the modern notion of tool, but also that of art. In *Technics and Time 1*, Stiegler demonstrates how *episteme* and *tekhne* are separated in philosophy, as *tekhne* becomes a mere tool. As he writes:

> If this question is not new it comes to us in an entirely original way in contemporary technics: the confidence that has ruled this question since Descartes, at least, no longer holds. This is also the case because the division originally made by philosophy between *tekhne* and *episteme* has become problematic. If the conditions of a new relation – economic, social and political – began with the Industrial Revolution, this novelty was actually declared a crisis only in the beginning of the twentieth century, with the First World War. (1998: 21)

If we begin to take the notion of a crucial genealogical rupture seriously, then *tekhne* as art, and more vitally as 'the art of living', comes to the fore. And the acceleration of modernity unites somewhat perversely *tekhne* and *episteme* through the 'art' of war. What this uncovers for readers of Levinas is that there is an intrinsic ethics at work here, that *tekhne* and *episteme* still hold to a 'regional ontology', of being as prior to ethics. There is no mention of ontology, and even if there was, would it not be possible to read Levinas's ethics 'before' ontology as a mode of *tekhne*? In other words, the question, or really, modality, of 'the art of living' is an ethical one – that of *relation*[22] to life. It is a matter of living, of action, of what Stiegler's later work will call political critique and action.

The final aspect of Stiegler's work and of the technological turn in philosophy involves his increasingly forceful critique of consumerism, globalization and capitalism, as developed in *The Crisis of the Industrial Democracies*, as technics continues its acceleration transforming the citizen into a 'proletarian consumer'. Before going on to develop a few keys points from this later work, it is crucial to point out how a reading of Levinas's thought might engage at the level of technics, at the social or global level, just as Freud later became interested in metapsychology with *The Future of Illusion* and *Civilization and its Discontents*. To phrase it differently, Levinas's ethics as it relates to technics might serve as the basis for an intervention into a Simulacrum that still has it *origins in ontology*, not ethics, whether it has lost the map (Baudrillard), or whether the Spectacle (technological reproduction) is conceived as a social relation rather than a mere image (Debord).

For Stiegler the relation of globalization, and the so-called digitalization of the world, constitutes a direct and emergent threat to the possibility of democracy and a non-programic future. In other words, it threatens a future that is reduced to calculation, rather than the open future that Derrida refers to as the to-come (*l'avenir*). Stiegler states, 'the collapse of the belief in politics has a history intrinsically tied to capitalism, to the industrial revolution, and to the fall of ontotheological-political metaphysics' (2011: 61). The consequences of this involve major three factors '1) the separation of capital and labour; 2) mechanization insofar as it permits this separation to spread (this is the proletarianization of the producers; and 3) the reconciliation of science and technics, which becomes technoscience and permanent innovation' (2011: 61). We can see here Stiegler's major concern with the reduction of *tekhne* to science and the relation of capital to the division of labour. What this strongly emphasizes is that *tekhne's* reduction opens doors to capital flows and quells the power of labour, and that this reductive and historical fact has major consequences for science and *tekhne* itself.

A final aspect of *The Decadence of Industrial Democracies* that I wish to address concerns Stiegler's reading the modern deployment of *tekhne* in terms of its disastrous effects and its contributions to globalization (led by the US), and the resulting proletarianization of the world. It is worth quoting Stiegler at length here:

The means of an ever-increasing circulation and deterritorialization, con-cretized through the intermediary of digitalization and the convergence of information and communication technologies, constituting a *planetary grammatization of behavior, of production and consumption*, that is, a planetary dis-existentialization of the gestures of work, or in other words, a planetary loss of *savoir-faire*, and constituting as well a par-ticularization of existence inducing a *planetary loss of savoir-vivre*, that is, a planetary loss of individualization, a generalization of the process of proletarianization to all modes of existence and substance. (2011: 63)

A crux of Stiegler's statement is how *tekhne* as digitalization combined with information and communication technologies is producing a new mode of de-existence, how such modalities are depriving human existence of libidinal forces, with the loss of *savoir-faire* and *savoir-vivre*, creating a new proletari-anization of all modes of existence and substance.

How does this relate to Levinas? If we go back to his critique of 'fundamental ontology' and his positing of the ethical relation as prior to Being, then rather than thinking the epistemological fact as the condition of Levinas's ethics, might it be possible to move Levinas's work into the region of global interdiction? That is to say, as capital, technics and digitalization 'de-exist' people and sub-stance, our task would be to disrupt the very concept of relationality as Being, moving the forces of capital with an ethics-of-interdiction. In other words, to culturally jam the registers that are destroying us. Remember that for Levinas there is nothing worse than to 'angle' another person, or the Other – the mark of Capital. In this manner, Levinas's thought must be a call to action (albeit through *reading* or other means, whether political intervention or art practice.)

QUESTIONS FOR FURTHER CONSIDERATION

1. Discuss how the problems of gender or race might be introduced into Levinas's ethics.
2. While Levinas's project clearly challenges traditional ethics, would you consider Levinas political? Explain.
3. Levinas's work is considered to be anti-humanist. He challenges the Enlightenment concept that 'man' is the centre of the universe. Can you think of any way in which Levinas might fall back into humanism?
4. Discuss the relationship between the Saying (performative) and the Said (constative). Is it possible to have one without the other? How would you write about Saying without describing it, without falling back into the Said?
5. The filmmaker Jean-Luc Godard once remarked: 'Tracking shots are a question of ethics.' Discuss how *The Sacrifice* might be read in light of Levinas and Godard from a filmic standpoint, in other words in terms of cuts, composition, panning, long takes, what might be occurring off camera, etc.

6. Choose another scene from *The Sacrifice*, such as when Otto (the postman) gives Alexander a map as a gift. How do you think Levinas would understand such a scene?

BIBLIOGRAPHY

Assoun, Paul-Laurent (1998) 'The Subject and the Other in Levinas and Lacan', trans. Dianah Jackson and Denise Merkle, in Sarah Harasym, ed., *Levinas and Lacan: The Missed Encounter*, Albany: State University of New York Press.

Austin, J. L. (1975) *How To Do Things With Words*, ed. J. O. Urmson and Marina Sbisa, Cambridge MA: Harvard University Press.

Bernasconi, Robert (1987) 'Deconstruction and the Possibility of Ethics', in John Sallis, ed., *Deconstruction and Philosophy: The Texts of Jacques Derrida*, Chicago: University of Chicago Press.

Bernasconi, Robert and Simon Critchley, eds. (1991) *Re-Reading Levinas*, Bloomington: Indiana University Press.

Blanchot Maurice (1982) *The Space of Literature*, trans. Ann Smock, Lincoln: University of Nebraska Press.

Blanchot, Maurice (1986) *The Writing of the Disaster*, trans. Ann Smock, Lincoln: University of Nebraska Press.

Butler, Judith (1993) *Bodies That Matter: On the Discursive Limits of Sex*, New York: Routledge.

Champagne, Roland (1998) *The Ethics of Reading According to Emmanuel Levinas*, Amsterdam: Rodopi.

Cixous, Hélène (1991) *Readings: The Poetics of Blanchot, Joyce, Kafka, Lispector, and Tsvetayeva*, Minneapolis: University of Minnesota Press.

Cornell, Drucilla (1999) *Beyond Accommodation: Ethical Feminism, Deconstruction, and the Law*, Lanham: Rowman & Littlefield.

Critchley, Simon (1999) *The Ethics of Deconstruction: Derrida and Levinas*, West Lafayette: Purdue University Press.

Derrida, Jacques (1978) 'Violence and Metaphysics', trans. Alan Bass, in *Writing and Difference*, Chicago: University of Chicago Press.

Derrida, Jacques (1983) 'Geschlecht: Sexual Difference, Ontological Difference', *Research in Phenomenology* 13, pp. 65–83.

Derrida, Jacques (1987) *The Postcard: From Socrates to Freud and Beyond*, trans. Alan Bass, Chicago: University of Chicago Press.

Derrida, Jacques (1988) *Limited Inc*, Evanston: Northwestern University Press, 1988.

Derrida, Jacques (1989) *Of Spirit: Heidegger and the Question*, trans. Geoffrey Bennington and Rachel Bowley, Chicago: University of Chicago Press.

Derrida, Jacques (1994) *Given Time: I. Counterfeit Money*, trans. Peggy Kamuf, Chicago: University of Chicago Press.

Derrida, Jacques (1995) *The Gift of Death*, trans. David Wills, Chicago: University of Chicago Press.

Derrida, Jacques (1999) *Adieu to Emmanuel Levinas*, trans. Pascale-Anne Brault and Michael Naas, Stanford: Stanford University Press.

Descartes, René (1996) *Discourse on the Method; and, Meditations on First Philosophy*, ed. David Weissman, New Haven: Yale University Press.

Dreyfus, Herbert (1991) *Being-In-The-World: A Commentary on Heidegger's Being and Time, Division I*, Cambridge MA: MIT Press.

Eaglestone, Robert (1998) *Ethical Criticism: Reading after Levinas*, Edinburgh: Edinburgh University Press.

Gibson, Andrew (1999) *Postmodernity, Ethics, and the Novel: From Leavis to Levinas*, London: Routledge.

Hegel, Georg Wilhelm Friedrich (1977) *Phenomenology of Spirit*, trans. A. V. Miller, Oxford: Oxford University Press.

Heidegger, Martin (1958) *What Is Philosophy?*, trans. William Kluback and Jean T. Wilde, New York: Twayne Publishers.

Heidegger, Martin (1977) 'On The Essence of Truth', trans. David Farrell Krell, in *Basic Writings*, San Francisco: Harper & Row.

Heidegger, Martin (1996) *Being and Time*, trans. Joan Stambaugh, Albany: State University of New York Press.

Heidegger, Martin (2001) 'The Origin of the Work of Art', in *Poetry, Language, Thought*, trans. Albert Hofstadter, New York: Perennial Classics.

Irigaray, Luce (1993) *An Ethics of Sexual Difference*, trans. Carolyn Burke and Gillian C. Gill, Ithaca: Cornell University Press.

Lacoue-Labarthe, Philippe (1989) *Typography: Mimesis, Philosophy, Politics*, ed. Christopher Fynsk, Cambridge MA: Harvard University Press.

Levinas, Emmanuel (1969) *Totality and Infinity: An Essay on Exteriority*, trans. Alphonso Lingis, Pittsburgh: Duquesne University Press.

Levinas, Emmanuel (1973) *Otherwise Than Being: or, Beyond Essence*, trans. Alphonso Lingis, Boston: Martinus Nijhoff.

Levinas, Emmanuel (1985) *Time and the Other*, trans. Richard Cohen, Pittsburgh: Duquesne University Press.

Levinas, Emmanuel (1986) 'The Trace of the Other', trans. Alphonso Lingis, in Mark C. Taylor, ed., *Deconstruction in Context: Literature and Philosophy*, Chicago: University of Chicago Press.

Levinas, Emmanuel (1987) 'Philosophy and the Idea of Infinity', in *Collected Philosophical Papers*, trans. Alphonso Lingis, Dordrecht: Martinus Nijhoff.

Levinas, Emmanuel (1996) *Basic Philosophical Writings*, ed. Adriaan T. Peperzak, Simon Critchley and Robert Bernasconi, Bloomington: Indiana University Press.

Lyotard, Jean-François (1984) *The Postmodern Condition: A Report on Knowledge*, trans. Geoffrey Bennington and Brian Massumi, Minneapolis: University of Minnesota Press.

Miller, J. Hillis (1987) *The Ethics of Reading: Kant, de Man, Eliot, Trollope, James, and Benjamin*, New York: Columbia University Press.

Norris, Christopher (1994) *Truth and the Ethics of Criticism*, New York: St Martin's Press.

Peperzak, Adriaan (1993) *To The Other: An Introduction to the Philosophy of Emmanuel Levinas*, West Lafayette: Purdue University Press.

Robbins, Jill (1999) *Altered Reading: Levinas and Literature*, Chicago: University of Chicago Press.

Stiegler, Bernard (1998) *Technics and Time, 1: The Fault of Epimetheus*, trans. Richard Beardsworth and George Collins, Stanford: Stanford University Press.

Stiegler, Bernard (2011) *The Decadence of Industrial Democracies*, trans. Daniel Ross and Suzanne Arnold, Cambridge: Polity Press.

Tarkovsky, Andrey (1986) *Sculpting in Time: Reflections on the Cinema*, Austin: University of Texas Press.

Wall, Carl Thomas (1999) *Radical Passivity: Levinas, Blanchot and Agamben*, Albany: State University of New York Press.

NOTES

1. Ontology is the study of being; it is considered to be the foundation of philosophy. Martin Heidegger, as we will see later in this chapter, complicates how ontology has been understood by philosophy since Plato.
2. The Other is an important notion in philosophy. The German philosopher Georg Wilhem Friedrich Hegel understood the Other as something to be overcome. For

Hegel, the Other must be posited in order to be overcome. For those interested in the complexities of Hegel's dialectic, see the *Phenomenology of Spirit* (Hegel 1977). For many twentieth-century French philosophers such as Levinas, Maurice Blanchot and Jacques Derrida, the Other is not something to be overcome, or understood, but rather something more radical. The Other for many poststructuralists is something estranged or outside of understanding, beyond meaning.

3. For example, Levinas's relation to gender, religion and animality are not explored here but are quite important. See Critchley (1999) for a reading of Derrida on Levinas about the importance of gender. Levinas's ethics, like Heidegger's Dasein, does not fully work through the implications of gender. Regarding animality, Critchley discusses Derrida and Llewelyn's criticism: 'One might conclude … as Derrida has recently done, that Levinasian ethics has no way of experiencing responsibility towards plants, animals, and living things in general and that despite the novelty and originality of Levinas's analysis of ethical subjectivity, he ends up buttressing and perpetuating a very traditional humanism, that of Judaeo-Christian morality. This issue is very sensitively discussed by John Llewelyn when he explores the question "Who is the Other (Autrui)?" by asking whether animals – dogs in particular – can obligate humans to the same degree as other human beings' (1999: 180).

4. Like Heidegger, Levinas is critical of philosophy. In the section on ontology, I will discuss some of the crucial differences between Heidegger and Levinas. Levinas, also like many poststructuralists such as Derrida, Lyotard, Nancy and Lacoue-Labarthe, is critical of the totalizing project of philosophy, especially as exemplified by Hegel. This thematic grouping of Levinas with Blanchot, Heidegger and many poststructuralists is provisional and only meant to show the common thread they share against the totalizing discourse of philosophy which culminates in Hegel's dialectic. The various critical differences and productive agons between these thinkers is, of course, crucial.

5. In the *Meditations*, René Descartes' famous phrase 'Cogito ergo sum' (I think, therefore I am) begins modern philosophy. Descartes, out to prove God's existence in the *Meditations*, begins by doubting everything except that he exists while he is thinking. The 'I', or subject, becomes foundational for Descartes, and the material world, which includes the body, becomes a *res extentia*, split from the 'I', the thinking subject. This begins the modern problem of the subject/object split. The problem of the subject has haunted all philosophers since Descartes.

6. *Being In The World* by Herbert Dreyfus (1991) is an excellent guide for those interested in reading Heidegger's *Being and Time* (1996). Dreyfus's book does a great job explicating the complexities of what Heidegger means by Dasein, equipmentality, and being-in-the-world.

7. See *Being and Time*, Division I, for the articulation of Dasein, and Division II for Dasein's relation to temporality.

8. For a detailed analysis of the performative and constative, see Austin's *How To Do Things With Words* (1975). Also crucial is Jacques Derrida's *Limited Inc.* (1988), which offers a 'deconstructive' reading of Austin and his student John Searle. See also, Judith Butler's *Bodies That Matter* (1993), esp. the chapter 'Paris is Burning', to see how the problematic of gender enters into the performative discourse.

9. For a complication of truth as representational see Section 44 of *Being and Time*, as well as Heidegger's *On The Essence of Truth* (1977).

10. Jill Robbins makes the point that 'The other is not a relation but a surplus radical asymmetry' (Robbins 1999: 4). Thus Levinas's 'relation', unmediated or predicated by ontology, is a non-relation, asymmetrical.

11. For Critchley, the Saying and the Said are of two different temporal orders, and although there is no way to escape the Greek *logos* that our language is inherently ontological, nonetheless the modes of synchrony and diachrony of the Saying and

Said differ. 'The Saying is a performative disruption of the Said that is instantly refuted by the language in which it appears' (1999: 164).

12. A crucial text which haunts and informs my own interest in mimesis is Lacoue-Labarthe's, *Typography: Mimesis, Philosophy, Politics* (1989).

13. The relationship between Derrida, Levinas and Blanchot is quite complex, and they do not have a unified notion of the 'literary'.

14. While these notes deal with specific thematic concerns in the film, a productive and developed reading of the filmic qualities of Tarkovsky is crucial. Such a reading might begin with Godard's well-known comment, 'Tracking shots are a question of ethics.'

15. Another productive reading could explore both the gift and the postman. See Derrida's *The Postcard* (1987) and *Given Time* (1994).

16. For more on the disaster, see Blanchot's *The Writing of the Disaster* (1986).

17. For a rigorous complication of Heidegger's question, see Derrida's *Of Spirit: Heidegger and the Question* (1989).

18. Stiegler has been a prolific writer and many of his works are now available in English translation.

19. It is crucial not to reduce Marx and Heidegger to the concept of tool-use, and especially to look at Division 1 of *Being and Time* for a better understanding of equipment, tool, hand and world in Heidegger.

20. Much of Heidegger's later work concerns questions of technics.

21. It is important to note that Michel Foucault in *Ethics* spends a great deal of time with this phrase. There is not enough space here to work through the nuances between Stiegler and Foucault on this issue.

22. See the earlier section on Levinas's notion of relation, especially to Being.

ECOCRITICISM

Kate Rigby

REMEMBERING THE EARTH

In 1756, the vicar of Selbourne planted four lime trees between his house and the butcher's yard opposite, '"to hide the sight of blood and filth"' (White quoted in Thomas 1983: 299). Gilbert White was a great naturalist who went on to write *The Natural History of Selbourne* (1789), a text much prized by ecocritics as environmental literature. White's arboreal screening out of the slaughterhouse is, in a sense, equally significant, for it exemplifies one of the key developments Keith Thomas charts in his history of changing attitudes towards the natural world in England between 1500 and 1800: namely, a growing uneasiness about killing animals for food. Towards the end of the eighteenth century this change in sensibilities led some, including the English poet Shelley, to become vegetarian.[1] The vast majority of people, including the vicar of Selbourne, nonetheless continued to eat animals. What changed instead was that slaughterhouses were banished from the public gaze, while meat increasingly was sold and prepared as faceless flesh – that is, minus the head. What concerns me here for the moment is less the ethics of meat consumption than the concealment of its price. For this kind of concealment would become characteristic of modern socio-ecological relationships on a range of geographical and temporal scales, whereby the benefits arising from ever more intensive and extensive exploitation of animals and the environment have accrued to a privileged minority, while the harms are passed on to others, human and otherwise, including future generations.

Since the eighteenth century, the necessity of recalling the true cost, both to subordinate humans and to the earth, of our production processes and consumption habits has grown in equal measure to its difficulty. For at the same time that the ecosystems sustaining all life on earth have become ever more critically endangered by our growing numbers and levels of consumption, ever more people (above all, those whose ecological debt is the largest) live at an ever greater remove from the natural world, unmindful of their impact upon their 'earth others'. As systems of production, consumption and exchange have become increasingly globalized, so too have the patterns of socio-ecological concealment. This has led to a proliferation of what feminist ecophilosopher Val Plumwood (2008) terms 'shadow places': places, that is, where people and environments, generally in developing countries, are exploited, and not infrequently poisoned, in the manufacture of cheap goods and the extraction of mineral resources, largely for the benefit of other, more affluent, nations and communities, which prefer to turn a blind eye to the true price of their petrol, cappuccinos and iPads. Today, the vicar of Selbourne's little screen of lime trees has been massively magnified by new forms of distancing – geographic, socio-economic, political, discursive, but above all, perhaps, that of a strategically cultivated ignorance – which separate, say, British motorists at the petrol pump from the despoliation of the land and lives of the Ogoni people of Nigeria as a consequence of what ecocritic Rob Nixon terms 'the ongoing romance between unanswerable corporations and unspeakable regimes' (2011: 105).

Within the academic institutions of the global North, the recollection of human dependence upon an increasingly endangered more-than-human 'mesh' (Morton 2010) has not come easily to those disciplines devoted to the study of cultural artifacts. Literary critics and cultural theorists in particular were notoriously slow to register those changes in thinking about the relationship of culture and society to non-human others and the environment which began to be articulated in neighbouring disciplines, above all philosophy, but also theology, politics and history, from the early 1970s. 'If your knowledge of the outside world were limited to what you could infer from the major publications of the literary profession,' observed Cheryll Glotfelty in 1996 in her introduction to the first ecocriticism reader,

> you would quickly discern that race, class and gender were the hot topics of the late twentieth century, but you would never know that the earth's life support systems were under stress. Indeed, you might never know that there was an earth at all. (Glotfelty and Fromm 1996: xvi)

There were in fact some isolated calls for an ecologically oriented criticism from the early 1970s.[2] However, it was not until the end of the twentieth century that the study of literature and the environment was finally recognized as 'a subject on the rise'.[3] By the beginning of the second decade of the twenty-first century, ecocriticism was acquiring considerable historical depth, international reach, and theoretical sophistication. Having begun to find a firm foothold in many universities throughout the world, environmental literary criticism now joins other ecologically oriented areas of study in what has become known globally as the transdisciplinary field of the Environmental Humanities.

In some respects it is perhaps not surprising that the study of literary texts should be coupled with such forgetfulness of other-than-human entities and processes. Although the practice of criticism has ancient origins in the exegesis of biblical and classical Greek texts, modern literary criticism only began to be institutionalized as an academic discipline in the early nineteenth century. This was precisely the time when a rigid separation began to be drawn between the 'natural' and the 'human' sciences. This is a divide that few literary critics and cultural theorists have dared to cross until relatively recently. The compartmentalization of knowledge effected by this divide is central to what Michel Serres terms the 'Modern Constitution', which sunders the human from the non-human realm, while defining society's relationship to the natural world in terms of mastery and possession (1995: 31–2). It is the Modern Constitution which facilitates also that characteristically modern (and especially urban) form of self-deception, whereby the consumption of meat can be disconnected from the suffering and death of animals. Thus, to regain a sense of the inextricability of nature and culture, *physis* and *techne*, Earth and artifact – consumption and destruction – would be to move beyond both the impasse of modernism and the arrogance of humanism.

What, then, might such a posthumanist, postmodernist remembering of the earth entail for the literary critic or cultural theorist? In her poem 'Parchment', Michelle Boisseau gives us some valuable leads:

> I'm holding in my hand the skin of a calf
> that lived 600 years ago, translucent
> skin that someone stretched on four strong poles,
> skin someone scraped with a moon-shaped blade.
> Here is the flesh side, it understood true dark.
> Here is the hair side that met the day's weather,
> the long ago rain. It is all inscribed
> with the dark brown ink of prayer,
>
> the acid galls of ancient oaks, though these reds,
> deluxe rivulets that brighten the margins,
> are cinnabar ground to a paste, another paste
> of lapis for these blue medieval skies,
> and for flowering meadows or a lady's long braids-
> the orpiment – a yellow arsenic –
>
> whose grinding felled the illuminator's
> boy assistants like flies, or the insect kermes
> whose pregnant bodies gave pigment, and the goose who supplied
>   quills, the horse its hair, and flax

the fine strong thread that held the folded skins
into a private book stamped with gold for a king. (2000: 177)

The parchment that Boisseau describes here is a product of *techne*, an artifact of considerable beauty, embodying something of the religious traditions and aesthetic sensibilities of a rich cultural tradition: it is, we learn, a late medieval illuminated prayerbook. In her poetic presentation of this prayerbook, Boisseau calls attention not to its meaning as a text, nor to its economic or antiquarian value, but to its materiality. Or rather, she asks us to reconsider its potential meaning and value in relation to its materiality, perceived in terms of the socio-ecological price of its production and consumption. Thus, she recalls the slaughtered calf, whose skin supplied the parchment, the oak trees, the insect-engendered galls from which supplied dark ink for the written text, and all the other animals, vegetables and minerals, which made possible the material production of this artifact. Recalling too the illuminator's boy assistants, who died 'like flies' from arsenic poisoning as a result of their labour, Boisseau reminds us that the price of production is borne by subordinate humans, as well as by non-human others. This link between social domination and the exploitation of nature is hinted at again in the close of the poem, where we learn the purpose for which this book had been produced at such cost: namely, for the private use of a king.

In one of his 'Theses on the Philosophy of History' Walter Benjamin observes that, to the historical materialist, there is 'no document of civilization which is not at the same time a document of barbarism' (1973: 258). Most ecocritics would agree with this, but they would add that there is also no work of culture which is not simultaneously exploitative of nature. This is of course also true of Boisseau's 'Parchment' (and, indeed, this essay), the writing, publication and distribution of which has taken its own toll on non-human others and the environment. And yet, the relationship between 'nature' and 'culture' is not one way. Of this too we are reminded by Boisseau's poem. For the written prayers and visual images contained in the book upon which the poet meditates convey ideas about nature, and about the relationship between nature, humanity and the divine, which crucially conditioned medieval perceptions of and interactions with non-human others and the environment, and which continue to resonate in complex and contradictory ways up to the present. The meanings discerned in such texts are not fixed, though, and those boy assistants are likely to have had a rather different take on the prayers they were helping to illuminate from that of the monarch for whom the book was intended. Their interpretive perspectives have nonetheless been rendered as invisible as their poisoned bodies within a dominant culture in which some voices count a lot more than others.

Culture, then, constructs the prism through which we know 'nature'. We begin to internalise this prism from the moment we learn to speak; the moment, that is, that we are inducted into the symbolic realm of the *logos*, the world shaped by language. 'Nature', which, as Raymond Williams has remarked, is 'perhaps the most complex word in the language' (1983: 219), is in this sense a cultural and, above all, a linguistic construct. The diverse physical realities of air, water, fire, rock, plants, animals, soils, weather, ecosystems, solar systems etcetera, to which I refer when I speak of 'the natural world' or 'earth', nonetheless precede and exceed whatever words might say about them. It is this insistence on the ultimate precedence and independent agency of the materiality of the more-than-human world vis-à-vis the ideations of human cultures, which signals the initial ecocritical move beyond the 'linguistic turn' ushered in by structuralism and poststructuralism and underpins ecocritical engagement with a variety of 'new materialisms' and 'critical' or 'speculative' realisms.[4]

It might be countered that at a time when there is no place on Earth that has not been affected in some way by humanity's alteration of the natural environment, as Bill McKibben (1989) has observed with respect to the global impact of anthropogenic climate change, the precedence of nature – those things, processes and interrelationships, that is, which have not been manufactured by humans – has now become questionable, at least on this planet. And perhaps, as Timothy Morton (2007) insists, the very concept of 'nature' is impeding our ability to think ecologically, summoning the phantasm of a stable and harmonious 'whole', which blocks our view of the multiplicity of diverse entities, whether naturally arising or man-made, with which we might be called to interact in a more ethically considered manner. It is however precisely the anthropogenic imperilment of so many of our Earth others, human and otherwise, which impels the ecocritical reinstatement of the environmental or non-human referent as a matter of legitimate concern. For the ecocritic, it is vital to be able to say, with critical realist Kate Soper, that 'it is not language that has a hole in its ozone layer; and the "real" thing continues to be polluted and degraded even as we refine our deconstructive insights at the level of the signifier' (1995: 151). Moreover, the fact that ever more of Earth's surface is currently being refashioned by *techne* does not mean that *physis* has ceased to exist. All human making, including the largely unintentional remaking (or rather, undoing) of Earth's ecosystems remains dependent upon physical processes which precede and exceed human knowledge and power. All human existence, meanwhile, remains interwoven, albeit often invisibly, with the life of countless non-human beings, including those dwelling within or upon our own bodies, who continue as best they can to pursue their own ends in the midst of an increasingly hostile environment.

Ecocriticism, then, remembers the earth by attending to the interconnectivities that link all aspects of human culture, including the production and consumption of literary and other kinds of texts, to other-than-human entities and processes. While acknowledging the role of language in shaping our view of the world, ecocritics seek to restore significance to those manifold more-than-human phenomena that exist beyond the page. In this way, ecocriticism has a vital contribution to make to the wider project of Green Studies, which, in Laurence Coupe's words, 'debates "Nature" in order to defend nature' (2000: 5). For many ecocritics, moreover, the defence of nature is vitally interconnected with the pursuit of social justice. As Scott Slovic (citing Walt Whitman) observed at the close of the last millennium, ecocriticism is 'large and contains multitudes' (1999: 1102). Ecocritics are increasingly many and varied, drawing on a range of analytical strategies and theoretical approaches, and addressing a diversity of cultural phenomena, from Shakespearean drama to wildlife documentaries, romantic pastoral to sci-fi ecothrillers, the Bible to Basho. This is a fast growing field, which cannot be explored fully within the limits of this chapter.[5] In what follows, I will nonetheless seek to trace some of the primary ways in which ecocriticism is forging new paths in the practice of literary studies.

CRITIQUING THE CANON

In 1967, the American historian Lyn White Jr. published a slim article entitled 'The Historical Roots of Our Ecologic Crisis' (White 1996). The fact that this key early work of ecological cultural criticism first appeared in the journal *Science* reflects the extent to which environmental problems were at that stage still seen as a largely scientific and technical issue. Yet the burden of White's article was precisely that science provided an inadequate basis for under-standing, let alone resolving, a crisis which was cultural and social in origin. Preempting Arne Naess' influential critique of 'shallow ecology' (1973), White argued that, 'what people do about their ecology depends on what they think about themselves in relation to things around them. Human ecology is deeply conditioned by beliefs about our nature and destiny – that is, by religion' (1996: 6). For this reason, White maintained that it was necessary to look to the dominant religious traditions of the West in seeking to identify the primary source of those attitudes towards the natural world, which in his view had led to the current crisis. The main target of White's critique is the Hebrew creation story in Genesis 1, which 'not only established a dualism of man and nature but also insisted that it is God's will that man exploit nature for his proper ends' (1996: 10). As White is well aware, however, the Bible, like all texts, is a complex and multivalent document, conveying highly mixed messages about the relationship between God, humanity and the rest of creation. In his analy-sis, the problem lay not so much with the biblical text itself, but rather with the way in which it began to be interpreted in Western Christianity from about the twelfth century: namely, as legitimating not only the scientific exploration, but above all the unlimited technological manipulation and ruthless economic exploitation of nature, which has today reached a level that would have been unimaginable, and quite possibly appalling, to the authors of Genesis.

White's article inaugurated the ecologically oriented critique of the way in which Nature is constructed in certain canonical texts of the Western tradi-tion. The first extended deployment of an ecocritical hermeneutics of suspicion to secular literature was Joseph Meeker's *The Comedy of Survival* (1972). Meeker's disapprobation falls in particular upon classical tragedy, which, he contends, reinforces the anthropocentric 'assumption that nature exists for the benefit of mankind, the belief that human morality transcends natural limitations, and humanism's insistence on the supreme importance of the individual' (1972: 42–3). Meeker is also highly critical of the pastoral tradition, which he sees as a form of escapist fantasy, valorizing a tamed and idealized nature over wild no less than urban environments. This kind of critique continues to have an important place in the ecological recasting of the canon. However, the charge that Christianity, or any other key element in Western culture (tragedy, pastoral, rationalist metaphysics, etc.) 'bears a huge burden of guilt' (White 1996: 12) for today's ecological crisis needs to be qualified in at least three ways.

Firstly, and most obviously, it is important to note that the West does not have a monopoly on ecological errancy. Many other cultures and societies have also failed to live sustainably in the past.[6] Secondly, Western religious and literary traditions are not monolithic ideological constructs, but complex and ambivalent cultural legacies. Christian arguments can be and have been called upon to justify very different, even contradictory, ways of relating to the natural world. Thus, for example, while Francis Bacon (1561–1626), the so-called 'father' of modern science, could appeal to the Bible in presenting the conquest of nature by Man as divinely ordained,[7] many of the opponents of precisely this kind of human chauvinism from the late sixteenth century onwards have also couched their arguments in Christian terms (Edwards 1984: 166–72). During the medieval period, too, divergent interpretations of Christian texts and traditions are evident even within the West, as White's own endorsement of St Francis as a 'patron saint for ecologists' (1996: 14) attests. Moreover, the fact that the period of the greatest despoliation of Earth has coincided precisely with the waning of the earlier theocentric view of nature as God's creation suggests, at the very least, that the culpability of Christianity is indirect.

There is finally also the tricky question of causality. While it might be true that 'what people do about their ecology depends upon what they think about things around them', as White puts it, we still have to ask what conditions the discursive practices and cultural traditions within which those thoughts are embedded. To leave the analysis on the level of cultural critique would be to fall prey to the fallacy of idealism, especially if there is any truth in the Marxist view that the material forces and relations of production are the real drivers of cultural and social change. Although we might not want to subscribe to the alternate fallacy of economic determinism either, it is important to acknowledge the influence of social, political and economic systems in the perpetuation, transformation and displacement of those views of nature which are conveyed by the texts of culture. The Baconian reinterpretation of Providence, in conjunction with the mechanistic and atomistic construction of nature that came to prominence in the seventeenth century, for instance, proved highly congenial to the laissez-faire mercantile capitalism, and associated colonialist ventures, that took off in northwestern Europe at the time. These socio-economic developments might not have *generated* the new conception of Nature as totally knowable, manipulable and predestined to be conquered and transformed by Man; but they almost certainly *guaranteed the success* of this view as a dominant paradigm in the modern era (Merchant 1980).

REFRAMING THE TEXT

Consideration of social context alone, however, cannot produce a fully ecological reading of cultural texts and traditions. Here too, White's brief article is instructive. A critique of capitalism is notably absent from his account. However, White's argument is in another respect profoundly materialist. For the aggressively human chauvinist interpretation of Genesis that emerged in the West was in his view connected, albeit indirectly, with something no less material than the nature of northern European soils. Unlike the lighter soils of the Mediterranean region, these are typically heavy and sticky, necessitating the use of a correspondingly heavy iron plough in farming the land effectively. Such a plough, 'equipped with a vertical knife to cut the line of the furrow, a horizontal share to slice under the sod, and a moldboard to turn it over' (White 1996: 8), appeared in northern Europe towards the end of the seventh century. Whereas the older wooden plough merely scratched the surface of soil, the new plough, which required eight oxen to pull it, 'attacked the land with such violence that cross plowing was not needed, and fields tended to be shaped in long strips' (White 1996: 8). Intriguingly, within about fifty years of the development of this plough, which, as White stresses, was unique to northern Europe, a change can be noted in the illustrated calendars of that region. In place of the old passive personifications of the seasons, the 'new Frankish calendars . . . show men coercing the world around them – plowing, harvesting, chopping trees, butchering pigs'. The burden of these images, in White's view, is that, 'Man and nature are two things, and man is master' (1996: 8).

Whether or not the connections that White makes between soils, ploughs, calendars, biblical interpretation and, ultimately, industrial modernity, can be substantiated, his introduction of earth as a *player* in his historical narrative is methodologically and philosophically significant. For White, as for subsequent ecocritics and environmental historians, other-than-human entities are no longer the passive recipients of human interventions and projections, but active participants in the formation and transformation of human culture and society. As Aldo Leopold observed in 1949, many historical events, 'hitherto explained solely in terms of human enterprise, were actually biotic interactions between people and land', the outcome of which was determined as much by the character of the land as by the culture of its human occupants (1998: 89). Transposed to literary studies, it is clear that this principle necessitates a radical shift in the way in which texts are interpreted and contextualized. This is the second way in which ecocriticism recasts the canon, and it demands of the critic an acquaintance with new areas of knowledge and understanding. Whereas, in the past, literary critics might have leant on history, philosophy or the social sciences in framing their readings of particular texts, ecocritics draw also on geography, ecology and other natural sciences, and science studies.

A striking example of this procedure is provided by Jonathan Bate (1996), when he rereads Byron's apocalyptic poem 'Darkness' (1816), together with Keats's idyllic ode 'To Autumn' (1819), against meteorological records for the places and time periods in which these texts were written. Pitting himself against the literary critical convention of reading apocalyptic writing such as Byron's either intertextually, with reference to earlier apocalyptic, or as a product of imagination, bearing a largely metaphoric relation to the world beyond the page, Bate explores what happens if Byron's image of a sunless Earth is taken literally. This leads him to the discovery that the highly inclement weather conditions described by Byron in his letters of the time, and confirmed by the meteorological records, can be traced to the eruption in 1815 of the Tambora volcano in Indonesia. This huge eruption caused an estimated 80,000 deaths locally, and lowered global temperatures for three years, leading to failed harvests, food riots and increased respiratory problems as far away as Europe. Bate's ecocritical strategy of foregrounding the role of the natural environment in the genesis of this text is entirely in keeping with the perspective of the poem itself, which dramatizes the impact on human cultural practices and moral values of a dramatic change in the natural environment: in this case, the loss of the life-giving rays of the sun, which, having eliminated all other sources of food, eventually drives a dwindling number of doomed survivors to cannibalism. Read in this meteorological context, 'To Autumn' also appears in a different light. Keats' pastoral idyll was written in the autumn following the first good summer since 1815, at a time when clear air and warm weather were especially important to its consumptive author. Far from being an escapist fantasy, this is in Bate's view a valuable 'meditation on how human culture can only function through links and reciprocal relations with nature' (1996: 440).

As another early ecocritic, Karl Kroeber (1994), observed, the literary critical preoccupations and disputations of the 1960s, 1970s and 1980s appear in retrospect to owe much to the ideological context of the Cold War. Focusing on questions of human creativity, human agency and human social relations, 'Cold War criticism' can also be seen to perpetuate that binary opposition of the human to the non-human, culture to nature, which has a long history in Western rationalism. By contrast, 'Global Warming Criticism', as Bate termed his new approach, attends to the inextricability of culture and nature, the primary sign of which he took to be the weather (Bate 1996: 439). Informed not only by meteorology and ecology, but also by the new science of non-linear dynamic systems popularized as 'Chaos Theory', Global Warming Criticism presupposes a natural world which can no longer be thought of as passive, orderly and compliant, but which is rather volatile, unpredictable, and responsive to our interventions in ways that we can neither foresee nor control. Acknowledging the ecologically embedded, embodied and hence vulnerable nature of human existence, Global Warming Criticism privileges those texts which can, as Bate puts it, enable us to 'think fragility' (1996: 447). Allied to an ethos of respect towards non-human others, this new critical paradigm has begun to generate its own counter-canon of literary texts that are seen to model a more ecologically sustainable mode of being and dwelling than that which has predominated in the lived reality of the modern era.

REVALUING NATURE WRITING

One of the seed-beds for ecocriticism, at least in the United States, was the study of a hitherto highly marginalized genre of non-fiction known as 'nature writing'. Among those who founded the Association for the Study of Literature and the Environment (ASLE) at the 1992 annual meeting of the Western Literature Association, several key players were scholars of nature writing, including ASLE's first President, Scott Slovic, and Cheryll Glotfelty, co-editor of the first ecocriticism reader and co-founder of *The American Nature Writing Newsletter*, which later became the *ASLE Newsletter*.[8] Nature writing figured prominently in ASLE's original mission statement, 'to promote the exchange of ideas and information pertaining to literature that considers the relationship between human beings and the natural world', and to encourage 'new nature writing, traditional and innovative scholarly approaches to environmental literature, and interdisciplinary environmental research' (quoted in Glotfelty and Fromm 1996: xviii).

This revaluation of nature writing, or, somewhat more broadly, 'environmental literature', constitutes the third way in which ecocriticism recasts the canon. In his landmark study of Thoreau and the 'environmental imagination', Lawrence Buell argued that an environmentally oriented work should display the following characteristics:

1. *The nonhuman environment is present not merely as a framing device but as a presence that begins to suggest that human history is implicated in natural history . . .*
2. *The human interest is not understood to be the only legitimate interest . . .*
3. *Human accountability to the environment is part of the text's ethical framework . . .*
4. *Some sense of the environment as a process rather than as a constant or a given is at least implicit in the text . . .* (Buell 1995: 7–8)

As Buell has emphasized in subsequent publications, there are many other ways in which a literary text might be 'bent towards' extra-textual landscapes, and other dimensions in which its 'environmentality' might be discerned (Buell 2005: 33). His earlier inventory of environmental literary desiderata, then, is best seen, not as prescriptive, but as descriptive: namely, of the kind of nature writing to which Buell's study is devoted, as exemplified above all by Thoreau's *Walden* (1854). Thoreau is the only author of environmental non-fiction to have been admitted to the canon of American literature. Buell none-theless redefines Thoreau's canonicity by reconnecting the 'order of the text' with the 'order of the body' (1995: 373): that is, by restoring flesh-and-blood readers and writers as agents in the world, while nonetheless recognizing that 'perforce they must operate and cooperate within the realm of textuality as a limit condition of their exchange' (1995: 384). In order to do this, Buell argues that it is necessary to consider not only the literary and scholarly reception of an author, but also their place in popular imagination and the lived practices that they modelled and inspired. In the case of Thoreau, this includes not only the (increasingly touristic) pilgrimage to Walden, but also countless practi-cal endeavours to find ways of living in closer communion with non-human others and more-than-human environments. Buell's reading of Thoreau and his reception is not entirely uncritical. However, he concludes by affirming that 'Thoreau's importance as an environmental saint lies in being remembered, in the affectionate simplicity of public mythmaking, as helping to make the space of nature ethically resonant' (1995: 394).

Although Buell advocates a form of criticism that directs our gaze beyond the page, he is also alert to the ways in which all writing and reading is sus-tained by a dense mesh of intertexts. Thus, he includes a fascinating Appendix to his study, in which he reconsiders the intertextuality of *Walden* in relation to the many forms of environmental non-fiction that were popular during Thoreau's time: literary almanacs, homilies celebrating the divine in nature, literary regionalism, the picturesque, natural history writing, and travel writing. Although some canonical texts are included here, such as Emerson's *Nature* (1836), Buell's inventory highlights the importance of a great number of other texts, which have generally not been valued as literature, from Charles Darwin's *Journal of Researches [. . .] during the Voyage of HMS Beagle* (1839) to Susan Fenimore Cooper's *Rural Hours* (1850). Environmental non-fiction, in Buell's analysis, turns out to be even more 'heteroglossic', in Bakhtin's terms, than the novel.[9] Buell's reconsideration of *Walden*'s many-tongued intertexts has also fostered further ecocritical interest in later environmental non-fiction, such as that of Mary Austin, John Muir, Aldo Leopold, Edward Abbey, Annie Dillard, Terry Tempest Williams and Barry Lopez.

Nature writing has long since surrendered the centrality that it was accorded in ecocriticism's early years in the US.[10] It nonetheless remains one significant line of inquiry within environmental literary studies, as well as occupying a new niche within the increasingly popular field of 'non-fiction' or 'life' writing studies.[11] Inspired by the work of Buell, Slovic (1992), and others, on North American nature writing, ecocritics elsewhere have begun to explore distinct varieties of environmental life writing in other national and regional literatures.[12] The work of this genre's most famous American progenitor, meanwhile, is being read ecocritically in a variety of new ways, such as Lance Newman's (2005) examination of the 'class politics' of nature in American Transcendentalism and Laura Dassow Walls' (2011) reframing of Walden Pond as a zone of natural-cultural hybridity. These scholarly re-evaluations of Thoreau accord with the impetus to re-integrate the social and the natural, the personal and the political, science and sensibility, that can also be traced in much contemporary nature writing, such as Richard Mabey's cultural history of 'outlaw plants' (2010) or Richard Kerridge's 'adventures with reptiles and amphibians' (2013). Nature writing, then, retains its ecocritical significance: but evaluations of what it is and can do are changing.

RETURNING TO ROMANTICISM

In addition to its revaluation of the previously neglected genre of nature writing, ecocriticism has also prompted a reconsideration of many canonical texts and traditions. Among these, European Romanticism, which forms another crucial strand in the intertextual mesh of Thoreau's writing, loomed particularly large in the ecocriticism of the 1990s. While this too is no longer so central within environmental literary and cultural studies, the return to Romanticism played an important role in the development of ecocritical theory and practice. Among other things, early ecocritical discussion of English Romantic poetry entailed a productive revaluation of the pastoral mode. As we have seen, pastoral comes off badly in Meeker's *Comedy of Survival*, as it generally does also in most leftist criticism, especially of the New Historicist variety.[13] It was nonetheless a leading British Marxist critic, Raymond Williams, who initiated a proto-ecocritical recuperation of Romantic (neo- or counter-)pastoral. In his account of the changing fortunes and perceptions of the country and the city, first published in 1973, Williams demonstrates that pastoral is potentially far more than an expression of conservative nostalgia for a lost agrarian past. He begins by observing that pastoral, which first emerged in Hellenistic Greek literature, may well have originated not in the escapist fantasies of an urban elite, but rather in the singing competitions of peasant communities themselves (Williams 1985: 14). Latin, and to an even greater extent Renaissance and Augustan, pastoral writing did nonetheless tend towards forms of idealization that elided the realities of rural life from the perspective of the labouring poor. In the 'green language' of Romantic neopastoral, however, above all that of early Wordsworth and his younger contemporary John Clare, himself a rural labourer by birth, Williams finds an important locus of resistance to the increasing commodification and degradation of the land, which was then occurring in many parts of England, and which is now going global. 'The song of the land', Williams concludes, 'the song of rural labour, the song of delight in the many forms of life with which we all share our physical world, is too important and too moving to be tamely given up, in an embittered betrayal, to the confident enemies of all significant and actual independence and renewal' (1985: 271).

Williams's plea for a revaluation of Romantic pastoral was largely ignored by Marxist critics in the following decades. Williams's lead has nonetheless been followed by some ecocritics. In his 1991 monograph on Wordsworth, programmatically entitled *Romantic Ecology*, for example, Bate endorses the value of Romantic pastoral as a type of environmental literature. In so doing, he affirms what is probably the dominant non-academic reading of Wordsworth against the New Critical and deconstructionist claim that what Romanticism really valorizes is not nature, but the human imagination and human language. Arguing also against the New Historicist counter-claim that the ideological function of Romantic imagination and pastoral was to disguise the exploitative nature of contemporary social relations, Bate repositions Wordsworth in a tradition of environmental consciousness, according to which human well-being and social equity is understood to be coordinate with the ecological health of the land. Thus understood, Romantic nature poetry stands in an ambivalent position to earlier pastoral writing, functioning simultaneously as continuation and critique. As Terry Gifford (1999) has argued, Romantic poetry is perhaps more accurately termed 'post-pastoral', or even, in the case of Blake, 'anti-pastoral'.[14]

The importance of Romanticism is explored further by Bate in *The Song of the Earth* (2000). Other ecocritics too have recognized in the Romantic tradition a valuable point of departure for rethinking our relations with the earth. Karl Kroeber, for example, acclaimed Wordsworth's 'Home at Grasmere' as a model of 'ecological holiness' as early as 1974, and Romanticism also provides the focus for his major work on *Ecological Literary Criticism* (1994). Historians of ecological thought have drawn attention also to the significance of Romantic 'natural histories' and German 'natural philosophy' to the emergence of a post-mechanistic, proto-evolutionary view of nature as a dynamic, autopoietic, unity-in-diversity.[15] Yet, while several ecocritical publications have continued and deepened this broadly sympathetic exploration of 'Romantic ecology' (e.g. Lussier 1999; McKusick 2000; Oerlemans 2002; Hutchings 2002), Greg Garrard's more cautious view of the Romantic legacy as 'both vital and ambiguous' (1998: 129) has been borne out in some more recent studies (Rigby 2014a). Romantic thought undoubtedly challenged the Cartesian dualism of mind and matter by positing human consciousness and creativity as a manifestation of potentials inherent in *physis*. However, this very naturalization of mind can lend itself to a celebration of *techne* at the expense of *physis*, as in the image of the 'good mine' in Shelley's poem 'Queen Mab' (1813), which embodies a symbiosis of mind and matter that ultimately confirms the '"omnipotence of mind"' (Morton 1996: 418). Clearly, Romantic holism does not always undo the hierarchies embedded in the oppositions that it strives to reconcile. Nor is the Romantic celebration of less technologically transformed landscapes entirely unproblematic either. It might be argued that the Romantic aestheticization of nature, whether 'beautiful' or 'sublime', has functioned historically not so much as a potential locus of *resistance* to its industrial exploitation, but rather as *compensation* for it. Under the Modern Constitution, it has been all too easy to move from the consumption of nature as raw material for economic production during the working week, to the consumption of nature, whether rural or 'wild', as an aesthetic experience on Sundays (Rigby 2004b: 220–1). In the context of British imperialism, moreover, Romanticism also played a politically ambiguous role, at times providing a locus of resistance to colonial violence, but at others becoming complicit with it, for example through the construction of notions of 'wilderness' that effaced prior histories of indigenous land-use (Hutchings 2009).

To draw attention to these problematic elements is not to negate the value of the ecocritical return to Romanticism. On the contrary: to the extent that its ambiguous legacies are still very much with us, such a reconsideration becomes all the more important. On closer analysis, it might appear that in some respects at least, Romanticism is part of the problem of Western modernity. In the meantime, though, as I discuss further below, ecocriticism has become a considerably more transhistorical and transnational affair, drawing inspiration from, as well as bringing a questioning gaze to, the texts and traditions of many other times and places.

RECONNECTING THE SOCIAL AND THE ECOLOGICAL

The Romantic affirmation of the ties binding human well-being to a flourishing more-than-human environment finds its critical counterpart in the recognition that 'ecological exploitation is always coordinate with social exploitation' (Bate 2000: 48). This is the point of departure for much recent ecocriticism that incorporates a concern with questions of class and race, gender and sexuality. This kind of eco-social critique is not entirely new. It is, for example, partially foreshadowed by Rousseau in his 'Discourse on the Origins of Inequality among Men' (1754). Paying close attention to Rousseau's voluminous footnotes to the work of Buffon and other eighteenth-century naturalists, Bate reads this text as an early 'green history of the world' (2000: 42), which shows how the progress of civilization in the domination of nature had been achieved at the price of increased social inequality, alienation and military conflict. This analysis is akin to what the German social theorists Theodor Adorno and Max Horkheimer would later term the 'dialectic of enlightenment' (1979 [1944]). By the time they were writing as Jewish Marxist exiles from Nazi Germany during the Second World War, this dialectic had, they believed, generated a whole new order of barbarism right in the midst of the technologically most advanced civilization in world history.

While Adorno and Horkheimer were primarily concerned with domination on the basis of race and class, they also pointed to connections between the domination of women and that of the natural world. The 'marriage of Mind and Nature', which Francis Bacon hoped would be effected by the new science and technology, was, they observed, 'always patriarchal' (Adorno and Horkheimer 1979: 4). This had implications for women as well as for non-human nature. Because of their close symbolic and to some extent also practical association with nature through the kinds of labour they have traditionally performed, women have been cast either as 'primitive' and potentially 'monstrous', hence part of that nature which was to be mastered by rational man, or as an alluring embodiment of that other nature to which rational man simultaneously longs to return. Such connections between the domination of women and nature have been explored more recently in far greater depth and detail by ecofeminist philosophers, historians, sociologists and critics.[16]

The first major work of ecologically oriented feminist literary criticism was Annette Kolodny's *The Lay of the Land* (1975). Here, Kolodny examines the metaphorization of the land as feminine in North American literature. In particular, she draws attention to the conflict between phallic and foetal attitudes towards the feminized landscape, whereby the impulse to penetrate and master the country as a whole has oscillated uneasily with a desire to preserve certain places perceived at once as 'virginal' and 'maternal'. Such privileged places are imaged as sites of (typically masculine) regeneration. This ambivalence, Kolodny suggests, might have its origins in universal aspects of the human psyche, but it is also conditioned by certain geographical, social and cultural contingencies. The metaphoric feminization of the land is likely to have rather different consequences depending on the place and perception of women in society, and in the patriarchal context of North America following white settlement it has contributed to the development of land-use practices that are both contradictory and ultimately unsustainable. Building upon Kolodny's work, Louise Westling (1996) critically examines variations on the trope of land-as-woman in the work of women as well as men writers, contextualizing her readings of nineteenth- and twentieth-century American literature in a 'deep history' of changing understandings of nature from prehistoric times through to the present. The nature and implications of the patriarchal association of women and nature have been explored further by other feminist ecocritics, including Patrick Murphy (1995) and Greta Gaard (Gaard and Murphy 1998), while Catriona Sandilands' (1999) theorization of a politics of coalition that is inclusive of queer aspirations has found a growing ecocritical resonance in the new millennium.[17] The intersections between other kinds of oppression in a range of socio-ecological contexts and literary texts are also being explored in the burgeoning fields of postcolonial ecocriticism and ecocritical animal studies, both of which are brought into conversation with feminist concerns by contributors to Gaard's, Estok's and Oppermann's anthology, *International Perspectives in Feminist Ecocriticism* (2013).[18]

While much work in the field of environmental justice criticism focuses on the uneven distribution of environmental harms,[19] another aspect of the exploration of interconnections between nature, gender, sexuality, race and class is the consideration of the extent to which those who stand in a different relation to non-human others and the environment from elite Western males on account of their occupation, social position, or cultural traditions might have valuable alternative understandings of the nature-culture complex. This consideration drives much ecocritical work focusing on environmental literature by women, Afro-American, Chicano and indigenous authors. None of these heterogeneous groups, it should be emphasized, constitutes a locus of pure difference: all live, to a greater or lesser extent, in more than one world, generally participating in some aspects of the dominant culture, while nonetheless also having access to alternative understandings and practices. Some recent writers perceive this inhabitation of multiple perspectives as at once alienating and liberating. One such writer is Gloria Anzaldúa, a 'border woman', who, as she puts it in the Preface to her autobiographical work, *Borderlands/La Frontera*, 'grew up between two cultures, the Mexican (with a heavy Indian influence) and the Anglo (as a member of a colonized people in our own territory)' (1987 Preface).

As a lesbian ecofeminist Chicana, Anzaldúa is further distanced from the patriarchal and heterosexist elements of the various traditions she inherits. On the other hand, she is also able to draw inspiration from other aspects of these traditions. Thus, for example, Anzaldúa reappropriates the Toltec Indian earth goddess, Coatlicue, as a model of female divinity and divine immanence, while simultaneously embracing Western discourses of personal and collective self-determination. Hybridity is also manifest in *Borderlands* on the level of the written language Anzaldúa uses, which shifts continuously between English, Tex-Mex, northern Mexican dialect, Castilian Spanish and Nahuatl. From an ecocritical perspective, what is particularly valuable in Anzaldúa's work is her interrogation of the patriarchal, capitalist and racist values that have contributed to the ecological destruction of the Rio Grande Valley and the impoverishment of its inhabitants. As Terrell Dixon observes: 'By voicing the damage that the dominant culture visits on those whom it marginalizes', Chicano and Chicana writing such as Anzaldúa's 'resists those national narratives that privilege metastasizing suburbs and environmentally debilitating consumption, and it emphasizes the lack of environmental justice in them' (1999: 1094). Dixon is among those ecocritics who believe that it is now necessary to turn our ecocritical attention 'from wide open spaces to metropolitan spaces' (Bennett 2001).[20] If, as is widely anticipated, ever more people come to live in cities in the new millennium, social ecocriticism with an urban focus is set to be a growth area in the years to come.

REGROUNDING LANGUAGE AND UNEARTHING ECOPOETICS

Although, as we have seen, ecocriticism often incorporates questions of social justice, it nonetheless differs from other forms of political critique in one important respect: namely, in so far as it also entails advocacy for non-human others. If, as Gayatri Spivak (1988) has argued, the human subaltern cannot always be heard without the mediation of more privileged supporters, how much more so is this true of the subordinated non-human? This is not to say, however, that nature is silent. Nor, despite all our best efforts at domination, is it truly subordinate (as we are forcefully reminded by every earthquake, volcanic eruption, passing comet, new epidemic, and extreme weather event). The perception that nature has indeed been enslaved is perhaps most readily arrived at by people inhabiting relatively gentle regions with the benefit of air-conditioning, electricity, supermarkets, flush toilets, and clean water on tap. Similarly, the view that nature is silent might well say more about our refusal to hear than about other-than-human beings' inability to communicate. Certainly, this view is not shared within animistic cultures, where, as Christopher Manes observes, human language takes its place alongside, and in communication with, 'the language of birds, the wind, earthworms, wolves, and waterfalls – a world of autonomous speakers whose interests (especially for hunter-gatherer peoples) one ignores at one's peril' (1996: 15). Contemporary biosemioticians, such as Jesper Hoffmeyer (2009), also testify to the abundance of signifying systems in the natural world. These range from the biological information system of the genetic code itself, through the production of a huge variety of indexical signs by all species of plants and animals, to the apparently intentional deployment of at least partially conventional signs by many birds and mammals. More generally, whole ecosystems are sustained by complex networks of communication and exchange between species and the abiotic elements of their environment. As Robert S. Corrington has observed, 'The human process actualises semiotic processes that it did not make and that it did not shape. Our cultural codes, no matter how sophisticated and multi-valued, are what they are by riding on the back of this self-recording nature' (1994: ix). This insight has significant precursors in Romantic thought and literature, but it began to be explored more rigorously in Maurice Merleau-Ponty's scientifically informed philosophical lectures on nature from the late 1950s, the ecocritical value of which has been revealed by Louise Westling (2014). For Merleau-Ponty (2003), human language is inherently embodied and gestural and retains certain continuities with the other modes of communication from which it evolved. It is on the basis of these continuities that humans are also able to communicate and potentially collaborate with some of our other-than-human animal kin.

If, for those who live under the conditions of Western modernity, nature is nonetheless experienced as 'silent', this is surely because they inhabit an increasingly humanized world as heirs to a cultural tradition, moreover, within which 'the status of being a speaking subject is jealously guarded as an exclusively human prerogative' (Manes 1996: 15). This restriction of language to the human sphere only began to predominate in the West in the wake of the Renaissance, and was never uncontested. But it probably has a far longer pre-history in the rise of literacy, whereby language becomes tied to the exclusively human practice of writing. A further shift occurs with the invention of alphabetical writing, when the textual signifier looses all iconic connection to the signified. David Abram has argued that it is above all at this moment that human language and culture appears to emancipate itself from the natural world (Abram 1996: 102). This liberation is nonetheless to a large extent illusory. Not only is our capacity to speak, write and create culture predicated upon vastly more ancient and complex other-than-human signifying systems. The particular languages that we use to communicate in speech and writing themselves bear the trace of the more-than-human environments in which they evolved. 'Language', as Gary Snyder puts it, 'goes two ways' (1995: 174). Although the relationship between spoken and written signifiers and their signifieds might be arbitrary, the distinctions that they signify are not necessarily or entirely so. Nor is the relationship between signifier and signified always arbitrary, as we are reminded by the existence of many onomatopoeic words in most, if not all, natural languages. Some writing systems, too, are mimetic of the world to which they refer through the use of pictographic elements. As Abram points out, even the alphabet, in its original Hebrew form, manifested residually iconic elements, and required the participation of the embodied subject in order for its vowels to be formed through the breath of speech (1996: 240–3). Many uses of language also manifest a two-way movement between world and word. In the oral traditions of indigenous peoples, for example, the world created verbally through story, song and ritual comprises a mnemonic of the physical world in which the speaking community dwells, encoding important messages about how to survive in the land with respect for its wider animal, vegetable, mineral and spiritual community (Abram 1996: 154–79).[21] Arguably, even the most highly intertextual and imaginative works of modern science fiction ultimately derive their imagery from terrestrial experience of a more-than-human world.

Jonathan Bate develops a further argument that a specifically literary use of language can reconnect us to the natural world in the final chapter of *The Song of the Earth*. Taking his cue from Heidegger, Bate privileges metrical writing, which, he suggests, 'answers to nature's own rhythms' (2000: 76). In a world where nature has been reduced to what Heidegger, in his 'Essay Concerning Technology' (1993 [1953]), terms 'standing reserve', poetry becomes all the more important in recalling and sustaining a non-instrumental relationship to the world. Poetry, in this view, does not name things in order to make them available for use, but rather in order to disclose their being in language (Bate 2000: 258). Poetry thus becomes a 'refuge for nature, for the letting be of Being' (Bate 2000: 264). Yet, there remains a certain tension between *logos* and *oikos*, the world of the word and the earth which sustains it, but from which it also, inevitably, departs. The poet *qua* poet, as Bate observes, dwells in the *logos*, rather than in any earthly place (2000: 149). Following Heidegger, Bate seeks to protect the *logos* of poetry from the machinations of technological reason. Poetic 'presencing', which discloses nature without 'challenging' it, is said to be opposed to technological 'enframing', which makes 'everything part of a system, thus obliterating the unconcealed being-there of particular things' (Bate 2000: 255). According to Hegel, however, this is precisely what we do whenever we use language. The particularity of the thing, as he rather drastically puts it in the *Jena System Programme* of 1803/4, is 'annihilated' whenever we subsume it under a designation, the signifying capacity of which is determined by a logic not its own, namely that of the linguistic system (Hegel 1975: 20). From this perspective, language is itself a system of enframing. Moreover, the specifically poetic use of language to speak of nature is not always innocent of instrumentalizing tendencies. This does not mean that we should abandon poetry. But it does mean that we need to be cautious about what we can expect of literary language (Rigby 2004a). Bate himself expresses an important reservation in acknowledging that what is disclosed in poetry is not Being in its fullness, nor even the singular being of particular entities, but only the trace of an experience, which is itself evanescent and always already conditioned to some extent by cultural constructs (2000: 281).

While it is important to relocate human language and literature, as advocated by biosemiotic ecocritics such as Wheeler (2006), within the wider signifying systems of the more-than-human world, it is also necessary to recall that there is more to this world than can ever be disclosed within the frame of human language.[22] We fall back into hubris if we follow Heidegger in claiming that 'only the word grants being to a thing' (Heidegger 1979: 164; my translation). Other entities in the natural world have their own systems of signification and can get along quite happily without the imposition of human designations. It is rather we who need words in order to share understandings about the world as we see it. In the view of some scholars in the burgeoning field of ecopoetics, moreover, it is not traditional lyric poetry, but more experimental uses of language that are best able to critically probe and potentially shift dominant understandings. Harriet Tarlo (2009), for example, makes a strong case for the use of found text (also referred to as 'cut ups' or 'recycles') to create open textual structures incorporating multiple voices and perspectives (including that of the reader), which are both imitative of, and continuous with, ecological networks of open-ended interdependency.[23] Juxtaposing and defamiliarizing diverse public discourses of nature, such works can also highlight our desensitization to environmental bad news stories, reminding us of our failure to act on what we know (Kerridge 2007). In refusing to occupy the cultural niche conventionally accorded to poetry in the lyric mode, avant-garde ecopoetics seeks to avoid becoming a 'tool for placation' (Kinsella 2009, 146). It is important to recall, however, that since the impact of any type of ecological art is ultimately decided on the level of reception, a variety of ecopoetic forms, as well as foci, are required in order to engage and inspire a range of differently situated recipients (Rigby 2015a). And while human articulate language might not be radically discontinuous from the other signifying systems that abound in the biosphere, the relationship between ecopoetics and the earth is complex, variable and highly mediated.

ECOCRITICISM IN THE ANTHROPOCENE: EXPANDING HORIZONS AND STORMY SKIES

The horizons of ecocritical scholarship have expanded rapidly in the twenty-first century. Within English-language ecocriticism alone, the historical range of environmental literary studies, initially largely restricted to the last two centuries, now reaches back to the medieval period (Rudd 2007; Siewers 2009), Roman pastoral (Saunders 2008), and Greek tragedy and ancient Sumerian epic (Westling 2014). Meanwhile, as ecocritical practices, and the professional associations that support them, have proliferated around the world, the literatures of many other linguistic and cultural traditions are now being studied from various environmental or socio-ecological perspectives (e.g. Goodbody 2007; Sivaramakrishnan and Jana 2011; Estok and Kim 2013). And in addition to this growing historical depth and international reach, ecocriticism's intellectual horizons too have been expanding through vigorous internal discussions and debates regarding underlying assumptions, political orientations, and methodological approaches.[24] While much (if by no means all) early environmental literary scholarship was marked by a certain wariness, or even hostility, towards theorization, there is now a growing body of ecocritical theory, informed by a range of philosophical, political and scientific perspectives, and engaged with a variety of other interdisciplinary areas of study.[25]

These expanding horizons currently place ecocritics in a better position to rise to the challenge posed to the literary critical establishment by Bate back in the mid-1990s: namely, to develop a form of literary scholarship – Global Warming Criticism, as he termed it – capable of responding to what is without doubt the greatest single socio-ecological crisis in era of the Anthropocene: the era, that is, in which industrial humanity's still largely fossil-fuelled practices of production and consumption have transformed our species into a geological force that is leaving its mark in this planet's rocky mantle and altering the future prospects of all life on Earth for millennia to come (Crutzen and Stoermer 2000). To grapple with anthropogenic climate change entails thinking in vastly expanded timescales, from a planetary perspective, and across disciplinary divides. As Timothy Clark observes in the *Cambridge Introduction to Literature and Environment*, getting a handle on global warming is extremely difficult, as its 'causes are diffuse, partly unpredictable and separated from the effects by huge gaps in time and space' (2011: 11), and, at the close of the first decade of the new millennium, relatively few ecocritics (albeit more than Clark acknowledges) had addressed it directly. Since then, however, as he rightly anticipated, many more have begun to do so, with projects ranging from the critical analysis of the diverse climate changed futures imagined within contemporary science fiction (e.g. Trexler and Johns-Putra 2011; Rigby 2012), through historical studies of literary responses to earlier climatic changes and weather surprises (e.g. Wood 2014), to theoretical reflection upon the new philosophies and methodologies that might help us to engage more effectively with this dire problem (e.g. Clark 2011; Morton 2013).

At the time of writing, it remains unclear whether sufficient political will can be mustered to limit global warming to the generally agreed guardrail of 2 degrees Celcius. What is increasingly apparent, however, is that the inevitable rise in global average temperatures, which has already been set in train by the growth in greenhouse gas emissions that began during the Romantic period and continues unabated, is already causing wide-ranging environmental changes, threatening an escalation of extinctions, melting polar and glacial ice, rising sea levels, and engendering an increase in the frequency and intensity of extreme weather events. In a perilously warming world, then, the ecocritical challenge is not only to consider how literary works of the creative imagination might help us to 'think fragility', with a view to averting further socio-ecological damage: it is also to consider how they might help us to prepare for, respond to, and recover from, those eco-catastrophes that are becoming increasingly common (Rigby 2014b). To do this with justice and compassion, moreover, requires that those patterns of concealment discussed at the beginning of this chapter are broken, in order to afford the voices of all those at risk, human and otherwise, a better chance of being heard.

NOTES TOWARDS A READING OF WORDSWORTH'S 'HOME AT GRASMERE'

Wordsworth's paean to his Lakeland dwelling-place was to be the first part of the first book of a long philosophical poem entitled *The Recluse*, of which *The Prelude* was the introduction. Wordsworth never completed *The Recluse*, and although his major autobiographical poem *The Prelude* was published posthumously in 1850, 'Home at Grasmere' only reached the public gaze in 1888, in a 'thin green volume of fifty-six pages bearing no editor's name' (Darlington 1977: 32). Most critics were initially unenthusiastic about this new addition to Wordsworth's by now increasingly popular and highly regarded published works (Darlington 1977: 460–2). Subsequently, however, 'Home at Grasmere' has come to be seen as standing 'securely on its own as Wordsworth's triumphant manifesto' (Darlington 1977: 32). From an ecocritical perspective, moreover, the choice of green for the cover of the first edition appears inspired: this is, as Karl Kroeber discerned as early as 1974, an exemplary work of Romantic ecopoetics.[26]

Until 1888, 'Home at Grasmere' existed in two main versions, one completed in 1806 (Ms. B) and the other in 1832 (Ms. D), in the form of two closely written, homemade notebooks without covers.[27] In view of Wordsworth's sparing use of writing materials and the frugality of his household as a whole, the ecological cost of the initial production of this text (if not its subsequent publication, republication and distribution) appears to have been slight.[28] What qualifies 'Home at Grasmere' as a work of environmental literature is nonetheless to be found primarily on the semantic level of the text, in the poet's explicit recollection of the wider ecological conditions of possibility for his work. The non-human environment certainly figures here as far more than a framing device for the exploration of narrowly human concerns. For the primary purpose of this poem is to render an account of how Wordsworth's life as a poet was enabled by the rural 'retreat' (147), 'this small Abiding-place of many Men' (146), 'the calmest, fairest spot of earth' (73), which he had made his home. Grasmere vale is nonetheless not presented as a place of delight for the poet alone. It is celebrated rather as a place where all manner of life, human and otherwise, might flourish; a place which seems even to take pleasure in its own existence:

> Dear Valley, having in thy face a smile
> Though peaceful, full of gladness. Thou art pleased,
> Pleased with thy crags and woody steeps, thy Lake,
> Its one green Island and its winding shores,
> The multitude of little rocky hills,
> Thy Church and Cottages of mountain stone –
> (116–21)

As this reference to the church and cottages indicates, the place to which the poet and his sister moved in 1800 was no 'wilderness', but rather a geo-cultural landscape, shaped by thousands of years of human habitation. Whereas other parts of northern England were caught in the first throes of industrialization, the Lake District was still overwhelmingly rural and by no means universally bent to human purposes. Its potentially treacherous mountain peaks, wooded hillsides, fast flowing streams and deep lakes are shown to retain their own agency, communicative potential and moral significance. Yet, while there is much that remains 'unappropriated' (74), here as elsewhere in Britain, the enclosure of formerly common land and the shift to a more intensive and commercialized form of agriculture were beginning to have an impact on the farming community. Grasmere's 'Church and Cottages of mountain stone' might be read as metonymic for a way of life that is construed as having arisen through a respectful process of negotiation with the physical environment of this particular bioregion. But among the 'untutored Shepherds' (428) who tended their small flocks on the hills and dales around Grasmere, Wordsworth perceived evidence of a mode of relationship to the land that he knew to be endangered. Indeed, it is perhaps precisely in the face of the changes that were underway elsewhere, and soon to encroach here too, that Wordsworth constructs this place as a 'shelter' (113) and 'last retreat' (147).

Wordsworth's Grasmere vale, however, is no pastoral idyll such as that projected by the idealizing poets of the Augustan age.[29] Although his first experience of the place as a 'roving School-boy' (2), recalled in the third person in the opening stanzas, was deeply delightful, the reader is reminded that the elements were not always kind here, as the speaker and his sister discovered when they first arrived in Grasmere in the middle of an especially harsh winter:

'Bleak season was it, turbulent and bleak, / When hitherward we journeyed, side by side' (152–3). Wordsworth's Lakelanders are no 'noble savages' either: 'ribaldry, impiety, or wrath' (344) are not unknown to them, and their lives are shown to be often hard, fraught with the personal suffering and economic hardships that are foregrounded in a number of his 'lyrical ballads'. Wordsworth nonetheless construes this as a place where most people can live in relative freedom and modest self-sufficiency, as well as in 'true Community, a genuine frame / Of many into one incorporate' (615–16). Significantly, this is an explicitly open community, welcoming strangers, 'come from whereso'er you will' (148), and comprising a heterogeneous more than-human collective:

> . . . a multitude
> Human and brute, possessors undisturbed of this Recess, their
>   legislative Hall,
> Their Temple, and their glorious Dwelling-place. (621–4)

Among the denizens of this wider collective, the poet focuses especially on the wild birds that frequent the shores of the lake and dwell in the woods and mountains. Within his more immediate community, he also honours individual domestic animals, such as 'the small grey horse that bears / The paralytic Man' (505–6) and 'The famous Sheep-dog, first in all the Vale' (510). Moreover, the poet stresses that he and his 'happy Band' (663) of family and friends were not alone in their affection for the more-than-human dimensions of their dwelling place. Although he acknowledges that the local farming community had a more practical relationship to the land than his own household, whose source of income came from elsewhere, he nonetheless insists that

> . . . not a tree
> Sprinkles these little pastures, but the same
> Hath furnished matter for a thought, perchance
> For some one serves as a friend. (441–4)

Wordsworth was himself an intentional 'reinhabitant', seeking to cultivate a sense of belonging to a particular place in a world that was increasingly characterized by dislocation and alienation.[30] Among the rural inhabitants of Grasmere he nonetheless encountered an older sense of place, incorporating an appreciation of the land as something far more than resource and commodity. Here, the land was still a storied place, traversed by pathways both literal and figurative, and studded with sites of narrative significance; here, the land could still be experienced as a 'nourishing terrain',[31] sustaining its inhabitants both physically and spiritually. And it is in this respect that Grasmere vale is disclosed as an immanently 'holy place' (277). 'Home at Grasmere' concludes with Wordsworth's famous poetic mission statement, which was published separately in 1850 as a 'Prospectus' to *The Prelude*. Here he proclaims that his great poetic work was to be a 'spousal verse', celebrating the marriage, 'in love and holy passion' of 'the discerning intellect of Man' with 'this goodly universe' (805–10). In this context, the significance of 'Home at Grasmere' lies in its demonstration of how the 'marriage' of the human mind and the natural world needs to emerge from an embodied experience in and of place. This poem is thus itself a 'spousal verse', celebrating the marriage of the poet with the place that modelled for him the partnership of humanity and nature, of which he proposed to write in his work.

From the perspective of a contemporary ecocritical hermeneutics of suspicion, there are nonetheless a number of problematic aspects of this text, beginning with the question of what might be occluded by Wordsworth's celebratory take on this 'individual Spot' (143). The poet reassures us that

> . . . Labour here preserves
> His rosy face, a Servant only here
> Of the fire-side or of the open field,
> A Freeman, therefore sound and unimpaired;
> That extreme penury is here unknown,
> And cold and hunger's abject wretchedness,
> Mortal to body and the heaven-born mind;
> That they who want are not too great a weight
> For those who can relieve . . . (359–67)

While it would doubtless be a category error to expect a detailed sociological analysis from what is essentially a song of praise, it is pertinent to consider to what extent Wordsworth glosses over the existence of certain forms of social domination and exploitation here, including those that render some people homeless, even in Grasmere. Secondly, Wordsworth's emphasis on the self-sufficient wholeness, as well as wholesomeness, of this place – 'A Whole without dependence or defect, / Made for itself and happy for itself, / Perfect contentment, Unity entire' (149–51) – effaces its inter-linkages with national and international socio-ecological developments. While the Wordsworths were making themselves at home in Grasmere, for instance, some of their countrymen were busily appropriating the land of indigenous people elsewhere in order to make themselves, and their domestic animals, at home in the colonies. And thirdly, turning from the text's context of production to that of its reception, we might wonder whether taking refuge in 'Grasmere', as it is recalled by Wordsworth in this poem, is for us, if not necessarily for him, to retreat from the pressing issues of the contemporary world in nostalgic reminiscence of a world that we have lost; one that probably never existed in quite the way that it is represented here. Ironically, Grasmere has itself in the meantime been transformed, not least by the growth of tourism, inspired in part by such a nostalgic urge and fuelled, ironically, by Wordsworth's own work.[32] Moreover, the tourists who once came by train from English towns now come by car, having frequently flown to Britain from other parts of the world, thereby adding to those carbon dioxide emissions that are changing Earth's climate and altering ecosystems, including those of the Lakes.

'Home at Grasmere' nonetheless also provides a hint as to how such problems of socio-ecological concealment and fossil-fuelled nostalgia might be redressed: namely, in calling upon its readers to pursue the good, here and now,

> Dismissing therefore all Arcadian dreams
> All golden fancies of the Golden Age,
> The bright array of shadowy thoughts from times
> That were before all time, or are to be
> Ere time expire . . . (625–9)

If, for contemporary readers, many of whom live under the 'black sky' (603) of today's growing cities, 'by the vast Metropolis immured' (597), Wordsworth's 'Home at Grasmere' has itself become an Arcadian dream, then we must endeavour to read it differently: not as a lost idyll, but as embodying an ethos of eco-social relationship that is more relevant today than ever. 'Home at Grasmere' cannot return us to Wordsworth's (partially imaginary) world. Read ecocritically, however, it might prompt us to consider the current threats to, and ongoing destruction of, numerous other such places of sustainable subsistence around today's world as a consequence of transnational processes of capitalist modernization. So too might it inspire us in the pursuit of greater justice and sustainability in those many and varied places, not only where we ourselves reside, but also those that we are unlikely ever to visit, but that support and/or suffer the consequences of the delocalized production processes and consumption habits with which all of our lives, to a greater or lesser extent, are enmeshed.

QUESTIONS FOR FURTHER CONSIDERATION

1. To what extent, and by what poetic means, does 'Home at Grasmere' disclose non-human agency, communicative potential and moral significance?
2. The metaphor of the 'marriage' of mind and nature that Wordsworth invokes here was also used by Francis Bacon as a model for science and technology. How does Wordsworth's conception of this 'marriage' differ from Bacon's? Does it seem to be any less patriarchal?
3. What role do class and gender play in Wordsworth's representation of life in Grasmere?
4. How do weather and climate figure in Wordsworth's representation of what it means to be 'at home' in Grasmere, and how might this be re-interpreted in the context of anthropogenic climate change?
5. In the final section of 'Home at Grasmere' that became the Prospectus to *The Prelude*, Wordsworth affirms the superiority of natural beauty, 'a living Presence of the earth', over artifacts made by humans (795–8). *The Prelude*, however, concludes with the assertion that 'the mind of man becomes / A thousand times more beautiful than the earth'

(Wordsworth 1971, lines 446–8). How would you account for the apparent contradiction between these two statements?

6. In what ways do you think that your response to 'Home at Grasmere' is influenced by the ecological and social context in which you yourself live, the place(s) in which you are (or are not) 'at home'?

BIBLIOGRAPHY

Abram, David (1996) *The Spell of the Sensuous: Perception and Language in a More-than-Human World*, New York: Vintage.

Abrams, M. H (1973) *Natural Supernaturalism: Tradition and Revolution in Romantic Literature*, New York: Norton & Co.

Adamson, Joni, Mei Mei Evans and Rachel Stein, eds. (2002) *The Environmental Justice Reader: Politics, Poetics, and Pedagogy*, Tucson: University of Arizona Press.

Adamson, Joni and Kimberley N. Ruffin, eds. (2013) *American Studies, Ecocriticism and Citizenship: Thinking and Acting in the Local and Global Commons*, New York: Routledge.

Adorno, Theodor and Max Horkheimer (1979) *Dialectic of Enlightenment* [1944], trans. John Cumming, London and New York: Verso.

Anzaldúa, Gloria (1987) *Borderlands/La Frontera: The New Mestiza*, San Francisco: Aunt Lute Book Company.

Armbruster, Carla and Kathleen Wallace, eds. (2000) *Beyond Nature Writing*, Charlottesville: University of Virginia Press.

Bacon, Francis (1870) *Novum Organum* [1620], in *Works*, vol. 4, ed. James Spedding, Robert Leslie Ellis and Douglas Devon Heath, London: Longmans Green.

Bakhtin, M. M. (1981) *The Dialogic Imagination. Four Essays by M. M. Bakhtin*, ed. Michael Holquist, trans. Caryl Emerson and M. Holquist, Austin: University of Texas Press.

Bate, Jonathan (1991) *Romantic Ecology: Wordsworth and the Environmental Tradition*, London and New York: Routledge.

Bate, Jonathan (1996) 'Living with the Weather', in *Green Romanticism*, Special Issue of *Studies in Romanticism* 35:3, ed. J. Bate, pp. 431–48.

Bate, Jonathan (2000) *The Song of the Earth*, Cambridge MA: Harvard University Press.

Benjamin, Walter (1973) *Illuminations* [1955], ed. and intro. Hannah Arendt, trans. Harry Zohn, London: Fontana.

Bennett, Michael (2001) 'From Wide Open Spaces to Metropolitan Spaces', *ISLE* 8:1, pp. 31–52.

Bennett, Michael and David Teague, eds. (1999) *The Nature of Cities: Ecocriticism and Urban Environments*, Tucson: University of Arizona Press.

Bicknell, Peter, ed. (1984) *The Illustrated Wordsworth's Guide to the Lakes*, Foreword Alan G. Hill, Exeter: Webb & Bower.

Boisseau, Michelle (2000) 'Parchment', *Poetry* CLXXV:3, p. 177.

Branch, Michael, Rochelle Johnson, Daniel Peterson and Scott Slovic, eds. (1998) *Reading the Earth: New Directions in the Study of Literature and the Environment*, Moscow: University of Idaho Press.

Buell, Lawrence (1995) *The Environmental Imagination: Thoreau, Nature Writing, and the Formation of American Culture*, Cambridge MA: Cambridge University Press.

Buell, Lawrence (2005) *The Future of Environmental Criticism: Environmental Crisis and Literary Imagination*, Oxford: Blackwell.

Campbell, SueEllen (1996) 'The Land and Language of Desire: Where Deep Ecology and Poststructuralism Meet' [1989], in Glotfelty and Fromm 1996: 124–36.

Campbell, SueEllen with Alex Hunt, Richard Kerridge, Tom Lynch and Ellen E. Wohl (2010) *The Face of the Earth: Natural Landscapes, Science, and Culture*, Berkeley: University of California Press.

Clark, Timothy (2010) 'Some Climate Change Ironies: Deconstruction, Environmental Politics and the Closure of Ecocriticism', *Oxford Literary Review* 32, pp. 131–49.

Clark, Timothy (2011) *The Cambridge Introduction to Literature and the Environment*, Cambridge: Cambridge University Press.

Cohen, Michael (2004) 'Blues in the Green: Ecocriticism under Critique', *Environmental History* 9:1, pp. 9–36.

Coole, Diana and Samantha Frost, eds. (2010) *New Materialisms: Ontology, Agency, and Politics*, Durham NC: Duke University Press.

Corrington, Robert S. (1994) *Ecstatic Naturalism: Signs of the World*, Bloomington: Indiana University Press.

Coupe, Lawrence, ed. (2000) *The Green Studies Reader: From Romanticism to Ecocriticism*, London and New York: Routledge.

Crutzen, P. J. and E. F. Stoermer (2000) 'The "Anthropocene"', *Global Change Newsletter* 41, pp. 17–18.

Cudworth, Erica (2005) *Developing Ecofeminist Theory: The Complexity of Difference*, Basingstoke: Palgrave Macmillan.

Darlington, Beth (1977) Introduction and Appendices to 'Home at Grasmere', *Part First, Book First of 'The Recluse' by William Wordsworth*, Ithaca: Cornell University Press.

Diamond, Jared M. (2005) *Collapse: How Societies Choose to Fail or Succeed*, New York: Viking.

DeLoughrey, Elizabeth and George B. Handley, eds. (2011) *Postcolonial Ecologies: Literatures of the Environment*, Oxford: Oxford University Press.

Dixon, Terrell (1999) Contribution to 'Special Forum on Literatures of the Environment', *PMLA* 114:5, pp. 1093–4.

Dixon, Terrell, ed. (2001) *City Wilds: Essays and Stories about Urban Nature*, Athens: University of Georgia Press.

Edwards, Keith (1984) *Man and the Natural World: Changing Attitudes in England 1500–1800*, Harmondsworth: Penguin.

Elder, John (1985) *Imagining the Earth: Poetry and the Vision of Nature*, Urbana: University of Illinois Press.

Estok, Simon C. and Won-Chung Kim, eds. (2013) *East Asian Ecocriticisms: A Critical Reader*, New York: Palgrave Macmillan.

Fletcher, Angus (2004) *A New Theory for American Poetry: Democracy, the Environment, and the Future of Imagination*, Cambridge MA: Harvard University Press.

Gaard, Greta and Patrick Murphy, eds. (1998) *Ecofeminist Literary Criticism: Theory, Interpretation, and Pedagogy*, Champaign: University of Illinois Press.

Gaard, Greta, Simon C. Estok and Serpil Oppermann (2013) *International Perspectives in Feminist Ecocriticism*, London: Routledge.

Garrard, Greg (1998) 'The Romantics' View of Nature', in David E. Cooper and Joy A. Palmer, eds., *Spirit of the Environment: Religion, Value and Environmental Concern*, London: Routledge.

Garrard, Greg (2012) *Ecocriticism*, 2nd edition, London: Routledge.

Garrard, Greg, ed. (2014) *The Oxford Handbook of Ecocriticism*, Oxford: Oxford University Press.

Gifford, Terry (1995) *Green Voices: Understanding Contemporary Nature Poetry*, Manchester: Manchester University Press.

Gifford, Terry (1999) *Pastoral*, London and New York: Routledge.

Gilcrest, David (2002) *Greening the Lyre: Environmental Poetics and Ethics*, Reno: University of Nevada Press.

Glotfelty, Cheryll and Harold Fromm, eds. (1996) *The Ecocriticism Reader: Landmarks in Literary Ecology*, Athens: University of Georgia Press.

Goodbody, Axel (2007) *Nature, Technology and Cultural Change in Twentieth-Century German Literature*, Houndmills: Palgrave Macmillan.

Goodbody, Axel and Kate Rigby, eds. (2011) *Ecocritical Theory: New European Approaches*, Charlottesville: University of Virginia Press.

Harrison, Robert Pogue (1992) *Forests: The Shadow of Civilization*, Chicago: University of Chicago Press.

Hegel, G. W. F. (1975) *Jenaer Systementwürfe I*, ed. K. Düsing and H. Kimmerle, in Hegel, *Gesammelte Werke*, Vol. 6, Hamburg: Felix Meiner.

Heidegger, Martin (1979) *Unterwegs zur Sprache*, 6th edition, Pfüllingen: Noske.

Heidegger, Martin (1993) 'The Question Concerning Technology' [1953], trans. William Lovitt, in *Basic Writings*, ed. David Farrell Krell, San Francisco: HarperSanFrancisco.

Heise, Ursula K. (2008) *Sense of Place and Sense of Planet: The Environmental Imagination of the Global*, Oxford: Oxford University Press.

Heringman, Noah (2004) *Romantic Rocks, Aesthetic Geology*, Ithaca and London: Cornell University Press.

Hoffmeyer, Jesper (2009) *Biosemiotics: An Examination into the Signs of Life and the Life of Signs*, Chicago: University of Chicago Press.

Hornung, Alfred and Zhao Baisheng, eds. (2012) *Ecology and Life Writing*, Heidelberg: Universitätsverlag Winter.

Hutchings, Kevin (2002) *Imagining Nature: Blake's Environmental Poetics*, Montreal and Kingston: McGill-Queen's University Press.

Hutchings, Kevin (2009) *Romantic Ecologies and Colonial Cultures in the British Atlantic World 1770–1850*, Montreal and Kingston: McGill-Queen's University Press.

Huggan, Graham and Helen Tiffin (2010) *Postcolonial Ecocriticism: Literature, Animals, Environment*, London: Routledge.

Iovina, Serenella and Serpil Oppermann (2014) *Material Ecocriticism*, Bloomington: Indiana University Press.

Kerridge, Richard (2007) 'Climate Change and Contemporary Modernist Poetry', in Tony Lopez and Anthony Caleshu, eds., *Poetry and Public Language*, Exeter: Shearsman Books.

Kerridge, Richard (2013) *Cold Blood: Adventures with Reptiles and Amphibians*, London: Chatto & Windus.

Kerridge, Richard and Niel Sammells, eds. (1998) *Writing the Environment: Ecocriticism and Literature*, London and New York: Zed Books.

Kinsella, John (2009) 'The School of Environmental Poetics and Creativity', *Ecopoetics and Pedagogies*, Special issue of *Angelaki* 14:2, pp. 143–8.

Knickerbocker, Scott (2012) *Ecopoetics: The Language of Nature, the Nature of Language*, Amherst: University of Massachusetts Press.

Kolodny, Annette (1975) *The Lay of the Land*, Chapel Hill: University of Carolina Press.

Kroeber, Karl (1974) '"Home at Grasmere": Ecological Holiness', *PMLA* 89:1, pp. 132–41.

Kroeber, Karl (1994) *Ecological Literary Criticism: Romantic Imagining and the Biology of Mind*, New York: Columbia University Press.

LeMenager, Stephanie, Teresa Shewry and Ken Hiltner (2011) *Environmental Criticism for the Twenty-First Century*, New York: Routledge.

Leopold, Aldo (1998) 'The Land Ethic' [1949], in Michael E. Zimmerman et al., eds., *Environmental Philosophy: From Animal Rights to Radical Ecology*, New Jersey: Prentice Hall.

Liu, Alan (1989) *Wordsworth: The Sense of History*, Stanford: Stanford University Press.

Lussier, Mark (1999) *Romantic Dynamics: The Poetics of Physicality*, New York: St. Martin's Press.

Lynch, Tom, Cheryll Glotfelty and Karla Armbruster, eds. (2012) *The Bioregional Imagination: Literature, Ecology, and Place*, Athens: University of Georgia Press.

Mabey, Richard (2010) *Weeds: The Story of Outlaw Plants*, London: Profile.

McGann, Jerome (1983) *The Romantic Ideology: A Critical Investigation*, Chicago: Chicago University Press.

McKibben, Bill (1989) *The End of Nature*, New York: Random House.

McKusick, James (2000) *Green Writing: Romanticism and Ecology*, New York: St. Martin's Place.

Manes, Christopher (1996) 'Nature and Silence', in Glotfelty and Fromm 1996: 15–29.

Marshall, Peter (1994) *Nature's Web: Rethinking Our Place on Earth*, New York: Paragon Books.

Mathews, Freya (2009) 'Introduction: Invitation to Ontopoetics', *Philosophy Activism Nature* 6, pp. 1–6.

Meeker, Joseph (1972) *The Comedy of Survival: Studies in Literary Ecology*, New York: Scribner's.

Merchant, Carolyn (1980) *The Death of Nature: Women, Ecology and the Scientific Revolution*, San Francisco: Harper and Row.

Merchant, Carolyn (1989) *Ecological Revolutions: Nature, Gender and Science in New England*, New York: Chapel Hill.

Merleau-Ponty, Maurice (2003) *Nature: Course Notes from the Collège de France*, ed. Dominique Ségland, trans. Robert Vallier, Evanston: Northwestern University Press.

Morton, Timothy (1994) *Shelley and the Revolution in Taste: The Body and the Natural World*, Cambridge: Cambridge University Press.

Morton, Timothy (1996) 'Shelley's Green Desert', *Studies in Romanticism* 35:3, pp. 409–30.

Morton, Timothy (2007) *Ecology without Nature: Rethinking Environmental Aesthetics*, Cambridge MA: Harvard University Press.

Morton, Timothy (2010) *The Ecological Thought*, Cambridge MA: Harvard University Press.

Morton, Timothy (2013) *Hyperobjects: Philosophy and Ecology after the End of the World*, Minneapolis: University of Minnesota Press.

Müller, Timo and Michael Sauter, eds. (2012) *Literature, Ecology, Ethics: Recent Trends in Ecocriticism*, Heidelberg: Universitätsverlag Winter.

Murphy, Patrick (1995) *Literature, Nature, and Other: Ecofeminist Critiques*, Albany: State University of New York Press.

Naess, Arne (1973) 'The Shallow and the Deep, Long-Range Ecology Movement', *Inquiry* 16:1–4, pp. 95–100.

Newman, Lance (2005) *Our Common Dwelling: Henry Thoreau, Transcendentalism, and the Class Politics of Nature*, New York: Palgrave Macmillan.

Nichols, Ashton (2004) *Romantic Natural Histories: William Wordsworth, Charles Darwin, and Others*, Boston: Haughton.

Nixon, Rob (2011) *Slow Violence and the Environmentalism of the Poor*, Cambridge MA: Harvard University Press.

Oerlemans, Onno (2002) *Romanticism and the Materiality of Nature*, Toronto: University of Toronto Press.

Phillips, Dana (2003) *The Truth of Ecology: Nature, Culture, and Literature in America*, Oxford: Oxford University Press.

Plumwood, Val (1993) *Feminism and the Mastery of Nature*, London and New York: Routledge.

Plumwood, Val (2008) 'Shadow Places and the Politics of Dwelling', *Australian*

Humanities Review 44, available at <http://www.australianhumanitiesreview.org/archive/Issue-March-2008/plumwood.html> (accessed 15 September 2014).

Rigby, Kate (2004a) 'Earth, World, Text: On the (Im)possibility of Ecopoiesis', *New Literary History* 35:3, 427–42.

Rigby, Kate (2004b) *Topographies of the Sacred: The Poetics of Place in European Romanticism*, Charlottesville: University of Virginia Press.

Rigby, Kate (2012) 'Utopianism, Dystopianism and Ecological Thought', in Michael Jacobsen and Keith Tester, eds., *Utopia: Social Theory and the Future*, Farnham: Ashgate.

Rigby, Kate (2014a) 'Romanticism', in Garrard 2014: 60–79.

Rigby, Kate (2014b) 'Confronting Catastrophe: Ecocriticism in a Warming World', in Westling, ed.

Rigby, Kate (2015a) 'Ecopoetics', in Joni Adamson, William Gleeson and Tony Pellow, eds., *Keywords in Environmental Studies*, New York: SUNY Press.

Rigby, Kate (2015b) *Dancing With Disaster: Histories, Narratives and Ethics for Perilous Times*, Charlottesville: University of Virginia Press.

Roos, Bonnie and Alex Hunt, eds. (2010) *Postcolonial Green: Environmental Politics and World Narratives*, Charlottesville: University of Virginia Press.

Rose, Deborah Bird (1996) *Nourishing Terrains: Australian Aboriginal Views of Landscape and Wilderness*, Canberra: Australian Heritage Commission.

Rudd, Gillian (2007) *Greenery: Ecocritical Readings of Late Medieval English Literature*, Manchester: University of Manchester Press.

Rueckert, William (1996) 'Literature and Ecology: An Experiment in Ecocriticism' [1978], in Glotfelty and Fromm 1996: 105–23.

Saunders, Timothy (2008) *Bucolic Ecology: Virgil's Eclogues and the Environmental Literary Tradition*, London: Duckworth.

Sandilands, Catriona (1999) *The Good-Natured Feminist: Ecofeminism and the Quest for Democracy*, Minneapolis: University of Minnesota Press.

Scigaj, Leonard (1999) *Sustainable Poetry: Four American Ecopoets*, Lexington: University Press of Kentucky.

Siewers, Alfred K. (2009) *Strange Beauty: Ecocritical Approaches to Early Medieval Landscape*, London: Palgrave Macmillan.

Serres, Michel (1995) *The Natural Contract*, trans. Elizabeth MacArthur and William Paulson, Ann Arbor: University of Michigan Press.

Seymour, Nicole (2013) *Strange Natures: Futurity, Empathy, and the Queer Ecological Imagination*, Chicago: University of Illinois Press.

Sivaramakrishnan, Murali and Ujjwal Jana (2011) *Ecological Criticism for our Times: Literature, Nature and Critical Inquiry*, Delhi: Authors Press.

Slovic, Scott (1992) *Seeking Awareness in American Nature Writing: Henry Thoreau, Annie Dillard, Edward Abbey, Wendell Berry, Barry Lopez*, Salt Lake City: University of Utah Press.

Slovic, Scott (1999) Contribution to 'Special Forum on Literatures of the Environment', *PMLA* 114:5, pp. 1102–3.

Snyder, Gary (1995) *A Place in Space: Ethics, Aesthetics and Watersheds*, Washington DC: Counterpoint.

Soper, Kate (1995) *What is Nature?* Oxford: Blackwell.

Spivak, Gayatri (1988) 'Can the Subaltern Speak?' in *Marxism and the Interpretation of Culture*, Basingstoke and London: Macmillan.

Tarlo, Harriet (2009) 'Recycles: The Eco-Ethical Poetics of Found Text in Contemporary Poetry', *Poetic Ecologies*, Special issue of *Journal of Ecocriticism* 1:2, pp. 114–30.

Thomas, Keith (1983) *Man and the Natural World*, New York: Pantheon.

Tredinnick, Mark, ed. (2003) *A Place on Earth: An Anthology of Nature Writing from Australia and North America*, Sydney: University of New South Wales Press.

Trexler, Adam and Adeline Johns-Putra (2011) 'Climate Change in Literature and Literary Criticism', *Wiley Interdisciplinary Reviews: Climate Change* 2:2, pp. 185–200.

Walls, Laura Dassow (2011) 'From the Modern to the Ecological: Latour on Walden Pond', in Goodbody and Rigby 2011: 98–112.

Westling, Louise (1996) *The Green Breast of the New World: Landscape, Gender and American Fiction*, Athens and London: University of Georgia Press.

Westling, Louise, ed. (2013) *The Cambridge Companion to Literature and Environment*, Cambridge: Cambridge University Press.

Westling, Louise (2014) *The Logos of the Living World: Merleau-Ponty, Animals, and Language*, New York: Fordham University Press.

Wheeler, Wendy (2006) *The Whole Creature: Complexity, Biosemiotics and the Evolution of Culture*, London: Lawrence and Wishart.

White, Lynn (1996) 'The Historical Roots of our Ecologic Crisis' [1967], in Glotfelty and Fromm 1996: 3–14.

Williams, Raymond (1983) *Keywords: A Vocabulary of Culture and Society*, rev. ed., London: Fontana.

Williams, Raymond (1985) *The Country and the City*, London: Hogarth Press.

Wood, Gillen D'Arcy (2014) *Tambora: The Eruption that Changed the World*, Princeton: Princeton University Press.

Wordsworth, William (1971) *The Prelude – A Parallel Text*, ed. J. C. Maxwell, Harmondsworth: Penguin.

Wordsworth, William (1977) 'Home at Grasmere', *Part First, Book First of 'The Recluse' by William Wordsworth*, ed. and intro. Beth Darlington, Ithaca: Cornell University Press.

NOTES

1. Shelley's participation in this 'revolution in taste' is explored by Timothy Morton (1994).
2. See in particular Meeker 1972, Kolodny 1975 and Rueckert 1996. Originally published in 1978, Rueckert's article includes the coinage 'ecocriticism'.
3. See e.g. the 'Special Forum on Literatures of the Environment', *PMLA* 114/5 (October 1999).
4. The first ecocritic to seek a point of connection between poststructuralism and radical ecological thought (specifically, Deep Ecology) was SueEllen Campbell in an article from 1989 (Campbell 1996). Among the many ecocritics who have since entered into conversation with poststructuralist thinkers, see e.g. Murphy 1995, Morton 2007, and the chapters by Elvey, Cahoon and Lussier in Goodbody and Rigby 2011. On the 'new materialisms' see Coole and Frost 2010. On 'critical realism' and the question of 'nature, see Soper 1995. On 'speculative realism' and ecological thought, see Morton 2013.
5. The scope and diversity of ecocritical work is evident in the earliest anthologies edited by Glotfelty and Fromm (1996) and Kerridge and Sammells (1998). For current directions see the important new anthologies from Oxford and Cambridge, respectively, edited by Greg Garrard (2014) and Louise Westling (2013).
6. See e.g. Diamond 2005.
7. In his *Novum Organum*, for example, Bacon proposed that through the arts and sciences, humanity could 'recover that right over nature which belongs to it by divine bequest', and should endeavour 'to establish and extend the power and dominion of the human race itself over the [entire] earth' (Bacon 1870: 114–15).
8. In 1995 Scott Slovic also took over from Patrick Murphy as the editor of the main ecocriticism journal, *Interdisciplinary Studies in Literature and Environment* (*ISLE*).

9. The term 'heteroglossia' was used by the Russian literary theorist Bakhtin to describe the many voices that vie with one another in the form of the novel, and, more generally, the inevitably contextual and intertextual nature of meaning (Bakhtin 1981: 259–422, and 428). See also Murphy 1995, for an ecofeminist deployment of Bakhtinian dialogics.

10. This demotion is evident, e.g., in Armbruster's and Wallace's programmatically entitled anthology, *Beyond Nature Writing* (2000).

11. See also ecophilosopher Freya Mathews' model of 'ontopoetic' life writing (2009), within which narrative agency is attributed to the more-than-human world itself, to the extent that this is reconceived, panpsychically, as a communicative order with an inner mentalistic dimension.

12. See e.g. Tredinnick's anthology of Australian and North American nature writing (2003); Campbell's multi-authored exploration of landscapes, science and culture around the world (2010); and Hornung and Baisheng (2012) on environmental life-writing in Europe, Asia and America.

13. See e.g. McGann 1983 and Liu 1989, and Bate's critique of the New Historicist take on Wordsworth (Bate 1991: 1–6).

14. For an extended ecocritical treatment of Blake, see Lussier 1999.

15. E.g. Marshall (1994) devotes three chapters to Romanticism in his history of environmental thought. On Romantic natural history, see also Nichols 2004, and, on both English and German Romanticism, Rigby 2004 and Heringman 2004.

16. On ecofeminist philosophy, see e.g. Plumwood 1993. For a historical perspective, see e.g. Merchant 1980 and 1989. On ecofeminist social and political theory, see e.g. Sandilands 1999 and Cudworth 2005.

17. See e.g. Seymour 2013.

18. See also Roos and Hunt 2010; Huggan and Tiffin 2010; and DeLoughrey and Handley 2011.

19. See e.g. Adamson, Evans and Stein 2002, and Nixon 2011.

20. See also Bennett and Teague 1999 and Dixon 2001.

21. Abram's ecophilosophy is based, in part, on his reading of the phenomenology of Merleau-Ponty, whose work is of considerable interest to ecocritics because of his emphasis on corporeality and the 'flesh of the world'. For an ecocritical engagement with Merleau-Ponty's phenomenology, see e.g. Scigaj 1999 and Westling 2013.

22. See also Gilcrest 2002 and Knickerbocker 2012.

23. See also Fletcher 2004 and Jonathan Skinner's on-line journal of avant-garde ecopoetics at http://ecopoetics.wordpress.com.

24. Among the first publications to trigger this productive process of ecocritical self-reflection were Phillips 2003 and Cohen 2004.

25. See e.g. LeMenager et al. 2011; Goodbody and Rigby 2011; Müller and Sauter 2012; Westling 2013; Adamson and Ruffin 2013; Iovino and Oppermann 2014; and Garrard 2014.

26. See also Bate 1991: 102–3 and Rigby 2004: 81–6.

27. This discussion follows Ms. D in the Cornell edition (1977); references to the text are given according to line numbers.

28. It should nonetheless be recalled that the material cost of production was also borne by Wordsworth's long-suffering wife Mary, who transcribed all of Ms. D and a substantial part of Ms. B. Wordsworth's devoted sister Dorothy also transcribed part of the latter, as did William himself.

29. Wordsworth differentiates his depictions of the Lake District from earlier pastoral writing in his allusion to 'The idle breath of softest pipe attuned / To pastoral fancies' (406).

30. On reinhabitation, see e.g. Elder 1985: 40–74, and Lynch et al. 2012, especially the contributions by Serenella Iovino and Bart Welling.

31. I take this phrase from the title of anthropologist Deborah Bird Rose's book *Nourishing Terrains* (1996).
32. In addition to his many poetic works celebrating life in the Lake District, Wordsworth also wrote an extremely popular *Guide through to District of the Lakes* (1835; Bicknell 1984). Wordsworth was nonetheless very concerned about the likely impact of mass tourism, which he feared would be encouraged by the projected construction of a railway linking the Lake District to the growing urban centre of Liverpool. See his letters to the *Morning Post* (1844) in Bicknell 1984: 185–98. For an ecocritical discussion of the *Guide* and Wordsworth's objections to the railway, see Bate 1991: 41–52.

MATERIALITIES, IMMATERIALITIES, (A)MATERIALITIES, REALITIES

CRITICAL MAKING IN THE DIGITAL HUMANITIES

Roger Whitson

In 'An Attempt at a Compositionist Manifesto', Bruno Latour calls into question the work of critique by invoking Nietzsche's hammer. 'What performs a critique', according to Latour, 'cannot also compose. . . . With a hammer (or a sledge hammer) in hand you can do a lot of things: break down walls, destroy idols, ridicule prejudices, but you cannot repair, take care, assemble, reassemble, stitch together' (2010: 475). Latour's argument mistakes a common philosophical reading of Nietzsche's metaphor for the actual uses of hammers, which often repair things. Rubber mallets align drywall, ball-peen hammers strike metal when forging tools or weapons, lump hammers affix concrete blocks together with masonry nails, framing hammers construct the frames of wooden houses, and upholstery hammers secure fabric to furniture. Even sledgehammers create and repair, by driving spikes into the ground and connecting railroads with ties. The reading of a hammer as a purely destructive tool doesn't exhaust Nietzsche's own use of the word in *Twilight of the Idols, or, How to Philosophize with a Hammer*. As Bernd Magnus and Kathleen Higgins point out, 'Nietzsche identifies his hammer with a "tuning fork", not with a sledgehammer', and Nietzsche's use of the hammer 'is ambiguous like [Martin] Luther's, in which the hammer both smashes the sinner's pride and provokes the beginning of a positive process of transformation' (1996: 53).

Latour's blind spot surrounding the actual use of a hammer is symptomatic of a theoretical tradition within the humanities that has little experience with articulating a critical language about the importance of making things.[1] This lack of experience causes misunderstandings between those who practise textual criticism and those who construct tools for work in the digital humanities like databases, digital archives, distant reading algorithms and social media applications. Part of this difficulty lies in the fact that the language of making is articulated in different ways by different practitioners. Stephen Ramsay calls it 'building/making' and, in an article written with Geoffrey Rockwell, appeals to 'the quality of the interventions', rather than the modality as determining the worth of non-textual artifacts produced in the academy (Ramsay and Rockwell 2012: 83). When Jentery Sayers asked 'why do you make things?' on Twitter for an article called 'Making Things in the Digital Humanities', Bethany Nowviskie related the feeling of making to her memories of childhood which 'smell like sawdust and wood polish. We make things in my family and I'm not happy if I'm not building' (quoted in Sayers 2013). The very different responses by Ramsay and Rockwell, on the one hand, and Nowviskie on the other, suggest that there is little consensus on what constitutes making, how making interventions work differently in scholarly objects, or what the stake is for scholars working with compositional processes made possible by different technologies. Further, these complications mean that many humanities scholars – used to dealing professionally with the standards of written scholarship – do not easily identify with the smell of a woodshop or the material instrumentality of tinkering despite the fact that some of them engage in these activities daily.[2]

I believe that the emerging field of 'critical making' can act as a conceptual bridge between making practices and critical theory. 'Critical Making', as defined by practitioners like Matt Ratto and Stephen Hockema, 'is an elision of two typically disconnected modes of engagement in the world – "critical thinking", often considered as abstract, explicit, linguistically based, internal and cognitively individualistic; and "making", typically understood as material, tacit, embodied, external, and community-oriented' (Ratto and Hockema 2009: 58). In 'Critical Making: Conceptual and Material Studies in Technology and Social Life', Ratto emphasizes 'critique and expression rather than technological sophistication and function' and argues that the 'shared acts of making' and 'practice-based engagement' 'rather than the evocative object' are the focus (2011: 253). Garnet Hertz sees critical making as 'hands-on productive work' that can 'supplement and extend critical reflection on technology and society'. Hertz, Ratto and Hockema articulate their theories of critical making out of the DIY ('do-it-yourself') maker movement, which encourages the return to a hands-on approach to technology that is often connected to computation. One example of this kind of work is the construction of interactive projects using Arduino microprocessors. Arduino allows makers to construct objects that can receive sensory input, make algorithmic decisions about that input, and respond using some kind of mechanism. Programmers have created interactive talking mirrors, robotic hands that mimic human gestures, and portable web servers. Still, as Hertz points out, there is a relative lack of critical reflection in DIY culture that, all-too-often, is dazzled by the newest gadget.[3]

I'd like to historicize critical making by looking at two nineteenth-century figures whose work helps to enrich and broaden the traditions already associated with the maker movement: the craft practices of illuminated printer William Blake and the computer programmer Ada Lovelace. David Gauntlett has previously identified textile-maker William Morris and art critic John Ruskin as pioneers of the maker movement who see 'creativity as part of everyday life, and as a binding force in "fellowship" – which today we would call "community"' (2011: 25). Yet both figures are also indebted to Blake's idea that making evocative objects is a critical intervention into culture. While Ada Lovelace is not often associated with the maker movement, it is my argument that her work with Charles Babbage's analytical engine combines issues of gender, aesthetics and computation that are important to understanding the combination of creativity and mathematics alive in the movement today. This article will first establish what critical making meant to Blake before moving to Lovelace. Throughout, we will focus on process as an important part of their interventions. My interest in process emerges from Glenn Adamson's observation that modernist art criticism sidelined 'physical consideration[s]' of process 'so that other qualities – opticality, transcendence, aesthetic resolution, conceptual depth – [could] take center stage' (2007: xix). I agree that aesthetic categories like transcendence, resolution and depth have been critiqued by many strands of critical theory; however, this critique has overwhelmingly been conducted at the level of conceptual and textual analysis. Many traditions of critical theory have thus carried with them the assumptions of modernist art criticism in practice, if not always in theory. This is one of the reasons why I consider critical making an essential part of the digital humanities: making with one's hands reveals the material basis of technologies that seem to melt into endless abstraction. The very same impulse to abstract concepts in modernist art criticism causes a sense of computation that, in the words of Friedrich Kittler, sees 'data flows once confined to books ... disappearing into black holes and boxes that, as artificial intelligences, are bidding us farewell on their way to nameless high commands' (Kittler 1999: xxxix). By challenging the dichotomy between critical theory and the haptics of making, critical making broadens the work of the digital in humanities disciplines while encouraging theory to embrace process as a critical and tactile act.

WILLIAM BLAKE, PROPHETIC MAKER

I must Create a System, or be enslav'd by another Mans
I will not Reason & Compare: my business is to Create.

Blake, Jerusalem, 10.20; E 153

William Blake's mythological figure Los utters this proclamation on the tenth plate of the epic *Jerusalem, or the Emanation of the Giant Albion*. Los's attitude to the connection between liberty and creativity encapsulates Blake's contradictory stance towards collaboration and critical inquiry. Over and over again in his writing, Blake's words and actions underline his radical separation from the thinkers and authors of his day. Saree Makdisi sees this as a kind of impossible history in which liberty is defined not as a freedom *from* the oppressive power of the state 'but rather in creative, affirmative, positive terms, as the power to constitute "the eternal body of man"; as the power to imagine, and to create through imagining; as the power to affirm life as being in common' (2003: 2).[4] Despite his dream of common existence, Blake is also often seen as a wandering, alienated eccentric – someone who always desires community but who is rejected time and again. In the review of the single public exhibition Blake undertook during his life, Robert Hunt calls him 'an unfortunate lunatic, whose personal inoffensiveness secures him from confinement' (in Bentley 1969: 283).

It might be that Blake's ideas were too esoteric to be taken seriously. Blake's approach to critical making also confused his contemporaries because it gave his words, images and ideas the ability to be decontextualized from their original environment and appear in new ones. For Blake, making is constructed as a critical conversation with the past – a belief he expressed in his visionary conversations with biblical prophets, angels and poets, and in the many forms of marginalia found in his books. 'Opposition is true friendship', as he refrains in *The Marriage of Heaven and Hell* (1982: 42). Yet for Blake, opposition is never framed in terms of destruction but as a potential outlet for creativity. We see this approach highlighted in *Milton: A Poem* where the eponymous epic hero comes into conflict with Urizen, Blake's lawgiver on the shores of Arnon. Instead of vanquishing his foe,

> Milton took of the red clay of Succoth, moulding it with care
> Between his palms: and filling up the furrows of many years
> Beginning at the feet of Urizen, and on the bones
> Creating new flesh on the Demon cold, and building him
> As with new clay a Human form in the Valley of Beth Peor. (1982: 112)

Milton sees critical making as renewal, one that 'creates new flesh', from older materials. Likewise, Blake's work renews itself across history by constituting a kind of pre-internet creative commons with artists, musicians and thinkers who appropriate and recreate his work. Blake's phrases show up on T-shirts, his images are incorporated into comic panels, and his ideas and characters are featured in pop music, advertisements and films. With Jason Whittaker I defined this tendency of Blake's art to reappear in new and strange places as *zoamorphosis*, in which the work 'encourages – even demands – that people create their own work in response to his visions' (Whitson and Whittaker 2012: 4). By encouragement, we mean that not only does Blake's verbal-visual art, in Mike Goode's words, have a 'delinquent tendency . . . to de-compose itself whenever and wherever it finds an audience', but that the entire Blakean corpus can be seen as a call to the 'Young Men of the New Age' to practice critical making (Goode 2012: 5). Blake's illuminated poems are not simply signs for decoding. They are also tools for making.

One of the many examples of the way Blake supplies tools for later artists can be found in the composition of John Barnard Garland's decoupage called the *Victorian Blood Book*. The book was held in the collection of novelist and travel writer Evelyn Waugh before appearing in the University of Texas's Harry Ransom Center. According to the description of the book found on the center's website, the decoupage 'was assembled from several hundred engravings, many taken from books of etchings by William Blake, as well as other illustrations from early nineteenth-century books'. Apart from listing the Christian and natural images found in the book, along with noting the well-known tradition of Victorian scrap-booking, the curators at Austin offer no other reading of the 'enigmatic object'. Further, the proto-surrealist aesthetic images found in the *Victorian Blood Book* must strike the Robert Hunts of the world as courting lunacy. I suggest that – as part of the decoupage tradition – Garland's book isn't meant to be read at all, but enacts a methodology of critical making that reanimates the past in order to create a relationship that is at once personal and bodily. Consider a page integrating Blake's work from his edition of Robert Blair's *The Grave* into the overall design (Figure 8.1).

Figure 8.1: John Bingley Garland, *Victorian Blood Book*, 'To Amy Lester Garland – A legacy left in his lifetime for her future examination by her affectionate father',
1854. Collage. Collection of Evelyn Waugh. Reprinted with permission by the Henry Ransom Center, University of Texas at Austin.

Figure 8.2: William Blake, *Frontispiece to Robert Blair's* The Grave. Engraved by Luigi Schiavonetti, 1808. Intaglio Print. Collection of Robert N. Essick. Copyright © 2014 William Blake Archive. Used with permission.

Blake's image can be found in the middle of Garland's page, which is borrowed from the frontispiece of *The Grave*. Blake's illustrations are, themselves, critical interpretations of Blair's poem. Blake was originally commissioned to do the work by Robert Cromek, who subsequently (and much to Blake's consternation) gave the work to engraver Louis Schiavonetti. Blake had produced a series of drawings for the planned illustrations with the expectation that Cromek would allow him to produce the final engravings. However, according to Alexander Gilchrist, Cromek found the sample of engravings Blake gave to him grim, austere and archaic, and that giving the work to Schiavonetti 'would insure the success of the designs with the public as Blake could never have done were he to have engraved them himself' (Gilchrist 1907: 36).

Whether or not Schiavonetti produced better versions of Blake's drawings is less important to me than the layering of critical making practice already apparent in the frontispiece design (Figure 8.2). Blair's poem is appropriately Gothic in tone, going so far as to invoke the 'Eternal King! whose potent arm sustains / The keys of hell and death!' (Harry Ransom Center 2009). Blake adds his own metaphysical speculations in the frontispiece by featuring a skeleton separated from both angelic horns and fiery brimstone through the thin cloth covering him. The cloth could be seen, most obviously, as a burial shroud. Yet we also know through the work of Tristanne Connolly that Blake often uses shrouds and clothing as visual signifiers for the opening of the body found in works like *The Book of Urizen*. 'Not only Blake's works', Connolly suggests, 'but also the bodies they depict, are meant to be entered; their insides are meant to be visible, not made impenetrable by layers of skin' (2002: 32). The burial shroud and skin are transformed in Blake's designs into phenomenological X-ray lenses that portray the inner processes of his bodies. Neither the shroud nor the skin separate us from the processes of life and death they are usually seen as concealing. Instead they are bridges to what is otherwise unknown, unobserved and unseen. Whereas Blair's poem features an invisible King acting as its muse and connecting the readers to the otherness of the grave, Blake shows us that this otherness is all around us – seeing that otherness only requires a form of transparency that is at the heart of Blake's artistic process. As we know from *The Marriage of Heaven and Hell*, Blake imagines his approach to printing as 'the infernal method, by corrosives ... melting apparent surfaces away, and displaying the infinite which was hid (1982: 39). In the frontispiece to *The Grave*, Blake shows us just how much critical work an illustration can provide by simply adding a thin layer of cloth.

Of course, Blake's intervention is utterly complicated by its placement in Garland's comparatively traditional religious decoupage. Rebecca Onion (2013) opines that the book 'may have been a betrothal present from a father to his daughter' and that 'the religious sentiments and related visual effects didn't startle his family at all'. The central added image in the page from Garland's book, a red cross dripping blood, appears in several of Garland's pages and acts as an organizing motif (Figure 8.1). Blood also drips from many of the leaves and a smaller red cross appears on one of the tulips. It is remarkable how the angel from Blake's drawing is positioned descending from the central bloodied cross and features a red cross on his chest with feet circled by smaller angels, while also emphasizing the covering of the leaf over the figure's once exposed genitals. Indeed, one must question how much Blake's insights about shrouds and skin survive its recontextualization in the scrapbook. Many of the inscriptions merely reinforce notions of messianic sacrifice presumably signified by the blood, while celebrating a form of doctrinal obedience that is very far from Blake's visionary critique of religious oppression. The inscription above the cross reads 'Blessed is the Man! that trusteth in the Lord! and whose Hope! The Lord is! (Jer: 17.07)' (Harry Ransom Center 2009). To the side beneath the list of contents for the Blood Book on the left side of the page, we see

> Shudder not!__to pass__The Stream!
> Venture!__all thy care__on Him!
> Him! whose dying Love!__and Power!__
> Still'd__its passing__Hushed its roar!
> Safe as the expanded Wave!
> Gentle! as the Summer's Eve!
> Not one object of his Care!
> Ever – suffered Shipwreck__there!__ (Harry Ransom Center 2009)

The poem expresses a particularly conservative religious view about the resurrection, but it also powerfully illustrates how Blake's images can be decontextualized and transformed. Blake's work provides Garland with the tools to produce the *Victorian Blood Book*. We might note, as the curators at the University of Texas do, the 'grotesque' and 'surreal' aspects of the decoupage while asking 'how does one "read" such an enigmatic object?' (Harry Ransom Center 2009). But these questions almost seem beside the point when confronted with the book's layers of visual information along with its dislocation and decontextualization of Blake's artwork.

Something provided Garland with the desire and the opportunity to appropriate Blake's work into his decoupage. How did he do it? Did he have a hitherto unknown copy of Blake's illustrations to *The Grave* that he cut up and rearranged? Is there a specific type of signification from the frontispiece that worked to provide Garland his intended effect? Literary scholars used to investigating works as completed artifacts might find 'reading' the scrapbook an arduous task, especially if they are too focused on whether or not Garland represented Blake accurately or what place Garland might have in Victorian literary history. A further complication is that the historical tradition of decoupage has been eclipsed in humanities departments by Roland Barthes' use of the term to refer to a phenomenological category in his essay 'Diderot, Brecht, Eisenstein'. The 'Organon of Representation', Barthes writes, 'will have as its dual foundation the sovereignty of the act of cutting out [*decoupage*] and the unity of the subject of that action' (1977: 69–70). However useful this concept has become in critical theory, the conceptual popularity of Barthes' concept erases the tactile process of making a material decoupage in the Victorian period – leaving that process to be described in popular how-to manuals that ignore the cultural implications of specific material processes.[5]

Judith Flanders' *Inside the Victorian Home* is one of the few critical books that provide a short historical reference to decoupage. It does so while mentioning the litany of impractical hobbies that were imposed upon women as domestic alternatives to the workplace (Flanders 2004: 197). What do we miss when we favour decoupage as a theoretical category instead of appreciating it as a craft methodology? By placing 'reading' as the central skill of critical theorists and deemphasizing process and tactility, makers argue that we ignore potentially fruitful aspects of critical engagement.

ADA LOVELACE, POETICAL SCIENTIST

For, in so distributing and combining the truths and formulæ of analysis, that they may become most easily and rapidly amenable to the mechanical combinations of the engine, the relations and the nature of many subjects in that science are necessarily thrown into new lights, and more profoundly investigated.

Ada Lovelace, 'Notes for L. F. Menabrea's "Sketch of Charles Babbage's Analytical Engine"'

Seemingly explanatory asides to a technical essay, Ada Lovelace's notes act in reality as small experiments in the creative power of machines and mathematics. Lovelace is seen as a pioneer in computing, and continues to inspire women to participate in the sciences.[6] Unfortunately, her fame is eclipsed by her more celebrated father Lord Byron, as beliefs about her skill are clouded by misgivings that she was not the mathematician she imagined herself to be. Lovelace's biographer Betty Alexandra Toole (2010) insists that claims of her overinflated ego are sexist and that her understanding of mathematics 'is evidenced by her use of imagination and quantitative skills . . . She used color [in her letters] and what were then considered vulgar instruments – compasses and protractors. She scolded her students for using indirect proofs when a direct proof should be used.' Lovelace integrated the imaginative and the quantitative in such a way as to insist that mathematical proofs could be 'reinforced by the apt use of metaphor' (Toole 2010). Her linking of the metaphorical and the computational helps connect nineteenth-century poetry to making practices within digital methodologies in the humanities and the sciences. Even so, there is a dearth of critical work on Ada Lovelace.

This lack is symptomatic not only of a disciplinary ideology within academia that has difficulty conceptualizing a 'poetical scientist', but also of the relatively small number of women participating within STEM disciplines.[7] Perhaps the closest that many literary scholars have come to appreciating the history behind Lovelace's life involves her appearance in William Gibson and Bruce Sterling's steampunk novel *The Difference Engine*, in which she gives a speech anticipating Gödel's theorem after her father rises to prominence as the head of the Industrial Radical Party. The novel portrays her many lovers, mathematical genius and gambling problem, but largely passes over her interest in art and poetry. Mick Radley, a spy and computer hacker (or clacker) in the novel, wistfully discusses how the machines Lovelace creates with Babbage 'built the world' and suppressed the revolutions he had hoped to inspire among the working poor (Gibson and Sterling 1991: 27). Gibson and Sterling depict Ada Lovelace as obsessed with mathematics, while their invention of the engine turned Britain into an oppressive society of surveillance, numbers and mechanisms by short-circuiting the century's bourgeois rebellions.[8] Of course, as Jay Clayton argues, Lovelace's real life is much more interesting, and her view of technology more nuanced. 'She simply does not fit any of the customary categories – either of her age or of our own.' Clayton reasons, 'if she contradicts the usual image of an upper-class Victorian woman, she equally fails to conform to the few roles we have imagined for women who were "ahead of their time"' (2000: 118). This inability to situate Lovelace's political positions parallels a difficulty in understanding her critical approach to making, because it infuses poetry and music with science and mathematics. By combining these worlds, Lovelace asserts creative possibilities for mechanisms and algorithms, yet also ignores the distinctions that have subsequently emerged between art and science.

Her notes for Menabrea's article illustrate how Lovelace was able to envision creative uses for Babbage's mathematical concepts, particularly the more complicated functions performed by the analytical engine. Babbage originally designed the difference engine as a machine to help tabulate polynomial functions for use by shipping navigators and scientists (Figure 8.3). The British government gave Babbage £7,500 to complete the project, but it stalled due to costs that escalated beyond that amount. During Lovelace's life, Babbage consequently never manufactured a calculating engine. Menabrea's article was completed in a time when Babbage sought funding to complete a proposed analytical engine, which promised to add foresight and reaction to the first engine's ability to calculate. In Henry Wilmot Buxton's words, Babbage had wanted nothing less than to replace 'the marvelous pulp and fiber of a brain [with] brass and iron' (1983: 48–9). Menabrea saw that the engine could offer 'rigid accuracy', 'economy of time' and 'economy of intelligence' to shipping calculations. Its value lay primarily in its use as a 'real manufactory of numbers, which . . . lend[s] its aid to those many useful sciences and arts that depend on numbers' (1843: 689). Menabrea recognized, moreover, that no one 'can forsee the consequences of such an invention', since 'many precious observations remain practically barren for the progress of the sciences, because there are not powers sufficient for computing the results'. His comments bordered on the utopian, as he exclaimed that the application of the machine to newer scientific problems would 'mark a glorious epoch in the history of the sciences' (1843: 689–90).[9]

Lovelace's notes tell a slightly different story. Not only does she realize that the engine has the potential to calculate solutions for numerical problems, she imagines that they *'weave . . . algebraical patterns* just as the Jacquard

PORTION OF BABBAGE'S DIFFERENCE ENGINE.

Figure 8.3: Benjamin Herschel Babbage, *Difference Engine No. 1*. Woodcut.
Harper's Magazine, 30:175 (December 1864), 34.

loom weaves flowers and leaves' (Menabrea 1843: 697). While Babbage was invested in logic, Lovelace turned increasingly to creative uses for computation. Her reference to the loom of Joseph Marie Jacquard is particularly apt, since Babbage based his first design for the difference engine on the punch cards used to control the processes of the loom. As punch cards proved to be foundational in standardizing the operations of Babbage's analytical engine, Herbert Sussman argues that the Jacquard loom 'could weave an infinite number of patterns through algorithms programmed into these cards that functioned as a form of external memory' (2009: 45). Yet Lovelace's analogical invocation of the Jacquard loom establishes a refreshingly poetic approach to its code. We see her imagination winding patterns of algebraical formulae like a weaver interlaces looms of thread to create artistic patterns of fabric, even as Babbage, Jacquard and Menabrea show more interest in the repeatable and industrial uses of their machines to mass produce cheap commodities.[10]

Lovelace's form of creativity is similar to Blake's since it relies heavily upon a critical approach to collaborating with other people. For instance, Menabrea argues that the central dilemma facing the development of correct tabular data is that most previous machines have depended upon 'the continual intervention of a human agent to regulate their movements, and thence arises a source of errors' (1843: 670). For Menabrea, this simply means that the Engine – which needs no human agent – frees up the operator to engage in reasoning and understanding and makes it less likely that errors will complicate mathematical processes. Lovelace expands this insight in her notes by speculating that the Analytical Engine 'is not merely adapted for *tabulating* the results of one particular function and no other, but for *developing and tabulating* any function whatever. In fact the engine may be described as being the material expression of any indefinite function of any degree of generality and complexity' (Menabrea 1843: 691). Here, she calls the engine a material creation of a function – imparting an agency to mathematics itself. In her definition of Lovelace's poetical science, Betty Elizabeth Toole suggests that this approach to studying mathematics gave Lovelace 'a broad vision of the future' (2010). But the integrative aspect of Lovelace's approach also allowed her to formulate the first computer program: an algorithm that uses the analytical engine to automatically generate Bernouli numbers.

Bernouli numbers are a sequence of rational numbers discovered in the seventeenth century by Jacob Bernouli and Seki Kowa. The number sequence is related to various mathematical theorems, including Fermat's last theorem and the Riemann zeta function. More important for our purposes is the fact that Lovelace uses a critical methodology to conceptualize a machine capable of generating numbers. This generation is particularly important in her understanding of the computer program. Whereas Menabrea and Babbage's realism sees calculating as the fundamental power of the engine, in that it could potentially model the fundamental structure of nature, Lovelace's poeticism underscores the primary importance of the engine as something that produces things.

Solutions are seen as the creative output of the engine, which, as she speculates, 'could compose elaborate and scientific pieces of music' (Toole 2010). As a poetical scientist, Lovelace sees no difference between an operator of the analytical machine tweaking algorithms and a musician tuning an instrument.

MATERIAL HISTORIES / DIGITAL HUMANITIES

Both Blake and Lovelace envision systems that involve creativity and a critical focus on material process. Critical making offers an alternative vision of the digital humanities as a discipline fundamentally interested in the critical understanding of material processes. Richard Sennett uses the term 'material consciousness' to designate methodologies that 'depend on curiosity about the material at hand', as well as to observe that 'we become particularly interested in the things we can change' (2009: 120). In this view, critical making takes on a Heideggerian orientation, in which 'the act of hammering itself discovers the particular "handiness" of the hammer' (Heidegger 1996: 65). We understand tools by using them, but the more we use them, the more they become invisible to us, until they reside simply as an unacknowledged extension of our bodies. Levi Bryant (2012) explains that 'the perpetual hammering on the metal of the anvil produces corporeal changes in the smith's body. His muscle structure, bone structure, and way of holding himself change over time.' Instead of simply being an image or a signifier of critique as a form of conceptual destruction, as in Latour's invocation of Nietzsche's hammer, critique emerges as a tactile methodology involved in investigating, speculating upon, and experimenting with material changes enacted by making processes.

Material changes are also *historical* and *sedimented* in nature, as Jussi Parikka explains in terms of the media archaeology field, which 'sees media cultures as layered, a fold of time and materiality where the past might be suddenly discovered anew, and the new technologies grow obsolete increasingly fast' (2012: 3). The folds of digital history are not linear, but anachronistic and – in the words of Erriki Huhtamo – include 'cyclical phenomena which (re) appear and disappear and reappear over and over again in media history and somehow seem to transcend specific historical contexts' (1997: 222). History does not, in Lori Emerson's words, 'reveal the present as an inevitable consequence of the past but instead . . . describe[s] it as one possibility generated out of a heterogeneous past' (2014). Critical making combines Derridean hauntology, Foucauldian (media) archaeology, Benjaminian now-time, the uncanny, and retrofuturism with figures like Sigfried Zielinski who, in *Deep Time of the Media*, urges historians to 'do some recycling [and] search through the heaps of refuse [in order to uncover] some shining jewels from what has been discarded or forgotten' (2006: 2).[11] History is material: formed from an ever growing pile of corpses and objects that decompose, mix together, are uncovered, repurposed, transformed, and make up the ground beneath our feet. 'Objects are never inert', Hertz and Parikka write in their aptly titled 'Zombie Media', 'but consist of various temporalities, relations, and potentials that can be brought together and broken apart. Things break apart anyhow – especially high technology – and end up as inert objects, dead media, discarded technology. Yet, dead media creeps back as dangerous toxins in the soil, or alternatively as zombie media recycled into new assemblies' (2012: 428–9). Blake's printing process might inspire new approaches to three-dimensional printing. Babbage's difference engine might find new life in steampunk design. The tendency of so many technologies to become invisible or abandoned requires a methodology that digs into the sedimented layers of digital history, breaks open objects, rewires and transforms them.

Consider the growing popularity of circuit-bending. Circuit-bending involves the breaking open of low-voltage consumer electronics to expose their circuit boards, then probing for potential connections between circuits – called bends – that can be stimulated with current to produce novel visual or audio effects. Circuit-bending pioneer Reed Ghazala describes it as a way to explore 'synthesis and experimental music', in which he could create 'all kinds of interesting sounds. Animals, insects, machinery, wind, thunder, and endless abstract, unrecognizable noises could be produced' (2004: 98). The spirit of circuit-bending is artistic, not scientific. Schematics are often not part of the process. Mistakes happen that fry circuits, cause electrocutions, start fires. Yet they also have a critical component. For Hertz and Parikka, bending experiments 'traverse . . . through the hidden content inside a technological system for the joy of entering its concealed underlayer, often breaking apart and reverse engineering the device'. They associate circuit-bending with 'early-20th-century wireless and radio culture', 'hobbyism, or DIY-tinkering that was typified in organizations like the Homebrew Computer Club' (2012: 426). They also suggest that it provides an image of digital culture that is 'customized, trashy, and folksy' (2012: 427). Imagine what a scholar or artist inspired by Blake's proto-surrealist visions might do with a 'bent' device like an X-Box Kinect, normally used to map motion for bodily-interactive gaming. For the Blakean interested in self-annihilation, other-bodily experiences, and a visionary materiality that Claire Colebrook calls 'haptic', in which 'the viewing eye [is allowed to] "feel" the scars and surfaces of the text', the Kinect might be an ideal device to bend (Colebrook 2012: 138). The connections between the body, printing and proprioception in Blake's work make the study of an altered sense of materiality central to understanding him. Altering the normal settings of the Kinect to map the body incorrectly could induce proprioceptive illusions and make the body seem out of joint with its environment, its time, or even with itself. The multitude of interactive devices surrounding us that locate and surveil our bodies, from motion detectors to GPS, webcams, digital cameras and tagging applications on Facebook, scream for a form of critical analysis that goes beyond written essays and starts engaging with objects, codes and electronic circuits. In other words, a folksy approach to critical making has the potential to challenge what Jonathan Crary has called a rising 'institutional intolerance of whatever obscures or prevents an instrumentalized and unending condition of visibility' (2013: 5).

The retrofuturist impulse of critical making can also help to nuance the futurism found in many discourses surrounding the digital humanities. I agree with the authors of *Digital_Humanities* when they suggest 'this is a galvanizing moment to be a humanist involved in devising, designing, and deploying new tools; in opening expanded modes of inquiry unthinkable in pre-digital conditions; and in forging innovative multimodal approaches to traditional questions' (Burdick et al. 2012: 9). A truly material approach to critical making mixes these innovative technologies and approaches with the various sedimented layers of digital history from which they emerge, fusing them together with wires, melted plastic and welded metal filler. Developing attentiveness to modality and materiality, perhaps heightened by the digitization of texts and the 3D printing of museum artifact models, also requires scholars to acquaint themselves with older tools and objects.[12] Matt Ratto and Megan Boler argue that critical making 'invites reflection on the relationship of the maker to the thing produced, reflection on how the elements (whether nuts and bolts, bits and bytes, or breath, blood, flesh, brain, and neurons) work together – in short, consideration and awareness of the mediated and direct experiences of interacting with the material world' (2014: 3). The true benefit of a making culture situated within the digital humanities is *networked* and *ecological* in character. Critical making encourages forms of scholarly collaboration that have previously been hidden under the modernist ideology of individual authorship and connects scholars with materialities obscured by discursive ideologies. While in the US the National Endowment for the Humanities looks increasingly to the digital humanities as a source for producing wealth in the form of the 'innovative' and 'new', critical making provides a vision of the field that – at once – pushes beyond traditional forms of discourse and resists the relentless and ecologically destructive late capitalist drive toward the dust-bin of history.[13]

QUESTIONS FOR FURTHER CONSIDERATION

1. Consider the 'critical' in Matt Ratto's definition of 'critical making'. Imagine yourself reading a poem and analyzing it critically. What is 'abstract, explicit, linguistically based, internal, and cognitively individualistic' about thinking 'critically'? How, by contrast, can we understand making – whether we are working on an experiment in a science class or painting a room of a house with our family or friends – as 'material, tacit, embodied, external, and community-oriented?' What is at stake in critical making when figures like Blake or Lovelace try to bring these modes of engagement together?

2. Memes in digital culture are seen as creative projects where users combine new ideas with common cultural images or sayings. Consider Charles Hancock's series of 'Blake memes' (http://blakememes.tumblr.com). Compare them to the memes he draws from (the trollface, the hipster, Y U No, the reaction guys) on Meme Generator (http://

memegenerator.net) How does Hancock use the memes he creates to critique Blake and his ideas?

3. Look at Blake's 'Proverbs of Hell' from *The Marriage of Heaven and Hell*. You can find the poem on the William Blake Archive (http://www.blakearchive.org/blake/erdman.html). Navigate: THE WORKS IN ILLUMINATED PRINTING / THE MARRIAGE OF HEAVEN AND HELL / Proverbs of Hell. Now, using the MemeGenerator or any other creative commons image (search for them at http://search.creativecommons.org), create your own Blake meme that illustrates, expands upon, subverts, or otherwise transforms the meaning of Blake's proverb. Explain how the practice of remaking Blake's work changes your interpretation or understanding of its meaning.

4. Ada Lovelace is an important figure in the digital humanities not only because she wrote the first computer program, but also because programming (like science) is often seen as a masculine practice. Why are science fields seen as masculine, while literary and arts fields are often seen as more feminine? What can be done about this perception?

5. It could be argued that Ada Lovelace's interest in developing 'poetical science' is due to the fact that she was part of a culture that did not distinguish science from the study of humanities fields like philosophy and literature. Consider Nick Montfort's 'Taroko Gorge' (http://nickm.com/poems/taroko_gorge_original.html) and Zach Whalen's ROM_TXT twitterbot (https://twitter.com/rom_txt) along with an interview where Whalen discusses his work (http://blogs.loc.gov/digitalpreservation/2014/05/when-literature-professors-bots-read-collections-of-roms-an-interview-with-zach-whalen). How are these projects forms of 'poetical science'?

6. Another example of critical making comes from Georgia Tech professor Hugh Crawford, who asks his students to build a replica of Henry David Thoreau's house after reading Thoreau's book *Walden* (http://www.thoreauhouse.org). Consider your favourite novel or poem and devise a project that combines a critical analysis of that work with a creative response. What material or tools (no matter how banal) are needed to complete the project?

BIBLIOGRAPHY

'The Ada Initiative' (2013) *Adainitiative.org*.
Adamson, Glenn (2007) *Thinking through Craft*, Oxford and New York: Berg.
Barthes, Roland (1977) 'Diderot, Brecht, Eisenstein', *Image, Music, Text*, trans. Stephen Heath, New York: Hill & Wang.
Benjamin, Walter (1968) 'Theses on the Philosophy of History', in *Illuminations*, ed. Hannah Arendt, trans. Harry Zohn, New York: Harcourt, Brace & World.
Bentley, G. E. (1969) *Blake Records*, Oxford: Clarendon Press.
Blake, William (1982) *The Complete Poetry and Prose of William Blake*, ed. David V. Erdman, Berkeley: University of California.

Burdick, Anne, Peter Lunefield, Johanna Drucker, Todd Presner and Jeffrey Schnapp (2012) *Digital_Humanities*, Cambridge MA: MIT Press.

Brooke-Smith, James (2013) 'Numbers, Medium, Nature: Wordsworth and Babbage Compose the Universe', *Romantic Circles Praxis* (April).

Bryant, Levi (2012) 'A Brief Note on Incorporeal Machines', *Larvalsubjects.wordpress. com*.

Buxton, Harry Wilmot (1983) *The Life of Charles Babbage MS Buxton 16 and 17, from the University of Oxford, Museum of the History and Science*, Oxford: University of Oxford, Museum of the History and Science.

Clayton, Jay (2000) 'Hacking the Nineteenth Century', in John Kucich and Dianne F. Sadoff, eds., *Victorian Afterlife: Postmodern Culture Rewrites the Nineteenth Century*, Minneapolis: University of Minnesota.

Clayton, Jay (2003) *Charles Dickens in Cyberspace: The Afterlife of the Nineteenth Century in Postmodern Culture*, Oxford: Oxford University Press.

Colebrook, Claire (2012) *Blake, Deleuzian Aesthetics and the Digital*, London: Bloomsbury Academic.

Connolly, Tristanne J. (2002) *William Blake and the Body*, Basingstoke: Palgrave Macmillan.

Crary, Jonathan (2013) *24/7: Late Capitalism and the Ends of Sleep*, London and New York: Verso.

Emerson, Lori (2014) *Reading Writing Interfaces: From the Digital to the Bookbound*, Minneapolis: University of Minnesota Press (Kindle edition).

Flanders, Judith (2004) *Inside the Victorian Home: A Portrait of Domestic Life in Victorian England*, New York: W. W. Norton.

Gauntlett, David (2011) *Making is Connecting: The Social Meaning of Creativity, from DIY and Knitting to YouTube and Web 2.0*, London: Polity.

Ghazala, Reed (2004) 'The Folk Music of Chance Electronics: Circuit-Bending the Modern Coconut', *Leonardo Music Journal* 14, pp. 97–104.

Gibson, William and Bruce Sterling (1991) *The Difference Engine*, New York: Bantam.

Gilchrist, Alexander (1907) *The Life of William Blake*, London: John Lane, the Bodley Head.

Goode, Mike (2012) 'The Joy of Looking: What Blake's Pictures Want', *Representations* 119:1, pp. 1–36.

Harry Ransom Center (2009) '"Victorian Blood Book" from the Library of Evelyn Waugh', *Hrc.utexas.edu*.

Heidegger, Martin (1996) *Being and Time: A Translation of Sein Und Zeit*, trans. Joan Stambaugh, Albany: State University of New York.

Hertz, Garnet (2012) 'Making Critical Making', in Garnet Hertz, ed., *Critical Making: Introduction*, Hollywood: Telharmonium Press.

Hertz, Garnet (2013) 'Critical Making', *Conceptlab.com*.

Hertz, Garnet and Jussi Parikka (2012) 'Zombie Media: Circuit Bending Media Archaeology into an Art Method', *Leonardo* 45:5, pp. 424–30.

Hertz, Garnet, Daniela K. Rosner, Steven L. Jackson, Lara Houston and Nimmi Rangaswamy (2013) 'Reclaiming Repair: Maintenance and Mending as Methods for Design', *CHI 2013 Extended Abstracts*, pp. 3311–14.

Holmes, Richard (2008) *The Age of Wonder: How the Romantic Generation Discovered the Beauty and Terror of Science*, New York: Pantheon.

Huhtamo, Erriki (1997) 'From Kaleidoscomaniac to Cybernerd: Notes Toward an Archaeology of Media', *Leonardo* 3:3, pp. 221–4.

Kirschenbaum, Matt (2006) *Mechanisms: New Media and the Forensic Imagination*, Cambridge MA: MIT Press.

Kittler, Friedrich (1999) *Gramophone, Film, Typewriter*, trans. Geoffrey Winthrop-Young and Michael Wutz, Stanford: Stanford University Press.

Kraus, Kari (2015) *Hopeful Monsters: Computing, Counterfactuals and the Long Now of Things*, Cambridge MA: MIT Press.

Latour, Bruno (2010) 'An Attempt at a "Compositionist Manifesto"', *New Literary History* 41:3, pp. 471–90.

Latour, Bruno (2011) 'Networks, Societies, Spheres: Reflections of an Actor-Network Theorist', *International Journal of Communication* 5, pp. 796–810.

Lovelace, Ada King and Betty A. Toole (1998) *Ada, the Enchantress of Numbers: Prophet of the Computer Age, a Pathway to the 21st Century*, Mill Valley CA and Sausalito CA: Strawberry; Critical Connection.

Mack, Eric (2013) 'Smithsonian Now Allows Anyone To 3D Print (Some) Historic Artifacts', *Forbes.com*.

Magnus, Bernd and Kathleen Higgins, eds. (1996) *The Cambridge Companion to Nietzsche*, Cambridge: Cambridge University Press.

Makdisi, Saree (2003) *William Blake and the Impossible History of the 1790s*, Chicago: University of Chicago Press.

Makdisi, Saree (2011) 'Empire and Human Energy', *PMLA* 126.2, pp. 318–20.

Manning, Hiram (1969) *Manning on Decoupage*, New York: Hearthside.

Menabrea, F. L. (1843) 'Sketch of the Analytical Engine Invented by Charles Babbage', trans. and notes Ada Lovelace, *Scientific Memoirs* 3 (1843), pp. 666–731.

Montfort, Nick, Patsy Baudoin, John Bell, Ian Bogost, Jeremy Douglass, Mark C. Marino, Michael Mateas, Casey Reas, Mark Sample and Noah Vawter (2013) *10 PRINT CHR$(205.5 RND(1));:GOTO 10*, Cambridge MA: MIT Press.

Onion, Rebecca (2013) 'The Creepy, Beautiful "Blood Book" Made By A Scrapbooking Victorian Gentleman', *Slate Magazine*, 31 October.

Parikka, Jussi (2012) *What is Media Archaeology?* London: Polity.

Pryce, Maggie and Nicki Dowey (2000) *Decoupage*, New York: Lorenz.

Ramsay, Stephen (2011) 'On Building', *Stephenramsay.us*.

Ramsay, Stephen and Geoffrey Rockwell (2012) 'Developing Things: Notes toward an Epistemology of Building in the Digital Humanities', in Matthew K. Gold, ed., *Debates in the Digital Humanities*, Minneapolis: University of Minnesota Press.

Ratto, Matt and Stephen Hockema (2009) 'FLWR PWR: Tending the Walled Garden', *Criticalmaking.com*.

Ratto, Matt (2011) 'Critical Making: Conceptual and Material Studies in Technology and Social Life', *The Information Society* 27:4, pp. 252–60.

Ratto, Matt and Megan Boler, eds. (2014) *DIY Citizenship: Critical Making and Social Media*, Cambridge MA: MIT Press.

Rawlings, Eleanor Hasbrouck (1975) *Decoupage: The Big Picture Sourcebook*, New York: Dover Publications.

Sayers, Jentery (2013) 'Making Things in the Digital Humanities', *Projectroomseattle. org*.

Sennett, Richard (2009) *The Craftsman*, Cambridge: Harvard University Press.

Solomon, Robert C. and Kathleen Marie Higgins (2000) *What Nietzsche Really Said*, New York: Schocken.

Sussman, Herbert L. (2009) *Victorian Technology: Invention, Innovation, and the Rise of the Machine*, Santa Barbara: Praeger.

Toole, Betty Elizabeth (2010) *Ada, the Enchantress of Numbers: Poetical Science*, Sausalito: Critical Connection (Kindle edition).

Whitson, Roger and Jason Whittaker (2013) *William Blake and the Digital Humanities: Collaboration, Participation, and Social Media*, New York: Routledge.

Zielinski, Siegfried (2006) *Deep Time of the Media: Toward an Archaeology of Hearing and Seeing by Technical Means*, Cambridge MA: MIT Press.

NOTES

1. I use Latour here fully knowing that he is generally very aware of materiality in his work. For example, he argues in the article 'Networks, Societies, Spheres: Reflections of an Actor-Network Theorist' that 'the expansion of digitality has enormously increased the *material* dimension of networks: the more digital, the *less virtual and more material* a given activity becomes'. Latour continues with a number of examples: When Harold Garfunkel described the skills necessary to 'pass' as a member of a society, you 'could say it was a totally intangible social phenomenon that could only be qualitatively described, but not today when every detail of your avatars on the Web can be counted, dated, weighed, and measured. Then you know that everything that before had melted into air has become fully incarnated. Go tell Google engineers that their vast arrays of servers are just virtual!' (Latour 2011: 802). My comment about Latour's discussion of the hammer, then, identifies a slip into the very form of abstract thinking he aligns with Garfunkel's print-inspired abstraction about social phenomena.

2. When Stephen Ramsay called out Alan Liu, who created and maintains the celebrated online academic portal *Voice of the Shuttle*, for trying to 'describe himself as not being a builder', Ramsay (2011) retorts that Liu 'can talk all he wants about being a *bricoleur*, but we can see the grease under his fingernails'. It's almost as if Liu, a scholar whose prolific work has transformed not only the field of British Romantic Literature but also that of New Historicism and the digital humanities, didn't want to get his hands dirty by identifying with maker culture. Since then, Liu has become even more involved in the digital humanities community, but his one-time reticence forms a model for the kinds of cultural divides apparent within humanities circles. Indeed, many digital humanities scholars appeal to forms of making as 'a new kind of hermeneutic', to use Ramsay's words (2011)

3. In their CHI 2013 position paper for the 'Reclaiming Repair Workshop', Hertz et al. discuss how the leading magazine of the maker movement, *Make Magazine*, 'tends to celebrate the creative process of invention and its tactical stance is just to make things' (2013: 1). They also claim that, in order to have impact upon culture, making 'needs to mobilize its material craft in the repair and hacking of society [and approach] the world as a system to be hacked' (2013: 2). Likewise, in the introduction to his *Critical Making* anthology, Hertz argues that *Make Magazine* avoids reporting on political forms of making like 'circuit bending work that is interested in opening up with the sealed black boxes of consumer electronics, media archaeological work that is interested in history and intervening and playing with it, or people that are into making custom "bespoke" things like lowrider cars or bikes' (2012: 2).

4. Makdisi recognizes the communities outside of Blake's historical period formed by his work. Specifically, Makdisi suggests that Blake 'is in many senses closer to T. S. Eliot or Wilfred Owen than to Charlotte Smith or John Keats; visually, he has far more in common with Pablo Picasso and Edvard Munch than with Thomas Gainsborough and Joshua Reynolds . . .; aurally he is close, on the one hand to Beethoven . . . and on the other hand to John Coltrane and Ornette Coleman . . .; philosophically, he is far closer to Benedict de Spinoza than to his contemporaries Jeremy Bentham and James Mill; politically he is the ally of Gerrard Winstanley rather than of Tom Paine' (2011: 319).

5. Some examples of these books include Eleanor Hasbrouck Rawlings's *Decoupage: The Big Picture Sourcebook* (1975), Maggie Pryce's *Decoupage* (2000), and Hiriam Manning's *Manning on Decoupage* (1969).

6. See for instance the Ada Initiative, a non-profit organization that 'supports women in open technology and culture through activities like producing codes of conduct and anti-harassment policies, advocating for gender diversity, teaching allies, and

hosting conferences for women in open tech/culture' (Ada Initiative 2013). One of their initiatives, AdaCamp, is an unconference dedicated to involving women in open source computing.

7. STEM refers to science, technology, engineering and mathematics. As many historians of science have noted, 'science' as a discrete field with a specific methodology did not exist prior to the Victorian period. For Richard Holmes, William Whewell was foundational in the professionalization of science as he 'proposed that, by analogy with the term "artist", they might form scientist' (2008: 449). As such, the branching off of science as a professional enterprise was less common during Lovelace's life than it would be later on in the century.

8. For Clayton, *The Difference Engine* unfortunately 'ends up affirming the alliance between technology and traditional Victorian assumptions about female sexuality, empire, and the police' (Clayton 2003: 190).

9. As James Brooke-Smith (2013) argues, Babbage saw machines as capable of 'mediating the world in such a way as to reveal its foundational logic and structure'.

10. This sense of code as music, text or poetry survives in the form of critical code studies, which according to the authors of *10 PRINT CHR$(205.5+RND(1)); GOTO 10* approaches computer code 'as a cultural text reflecting the history and context of its creation'. Codes are, further, 'embedded with stories of a program's making, its purpose, its assumptions, and more' (Montfort et al. 2013: 3).

11. Zielinski's understanding of recycling draws from Benjamin's angel of history who 'sees one single catastrophe which keeps piling wreckage upon wreckage and hurls it in front of his feet' (Benjamin 1968: 257).

12. On 13 November 2013, *Forbes* reported that the 'Smithsonian Now Allows Anyone to 3D Print (Some) Historic Artifacts', and argued that 'the benefits for the general public who might not otherwise ever be able to the Smithsonian to see these artifacts up close is obvious' (Mack 2013). The article also mentions the use of the printer for educational purposes and as an alternative to the 'full excavation and potentially damaging removal and relocation of precious artifacts'.

13. See Hertz and Parikka (2012: 425), where they argue that critical making protests the ideology of planned obsolescence, or 'artificially decreasing the lifespan of consumer commodities – as with new fashions that make old clothing appear outdated [which] increases the speed of obsolescence and stimulates the need to purchase'.

(A)MATERIAL CRITICISM

Tom Cohen

1

One is always, tradition suggests, after 'materiality' – that is, not only in pursuit of a promised ground or ontology that is also worldly, associable with reference and the 'thing', historical process or analysis, a real, but temporally after (as the model of the hunt suggests too), as though the term were bound nonetheless to linguistic traces, to something anterior to figurative systems.

The chapter I propose will track a key path by which the term 'materiality' is put in play on the coming horizons by a hybridization of the Marxian with the deconstructive traditions. With this in mind, I begin with a brief review of continuing spells that the word 'materiality' holds over sociological and political criticism – and why that seems at an impasse. The Aristotelian *hule* – one *ur*-term for 'matter' (linked to the stuff of wood) – was itself made possible by a Platonic binary in which it had been sustained by opposition to variable others (mind/body, spirit/matter). It promised a non-human – which is to say, extra-linguistic – or mute real whose legacy would be heard in the dialectical appeal of classical Marxism, for which 'material' and economic processes mapped along abstract schemata (base/superstructure) might both interpret and execute a programmed narrative for the overcoming of capitalist models. Can the term be used as a tool of reading or literary analysis, however, in an era of so-called 'globalization' where, to use Avital Ronell's term (1989), 'switchboards' of teletechnicity disperse and reroute notions of fixed historical events and material facts, redirecting definitions of memory, the 'human', the 'event' and performance?

To mark a use of 'materiality' in the afterlife of this term, we might speak of a certain *(a)materiality* – a ghostly materiality, perhaps, that persists in the cancellation of past associations with or promises of the irreducible real. Yet it may be here that the appeal of this term, still, to critical and 'literary' reading may find resonance, rather than in the archival and 'dialectical materialist' traditions that have used this assertion of ground as an appeal to historical fact. Rather than asserting a referential real or economic processes as the ontological ground of reference, such (a)materiality might locate itself at the junctures between linguistic performance and historial events, anterior programmes and mnemotechnic projections, inscription and 'experience'.[1] After reviewing one direction that such a prospect leads, I will suggest possible ways in which such (a)materialist reading strategies – when applied to canonical works, in this case Faulkner and Hitchcock – might partake of an ongoing epistemo-political transformation in post-humanist critical culture.

The term 'materiality', it turns out, persists today with a lure tied to various epistemo-critical programmes (historicism, pragmatism, empiricism, etc.) and thus this rich and diverse set of critical traditions maintains the 'ideological' mystifications of a metaphysical model. To displace these, we might appeal to directions indicated by Walter Benjamin's trope of 'materialistic historiography', and to where that model demands a return to a conception of the material event bound to inscription, memory, temporality and political intervention. How is this complicated, or translated, by contact with the problem – proper to linguistic and literary studies to come – of the 'materiality' of inscriptions? The latter phrase comes from Paul de Man, who in this respect is a continuer of Benjamin's project – although directing the latter from metaphoric grandeur to the engineering involved in a close reading of, and intervention in, potential programmes which generate world-views and perception. The topic shifts from tracking 'ideology' to intervening within a historial programme.

BENJAMIN'S LEAP

Rather than name and guarantee unfettered access to a mute real, the 'materiality' of language and mnemonics complicates future horizons of this tradition irremediably – at once suspending and reinscribing it, transitionally, in and as a kind of (a)materiality. On the one hand, we may point to the brute material networks that sustain linguistic memory and programme perception (or hermeneutics), such as so-called 'material' signifiers – letters, sounds, inscriptions. On the other, this reflexive turn seems to precede and itself produce various systems of reference, value or association. 'Materiality' would seem an effecting-effect produced within and by signifying networks already replete with mnemonic imperatives, hermeneutic assignations, tropes.[2] 'Materiality', as (a)materiality, enters the new century burdened by this ghostliness: as a term, it is retired with the classic metaphysical monuments, yet rather than disappear, it mutates, marks that absence, and appears re-engaged around a problem of interest to reading: how do we track an (a)material and mnemonic effect that precedes and programmes figurative systems, particularly if it itself is defined by the absence of metaphor, something prefigural, like the black-hole and facticity of an inscription?[3] What, in the critical and 'literary' reading practices of an era programmed less by the hegemony of the Book than teletechnicity and mnemotechnics more generally, might 'materiality' come to signify? Why, moreover, must a reinscription of this term alter not only our conception of the 'literary', or the event, but temporality, signalling an intervention in how past and future might be structured or produced?

We may root this discussion – at the juncture between rethinking Marxian and linguistic problematics – in directions indicated by Walter Benjamin's work. In his 'Theses on History', for example, he introduces the trope of a 'materialistic historiography (*der materialistischen Geschichtsschreibung*)' (Benjamin 1968: 262; 1961: 278) as one name for an engagement with historial networks that links linguistic performance – an intervention in reading and writing – to a redeployment of Marxian and theological figures. His programme suspends linear historical narratives and condemns 'historicism' – a term encompassing various epistemological regimes that archive history and its 'facts' – as complicit with a 'fascist' current in political thought. He seems to envision a return to a conception of the material event bound to inscription, memory, temporality and political intervention. This last is imperative, for Benjamin, by repeating the odd phrase 'materialistic historiography' rather than 'historical materialism', say, seems to invoke a type of writing of history (*graphy*), of the 'present(s)', multiply and mutually encased, that stands to reinscribe the past epistemo-critical programmes (politics, here, is conceived of also as an epistemological regime), and alters the site where inscriptions are encountered as already installed. Benjamin not only dovetailed the thinking of philosophic concepts with a meditation on linguistic performance (or literature), but identifies a moment in this conjuncture where received 'history' in the form of mnemonic programmes may be performatively contested, interrupted, opened to recasting. As such, the 'materiality' appealed to would seem to be located not in the world's objects but in *mnemonic* constellations and representational regimes, which for Benjamin programme the senses (or 'sensoria'). Which is also to say programme models of reading, archivism, the legislations of reference. If history is not a string of occurrences that have been mythologized and recorded but is an effect produced (within a certain archive), what strategies for turning that system back on itself stand to performatively intervene at some seemingly pre-originary site where mnemonic regimes are installed or set – offering a break with them? 'Materialistic historiography' wants to name what Benjamin sweepingly opposes to 'historicism', in the same way that a *performative* reading or reinscription which would have the potential to rewire history stands opposed to the archival machines which store and legitimize an older regime's programmes ('humanism', or 'empiricism', or 'pragmatism', and so on). The material appears used to conjure what is prefigural, invoking the impasse of how matter is personified to begin with, how 'man' is positioned, the 'human' constructed, the living and the dead assigned in performative language:

> Materialistic historiography, on the other hand, is based on a construc-
> tive principle ... Where thinking suddenly stops in a configuration
> pregnant with tensions, it gives that configuration a shock, by which it
> crystallizes into a monad. A historical materialist approaches a historical
> subject only where he encounters it as a monad. (Benjamin 1968: 262–3)

Monad, that is, as an irreducibly individual nexus or node of proactive historial networks, both anterior and still virtual. Because the 'past' is addressed as
sheer anteriority, the '(a)material' trace is bound to where the past, *was*ness
(in Faulkner), is also managed and produced. Benjamin's Marxian trope of
'materialistic historiography' weaves together the structure of mnemonic relations with an experience of, and intervention in, their networking – where the
patterns for otherness, interpretation, temporality and so on would have been
installed. Because such a project is aimed at a pragmatic intervention this '(a)
materiality' may be said, in one idiom, to lie at a site or non-site of prefigural
inscription. 'Materialistic historio*graphy*' appears a virtual technique of historial intervention intended not only to counter the spell of historicism ('where
historical materialism cuts through historicism' [1968: 255]), of received narratives of linear time as an empty 'continuum' ('telling the sequence of events
like the beads of a rosary' [1968: 263]), but as what stands to alter anteriority
('the dead') by way of a certain caesura-effect, or 'standstill', in which pasts
and futures offer themselves as *virtual*. Elsewhere in Benjamin, this project of
an intervention that critically and performatively turns back on the archival
machines to produce another set of possible futures might seem to be called
allegory, even *cinema*, and *translation* at times – for which the term 'materialistic historiography' seems a final avatar.

PHANTOM BODIES

What is an inscription if one can only point to a brute fact of mnemotechnics,
against which memory and 'experience' might appear programmed? Is there a
body or a horde of anterior inscriptions by which this '(a)materiality' can be
thought? The phrase 'materiality of inscription' derives from the late work of
de Man (1996), at a point in his work in which a redefinition of the 'aesthetic'
becomes a dominant theme. De Man may in this respect appear a continuer
of Benjamin's project – as if redirecting the latter's metaphoric sweep to the
sort of unglamorous micrological engineering Benjamin shied from. When
Benjamin speaks of turning 'the symbolizing into the symbolized' (1968: 8) he
implies that (a)material linguistic traces have been raised into a movement of
active reading, at a prospective site of reinscription. It is not accidental that de
Man's 'materiality of inscription' – what Derrida interprets in 'The Typewriter
Ribbon' as a 'materiality without matter' (Cohen et al. 2001: 277–360) –
emerges in association with a rethinking of the category of the aesthetic itself,

in which the latter term appears to shift from a zone of Schillerian 'play' to a site where signs are phenomenalized, the senses or perception (*aistbanumai*) programmed. Hence the translation here, where 'materiality' now indicates an irreducible trace in which the anchors of memory and the 'human' are deanthropomorphized, defaced. What has been called this other (a)materiality thus supposes linguistic networks that precede the historical form that the 'human' takes, repositioning the 'material' in an experience of the non-living as well. In this movement or process one might want to speak of a broader conceptual transformation, or *translation*, in which a certain (a)materiality is itself foregrounded – be it as networks of sound, the letter, inscription, agency and so on.[4] These micrological players, however, rather than constituting a new corporeality of the text, say, tend to dismember any notion of the body that does not acknowledge the term's phantasmal, semiotic, multiple, inscribed and deanthropomorphized implications, bodies traversed by technicities before which there would be no pure (phenomenological) perception or 'experience'. This non-site for the installation of inscriptions organizing any narrative of events might suggest the '(a)materiality' which everyone, all along, was after; but such would *appear* always, *also*, bound to the movement of a trace that is prehistorial and prefigural.

This '(a)materiality' problematizes certain humanist appropriations of the term (materiality) that have been reinvested in the *body*. Cultural studies has gone far in complicating this figure, which has involved studies of pain (Scarry 1985), different ways that bodies are marked and materialized as 'identities', and the priority of techno-bodies and machinal figures – of which Haraway's 'cyborg' is but an early, genderized variant. But to invest 'body' with the legacy of materiality, as though a reversal of Platonic binaries were at issue, has been to risk returning to the figure an aura of the whole, the organic, the sensible, the present and so on, the reinvestment of a metaphysical site for the real, not to mention falling back into one or other variant phenomenologies. A departure from this tradition, with its great variety of bodies, has been Judith Butler's work on gender performance, where, as in *Bodies That Matter* (1993), an altered figure of 'materiality' would be restituted conceptually. In *Gender Trouble* (1990), an appeal is made to how the body is 'inscribed', realized through marking systems or performed.[5] In *Bodies That Matter*, Butler remarks: 'to warn against an easy return to the *materiality* of the body or the materiality of sex ... To return to matter requires that we return to matter as a *sign*' (1993: 49). For mutually contesting, colonializing and erasing networks of signification to be always already in play, 'body' must be configured as a site undefined outside of 'matter as a sign', and the question of matter converts into a 'materialization' of inscriptive, mnemotechnic effects, that is, the phenomenalization of '(a)material' signs.[6]

A work that takes up the Marxian legacy at a point of its recently declared death with the collapse of Soviet communism and the onset of global capitalism, Derrida's *Specters of Marx* draws implicitly on Benjamin's 'Theses' for inspiration – particularly in the recursive use of a 'messianism without the messianic', which echoes and unpacks Benjamin's phrase 'weak *Messianic* power' (1968: 254).[7] Derrida's spectrality, for which any 'present' would be reconceived as a network of traces, identifies the prospective site of reinscription in the traffic of spectres. That site would be sought after or projected by Benjamin's text ('leap', 'shock', 'translation') and is linked to that Marxian motif most to be prized by his various heirs, the claim to historial intervention. For Derrida, 'Marx is one of the rare thinkers of the past to have taken seriously, at least in its principle, the originary indissociability of technics and language, and thus of tele-technics (for every language is a tele-technics)' (1994: 53). Such a specialized 'materiality' in the absence of this last term involves a translational task that would presage a new politics 'to come' (including a politics of memory) in which these programmes or legacies are transposed into other models of the event, alterity, 'experience', economy, ethics and so on.[8]

Can the confluence of these vectors – the epistemological revolution surrounding the materiality of language and the interventionist critique of leftist thought – open new projects of reading, and specifically reading 'literary' works? The 'materialistic historiography' that Benjamin proffered is a proactive agenda that eschews historicist archivism. It implies a 'moment' of passage in which a radical desemanticization of received reference or hermeneutic systems accompanies a recalibration of perception as such – rather than deriving from 'material' facts the latter appears to occur as the phenomenalization of signifying regimes, a reversal of the position of the 'aesthetic' itself. The disjuncture or caesura that it would practise proposes to alter anteriority itself, in an instantiation of suspense or rupture within current trace-chains. If tropes in general bring to mind colour, the iridescence of the rainbow, the prefigural bears the contradiction of appearing to precede light itself, or to be the latter's technical base. Bringing the virtual blackness of a trace or mark which in effect precedes phenomenality into contact with mimetic reading models induces a 'translation' effect in the model of reading – the attempted installation of a prospective, 'new' reading contract, and with it a conception of historial agency.[9] It does so, at first, by turning to the long occluded elements of material labour, bearers of 'sense', slave agencies (marks, sound, inscription) within the mimetic or referential regime.[10] This is perhaps what de Man terms an 'epistemological critique of tropes': that is, repositioning reading outside of the humanist or Schillerian models of relapse – the 'human' being for de Man a by-product of this structural hermeneutic relapse before (or after) a material event (a mnemonic intervention in the archive). This passage, or translation, involves a supposed movement from a system of tropes to something else called the 'performative'.[11] Performative, for de Man, might be heard multiply, as implying the actual act of a historial event – which cannot be reversed – and performative in the positional sense of inhabiting the mutant facades and faces of so-called 'speech acts'. Tracking (a)materiality leads to unstable sites, since rather than presenting us the referential ground, it tends to open onto the ways in which the archive is itself managed or produced: that is, the site of pre-recordings, Althusserian rituals, installed hermeneutic systems. Reading 'materially' within this problematic entails reading with – and against – inscriptions and models of inscriptions, tracking where this model begins to install another system of reference, agency, perception, temporality and so on. It examines where such has always been in place within the traditions of the Book that have shaped global memory and is aware that all of this takes place within a transformation underway towards the tele-technological archive, a broad re-imprinting of (a)material memory across cultural archives. In the process of this review, it becomes apparent that rethinking the (a)material in this way involves rewriting the entire category of the aesthetic itself, the site of imprinting from which the senses (and, hence, hermeneutic models) appear programmed historially.

READING (A)MATERIAL(LY)

Reading is here conceived of actively as one name for a site in which legacies are relayed, constellations of 'textual' events reconfigured, hermeneutic regimes reimprinted, or, alternately, where epistemo-linguistic ruptures occur in which reinscriptions become possible – a moment to which Benjamin will attach terms like 'shock' or 'caesura'. If there is a 'materiality' to which reading is directed, a moment in the experience of memory and sign systems that moves us from a mimetic to a performative model of the text as virtual or historial event, then it may impact the identity of 'literature' as an institution. Such a project seems itself, in part, to participate in a broader translation of textual legacies into the terms of technicity that are likely to dominate (again) coming hybridizations of science and once humanistic discourses.

How do we read 'materially', or (a)materially? How is such an approach – in which the borders of life and death, human and non-human, historial and hyperpolitical become porous – once again likely to have dominance in various manifestations of discourse, as just mentioned? Let me only suggest one possible approach to this, which might demonstrate how two seeming extremes – the claim to intervention in history, and the agency of desemanticized traces – interface. The 'material' would at first retain its old associations: the lower order in a binary, the promise of what is, of *hule* or matter, appearing in a slave (again lower) position to a master.[12] What Benjamin's 'historiography' would indicate is that this direction cannot be engaged without the received orders of temporality and historial mapping becoming disarticulated. An approach to texts is summoned that might desire to be void of aura, or anthropomorphization, in which the 'human' is open to redefinition when traversed by the traces of its non-human (undead, material) others. The implication is that after 'materialism' is closed as a metaphysical-referential promise, one nonetheless draws closer to another sort of (a)materiality in which the divide between the 'human' domain delineated by the ejection of its specular non-human others or organizing dyads has been dismantled – the borders as if between human and animal, living and dead, past and to come – in the optioning of an altered (a) terrestriality that is traversed by these categories.

Which is why this (a)materiality swerves against the tendency of cultural studies to relapse into humanist, mimetic, descriptive terms in which received models of reference retain (historicist) dominance. We have suggested that if the term 'materiality' has a future for literary and cultural studies – if they are called that – in an (a)material sense that derives from a coalescence of deconstructive and Marxian discourse, such a trajectory leads into a rewriting of this historical archive in the process. It involves epistemo-political consequences and resistances. I will attempt, at this point, a short reading – or perhaps two – using canonical texts in this regard: Faulkner (*Go Down, Moses*) and/ or Hitchcock (the first *Man Who Knew Too Much*). The former allows a brief encounter with the ideology of 'race', the latter with the metaphysical categories of the idea, the eye, visibility, knowing (Benjaminian 'cinema'). I will call this project, derived from the tradition of rethinking allegory (Benjamin, de Man), allographical. Such a project, I will suggest in conclusion, makes claims on how we address the (a)materiality of the human, the animal, temporality, the political, mnemotechnics, the sensorium, the aesthetic and so on – while relinquishing the term 'materialist' in its ontological sense. In the two sketches offered, strategies of reading are suggested in which two different epistemo-political problems are addressed: that of the hermeneutic pursuit as a ritualized model (Faulkner), and that of the light and solar poetics as the ideology of cognition and visibility in the West (Hitchcock). If the first example disarticulates the premise of 'literature' as a received institution, the second undoes received models of temporalization before a principle of repetition at once formalized by the cinematic machine (one literalizing on celluloid the facticity of an inscription that precedes phenomenalization) and yet Nietzschean in its consequences.

2

Engaging in (a)materialist readings of canonical works can suggest a translation of sorts – as though from familiar referential reading models to others in which a mnemonic trace void of semantic depth emerges. Such a trace brings together two apparent functions: it remarks the 'material' dimension of language and ruptures merely symbolic or figurative networks. It's identification inevitably involves an *active* renetworking, even as such a trope of the material reflexively inverts the referential, grounding and historicizing associations the term was once heralded to invoke. As in Benjamin's theorization of 'cinema', such a (non)figure may also suggest a site beyond *aura* when the latter is heard or understood as a discourse of (human) personification. Hence (a)materialist reading leaves the humanism of classical hermeneutics and may be called alloanthropomorphic.

NOTES TOWARDS AN (A)MATERIALIST READING OF FAULKNER

The case of Faulkner is instructive, since the dominant Americanist interpretations issue from a grand territorial assertion: Faulkner's regionality and value as a representational author has long inscribed his reception and interpretation in a quasi-realist logic that seems, in turn, to sustain his value as a regionalist author, even as it contains the performative transgressions his work seems to gamble its import on. This is certainly the case with Go *Down, Moses* (1973), a work generally cast as a work of decline, but also (if contradictorily) a return to nineteenth-century realist narrative – particularly in its treatment of race and black figures – from the 'modernist' stylistic experiments. That is, authorial decline corresponds to a supposed return to hermeneutic proprieties. What is interesting, here, is what is defended against by the hermeneutic guardians: a text where an (a)material trace and the history of racial justice collude in their opposition to a plantation-era hermeneutic that manages or had managed property, definition, time, the Book, race definition, family and so on.

Both assumptions are directly questioned by the title of what is neither given as a 'novel' (rather, an allochronic network of seven tales) nor a collection. Indeed, if anything, the segments probe the parameters of received history and the era of 'the Book'. The 'going down' of the Mosaic author is both 'Faulkner' and a *going under* of the Mosaic laws of reading (and we can hear a Nietzschean resonance to 'going down'). It is not accidental that the last and titular text, 'Go Down, Moses', speaks of a lawyer whose 'serious vocation was a twenty-two-year-old unfinished translation of the Old Testament *back* into classic Greek' (1973: 371) – that is, a translation from an authoritative originary language which was not one (English, Old Testament) back into a pre-originary, aesthetic language which, too, was never original. The vocation of the lawyer, from the position of the law, presupposes an endless translation into an infra-linguistic space – what Benjamin, in his essay on 'Translation', may have termed 'pure language', the pure (a)material traces out of which languages (if such are at all discrete or extant) are materialized, or figuration, memory, and so on, spawned.

Among other things, such a *translation effect* suggests that the way we have understood reference – history, anteriority – to operate in Faulkner is passive and regressed. A supposed return to historical realism around the representation of blacks (starting with the ante-bellum economy of the old McCaslin twin brothers in the opening tale 'Was') coincides with a divestment of that as the product of a ritualized slave economy. Since the black, like the animal, does not participate in the language of the white fraternal order – in 'Was', as though sterile (twin males co-habitating), bound to a plantational fiction, he is utterly ritualized. Indeed, blackness moves through the work in a manner always also dethreading the referential regime of the white masters – and, perhaps, nowhere more than in 'Pantaloon in Black', where the titanic black labourer Rider's name seems to echo, unexpectedly, both *reader* and *writer*.[13]

(If reading – and, for that matter, writing itself – marks the incessant rethinking, bureaucratization, and recalibration of anterior traces that event can suggest a non-site where referential and epistemo-critical programmes are either enforced or recast.) Like 'Moses' before the Jordan River, the work can seem to disown and dissolve the supposedly (pre- and post-)modernist writing project that bears Faulkner's signature, anticipating a different 'law' of reading to come which it cannot designate. Such an other law, which is announced in a sense in the book's title, does and does not arrive. The work seems to poise itself before (and after) this translation. It is, moreover, connected to a site where the once slave status is associated with a material order of signifying trace. The black corresponds not only with the prefigural status of the animal – as bearer (horse), ritual prey (fox, runaway slave) or object of the hermeneutic hunt (bear) – but with the (a)material traces of what is called 'earth', with spectrality, with the sterility of hermeneutic ritual, with a precession of narrative history, with the way that aural and scriptive signifiers are re-empowered, with a recalibration of non-linear time.

It is not accidental that 'Was' names, innocently enough, sheer anteriority. The ante-bellum setting records the sterile rituals of the hunt in the hands of the phantasmal old twins – referencing a preoriginarily absent patriarch ('Old Carothers') whose legacy, clearly, paralyses both. But this setting is not, as is thought, that of (a) historical fiction. Rather it mimes the commodity of that 'genre' – a frontier tale – to put into play a post-contemporary gamble (the performative moment of the work, in this way, always puts something, and itself, at risk). The opening 'hunt' for a released and retrieved fox mirrors the ritual pursuit and return of the escaped slave, Tomey's Turl (half-brother to the twins). This ritual seems that of a modernist hermeneutics, letting the slave term escape (the material trace) only to return it in a pre-programmed interpretive notion of *reference* and property – one that is repetitive, sterile, poised before a cataclysm (or civil war). The black, like the fox, partakes of this escaped, desemanticized order, much as blackness itself appears prefigural, inscriptive, at the worm-hole of a representation or plantation system of 'meaning'. 'Was' puts anteriority, the received regime of memory management (or reference), into crisis, even as the definition of 'was' itself lingers without referential transparency. That is, if 'Was' indicates a comic view of what was, the structure of wasness is in question; if 'Was' is a genre tale (say, frontier comedy), it also declares that genre – historical fiction, regional hermeneutics – as over, past, gone down. As *was*. The (a)materialist reading that opens this transition in Faulkner involves a desemanticization and reinscription of the narratives traversed (including that 'of' Faulkner's own production and reception). The tale brings an entire system close to or beyond the point of dissolution – at a poker game between Hubert Beauchamp and the dexterous Uncle Buddy – in which the entire alignment of white and black property is at stake together with the prospective union of the absurd belated couple (Uncle Buck, Sophonsiba Beauchamp) on which the possibility of a future, or even the book itself (Isaac), depends. The system moves to the place of translation and draws back – Uncle Bud appears to bluff effectively in the poker game in which past and future are at risk, Hubert retreats, Uncle Buddy for now returns to the plantation, having escaped Sophonsiba's trap (which, since the book's narrative is written, and Isaac is born, we might assume occurs in a later interspace or *elsewhere*). The plantation economy and its sterile rituals seem restored for the *twins* – themselves tropes for a dialectical history at aporia (Greek/Biblical, Aesthetic/Ideation, Inside/Outside, and so on).

The only mention of the name 'Moses' in the work occurs here, and it is assigned to a ludicrous old hunting dog capable of chasing a fox around the house. He is called 'old Moses', as though discreetly enough an entire Mosaic metaphysics were assigned this role of the hermeneutic set-up linked to sterile ritual returns of escaped slave figures:

> And when they got home just after daylight, this time Uncle Buddy (that is, Amodeus) never even had time to get breakfast started and the fox never even got out of the crate, because the dogs were right there in the room. Old Moses went right into the crate with the fox, so that both of them went right on through the back end of it. That is, the fox went through, because when Uncle Buddy opened the door to come in, old Moses was still wearing most of the crate around his neck until Uncle Buddy kicked it off of him . . . and they could hear the fox's claws when he went scrabbling up the lean-pole, onto the roof – *a fine race* while it lasted, but the tree was too quick. (1973: 28)

The tree now appears a technical term. When animals (or escaped slaves) are run down, they get trapped at the top of a tree. No exit. That is, the lower or material term (the material signifier as aural or scriptive trace) arrives at the referential site of the signified, is itself caught as referent, what Benjamin called 'to turn the symbolizing into the symbolized' as the predicate for allegorical transformation – the reinscription or reprogramming of perception, the past or the aporetic predicate for such a re-gambling (in which virtual futures, as well, are at risk). In the above passage we see another example of this assertion, for one cannot not hear an aural transposition in 'a fine (t)race', particularly one that here was 'too quick', too safe, too predictable. For 'race' must echo, somehow, so-called racial difference and its hierarchies or conceptual stability: the site of race difference (and the determination of the human master as the sterile white brotherhood's narrative machine) appears linked to, or generated by, a hermeneutic system of property and propriety, a machine of the hermeneutic hunt as pre-ordered ritual. This 'race' has aesthetic properties. It mimes a model of reading which is ritualized, with memory predicting the rigged repetition as play. It is ritual as a game at this point, 'too quick'. 'Race' operates at the top of the tree, caught in this exposed impasse – perforated with diverse referents that, also, are at a point of disappearance (like the plantation economy designated the pre-modernist, and perhaps modernist and even postmodernist reading model, all the same suddenly). It is an *aesthetically* determined term or concept too, understanding 'aesthetic' to retain the Greek traces having to do with perception or the programming of such. The mnemonic hunt on which the routines of an older reading model depended, 'old Moses', appears unpredetermined, traversed by marking systems that necessitate readings, other assignations of reference, other conceptions of 'literature', as (historical) institution, anteriority and so on. At stake in the outcome of this gambling in and with 'was', as a term, is nothing less than the model of history itself – as is clearer in 'The Bear' – and with that temporalization, the 'Americanist' hermeneutic template, the event of performative writing or reading. One can predict more readings of this sort in the twenty-first century which break with prescribed programmes of history, reference, 'reading', mnemonic management.

NOTES TOWARDS AN (A)MATERIALIST READING OF HITCHCOCK

An evacuation of solar poetics can be seen, and differently ascribed an (a) materialist import, in select cinematic writing – and certainly that oeuvre most aware of these issues, Hitchcock's. 'Solar poetics' can be heard as a general figure for the ersatz Platonic assumption of an origin of light, the sun, from which both the plenitude of sense and the transparency of the visible – ocularcentrism, on which much of so-called film theory depends – derive. An example would be the first *Man Who Knew Too Much* (1934). The narrative is filed as 'about' the kidnapping of a child to silence parents who have been passed the secret of an assassination attempt that could precipitate a world war (notes Agent G). That information is passed in a writing hidden in a razor referencing a temple of sun-worshippers in Wapping, with a sketch of a pyramid before a sunburst. It is read in an Alpine resort, at St Moritz, before a closed door in which the hotel police present a cacophony of language types (German, Italian, French, English). 'Knowing too much', which silences a certain subject in Hitchcock, as with too many movements of a writing to speak (a recurrent problematic that takes various forms and is inscribed in a Hamlet-referenced paradigm), may appear linked to a Babel of languages resolved to aural-signifiers, an English become alien, or as Hitchcock says to Truffaut, dialogue understood primarily as sound. In the so-called West, of course, *knowing* has always been linked to light, to the sun (or sun-worship) and to sight – the *eidos* being that which would be visible, the 'idea'.[14] But the pyramid suggests not a Greek but an Egyptian problematic – as of the hieroglyphic metaphors used in the early years of cinema to conjure to new media's (*ur*-scriptive) powers before the onset of sheer commercialism. If 'knowing' is linked to the pretext of transparent sight or vision, the apparent predicate of cinema (or cinema as a mimetic medium), it is put in question by this most theoretically invested of auteurs. Instead of the eye, reading, we witness interrupted reading, as in Hitchcock's cameo in his 'first' talkie, *Blackmail*. In that cipher–cameo Hitchcock is interrupted reading by a bullying boy on an Underground train

– the clacking of tracks and lights in attendance (what makes the 'train', static in movement, a premier prefigural trope for the transport of cinema). Sound is generated from machinal intervals, sight from the interruption of 'light', inter-valed with absence or blackness.

Thus the temple of sun-worshippers must be examined, even as it is the front for the assassins. For on the one hand, it names a duped contingent. The wor-shippers are like a cinematic audience from whom money is collected (tickets) in a ruse – they come for the light, the sun, but the whole is a front, and that for an assassination attempt (a certain Hitchcock is always to be identified with the plot of world disruption). Moreover, the figure of the sun returns us to the earlier marksmanship contest between Jill and Ramon (the would-be assas-sin), which involves clay pigeons, black disks traversing the sky and shot at. Numerous black suns – or the prefigural mark or simulacrum that undoes or precedes the solar fiction of originary light or unveiling. Shot at, another black sun returns, as if shooting this mark – which does not take place once and for all – triggers an assault on how time, anteriority, or the trace is managed. This hyperbolic or Hyperion-like subtext is registered in terms like 'jumper' and references to Spring, a 'knowing *too much*' that both is a knowledge of excess and the undoing of a (political) model of the senses, of knowing, of sight. As this black sun or black trace is released across Hitchcock – for it accords with the little black dog that ran out on the white snow to occasion the opening fall of the agent Louis-Bernard in the opening – it recurs in transformative chains. Clearly imbued with the power to infect any sound or marking system as an (a)material trace that (like an escaped slave) stands in excess of the referential order it nonetheless precedes, this prefigure recurs in these early films as a black trace, a dog, a cat, chocolate, excrement, black buttons or marbles, sheer sound (*Secret Agent*). Included in the pop cultural catalogue Hitchcock wants at stake is 'Western' cultural history and memory preceding the scriptive origin of writing in the Egyptian hieroglyph. Without going into the panoply of signature-effects in Hitchcock – modes of writing which expose and dissolve the mimetic fiction of photography itself (Hitchcock dismissed other films as pictures of people talking) – it is interesting that, at the end of *Blackmail*, the blackmailer Trac(e)y seems to precede the Egyptian wing of the British Museum (through which he is chased), to fall through a glass copula to the Universal Reading Room. In the same vein, Mr Memory in *The 39 Steps* will seem to reference Mnemosyne, the Hesiodic muse, reduced to a recording machine of mere 'facts' – inscriptions or the pretext of photographic images, mechanical and (a)material. In the first *Man Who Knew Too Much* (and, uniquely in Hitchcock, the work generated a remake, as if an endless series of such could not satisfy the import of the narrative), 'knowing' is also referenced to a look on various faces of people who, shot, will die imminently. In each case (Louis-Bernard, Nurse Agnes), the face does not cognize anything: this 'death' is not biological, it precedes the opposition life/death, nodding towards the spectral space of cinema whose logics will be targeted repeatedly (*Rebecca*,

Vertigo, Psycho, Family Plot), the séance nature of the 'cinematic' event. In *To Catch a Thief*, this black cat will be allied with the theft of diamonds, sex, meaning, history and light itself, a neo-promethean post-historial impasse.

This prefigurative agent that reduces reference systems to a skein of traces places temporality in question, even as it does identity, sight or for that matter gender markings. It does so, moreover, through an interrogative alliance between language reduced to its (a)material elements and mnemonics, opening a site for the recalibration (or reinscription) of these. It assumes a parallel between the experience of cinema as an artificed memory and sensorium and the way that a 'consciousness' which is the effect of (a)material traces that are neither living nor dead operates.

CONCLUSIONS

In each of the above an element appears identified that, while excluded from the chains of figural meaning proper (the slave, the black sun), is marked, and reflexively modifies or vacates the assumed referential programme or grid – that 'Was' is *about* a frontier, that cinema relays mimetic facts. In raising the symbolizing or (a)material mark or phoneme to the level of the signified, the textual event reconfigures itself and the older territoriality of sense is rewired through that performative factor. Reading becomes micrological and, at the same time, stands to recast inherited models of history, knowledge, time, perception and memory in what de Man perhaps calls an opening 'epistemological critique of tropes'. No alteration, no intervention, without a recasting of the programmatic or mnemonic regime (or ritual). To call this the predicate of (a) material reading may be misleading if the term 'material' does not go through an equivalent translation where the term returns, if at all, to mark a space that would never be attached to the earlier concept of the term (hence what Derrida calls, in speaking of de Man, a 'materiality without matter'). A term that had guaranteed reference – going back to the Aristotelian *hule* – has shifted, by designating a supposed 'materiality of inscription' that precedes mnemonic programme. According to this mode of thinking, whatever would reinscribe the site of conceptual terms or global memory would have to pass through this non-site.

QUESTIONS FOR FURTHER CONSIDERATION

1. What sorts of 'materiality' can be referenced to language and how does that complicate, or displace, any transparent use of the term?
2. What sort of mnemonic agency does an appeal to a 'materiality of inscription' suggest, and how might texts be considered events?
3. Why does what is called '(a)material' here make its appearance with a suspension of affirmed referential objects, matter and so on – as if a desemanticizing moment attends this advent?
4. What, in the Faulkner and Hitchcock texts examined, might be the connection between the role of the escaped slave in the first and the black sun as a visual trace in the second?

BIBLIOGRAPHY

Althusser, Louis (1971) *Lenin and Philosophy and Other Essays*, trans. B. Brewster. New York: Monthly Review.

Apter, Emily S. and William Pietz, eds. (1993) *Fetishism as Cultural Discourse*, Ithaca: Cornell University Press.

Aristotle (1960) *Metaphysics*, trans. Richard Hope, Ann Arbor: University of Michigan Press.

Benjamin, Walter (1961) *Illuminationen*, Frankfurt: Suhrkamp.

Benjamin, Walter (1963) *Ursprung des deutschen Trauerspiels*. Frankfurt: Suhrkamp.

Benjamin, Walter (1968) *Illuminations*, ed. Hannah Arendt, trans. Harry Zohn, New York: Schocken.

Benjamin, Walter (1977) *The Origin of German Tragic Drama*, trans. J. Osborne, London: Verso.

Bergson, Henri (1988) *Matter and Memory*, New York: Zone Books.

Bloch, Ernst et al. (1980) *Aesthetics and Politics*, trans. Harry Zohn, London: Verso.

Butler, Judith (1990) *Gender Trouble*, New York: Routledge.

Butler, Judith (1993) *Bodies That Matter: On the Discursive Limits of 'Sex'*, New York: Routledge.

Cadava, Eduardo (1997) *Words of Light: Theses on the Photography of History*, Princeton: Princeton University Press.

Cochran, Terry (2001) *Twilight of the Literary: Figures of Thought in the Age of Print*, Cambridge: Harvard University Press.

Cohen, Tom (1998) *Ideology and Inscription: 'Cultural Studies' after Benjamin, de Man, and Bahktin*, Cambridge: Cambridge University Press.

Cohen, Tom, Barbara Cohen, J. Hillis Miller and Andrzej Warminski, eds. (2001) *Material Events: Paul de Man and the Afterlife of Theory*, Minneapolis: University of Minnesota.

Davis, Paul and John Gribbin (1991) *The Matter Myth: Towards 21st Century Science*, Harmondsworth: Penguin.

de Man, Paul (1986) *The Resistance to Theory*, Foreword by Wlad Godzich, Minneapolis: University of Minnesota Press.

de Man, Paul (1996) *Aesthetic Ideology*, ed. and intro. Andrzej Warminski, Minneapolis: University of Minnesota Press.

Derrida, Jacques (1994) *Specters of Marx: The State of the Debt, the Work of Mourning, and the New International*, trans. Peggy Kamuf, intro. Bernd Magnus and Stephen Cullenberg, New York: Routledge.

Derrida, Jacques (1995) *On the Name*, ed. Thomas Dutoit, trans. David Wood, John P. Leavey Jr. and Ian McLeod, Stanford: Stanford University Press.

Ezell, Margaret, J. M. O'Keeffe and Katherine O'Brien, eds. (1994) *Cultural Artifacts and the Production of Meaning: The Page, the Image, and the Body*, Ann Arbor: University of Michigan Press.

Faulkner, William (1973) *Go Down, Moses*, Vintage: New York.

Haraway, Donna (1991) *Simians, Cyborgs, and Women: The Reinvention of Nature*, New York: Routledge.

Hennessy, Rosemary and Chrys Ingraham, eds. (1997) *Materialist Feminism: A Reader in Class, Difference, and Women's Lives*, New York: Routledge.

Irigaray, Luce (1985) *This Sex Which Is Not One*, trans. Catherine Porter, Ithaca: Cornell University Press.

Jameson, Fredric (1991) *Postmodernism, or, The Cultural Logic of Late Capitalism*, Durham NC: Duke University Press.

Kittler, Friedrich A. (1997) *Literature, Media, Information Systems*, Amsterdam: G+B Arts International.

Marx, Karl and Friedrich Engels (1998) *The German Ideology: Including Theses* on *Feuerbach and Introduction to the Critique of Political Economy*, Amherst: Prometheus Books.

Miller, J. Hillis (1999) *Black Holes*, Stanford: Stanford University Press.

Montag, Warren (1995) '"The Soul is the Prison of the Body": Althusser and Foucault, 1970–75', *Yale French Studies* 88, pp. 53–77.

Moser, Paul K. and J. D. Trout, eds. (1995) *Contemporary Materialism: A Reader*, New York: Routledge.

Ronell, Avital (1989) *The Telephone Book: Technology, Schizophrenia, Electric Speech*, Lincoln: University of Nebraska Press.

Scarry, Elaine (1985) *The Body in Pain: The Making and Unmaking of the World*, New York: Oxford University Press.

Sim, Stuart (2002) 'Chaos Theory, Complexity Theory and Literary Criticism', in Julian Wolfreys, ed., *Introducing Criticism at the 21st Century*, Edinburgh: Edinburgh University Press.

Spivak, Gayatri Chakravorty (1999) *A Critique of Postcolonial Reason: Toward a History of the Vanishing Present*, Cambridge MA: Harvard University Press.

Sprinker, Michael, ed. (1999) *Ghostly Demarcations*, New York: Verso.

Truffaut, Francois (1967) *Hitchcock*, New York: Simon & Schuster; revised edition 1984.

Voloshinov, V. N. (1973) *Marxism and the Philosophy of Language*, trans. I. R. Titunik and L. Matejka, New York: Seminar Press.

Weber, Samuel (1996) *Mass Mediauras: Form, Technics, Media*, Stanford: Stanford University Press.

NOTES

1. *Mnemotechnic* is here used to suggest the manner in which memory itself is connected entirely to systems of marks, traces, writing, archives or regimes that implicitly organize and programme not only sensation and reference but cultural truths, reference and so on. As a technic, something 'material' in the sense of being associable with exterior marking-systems, it is a site that can be addressed as open to disinscription and reinscription.

2. For one recent account of the 'material' basis for the transformation of an era of the Book into that of teletechnological media, see Cochran 2001.

3. Stuart Sim, in his contribution to the first edition of this volume, 'Chaos Theory, Complexity Theory and Literary Criticism', references Davis and Gribbin's *The Matter Myth: Towards 21st Century Science*, to address the 'death of materialism' (Davis and Gribbin 1991: 2) and its impact on Marxist criticism: 'The death of materialism is not good news for Marxism, which still essentially adheres to a mechanistic world view, with broadly determinable patterns of cause and effect, and whatever undermines Marxist philosophy also undermines Marxist critical theory, the authority of which derives from the philosophy in the first instance' (Sim 2002: 97). The most traditional forms of 'materialist' analysis continue, in this genre, to be mounted as archivally significant political analyses, such as is the case for the linkage of 'Marxism' to feminism in Hennessy and Ingraham's collection, *Materialist Feminism: A Reader in Class, Difference, and Women's Lives* (1997).

4. When Benjamin speaks in his essay on 'Translation' of turning 'the symbolizing into the symbolized' (Benjamin 1968: 8), he implies that (a)material linguistic traces have been as if raised from the lower or servant position to a vortex of signification.

5. In *Gender Trouble*, Butler critiques Foucault's invocation of inscription, to single out conception that takes a 'body' for granted that precedes the field of cultural inscription, a Foucault who 'points to the constancy of cultural inscription as a "single drama" that acts on the body . . . By maintaining a body prior to its cultural

inscription, Foucault appears to assume a materiality prior to signification and form' (Butler 1990: 128). Butler critiques Irigaray's appropriation of the Platonic *Khora* to bring the figure of matter together with its inherent pun on mater, or female figuration, in the same vein (1990: 46–8). For an inverse take on *Khora* from the *Timaeus*, where 'materiality' emerges as a figure for a site of preoriginary inscription, a matter that is no mater, or mother, see Jacques Derrida's *Khora* in *On the Name* (Derrida 1995). For a valuable interpretation of Butler's contribution at this juncture, see the extended treatment of her work in this volume's chapter on 'Gender and Transgender Criticism', by Sarah Gamble.

6. A precursor of this tradition coming out of or citing Marxian thought, in which the materiality of differential signs is expounded, would be Voloshinov's *Marxism and the Philosophy of Language* (1973) – where the term 'sign' is both evacuated (being without inside or out, signified or signifier as such) and returns as a tropological place-holder. The place of this work within the Bakhtinian authorship helps explain the possibility of reading Bakhtin's work as a proto-Benjaminian project.

7. This phrase invokes the destructuration of received temporal models when the structure of the promise (that does not arrive), essentially that of radical performativity, is deployed to rethink the problematic of the event. For a series of counterstatements, and discussions, surrounding Derrida's rereading of Marx see Sprinker 1999.

8. How, Derrida asks in 'The Typewriter Ribbon', 'is one to reconcile with the machine a thinking of the event, the real, undeniable, inscribed, singular event, of an always essentially traumatic type' (Cohen et al. 2001: 336).

9. For one use of the figure 'black hole' as a trope for where the trace of the material may appear known through a representational implosion and absence, rather than a promised referent, see Miller 1999.

10. One may think of the 'materiality' of language in the manner that Benjamin conceives, in his 'Task of the Translator', of a 'pure language' or *reine Sprache*, an inter-space of all supposed 'mono' languages (Benjamin 1968: 69–83). 'Pure language' would, then, be the opposite of idealized meaning, indeed void of 'meaning', evoking instead a materiality-effect of all traces and bearers of mnemonic effect, such as marks and sound and inscriptions.

11. The 'movement', or 'passage', is presented as from 'cognition' or figuration to 'the materiality of something that actually happens, that actually . . . occurs materially' (de Man 1996: 132). This movement as if away from figuration or systems of tropes occurs by way of what de Man terms an 'epistemological critique of tropes' (1996: 133): that is, in 'Kant and Schiller', positioning a reading outside of the humanist or Schillerian models of relapse from a Kant whose 'materialism [is] much more radical than what can be conveyed by such terms as "realism" or "empiricism"'. This 'relapse' is 'a kind of reinscription of the performative in a tropological system of cognition again' (1996: 133). The 'human' for de Man is not a given but a phantom by-product of this structural hermeneutic relapse before (or after) a material event (a mnemonic intervention in the archive), hence reading by inscription continues to use the term 'material' to indicate the non-human, or a perspective from which 'there is, in a very radical sense, no such thing as the human' (de Man 1986: 96).

12. Only now it would be foregrounded, raised to the order of a signified in a process in which the signified is not *represented* (if anything, the signifier or 'symbolizing' is dissolved along with the bi-partite Saussurean model of 'sign'). The logic of 'allegory' that Benjamin develops as another nomadic assault on this transformation of programmes must be understood as other than representational – that is, a movement that negates what it represents, alters its own archival reserve (itself), in a process initially destructive. As Benjamin puts it in the *Trauerspiel*: Allegory 'means precisely the *non-existence* of what it (re)presents' (*Und zwar bedeutet es genau das Nichtsein dessen, was es vorstellt*) (1977: 233; 1963: 265).

13. A further unpacking of the title 'Pantaloon in Black' would focus on the panta-loons, leg-trousers, in which the echo of *panta* (all) is heard across a serial use of 'panting' in the text. This isolation of the syllable-word-sound *panta* migrates, too, into the *pensere* of thought (confirmed by Rider's final reported words: 'Ah just cant quit thinking' (159)) and *the phainesthai* of appearance, phantasm, phenom-enalization. Such a reading might suggest that, within the pantomimetology of the text read as performative event (in 'Faulkner', in the canon and archive virtually, and so on), what the writing pursues is a reinscription of the laws of phenomenality parallel to the destruction of an entire history (of which the author, 'Faulkner', is also a product).

14. For an important reading of the technicity of 'light' and photography in a Benjaminian vein, see Cadava 1997.

DELEUZEAN CRITICISM

Claire Colebrook

Above all else, Gilles Deleuze was a philosopher. His works always insisted on the power of philosophy to question and transform life. But Deleuze also thought that philosophy could only be truly transformative if it encountered other powers, such as the powers of art, cinema, literature and science (Deleuze and Guattari 1994).

Before looking at how we might 'translate' Deleuze's philosophy into literary theory it is necessary to consider just what the concept of 'literary theory' presupposes about the relation between philosophy and literature. 'Theory' is derived from the ancient Greek 'theoria' – a mode of elevated looking that intuits the stable truths behind the flux of appearances. Theoria is therefore connected with the privileging of *being* – or what remains the same and knowable – over *becoming*. Following the French philosopher Henri Bergson (1859–1941), Deleuze argued that it is theoretical knowledge that fixes and spatializes the temporal flow of life. For practical purposes we do not attend to the fluxes of difference that make up the real. Instead, we perceive a world of determined and stable beings. Deleuze's own work has insisted that we need to take philosophy and all thinking beyond the narrow viewpoint of conceptual knowledge. Philosophy, from Plato onwards, has been *theoretical* because it intuits or sees the truth of *what is*; it is elevated above the flux of perceptions to discern those truths and forms that make perception possible. In this respect, most philosophy has been committed to *transcendence*, or what lies outside experience and remains the same. Indeed, philosophy has always formed its *transcendental* or grounding questions on the basis of some *transcendent* or external being. The relation, and difference, between transcendent and transcendental is crucial in Deleuze's philosophy. We may have experiences within the world – of this or that *transcendent* or external object – but philosophy reflects upon how we see or know anything at all. Philosophy, from Plato to Deleuze, has affirmed its *transcendental* potential: rather than being concerned with any given or *transcendent* thing, it asks how the experience or being of things, in general, is possible. This is transcendental questioning, which does not begin from any already given term within the world but asks how anything like a world, experience or being could exist at all. Whatever transcendent events we perceive within the world, we can always adopt a transcendental viewpoint: how are such events possible?

That identity not be first, that it exist as a principle but as a second principle, as a principle *become*; that it revolve around the Different: such would be the nature of a Copernican revolution which opens up the possibility of difference having its own concept, rather than being maintained under the domination of a concept in general already understood as identical (Deleuze 1994: 40–1).

According to Deleuze, Western thought has more often than not failed to ask properly transcendental questions. We usually begin from some transcendent term, or 'plane of transcendence'; we presuppose the mind of man, or matter or the perceiving human eye. To think transcendentally requires, Deleuze insists, a commitment to immanence. This is a refusal to explain life by some outside or transcendent plane; it is to think the power of life on its own terms, without subordinating life to an already existing image (Deleuze and Guattari 1987: 499). A truly transcendental viewpoint does not accept that the world that we experience at a day-to-day level is the truth or whole of life. In order to arrive at the very life of things we need to go beyond any single or specific event and ask how events, differences and 'singularities' are possible.

Literary theory has tended to expose the practice of traditional literary criticism to these sorts of transcendental considerations. How is meaning or reading in general possible? With literary theory we do not just read or interpret a text as though its meaning were simply something 'there', or transcendent, waiting to be discovered. *Theory* demands that we account for *how* we read or see a text, how we generate the meanings that we do. It demands that we reflect upon our practices and our point of view as readers and interpreters. Once we recognize the possibility of theory – that we always approach the text from some point of view – then we also admit that any interpretation that claims *not* to have a theory is merely blind to the decisions and assumptions it must make in order to read. Given this claim of theory in general – that reading is always a decision in relation to a text – what sort of theory does Deleuze offer? To begin with we can note that Deleuze tries to overcome the idea of a theoretical viewpoint, and this also includes the concepts of meaning and interpretation. Far from *deciding* what a text means from some separate point of view of judgement, and far from making sense of a text, Deleuze's own practice of reading was one of *encounter*: what does this text *do* to thinking? And sense, for Deleuze, is not something a reading uncovers. We do not see text or hear sounds and then shuffle through our memory bank to match it to some meaning. Sense is not something we consciously decide upon, interpret or intuit through a theory. Sense is a virtual plane or whole opened up by a text that confronts us or does violence to our presuppositions.

We can read a sentimental novel or attend a performance of a Romantic opera and find ourselves moved to tears or have our heart rate elevated by anticipation and desire for narrative resolution; we are not interpreting this work – finding some signification behind its signs. The work offers itself as a whole world of affects and senses: a sense of love, loss, cliché or even cloying sentimentality. It is not that we *feel* love or are in love, but we experience the *sense* of love. Now for Deleuze this means that the point of view of the separate and disengaged subject of theory, the subject who decides upon or interprets, does not go far enough in asking the transcendental question. Before there are subjects who perceive and form theories Deleuze insists on the impersonal domain of sense: on affects of love, for example, that are felt as such, without being the love *of* this or that person for this or that beloved. This is why art – as the creation of affects – is so crucial for Deleuze's philosophy of immanence. For it is only if we move beyond theory and the judging and interpretive point of view to those senses and affects that invade us and produce us that we will arrive at thinking life itself, and not any of its organizing or transcendent terms.

Many philosophers of Deleuze's generation, particularly Jacques Derrida and Michel Foucault, questioned the status of philosophy as transcendental. Philosophy could not be some pure theory separated from the particular events and texts of this world. Philosophy had its own textual conditions (its use of metaphors, figures, syntactical idiosyncrasies and embedded norms) along with specific historical conditions, such as what constitutes a legitimate question for any epoch. On the one hand, then, the twentieth century saw an emphasis on theory: on reflecting upon the conditions and decisions that form philosophy and judgement. For Derrida this meant looking at textual conditions or the way syntax and language determined decisions. For Foucault this meant looking at the historical a priori, or all the ways in which thinking was determined by the 'unthought', including spatial, technical and material conditions. For Deleuze, by contrast, far from abandoning the possibility of a philosophy capable of thinking the very genesis of life, Deleuze insisted that we should not collapse transcendental questions – questions about life *as such* – into worldly questions. Philosophy for Deleuze is not just another form of writing or textuality; it has a power to think beyond any actual or given differences. Where Deleuze differs from many of his contemporaries is in his insistence on the force and essence of philosophy and its difference from the force and essence of literature. This has two important consequences.

First, Deleuze insists in general on a philosophy of transcendental empiricism. It may be that any philosophical text will have elements of the literary about it, but this does not mean we cannot intuit essentially philosophical tendencies. An essence for Deleuze is not some isolated and unchanging thing, such as the supposed essence of 'human nature'. An essence is a capacity, tendency or power to become. The essence of philosophy does not lie 'in', say, the works of Plato; it is a power to produce philosophical problems, both in the actual texts of the past and the potential texts of the future. Philosophy and literature differ in their powers or potentials. A novel may have passages of philosophical reflection but what makes it a novel or an instance of literature is its specifically artistic power: its power to create sensations and affects beyond the reader's own world. I read a novel such as Charles Dickens's *Bleak House* and perceive a sense of disorder, futility, stultification and hopelessness, a sense that is conveyed through images of mud, slime, delay and obstruction. Literature has this power to release sense from specific persons and situations and give us a general affect.

Philosophy, also, has its own power which can be discerned or intuited even if all the texts of actual philosophy are mixed with scientific and literary elements. It is the power to create concepts. Such concepts do not label things. Rather, creating a philosophical concept entails thinking beyond things to the forces or tendencies that make things possible. A concept does not label an event within the world; it allows us to think of the world in a new way. The concept of 'desire' in psychoanalysis, for example, does not generalize or label a collection of things *within the world*. It is desire that produces bodies, passions, perceptions, images, histories, fantasies and human societies (Deleuze and Guattari 1983: 30). Deleuze's philosophy of desire is *transcendental* because it refuses to reduce life to any of its already existing manifestations. It strives to think the hidden or virtual potential of life, above and beyond any living thing. Philosophy is the tendency to create concepts that allow us to think this virtual life.

Second, a transcendental approach does not end with the power of philosophy. Life, according to Deleuze, can express or become through different and divergent tendencies; indeed, it may well be impossible to combine the perceptions of science, art and philosophy into one coherent world. Literature or art are specific tendencies and should not be seen as the stylistic expression of scientific or philosophical ideas. Whereas philosophy is the power of producing concepts (enabling us to think the whole of life), and science is the power of producing functions (allowing us to form practical observations and laws that organize life), art produces affects and percepts. We will look at this in far more detail below, but to do so we need to add more concepts to Deleuze's project of transcendental philosophy: the concepts of univocity, empiricism and immanence.

Concepts, Deleuze argues, are never isolated entities. A concept allows thought to move around and create, but it can do so only by producing a 'plane': a series of interconnected moves that allow us to ask meaningful questions. How could we have the philosophical concept of 'mind', for example, without the connected concepts of logic, knowledge, certainty, thoughts and individuals? And all these concepts presuppose a certain drama or image of thought (Deleuze 1994: xx), such as a philosopher alone in her study asking what is really true. For Deleuze, recognizing these planes or unstated pre-suppositions and images means exploring the sense within which we move and think. Sense is neither stated nor represented, but it has to be there as a medium in order to state or represent. We could not have the concept of mind without the assumption that it makes *sense* to ask certain questions. We have the concept of mind in response to certain problems. If I ask, 'How do I know the experiences I have are real?' then this can only make *sense* if we assume a mind disengaged from a world, a subject set over against experience. Before there can be decisions about truth or falsity there has to be this milieu of sense. This attention to sense gives us a transcendental method, for as we ask more and more questions and create further problems we free ourselves from dogma and opinion and begin to *think*. No concept makes sense without some presup-posed plane; these are not personal presuppositions, for there has to be some milieu of sense before there can even be the concept of the person.

Deleuze's own concepts of univocity, empiricism and immanence are created across the plane of his own philosophy, although he also tried to create mul-tiple planes and even co-authored a work called *A Thousand Plateaus*, which was not a coherent thesis so much as the creation of diverging problems. Univocity is a commitment to *one* being with no outside or external viewpoint (Deleuze 1994: 35). Western thought has tended to be *equivocal*, dividing being into two hierarchized substances, such as mind and matter, reality and illusion, creator and created, actual life and virtual life, or subject and being. For Deleuze equivocity *cannot* make sense. To say that something is *is* to admit its existence or being. If I say that something *is* an illusion, a fiction, an error or even an evil, then I already acknowledge its force and its reality. For Deleuze there is one being that includes ideas, matter, the future, difference, the past, stories, representations, particles and concepts. And if perceptions are them-selves real then it also makes no sense to see them as images or copies *of* the real. The real itself is just the totality of possible perceptions and events, with the totality being necessarily open to further difference and perception. This is univocal being, with no substance being elevated above, or given priority to, any other: 'Univocity of being thus also signifies equality of being. Univocal Being is at one and the same time nomadic distribution and crowned anarchy' (Deleuze 1994: 37). Minds are not pictures of reality, nor is reality a projection of mind; mind and matter are different expressions of the one life.

Univocity therefore leads to immanence. Western thought has been enslaved to transcendence: the idea that there is some outside or external world to be known, the idea that being simply *is*, or that it transcends us and that we somehow have to break through images and becoming in order to get to the real and transcendent world. (Deleuze and Guattari, 'Transcendence: a Specifically European Disease', 1987: 18). Against this, Deleuze insists on immanence. There is not a transcendent real world outside or beyond images and perceptions. Being *is* perception. This does not mean that being is a mental event or something inside our heads. If we thought this then we would still be grounding the world on some privileged external point – such as the mind, brain or human perception. To say that being *is* perception is to say that life as such is imaging and perceiving: sound waves, light waves, genetic mutations, nucleic acids and proteins, computer errors and viruses all 'perceive' each other in the dynamic whole that is life. The human brain is one point of perception among others, with the peculiar capacity to form a concept or idea of this whole imaging process. There is, for Deleuze, just one immanent life, an open whole precisely because there is no single point, no transcendent outside, that can act as the ground or viewpoint for any other. Each event in life perceives its own world, and there are as many worlds as there are potentials for perception: plant worlds, animal worlds, fictional worlds, the worlds of the microscope and other machines.

Univocity and immanence, in turn, connect with empiricism. Empiricism is opposed to idealism. Idealism insists that any world or experienced thing is known *as* something and is therefore determined and made possible by the idea we have of it. Deleuze's empiricism argues the contrary. It is not that there is a mind, language or culture that constructs or determines a world. Mind, ideas and languages are effects and creations of life (Deleuze 1994: xx). This argument is explored most imaginatively in two of the books Deleuze co-authored with Félix Guattari: *Anti-Oedipus* and *A Thousand Plateaus*. Mind and language are described here as effects of a general and inhuman desire. Life begins as an 'intense germinal influx' – an open whole of becoming, creation and interaction (Deleuze and Guattari 1983: 164). We need to get rid of the idea of pre-human life as an undifferentiated chaos (Deleuze 1988b: 103). For Deleuze and Guattari the pre-human is intensively diverse, mobile and creative of differences far too rich for any single human eye or language.

From the pre-human complex of flows, relative points of stability gradually form, such as tribes or territories. These blocks of assembled bodies create further marks and differences, such as scarring, tattooing and body-painting, which organize and code the genetic differences or the germinal influx. Once these territories become relatively stable it is possible for one body or mark to organize the whole; one body *deterritorializes* to become a leader or author of the assemblage. This body that leaps outside the territory can, through even further force and desire, construct an image of law or separate power: the king's body is the sign of a divine right not reducible to the material body. This gives life a virtual centre or governing origin. Deleuze and Guattari's main point is that such a virtual body that enslaves life is actually created from desire and the imagination, from perception and excess: it is by taking more than the other bodies, and by *not* producing, that the royal body becomes law. When, in modernity, we overthrow such divine origins and assert the rights of 'man' or the 'subject' we have merely taken one point of transcendent illusion and substituted another. We are still subjected to transcendence: the illusion that there is some image within life – the subject – that is the point of explanation for life in general, 'the ultimate private and subjugated territoriality of European man' (Deleuze and Guattari 1983: 102).

The task of literary theory, therefore, should be the destruction of this subjection to transcendence. This requires two moves. First, there is no such thing as theory. There is no privileged point or origin from which life might be judged. There are theoretical concepts and tendencies, but if these become 'a' theory then they lose their power to theorize: to think beyond already given images. Instead of trying to step outside the whole of life to establish a point of theory and reflection we need to create concepts – such as Deleuze's concept of desire – that enable us to think of life as an infinitely complicated, inhuman, differing and open whole. Second, instead of thinking of language as a 'signifier' used by the subject (or culture) to represent and determine the world, we need to see language as a flow of signs alongside other signs, signs which themselves are effective and productive without being *meaningful*. Instead of interpreting a text by asking what it means or wants to say – as though the text were a way of getting to the world – we need to see what a text does as an event of becoming, as itself a 'world'.

STYLE

The usual understanding of style is tied up with traditional and, for Deleuze, debilitating metaphysical notions of transcendence, equivocity, subjectivism and representation. If we imagine that there simply *is* a transcendent or external world that is then represented, then we will imagine style as some type of secondary ornament or overlay. There would be being and then its various styles of existence, or the representation of being supplemented by stylistic differences. Good thinking would supposedly represent the world with as little difference as possible. The model of truth would be the universal proposition that can and must be agreed upon by all subjects: propositions in accord with a purely formal logic free of stylistic content. On this picture, style would be in danger of distorting truth and the straightforward presentation of the world. To understand style in this way is to see difference as negative. It is as though there is a self-same world that could be represented through this or that different style. The differences of style would then be grounded on some prior sameness.

Such an understanding of style also commits us to subjectivism. There would be an original point or ground – the subject – which forms the basis for various differentiating statements. Bear in mind that the 'subject' refers to the 'I' who speaks, the subject of the sentence that can then be predicated, and to the ultimate ground – the subject of discussion. Deleuze wants to think style independently of all these senses: a style freed from a subject's point of view, a mode of writing that does not use the subject/predicate form of the proposition, and a mode of thinking that does not refer difference and variation back to some prior ground. The subject is that which precedes or stands outside various acts of predication, difference and style. The act and event of style is thereby subordinated to what it creates. This concept of the subject also ties in with equivocity: we imagine an actual world of being or material substance, and then a world of representation. Such a metaphysics for Deleuze is not only in error – for it makes no sense to posit a 'real' world *behind* thoughts, style and representation. Thinking, styles and images are themselves fully real and part of life, not supplements added onto life. 'Becoming produces nothing other than itself. We fall into a false alternative if we say that you either imitate or you are. What is real is the becoming itself, the block of becoming, not the supposedly fixed terms through which that becoming passes' (Deleuze and Guattari 1987: 238).

The metaphysics of equivocity, which separates being from its stylistic differences, is also *reactive*. It enslaves the active creation and becoming of life to one of its created terms. A certain style of speech and existence produces the concept of the subject, and we then imagine that the subject preceded and grounded becoming and creation. But any such transcendent ground or external point from which we might judge life is, Deleuze insists, itself an event in the differential flow of life.

The standard notion of point of view – that there is a subject who speaks and predicates an outside world or who lies behind perceptions – needs to be supplanted by an *immanent* understanding of style. If there are just perceptions and differences, without preceding subjects, then we can imagine a world of interacting variations rather than fixed beings and relations. 'What is called a style can be the most natural thing in the world; it is nothing other than the procedure of continuous variation . . . Because a style is not an individual psychological creation but an assemblage of enunciation, it unavoidably produces a language within a language' (Deleuze and Guattari 1987: 97). Here, style is not an ornament or affect used by subjects to express their point of view. Style is the difference of life itself from which subjects are effected: 'man' is the creation of certain styles of speech, action, anticipation and social connection. Animals have their own style: becoming-animal. We can imagine human life abandoning the concept of the subject and creating in other ways, such as becoming-woman: 'Language must devote itself to reaching these feminine, animal, molecular detours, and every detour is a becoming-mortal . . . Syntax is the set of necessary detours that are created in each case to reveal the life in things' (Deleuze 1997: 2). Life as a whole is nothing more than stylistic variation, a potential to create ever more differences and perceptions. For each style of becoming can cross with other styles to create even further differences. A cat is a style of becoming-animal – a collection of moves, habits, preferences, capacities and potentials – including the potential to create styles in other styles of life. If a cat's perceptions and world are perceived by a poet then we might have a literature that no longer speaks with the voice of man. When T. S. Eliot (1888–1965) wrote *Old Possum's Book of Practical Cats* (1939) he did not describe or list propositions about cats, nor did he speak 'like' a cat. He allowed one style of life – human speech – to intersect with another – cat-life, and this produced a poetry that was certainly not 'about' the world so much as creative of a world.

Literary style, for Deleuze, is not a medium or vehicle that authors use to express ideas. Style is not a way of depicting life; style produces life and points of view:

> That is what style is, or rather the absence of style – asyntactic, agrammatical: the moment when language is no longer defined by what it says, even less by what makes it a signifying thing, but by what causes it to move, to flow, and to explode – desire. For literature is like schizophrenia: a process and not a goal, a production and not an expression. (Deleuze and Guattari 1983: 133)

Free-indirect style, dominant in the literary modernism of the early twentieth century was a crucial manoeuvre in liberating style from the subject. In free-indirect style the text is neither in the first person – referred back to the expressing 'I' – nor in an omniscient third person who could oversee and speak objectively about characters and the world. Omniscient narration uses a language that would not be spoken by the characters themselves to describe their thoughts and actions. Much of the satire of Henry Fielding's *Tom Jones* is achieved by the narrator being able to view and describe all the motives and psychological depths that characters themselves might deny:

> The extremes of grief and joy have been remarked to produce very similar effects, and when either of these rushes on us by surprise, it is apt to create such a total perturbation and confusion that we are often thereby deprived of the use of all our faculties. It cannot therefore be wondered at that the unexpected sight of Mr. Jones should so strongly operate on the mind of Molly and should overwhelm her with such confusion that for some minutes she was unable to express the great raptures with which the reader will suppose she was affected on this occasion. (Fielding 1994: 190)

In so doing traditional omniscient narration creates a confident shared viewpoint between reader and narrator; we have satire because 'we' can see the motives behind actions and are thus able to discern the difference between the style the character presents and their actual intentions.

Free-indirect style, by contrast, employs the idiosyncrasies and verbal tics of a character in order to describe or speak about that character. *Simple* free-indirect style would therefore use a dialect to describe a character from a particular region, or it may even be quite subtle and express the values or inflections of the described character. In D. H. Lawrence's 'Jimmy and the Desperate Woman' the narrative voice moves seamlessly between words that would seem to be alien to the described character and near-exclamations that would be inwardly spoken by the character himself. The following sentences trace the very eye of the character, making their way through the description in the same way that an eye makes out and assesses details, with a 'yes' when something is identified.

> At last he came in sight of a glimmer. Apparently, there were dwellings. Yes, a new little street, with one street-lamp, and the houses all apparently dark. He paused. Absolute desertion. Then three children. (Lawrence 1950: 115)

This is not a narrator who has the plot and details spread out in advance from a single viewpoint. Instead of sentences and propositions grounded in observers there are detached perceptions: 'Absolute desertion'; 'Then three children'. It is impossible to say *who* is seeing or saying these 'percepts': the narration is just the list of the character's perceptions, but the character is presented, himself, as an assemblage of perceptions. Free-indirect style is located neither within the subject, nor above the subject in a describing narration; it is a style of writing that displays the production of selves and locations through perceptions and expressions:

> It is for this reason that indirect discourse, *especially free indirect discourse*, is of exemplary value: there are no clear, distinctive contours; what comes first is not an insertion of variously individuated statements, or an interlocking of different subjects of enunciation, but a collective assemblage resulting in the determination of relative subjectification proceedings, or assignations of individuality and their shifting distributions within discourse. Indirect discourse is not explained by the distinction between subjects; rather, it is the assemblage, as it freely appears in this discourse, that explains all the voices present within a single voice . . . (Deleuze and Guattari 1987: 80)

Style, for Deleuze, is not what we use in order to speak; it is style that enables the creation of a 'we' and a shared mode of speech. For this reason, Deleuze writes of literature's production of a 'people to come': 'Health as literature, as writing, consists in inventing a people who are missing. It is the task of the fabulating function to invent a people . . . The ultimate aim of literature is to set free, in the delirium, this creation of a health or this invention of a people, that is, a possibility of life' (Deleuze 1997: 4). There are not communities of speakers who share an identity and then speak; rather, through the production of styles relatively stable identities are created, but such creations are always open to future mutation and difference. Free-indirect style is important in this regard precisely because it shows the ways in which styles of speech are never fully or exhaustively owned by speakers. Speech and style bear their own force; to adopt a style of speech is to become in a certain way, to take part in a specific territory and to reinforce and reconfigure tendencies and habits:

> for speaking is no less a movement than walking: the former goes beyond speech toward language, just as the latter goes beyond the organism to

a body without organs ... Creative stuttering is what makes language grow from the middle, like grass; it is what makes language a rhizome instead of a tree, what puts language in perpetual disequilibrium: *Ill Seen, Ill Said* (content and expression). Being well spoken has never been either the distinctive feature or the concern of great writers. (Deleuze 1997: 111)

What free-indirect style then creates is the idea of a language freed from voice and subject: an 'it speaks', 'speaking' or 'to speak', rather than an 'I speak'. We can also note, here, a point about Deleuze's approach to history. If we see the power of modernist free-indirect style, this does not mean that we should try to re-create the very styles of modernism as *the* style most appropriate to Deleuzean criticism. Rather, if we see how modernism uses style to transform the concept of style – style is no longer spoken by the subject but creative of subjects – then we will be able to ask how we might repeat modernism's essence. Far from creating modernist works this would require reading the texts of today, or the past, with a sense of how style might work, what style might do – and not what style represents or reflects. How could other styles transform the very potential of style?

AFFECT

In *Anti-Oedipus* Deleuze and Guattari describe or imagine the 'intense germinal influx' or life as an inhuman swarm of differences: forces that attract and repel each other to produce points of relative stability, bodies or territories:

In a word, the opposition of the forces of attraction and repulsion produces an open series of intensive elements, all of them positive, that are never an expression of the final equilibrium of a system, but consist, rather, of an unlimited number of stationary, metastable states through which a subject passes. (Deleuze and Guattari 1983: 19)

Bodies, subjects or points of view are produced through the connection of intensities: the eye meets with light and in this attraction the eye becomes an organ of vision and the light waves become visible. For Deleuze, the world we know through relations – the world our eye sees, our ear hears, our mind imagines and our body feels – is the *actualization* of flows of difference. Light waves become visible when attracted by the eye, but the differences of light waves have other potentials – to be actualized as felt heat, just as sound waves can be visible for a bat who 'sees' through sonar. It is not that there are related points – eye and world – which *then* meet through affect. Rather, there are affects – sensibilities *to be* heard, seen or perceived – that produce the seeing eye, the thinking mind and the acting body: 'The mind begins by coldly and curiously regarding what the body does, it is first of all a witness; then it is affected, it becomes an impassioned witness, that is, it experiences for itself affects that are not simply affects of the body, but veritable *critical entities* that hover over the body and judge it' (Deleuze 1997: 124).

Human life emerges from the intense germinal influx through the territorialization of affect. From a large range of affects – all the potential differences that the human body encounters – certain regularities are invested. The eye is drawn again and again to the same image, the mouth again and again to the same body part; this repetition *creates* difference. In repeating an affect, such as the eye re-finding an image, the image can become a sign, a symbol, a totem. The mouth that seeks the breast creates a relation between mother and child, a family, a culture. The repetition of affects produces distinct terms, with each term itself capable of further connections and creations. A tribe is formed by investing in the affect of a sound (a drumbeat). 'England' is formed by the investment in affects: the colours of the flag, the sounds of the national anthem, the continual quotation of phrases from Shakespeare. Such affects are not symbols *of Englishness*; Englishness is just the collection of bodies investing in certain repeated affects. Affects are those events of intersection prior to human thought. The eye that meets with light, the ear that hears, the body that starts or jumps from shock – all these are the affects from which we are formed.

Deleuze and Guattari define philosophy as the creation of concepts, concepts such as 'the intense germinal influx' or 'Being', which enable minds to think the virtual whole of life, virtual because such a whole could never be presented as an actual thing: 'the Whole is only virtual, dividing itself by being acted out. It cannot assemble its actual parts that remain external to each other: The Whole is never "given." And, in the actual, an irreducible pluralism reigns – as many worlds as living beings, all "closed" on themselves' (Deleuze 1988b: 104).

Art, by contrast, creates affects and percepts. This is more than saying that art is affective (making us feel something), and it is more than saying that art is non-conceptual (presenting colours and sounds rather than meanings or ideas). Art may present colours we *perceive*, but it engages with *percepts* when it presents colour not just as an actual thing but as a potential or power for perception. A Rembrandt portrait is not just a dark canvas; we do not just see dark paint; we see what darkness can do. We can imagine a young painter seeing a Rembrandt who responded not by forging a painting (banal repetition) but by being provoked into taking darkness even further. Such repetition would respond to the percept: what is perceived is not just the actual and present – these dark shades – but an *Idea* of darkness, or what darkness might become: darkness as a virtual power *to differ*.

The problem, for Deleuze, that dominates common sense and everyday life, and that thereby leads to unthinking philosophy, is the lazy and undifferentiated attachment of concepts to affects and percepts. Green means go; darkness means negativity; 'man' is white; tartan, haggis and Burns are what it means to be Scottish. We no longer encounter affects – allowing ourselves to respond, become or question differences. We attach affects habitually to everyday concepts; we pass all too readily from affect to concept. For Deleuze this is the banality and rigidity of opinion, which underpins a society geared to 'communication' or the maximum circulation of information *without* ambiguity or distortion. Concepts are easily attached to affects: the 'foreigner' is a label for certain smells, sounds, gestures and rhythms. Similarly, certain affects are directly attached to concepts. Such attachments stop us from thinking. Deleuze and Guattari cite the example of the smell of cheese (Deleuze and Guattari 1994: 146). The everyday man of opinion moves directly from affect – the nostrils recoiling at the smell – to concept: this cheese *is* disgusting or inedible. Common sense and opinion create a single, universal point of view of agreement, from which all affects are immediately recognized and judged:

> In every conversation the fate of philosophy is always at stake, and many philosophical discussions do not as such go beyond discussions of cheese, including the insults and the confrontation of worldviews. The philosophy of communication is exhausted in the search for a universal liberal opinion as consensus, in which we find again the cynical perceptions and affections of the capitalist himself. (Deleuze and Guattari 1994: 146)

Art, by contrast, dehumanizes affect, liberating affects from everyday recognition (Deleuze and Guattari 1987: 320). 'One' thinks that darkness means negativity, but art can create a canvas of darknesses taking the eye beyond a darkness that can be recognized as meaningful. Art carries affects to their 'nth' power; the eye feels a darkness beyond comprehension and habitual recognition. Often, the eye that views art, not only does not know what it is seeing, but also fails to know what *seeing is*: just how is one to view this? Poetry also does violence to the everyday language of opinion – the language that for the most part enables us not to think or see. By disengaging affect from concept, literature moves in two directions. The eye can see again. Language is no longer description, passing from what we see to what we say; language 'stutters' (Deleuze 1997: 55). The words we say become noise or affect themselves in their difference from what is seen. The visible and articulable separate into two directions (Deleuze 1988a). Words themselves become sound, noise, rhythm or stuttering; but in *not* seeing, designating or referring to the actual world, words can also open us up to the unseen, worlds beyond our present point of view:

> The work of art leaves the domain of representation in order to become 'experience', transcendental empiricism or the science of the sensible ... Empiricism becomes truly transcendental, and aesthetics an apodictic discipline, only when we apprehend directly in the sensible that which can only be sensed, the very being *of* the sensible: difference, potential difference and difference in intensity as the reason behind qualitative diversity ... The intense world of differences, in which we find the reason behind qualities and the being of the sensible, is precisely the object of a

superior empiricism. This empiricism teaches us a strange 'reason', that of the multiple, chaos and difference (nomadic distributions, crowned anarchies). (Deleuze 1994: 57)

NOTES TOWARDS A READING OF JAMES JOYCE'S *DUBLINERS*
Style

Free-indirect style presents language that is not so much owned by speakers as it is definitive of a certain locale or habitus. James Joyce's (1882–1941) *Dubliners* does not just describe the people of Dublin using verbal tics, although he does do this. (One character refers to a carriage with 'rheumatic wheels'.) *Dubliners* 'speaks' in the voice of newspapers, cheap novels and the hackneyed phrases owned by no one. These are phrases that circulate and *create* territories, without being intended from a single point. Think of the way bodies of football supporters are produced *as* a body through the chanting of rhythms, the wearing of colours and the assemblage of bodies. This is what Deleuze refers to as a collective assemblage created through investments in intensities and affects. The group does not precede and author the signs of identity; the signs do not refer back to a group; the group is the effect of a collection or assemblage of signs: '*Signs do not have objects as their direct referents*. They are states of bodies (affections) and variations of power (affects), each of which refers to the other. Signs refer to signs ... Signs are effects: the effect of one body upon another in space, or affection; the effect of an affection or duration, or affect' (Deleuze 1997: 141). The styles of *Dubliners* are not so much expressions of specific speakers as productions of a place or territory (a territory that would be *de*territorialized if it were then grounded on one single term, such as the 'Irish spirit'). Deterritorialization takes one body of the assemblage – such as the speaking voice – and uses it to explain the assemblage as a whole; this is what happens when the subject or a community is seen as the author and ground of signs, rather than as an effect of intensities. Joyce works against this tendency to produce a grounding Irish spirit; his stories present the affects and styles from which identities are retroactively assumed.

In 'A Painful Case' Mr Duffy has just read a newspaper report, contained in full in the story, of the death of a woman with whom he had been involved. The following passage is technically in the third person, but is expressive of Mr Duffy's moral outrage, employing his condemnatory tone and 'elevated' position. What Mr Duffy most objects to is not the death itself, so much as its description in a language which is devoid of moral judgement. The narrative voice that speaks is not just that of Mr Duffy; by adopting the viewpoint of consensus – 'Evidently' – it is a voice that confidently speaks for all such upright members of 'civilisation':

> The threadbare phrases, the inane expressions of sympathy, the cautious words of a reporter won over to conceal the details of a commonplace vulgar death attacked his stomach. Not merely had she degraded herself;

she had degraded him. He saw the squalid tract of her vice, miserable and malodorous. His soul's companion! He thought of the hobbling wretches whom he had seen carrying cans and bottles to be filled by the barman. Just God, what an end! Evidently she had been unfit to live, without any strength of purpose, an easy prey to habits, one of the wrecks on which civilisation has been reared. (Joyce 1995: 108)

It is often said that modernism is avowedly elitist and dismissive of the masses (Carey 1992). This would certainly be the case if it criticized the voices of the city and populace through the creation of a higher and judging point of view. However, modernism's use of style frequently adopts the tone of bourgeois elitism and threatened narrow-mindedness, not to appeal to an existent 'we', but to signal the illusion and specificity of any supposed voice of man in general. T. S. Eliot, Ezra Pound and Virginia Woolf may not have been populists but the voice of parochial derision so often adopted in their works is by no means exhaustive of the narrative voice, a voice which is always interspersed with quotation, allusion and misread repetitions. To read in a Deleuzean manner is to reread: far from looking back at modernism's elitist intent we can see the necessary failure of any voice that imposes itself from on high. For, once expressed as style, manner and text the supposed universality or 'height' of voice is also contaminated by the depths: its emergence from sound, noise, received fragments and unthought inclusions. As Deleuze and Guattari argue in *Anti-Oedipus*, racism does not work by exclusion but by inclusion (Deleuze and Guattari 1983: 85): assuming a voice of white, middle-class agreement and civilization as the voice of 'us' all.

Free-indirect style demonstrates that the man of reason is a specific style and manner of voice; the very citizen who would set himself above the inanity of the press and mindlessly circulating language is created through a no less repeatable style and manner: 'Just God, what an end!' Mr Duffy is the virtuous bourgeois soul who laments the fall of language into mere rhetoric and repetition. Free-indirect style, far from striving to find a point of origin and genesis *outside* style and repetition, adopts already-given styles – such as the moralism of Mr Duffy – to show how style produces and creates character.

Free-indirect style allows the thought of a difference that does not differentiate some prior sameness. There is no normal humanity or presupposed 'we' behind the dialects of *Dubliners*. The human is nothing more than its various stylistic differences. The concept of the human or the concept of some underlying subject or nature is destroyed through a style, such as free-indirect style, that affirms and multiplies differences rather than subordinating differences to some governing point of view.

Affect

There is a standard idea of realist fiction, where the voice of the text follows or views the scene and speaks what it sees. Joyce adopts this connection between viewing eye, speaking voice and organized affect in 'Ivy Day in the Committee Room' from *Dubliners*:

> A denuded room came into view and the fire lost all its cheerful colour. The walls of the room were bare except for a copy of an election address. In the middle of the room was a small table on which papers were heaped.
>
> (Joyce 1995: 113)

The room itself bears the affect; the 'cheer' is not felt by any of the characters but is attributed to an object. The bare walls, heaped papers and waning fire given an affect of desolation, an affect that is not felt by any subject – neither narrator, nor reader, nor character. The redundant messages, discarded papers and unnoticed objects create an affect of emptiness, even though the characters speak vociferously and with a tone of conviction. Joyce presents an emptiness that will come to overtake the bodies in the room. By describing impersonal affects the voice of the story allows the characters' voices to appear as so much noise. The true power of literature lies in freeing affect from its organization by regular opinion. Great literature, for Deleuze, does not express who 'we' are, but produces new affects freed from subjective recognition: 'literature . . . exists only when it discovers beneath apparent persons the power of an impersonal – which is not a generality but a singularity at the highest point: a man, a woman, a breast, a stomach, a child . . . It is not the first two persons that function as the condition for literary enunciation; literature begins when a third person is born in us that strips us of the power to say "I"' (Deleuze 1997: 3). This is precisely what Joyce's *Dubliners* goes on to do. It uses the descriptive affects of realism, where a world of sensations creates a general affect – a room of empty phrases, hopelessness and vacuity. After the description of the room, the characters of 'Ivy Day in the Committee Room' exchange their opinions – their ready-made phrases lining up candidates on one side or the other of politics. This is a politics of opinion – allegiances to single images such as the ivy-leaf lapel badge, and to the memory of Parnell. It is *paranoid* in Deleuze and Guattari's sense; it subjects itself to images and voices from outside, such as the spirit of Ireland: 'All paranoiac deliriums stir up similar historical, geographical and racial masses' (Deleuze and Guattari 1983: 89). But Joyce's description of the scene is *schizoid*; it pulls apart all the phrases, affects and images that create political groupings, all the ways in which these bodies form themselves *as* Irish through attachments to badges, phrases, remembered persons and anthems. 'If schizophrenia is the universal, the great artist is indeed the one who scales the schizophrenic wall and reaches the land of the unknown, where he no longer belongs to any time, any milieu, any school' (Deleuze and Guattari 1983: 69). The whole point of this political scene as presented by Joyce is that the politics is not one of ideas or beliefs. The dialogue 'lists' perceptions and revulsions, commitments and prejudices as so many unthought and pre-personal attachments: desires that have become fixed through the repetition of banal phrases and anecdotes. Joyce is not analysing the beliefs or psyches of these characters so much as styles of speech that operate in compelled and automatic rhythms:

> 'What did I tell you, Mat?' said Mr Hynes. 'Tricky Dicky Tierney'.
>
> 'O, he was tricky as they make 'em,' said Mr Henchy. 'He hasn't got those little pigs' eyes for nothing. Blast his soul! Couldn't he pay up like a man instead of: "O, now, Mr Henchy, I must speak to Mr Fanning . . . I've spent a lot of money"? Mean little schoolboy of hell! I suppose he forgets the time his little old father kept the hand-me-down shop in Mary's Lane.'
>
> 'But is that a fact?' asked Mr O'Connor. (Joyce 1995: 116)

After the circulation of so much dialogue, so much language that flows in a habitual and near machine-like manner, the characters open bottles of stout by placing the bottle over the fire, allowing the gas to expand to produce a 'Pok!' The mere noise of speech becomes interspersed with the literal hot air from the bottles and a similarly compelled and automatic sound from the bottle. Joyce writes the noises of life, rather than speakers, into his stories.

According to Deleuze, we really begin to think when we ask of language, not 'what does it mean?' or 'who speaks?', but 'what does it do?' or 'how does it work?' (Deleuze and Guattari 1983: 109). In *Dubliners* Joyce looks at the way meaningless affects create social groupings. We have to ask: would exhaustive footnotes that described the political context of this story make what the characters say any more meaningful? I doubt it. Joyce presents the voice of Ireland, his own language, as a foreign language (Deleuze 1997: 113). Language seems to operate through and across these voices. The bodies in the room line up behind this or that opinion, this or that badge or poster; far from giving us a sense of character and distinct persons, we get the circulation of phrases that pass from point to point: Mr Henchy, Mr Hynes, Mr O'Connor. The story concludes with the recitation of a hymn to the remembered leader Parnell, a recitation that only briefly interrupts the further 'Pok!' of bottles and hot air, and the final recognitions of opinion:

> 'What do you think of that, Crofton?' cried Mr Henchy. 'Isn't that fine? what?'
>
> Mr Crofton said that it was a very fine piece of writing. (Joyce 1995: 116)

For Deleuze, politics is not about the exchange and recognition of opinions among persons. To really think politically we have to look at affects: all those investments that *create* personal positions and groupings. Joyce gives Dublin as a territory of affects: a style of speech, an investment in certain images, ceremonies, bodies (Parnell) and rhythms (from political anthems to religious services). Politics has less to do with competing ideas and beliefs and more to do with affect. Joyce's 'Ivy Day in the Committee Room' describes a political territory, but does so *micropolitically* – not referring to the ideas or meanings held by characters, but to the formation of characters through the repetition of noises, gestures and symbols. Affective analysis, or diagnosis, pervades Joyce's writing.

> ... the writer as such is not a patient but rather a physician, the physician of himself and of the world. The world is the set of symptoms whose illness merges with man. (Deleuze 1997: 3)

Joyce both repeats the sounds that make up who we are – the rhythms of nationalism, the Church service and newspaper headlines – and creates and adds inhuman affects and pulsations: the 'Pok!' of hot air from bottles in *Dubliners*, the animal, machine and bodily noises of *Ulysses*, and the language of human speech in *Finnegans Wake* that mutates as it speaks, blurring the boundaries between textual accidents, human slips and idiosyncratic intentions. Such texts do not describe so much as create and open up worlds.

QUESTIONS FOR FURTHER CONSIDERATION

1. One of Deleuze's main objectives was to think *difference itself*, beyond the human point of view. For this reason he favoured literature that looked at machines, animals and all sorts of 'inhuman' desires. To what extent is such a project *utopian*? Would it be possible to achieve an inhuman viewpoint, or is this something writing can only work towards?
2. In his own time Deleuze argued that cinema, with its capacity to present images of time and becoming, provided new ways of thinking about art and philosophy. To what extent is recent fiction and art 'cinematic' – using images and sequences that are not tied to logical or unified order?
3. Deleuze argues that far too much emphasis was placed on metaphor and signification, or looking at what images and signs referred to. Instead, he suggested that we should look at the power and force of words and images themselves. Does this limit us only to very modern forms of art – such as modernism – or could we reread traditional works less for their meaning and more for their capacity to create affects?
4. Because of Deleuze's attack on the notions of representation and signification he is often criticized for being a *literal* philosopher: trying to think life itself rather than images of life. Deleuze's work is therefore out of step with a tendency of literary, social and political *theory* that stresses that we need to recognize and reflect upon our point of view rather than aim for a view from 'nowhere'. Do you think this criticism of Deleuze is valid?
5. In *What is Philosophy?* Deleuze and Guattari argued for distinct powers of literature, art and philosophy. No text may be purely artistic but we can discern distinctly artistic tendencies. Often, though, we

read literature to demonstrate ideas and concepts. Is it possible to read with a view to distinct tendencies in literature? Could we, for example, read Virginia Woolf's *Mrs Dalloway* for its feminist philosophy on the one hand, and its affects or impersonal styles on the other?

BIBLIOGRAPHY

Carey, John (1992) *The Intellectuals and the Masses: Pride and Prejudice Among the Literary Intelligentsia: 1880–1939*, London: Faber & Faber.

Deleuze, Gilles (1984) *Kant's Critical Philosophy: The Doctrine of the Faculties*, trans. Hugh Tomlinson and Barbara Habberjam, London: Athlone.

Deleuze, Gilles (1986) *Cinema 1: The Movement-Image*, trans. Hugh Tomlinson and Barbara Habberjam, Minneapolis: University of Minnesota Press.

Deleuze, Gilles (1987) *Dialogues with Claire Parnet*, trans. Hugh Tomlinson and Barbara Habberjam, New York: Zone Books.

Deleuze, Gilles (1988a) *Foucault*, trans. Sean Hand, Minneapolis: University of Minnesota Press.

Deleuze, Gilles (1988b) *Bergsonism*, trans. Hugh Tomlinson and Barbara Habberjam, New York: Zone Books.

Deleuze, Gilles (1988c) *Spinoza: Practical Philosophy*, trans. Robert Hurley, San Francisco: City Light Books.

Deleuze, Gilles (1989a) *Cinema 2: The Time-Image*, trans. Hugh Tomlinson and Robert Galeta, Minneapolis: University of Minnesota Press.

Deleuze, Gilles (1989b) *Masochism: Coldness and Cruelty*, trans. J. McNeil, New York: Zone Books.

Deleuze, Gilles (1990) *The Logic of Sense*, trans. Mark Lester, ed. Constantin V. Boundas, New York: Columbia University Press.

Deleuze, Gilles (1991) *Empiricism and Subjectivity: An Essay on Hume's Theory of Human Nature*, trans. Constantin V. Boundas, New York: Columbia University Press.

Deleuze, Gilles (1992) *Expressionism in Philosophy*, trans. M. Joughin, New York: Zone Books.

Deleuze, Gilles (1993) *The Fold: Leibniz and the Baroque*, trans. Tom Conley, London: Athlone Press.

Deleuze, Gilles (1994) *Difference and Repetition*, trans. Paul Patton, New York: Columbia University Press.

Deleuze, Gilles (1995) *Negotiations 1972–1990*, trans. Martin Joughin, New York: Columbia University Press.

Deleuze, Gilles (1997) *Essays: Critical and Clinical*, trans. Daniel W. Smith and Michael A. Greco, Minneapolis: University of Minnesota Press.

Deleuze, Gilles (1999) 'Bergson's Concept of Difference', trans. Melissa MacMahon, in John Mullarkey, ed., *The New Bergson*, Manchester: Manchester University Press.

Deleuze, Gilles (2000) *Proust and Signs*, trans. Richard Howard. London: Athlone.

Deleuze, Gilles and Félix Guattari (1983) *Anti-Oedipus: Capitalism and Schizophrenia*, trans. Robert Hurley, Mark Seem and Helen R. Lane, London: Athlone.

Deleuze, Gilles and Félix Guattari (1986) *Kafka: Toward a Minor Literature*, trans. Dana Polan, Minneapolis: University of Minnesota Press.

Deleuze, Gilles and Félix Guattari (1987) *A Thousand Plateaus: Capitalism and Schizophrenia*, trans. Brian Massumi, Minneapolis: University of Minnesota Press.

Deleuze, Gilles and Félix Guattari (1994), *What is Philosophy?*, trans. Hugh Tomlinson and Graham Burchell, London: Verso.

Eliot, T. S. (1939) *Old Possum's Book of Practical Cats*, London: Faber & Faber.

Fielding, Henry (1994) *The History of Tom Jones* [1749], Harmondsworth: Penguin.
Joyce, James (1995) *Dubliners*, ed. Andrew Goodwyn, Cambridge: Cambridge University Press.
Lawrence, D. H. (1950) *The Woman Who Rode Away and Other Stories*, Harmondsworth: Penguin.

SPACE, PLACE AND MEMORY

CHAPTER

11

AFFECT THEORY

Christine Berberich

Affect is diverse and multiple.

David Crouch (2010: 132)

The writing of this chapter coincided with my first camping trip in years. Having been subjected to relentless petitioning by my son for what felt like months, I gave in and vaguely promised to organise a two-night camping trip to celebrate his eighth birthday. Not being a camping enthusiast, nor a particularly outdoorsy person in the first place, I was slightly apprehensive – the prospect of spending a night in a soggy tent that was at risk from being blown away in an unseasonal thunderstorm was not particularly enticing; nor was the thought of sharing rudimentary bathroom facilities with strangers. I do like my home comforts. Imagine my unadulterated joy when – by sheer coincidence – I stumbled over a website advertising 'glamping trips': camping that seemed to be made specifically for people like me, no, *just* for me, offering stunning locations and *furnished* tents, with proper beds, and duvets, a stove inside the tent, and the option of having breakfast delivered in the morning. Ever the magnanimous mother I jovially promised the camping trip, and booked a two-night stay in a yurt in rural Hampshire. Happy child. Gloating mother. Result.

*

Fast forward a few weeks and the big trip has arrived. Our yurt is picturesquely situated in a quiet wood, entirely 'off grid' as the owners enthusiastically assure us. There is a fire roaring in the fire pit, the bed is nicely made up and the promise of twinkling fairy lights even make the prospect of trips to the euphemistically styled 'compost toilet' bearable. All is great. The child is ecstatic about this truly idyllic camping site. We breathe in deeply, and willingly let ourselves be affected by our leafy environment. This is true mother-and-son bonding time. We kick off our shoes. We play. We explore the wood. We zoom across the little stream on a zip wire, the inner Tarzan within us unleashed. We eat a delicious dinner by the campfire, wholeheartedly agreeing that food tastes so much better in the great outdoors, feeling completely and utterly in tune with our environment. This is, in fact, the Good Life. The things we usually take for granted – electricity, hot water on tap, too many TV programmes, telephone, compulsive email checking – seem far away, and in a good way.

And then the shadows become longer, and night starts to fall. Around us, the forest turns dark and darker, and comes alive – but in a different, disconcerting way from its lushly green day-time self. And this is when things start to change and shift.

*

As I lay sleepless and rigid in my bed in the middle of a seemingly vast and hostile forest, I experience what can only be described as an out-of-body experience. Floating above the bed, I look down at myself, eyes staring unseeingly into the darkness, fear and panic written large on my face as I realise that we are entirely alone in this stretch of the forest. The French philosopher Gaston Bachelard has written about '*the immensity of the forest*', an 'immensity' that 'originates in a body of impressions which, in reality, have little connection with geographical information. We do not have to be long in the woods to experience the always rather anxious impression of "going deeper and deeper" into a limitless world' (1994: 184). As I lay there, I feel an enormous sense of alienation from my environment, and am struggling to keep a sense of perspective. My already feverish imagination goes into overdrive: as my eyes seek to penetrate the unaccustomed darkness of the forest night, devoid of the permanent light pollution of the city, they become useless tools in trying to locate myself within this new and entirely unfamiliar territory. My panicked brain seeks information from other sources. My sense of hearing becomes acute as I wince at every noise, even the smallest of them magnified in the eery night-time forest. My night has been stripped off its usual noise accoutrements – cars passing the house; people loudly laughing on their way home from the pub; neighbourhood dogs barking; a police siren a few roads away. Like my eyes, confronted with unbroken darkness, my ears struggle to make sense of the new and unfamiliar noises they encounter: what is that shuffling noise just outside the yurt? Was that the call of an animal? Why did that branch snap? The darkness and silence I should willingly embrace to grant me a deep and undisturbed night's sleep feel, instead, *unheimlich*, threatening; the 'immensity' of the forest is simply too immense, too removed from what I'm familiar with, to allow me to relax.

In my mouth, I taste my own fear.
Sleep eludes me.

*

For some readers, this might be an amusing anecdote, a whimsical introduction at odds with the objective and critical tone of academic writing. For me, though, it was an example of 'affect' in action. It forcefully brought home the 'personal' aspect of Affect Theory, and dissociated it from the theoretical space it had occupied for me before as a bourgeoning form of academic inquiry. As I was huddled bleary-eyed around a steaming cup of coffee in the bleak light of dawn, I realized that my previous over-romanticized and sublime notion of being one with nature – that had seemed within all-too-easy reach the previous day – had been challenged and turned into a much more complex one throughout the night. The forest had acquired a new meaning. It had turned into a place of inexplicable shadows and unfamiliar noises; it had assaulted my senses, made me more aware of them, queried their reliability, forced me to question what I considered familiar, and pushed me to the edge. In short: it had affected me deeply, and in ways I hadn't anticipated.

At its most basic, 'affect' refers to the senses and the personal, to things that move us, not only in extraordinary situations (as I had encountered in the forest that night) but, most particularly, in the everyday and ordinary. The American anthropologist Kathleen Stewart, one of the leading Affect Theorists, defines affects as:

> the varied, surging capacities to affect and to be affected that give everyday life the quality of a continual motion of relations, scenes, contingencies, and emergences. They're things that happen. They happen in impulses, sensations, expectations, daydreams, encounters, and habits of relating, in strategies and their failures, in forms of persuasion, contagion, and compulsion, in modes of attention, attachment, and agency, and in publics and social worlds of all kinds that catch people up in something that feels like *something*. (2007: 1–2)

The previously unconsidered or ignored can, in Stewart's view, in a different situation and an entirely unexpected way, become something significant, something with a different meaning. It can change our perception of the thing itself, of ourselves, and of the world at large around us. Similarly, the Cultural Geographer John Wylie points out that 'an affect is an intensity, a field perhaps of awe, irritation or serenity, which exceeds, enters into and ranges over the sensations and emotions of a subject who feels', and that 'Affect thus denotes the shifting mood, tenor, colour or intensity of places and situations' (2005: 236). However, affect is by no means solely reduced to the purely haptic and needs to be strictly differentiated from mere emotion; affect goes above and beyond a passive 'being affected' by something. In fact, Gilles Deleuze and Félix Guattari contend that 'affects are no longer feelings or affections;

they go beyond the strength of those who undergo them. Sensations, percepts and affects are beings whose validity lies in themselves and exceeds any lived' (1994: 164). For Deleuze and Guattari, affect gives new meanings to things but, simultaneously, makes them independent from the very thing that gave them this meaning in the first place. Importantly, Gregory J. Seigworth and Melissa Gregory, editors of *The Affect Theory Reader* that brings together the leading theorists in the field, highlight that affect is 'at once intimate and impersonal', both 'a body's *capacity* to affect and to be affected' (2010: 2). Affect is thus multi-dimensional, both active and passive, taking on a life of its own and developing further and in unanticipated ways. For Sara Ahmed, 'to be affected by something is to evaluate that thing. Evaluations are expressed in how bodies turn towards things. To give value to things is to shape what is near us' (2010: 31), and Michael Hardt similarly asserts not only 'our power to affect the world around us and our power to be affected by it' but also, importantly, 'the relationship between these powers' (2007: ix). This concept goes back to Baruch Spinoza's ideas on *affectus* and *affectio* that differentiated, as Megan Watkins outlines, between 'the force of an affecting body and the impact it leaves on the one affected' (2010: 269).

For Seigworth and Gregg, this process, this relationship, is an 'affective bloom space' (2010: 9), a space everybody can contribute to and participate in, especially if we, as Ahmed, '[think] of affects as contagious' (2010: 36). As such, the 'promise' and 'potential' of affect (Seigworth and Gregg 2010: 2, 12) is effectively 'limitless' (Anderson 2010: 166).

This seemingly subjective approach to life and the world has, in the words of Patricia Clough (2007), inspired a veritable 'affective turn' within the Academy, thus inspiring the – potentially over-simplified and restrictive – singular term *Affect Theory*. 'Affect' is now applied by a wide variety of academics across the humanities and social sciences, from cultural studies and literature to sociology, anthropology and human geography; creative practitioners such as filmmakers, photographers, creative writers, sound artists or dancers push its boundaries. For many scholars, Affect Theory is a turn away from what they consider restrictive concepts and theories of the -ism kind: postmodernism, poststructuralism, posthumanism. Brian Massumi's influential study *Parables for the Virtual: Movement, Affect, Sensation*, for instance, again focuses on the wide potentiality of affect – 'the turbulent soup of regions of swirling potential' that, unlike other theories, offers escape from confinement (Massumi 2002: 34). Similarly, David Crouch consciously directs his research away from 'particular labeled area[s] of big theory' towards articulating 'flows, processes, complexities, action' (2010: 2). It is this very diversity of affect – or rather the multitude of diverse affects – that makes it difficult to pinpoint the concept in an all-encompassing definition and also suggests that, rather than resulting in a single overarching 'Affect Theory', it has engendered many different kinds of affective engagements that allow for a 'commingling', in Crouch's terms (2010: 4), of multiple affects, sensations and experiences. The list of critical thinkers who have contributed to developments in Affect Studies – Eve Sedgwick, Kathleen Stewart, John Wylie, Michael Hardt, Lauren Berlant, Brian Massumi, Elspeth Probyn, Ben Highmore, Patricia T. Clough, Laurence Grossberg, to name but a few – as well as their many respective subject areas shows that Affect has become a force to be reckoned with (see also Berberich, Campbell and Hudson 2013 and forthcoming). Individual scholars further enhance the study of Affect(s) with their own interpretations of it – ranging from Jane Bennett's notion of enchantment, the ability 'to be struck and shaken by the extraordinary that lives amid the familiar and everyday' (2001: 4), to David Crouch's idea of 'flirting with space' to 'influence and affect . . . the meaning and value of things and the way things happen' (2010: 125).

Increased academic interest in and curiosity about affect has in recent years resulted in a spate of cross-disciplinary conferences on the topic, and has also engendered a number of creative-critical publications (see Seigworth and Gregg 2010; Berberich, Campbell and Hudson, 2013 and forthcoming) that actively try not only to focus on and foster debate on affect *per se* but also to engage with it during the very writing process, resulting in, effectively, a new academic discourse that foregrounds the human experience, and that, at first glance, seems to be more subjective and lack the traditional academic objectivity and rigour. However, as Dewsbury et al. point out, this new discourse can be a 'field of potential', 'not a method in the traditional sense, but a matter of finding a way of going-on, a way of getting somewhere' that, effectively, blends critical and creative registers (2002: 439). They urge for a 'resolute experimentalism' (2002: 440), and much recent writing on 'Affect' thus not only pushes the boundaries in terms of content but also through its linguistic register that blends the academic with the creative, the haptic with the critical.

It is precisely this emphasis on the creation of a new language that also stands at the forefront of many recent travel accounts. Among the plethora of texts in this genre-crossing writing stand out some that do not only focus on the journey itself but that try to develop a new language in dealing with the *affective effect* the journey has on the individual and whose engagement with the landscape surrounding the traveller transcends mere travel description and, instead, turns into a metaphysical assessment of the self in the world at large and the landscape in particular. It is, in particular, writing on physically *walking* the land that stands out and that will be the focus of the ensuing case study. The past few years have seen a multitude of publications about walking journeys criss-crossing in particular the English countryside. Some recent examples include journalist Peter Mortimer's book *Broke Through England*, first published in 1999, Simon Armitage's *Walking Home* of 2012, and Charlie Carroll's 2013 publication *No Fixed Abode: A Journey Through Homelessness from Cornwall to London*. Mortimer's book is the account of the gruelling 500 miles he walked from Plymouth to Edinburgh without a single penny, entirely relying on the kindness of strangers. Carroll similarly abandoned home comforts and worldly goods to join the large number of homeless people living rough and walking across the country in search of food and shelter. Armitage focuses on his pilgrimage, so to speak, along the Pennine Way, which he walked, unusually, from North to South, and which he undertook in the age-old tradition of the troubadour, singing, almost literally, for his supper and a bed for the night. All three authors similarly assert the complete departure from their everyday routine and life that their respective walks mean to them and, in particular, the intense psychological effects that days spent by themselves in isolated places, navigating difficult terrain, combating bad weather and reaching the limits of their strength has on them. Their narratives thus combine the traditional travelogue with a more personal, more introspective assessment of the self and identity.

Of course, travelogues such as these are not new but are, rather, steeped in the romantic tradition. Rebecca Solnit's 2001 work *Wanderlust* demonstrates that for Romantic poets, William Wordsworth most prominent among them, walking was 'a mode not of traveling, but of being', a mode Wordsworth made 'central to his life and art to a degree almost unparalleled before or since' (2002: 104). Wylie asserts that 'to walk in the English countryside involves at least some attunement with the various sensibilities still distilling from sublime and romantic figurations of self, travel, landscape and nature', sensibilities closely linked to masculine pursuits of solitary walking (2005: 235, 237), and Tim Edensor points out that walking 'is beset by conventions' that have to do with both romantic traditions but also regulations about '"appropriate" bodily conduct, experience and expression' (2000: 83). Included in these 'conventions' is, undoubtedly, the fact that 'the countryside' is a highly politicized concept, closely linked to notions of ownership and power, but also to public and preconceived notions about what exactly it constitutes. Crouch, for instance, points out that 'conceptual debate on landscape has emphasized a relative stability' that is 'familiarly presented in terms of powerful ideologies as sites of representation imposing social relations even to the point of claiming national identity' (2010: 104). Walking the land, however, unsettles the 'considerable popular purchase' that the word 'landscape' entails (Crouch 2010: 105) as it forces the walker to think about practical things: orientating him/herself in a potentially unfamiliar environment; focusing on the movement of the body. According to McNaghten and Urry, 'the body senses as it moves' (2000: 8), as the walker is constantly confronted with new experiences, new sights, sounds and smells. According to Edensor, walking in the country thus 'possesses the potential for disruption' (2000: 102) and it is this disruption that allows for new affective experiences. Solnit explains that 'Walking, ideally, is a state in which the mind, the body, and the world are aligned, as though they were three characters finally in conversation together, three notes suddenly making a chord' (2002: 5). For her,

> the rhythm of walking generates a kind of rhythm of thinking, and the passage through a landscape echoes or stimulates the passage through a

series of thoughts. This creates an odd consonance between internal and external passage, one that suggests that the mind is also a landscape of sorts and that walking is one way to traverse it. (2002: 5–6)

A walk thus becomes a journey in more than just one sense of the word: a journey not only through physical space (i.e. the countryside) but a journey through different experiences, thoughts and emotions that change our perceptions not only of the land we traverse but also ourselves. For the walker this ultimately means not only *feeling* but also actively *creating* their own geographies. No two journeys are the same; there are always different experiences, different emotions as the body responds to different stimuli – the weather, the condition of the path, the encounter with others along the way. And as we follow the traces of those before us in well-trodden paths, so we, in turn, leave our own footsteps: we are affected by the land around us but, in turn, also affect it ourselves. Moving through space, encountering new places, battling with a wide variety of experiences enables the walker to listen to and into the body, to engage with haptic experiences in a new way. To *write* about those affective experiences then means a critical assessment of not only the experiences of the physical and metaphysical journeys but also their affects on the individual's identity and sense of being both with and in the world.

One recent text that stands out in this respect is Robert Macfarlane's *The Old Ways* of 2012. Macfarlane summarizes his writing as 'travel writing, natural history, documentary fiction, cultural history, chorography, biography, bio-geography, psychogeography, auto-biopsychogeography, deep topography, pastoral, post-pastoral, anti-pastoral, (regrettable) bouts of Baedeker, memoir, folklore, folk song, sub-shamanic paeans and pseudo-paeans ...' (Stenning 2013: 77). This merging of genres indicates clearly Macfarlane's attempts to engage with landscape in a new way, as a merging of genres and disciplines that defy and transcend boundaries and for which, effectively, a new language and critical framework has to be developed. At the forefront of Macfarlane's work stands his *own* engagement with the landscape he traverses. For him, it is not only a question of landscape affecting him but also of him, in turn, affecting the landscape – Spinoza's *affectus* and *affectio* again – of leaving his own tracks and traces that merge and mingle with millions of others before him (he says, at the very beginning of his account, 'To all these marks I added my own' [Macfarlane 2012: 7]), thus contributing to the multifarious and rhizomatic histories of place. By walking the land, by leaving his tracks, Macfarlane is literally inscribing himself into the land, affected by its histories but, in turn, affecting these histories himself.

Macfarlane views his walks along old English ways and paths as a 'pilgrimage' (Stenning 2013: 78), a term often used by writers travelling around England on foot – a pilgrimage, importantly, that, according to Macfarlane, helps show 'how we use landscape to make sense of ourselves' and, importantly, make sense 'of the world' too (Stenning 2013: 78, 82). In a departure from other travel accounts, and probably more in keeping with psychogeography, Macfarlane does not attempt to recount the experiences of long journeys. Rather, he picks out specific walks or paths with particular resonance in English mythology; the Icknield Way, for instance, the oldest of England's fabled chalk paths, with its 'origins and history . . . shrouded in myth and confusion' (Macfarlane 2012: 41). He focuses on the small-scale, recounting not only what he sees, but also what he hears – ghostly, inexplicable sounds at night that he later learns are linked to ancient hauntings – touches and feels, what he experiences with all his senses. His article 'A Counter-Desecration Phrasebook' of 2010 is a rallying cry for the invention of a new *affective* language in our engagement with landscape in order to do justice to the whole spectrum of sensual experiences with language. Macfarlane had taken as his starting point the demand for 'a new nomenclature of landscape' (quoted in Smith 2013: 5), issued by the environmental campaigner Finlay MacLeod. Macfarlane's emphasis on language ranges from the reintroduction of almost extinct words denoting landscape (in fact, *The Old Ways* includes a nine-page glossary of countryside and walking-related terminology ranging from '**albedo** The proportion of light reflected from a surface' to '**zawn** (Cornish) A fissure or cave in a coastal cliff' [2012: 365–73]) to a more open acknowledgement of how landscapes *affects* us. 'We are adept, if occasionally embarrassed, at saying what we make of places', he says, 'but we are far less good at saying what places make of us' (2012: 27). Jos Smith refers to Macfarlane's focus on 'naming' as 'an insight into careful acts of attention' (2013: 6). What Smith calls 'careful acts of attention' I argue should be referred to as manifestations of 'affect', as personal insights or epiphanies entirely reliant on the senses, the seeing, the hearing, the touching and feeling. For Macfarlane, walking through the English countryside becomes 'ways of feeling, being and knowing' (2012: 24).

In his pursuit of greater insights and understanding, paths, for Macfarlane, play a major role. Tim Ingold asserts that 'Life is lived . . . along paths, not just in places . . . It is along paths, too, that people grow into a knowledge of the world around them, and describe this world in the stories they tell' (2007: 2). For Macfarlane, paths have a quasi-poetic quality: 'Pilgrim paths, green roads, drove roads, corpse roads, trods, leys, dykes, drongs, sarns, snickets – say the names of paths out loud and at speed and they become a poem or rite – Holloways, bostles, shutes, driftways, lichways, ridings, halterpaths, cartways, carneys, causeways, herepaths' (2012: 13). They are more than simply natural entryways into landscape that allow the walker, at the most basic level, to get from A to B. For the attentive walker, according to Macfarlane, they do not only connect places and allow for easier navigation of potentially difficult terrain but also allow for the exploration of *imagined* terrains, as pathways not only forwards in space but also backwards into histories. Wylie asserts that, in purely physical terms, 'the walker is poised between the country ahead and the country behind, between one step and the next' (2005: 237). But this *physical* experience also extends to the *haptic* experience of the senses in that the walker reflects on those who have trodden the path before him, and those that might come after. Macfarlane himself ponders that, when out walking, 'the eye is enticed by a path, and the mind's eye also. The imagination cannot help but pursue a line in the land – onwards in space, but also backwards in time to the histories of a route and its previous followers' (2012: 15). While walking across the South Downs, Macfarlane repeatedly and extensively refers to the walks and work of the poet Edward Thomas, whose writing and thinking about being in the landscape clearly inspired Macfarlane not only to retrace his steps but also, effectively, to create a work of 'biogeography' (2012: 33) of the poet's life that assesses Thomas in terms of space, place, and his own affective ponderings about self and landscape. Macfarlane explains that, for Thomas, 'paths were imprinted with the "dreams" of each traveler who had walked it, and that his own experiences would "in course of time [also] lie under men's feet"' (2012: 44). This awareness of those who have walked the land before us and the traces they have left is not generally one often and openly engaged with in Western cultures, although it is common in some indigenous cultures such as the Australian Aboriginals, for instance, who follow the Songlines of their ancestors (see also Macfarlane 2012: 28–31). Macfarlane thus effectively traces Thomas's dreamlines, and Thomas himself can be seen to be 'ghosting' the book, an omni-presence having inscribed his footsteps into the very landscape that Macfarlane is now traversing, and so accompanying, 'haunting' him in his walks. And for many walkers, 'to be haunted' and, in turn, 'haunting' the landscape becomes an important component of their respective walks. Referring back to Derrida and reflecting on his own walking experiences, Wylie points out that 'I became more ghostly with every passing step', comparing his walk along the South West coast path as a 'continual passing through' but ultimately concluding that 'to be spectral, however, is not to vanish but to haunt' and that 'to haunt a landscape is to supplement and disturb it' (2005: 245–6). Through affective engagement, landscapes can be seen as ghostscapes: not 'ghostly' in the sense of being deserted, devoid of human life, desolate, but rather in the sense of being spaces that have influenced – but that have also been influenced by – generations before and those yet to come, and where we can see, hear, touch, feel and taste faint traces of the past. By adding his own footsteps to those of Thomas and countless other walkers before him, Macfarlane actively inscribes himself on the Icknield Way, too, adding yet another history, and yet another layer to the landscape around him, and leaving it for future walkers to detect, to decipher, to affectively engage with. In that way, both Thomas and Macfarlane assert, old paths survive, even if concreted over or built upon: they survive as shadows, or faint echoes, as 'certain kinds of knowledge which exceeds the proportional and which can only be sensed, as it were, in passing' (Macfarlane 2012: 51).

For Macfarlane, walking thus 'enables sight and thought rather than encouraging retreat and escape' (2012: 24), and it is important to comprehend that he does not necessarily use the word 'sight' to indicate seeing with the eyes. His account is full of references to the 'footfall as knowledge' (2012: 28) or 'footfall as a way of seeing the landscape; touch as sight' (2012: 29). With this he also has been influenced by Thomas who, famously, taught his wife Helen to walk '"with [her body], not only with [her] legs", feeling the landscape as she walked over it' (2012: 312). Macfarlane thus advocates freeing ourselves from preconceived notions – 'how can feet see?' – and allowing ourselves to absorb and be absorbed by the landscape around us in a way that sees a merging of geography and self: 'what do I know when I am in this place that I can know nowhere else?' and 'what does this place know of me that I cannot know of myself' (2012: 27) he asks. Wylie explains that 'through a walking narrative [the] subject may be disassembled and differently cohered and scattered' (2005: 237). Walking for Macfarlane is thus a multi-sensory experience that takes in seeing, feeling, hearing, touching, and that affects and alters the individual, and this is what Crouch means when talking about 'flirting with space': 'Flirting offers a means through which to explore the character of living spacetime through a number of threads that connect everyday living and our feeling and thinking . . . Flirting with space is a vehicle to explore the dynamics of what is happening and how that flirting can affect things' (2010: 2–3). Things, people, places, stories we thought we knew change shape, take on different meanings, alter our own perceptions. Nothing is set in stone. No experience is the same. Affect changes our perception of the world.

For Macfarlane, the act of walking is thus not only an actual negotiation of space but a 'whole-body experience' that transcends the boundaries we normally function within. An early morning near a long barrow on the Icknield Way gives him 'the feeling of walking in cool water. Among the trees, a taste of moss in the mouth; green silence' (2012: 52). Bodily sensations usually considered 'normal' are being changed and subverted through his intensive and affective engagement with the landscape around him: while we might generally 'touch' or 'feel' moss, the sensations for him become so intense that he professes to 'tasting' it; the silence surrounding him – usually something that is heard, or rather that is conspicuous by the very absence of sound – acquires a colour, becomes something that can be 'seen', and, with 'green', a colour that is generally considered as soothing, as expressing hope, balance and harmony. In our generally noisy and increasingly busy world, Macfarlane's close encounters with landscape offer him a chance to pause; to reflect; to reassess.

For Macfarlane, places that trigger experiences like that are 'border crossings' (2012: 78). He explains that 'we lack – we need – a term for those places where one experiences a "transition" from one known landscape [into another]: somewhere we feel and think significantly differently' (2012: 78). Lone Bertelsen and Andrew Murphie, referring back to Félix Guattari, write that 'affects are *transitions* between states' and that 'a "logic of affects" might even argue that "states" are themselves slow, refrained, or looped affects – in short, passages' (2010: 145). For Macfarlane, these border crossings and transitions are unpredictable but they 'exist even in familiar landscapes' (2012: 78), the unexpected in the expected, so to speak. Kathleen Stewart similarly writes about moments of the-unexpected-in-the-ordinary in the 'Perfectly Ordinary Life', describing them as 'a taste for the miniature, a passion for secrets, a place where desires float free. Life seized in the sidelong glance, the glimpse of something brooding, inexplicable, beautiful. The hunch that everything might become clear if we just keep watching for the faces in the trees' (2003, n.p.). For Roland Barthes, such moments or thresholds create an 'inventory of shimmers' (2005: 77) that examine the intersection between ordinary life and extraordinary encounters and exchanges with the world around us. These transitions, glimpses, shimmers beyond the expected can sometimes have disconcerting, almost otherworldly results for Macfarlane, especially while walking along mythical old English paths. Describing a walk along the Broomway in coastal Essex, allegedly the 'deadliest path' (2012: 59) in Britain and one that can only be navigated at low tide, Macfarlane's language changes from that of hopeful greens and soothing tastes of moss to one of disorientation and dread. He labels the path 'the unearthliest path I have ever walked' (2012: 60) and his language reflects his feeling of unease of navigating a path that becomes subsumed by rising tidal waters within minutes and has cost the lives of many walkers. His narrative, even with the reflective distancing of the writing process, abounds with words such as 'worried', 'anxious', 'confused' (2012: 73) as he strikes out 'barefoot over and into the mirror-world' (2012: 72) of the receding tide, out into what is, effectively, the open sea, his choice of words reflecting his vulnerability – 'barefoot' – in a world lacking perspectives. The Broomway, devoid of traditional markers for orientation that other paths and landscapes afford, disorients Macfarlane and plays tricks on his perception. 'I was experiencing a powerful desire to walk straight out to sea and explore the greater freedoms of this empty tidal world' (2012: 73) and

> my brain was beginning to move unusually, worked upon and changed by the mind-altering substances of this off-shore world, and by the elation that arose from the counter-intuition of walking securely on water. Out there, nothing could be only itself. The eye fed on false colour-values. Similes and metaphors bred and budded. Mirages of scale occurred, and tricks of depth. (2012: 74)

Again, Macfarlane's affective language expresses his disorientation. The landscape he finds himself in assumes drug-like qualities that act strangely on and unhinge his mind, filling him with ecstasy at seemingly achieving almost god-like abilities such as walking on water. The fact that he refers to the Broomway and its surroundings as an 'off-shore world' clearly signals that he considers it to be set apart from the 'normal' world and that it achieves quasi-otherworldly status. The Broomway thus becomes a transitional space for Macfarlane, a border crossing, a 'rite of passage', 'leaving known places outlandish or quickened, revealing continents within counties', a 'xenotopia' (2012: 78) within the otherwise known landscape of coastal Essex. The receding water and its strange reflections, the coastal fog and mist, the distortion of sound out on the tidal flats, all affect Macfarlane both negatively – he professes to being scared of losing his way – and positively as it fills him with an unexpected euphoria. He summarizes the affect acting on him during that walk: 'Felt pressure, sensed texture and perceived space can work upon the body and so too upon the mind, altering the textures and inclinations of thought' (2012: 77) and 'when I think back to the outer miles of that walk, I now recall a strong disorder of perception that caused illusions of the spirit as well as the eye. I recall thought becoming sensational; the substance of landscape so influencing mind that mind's own substance was altered' (2012: 75). The solitary walker on the treacherous Broomway struggles to cope with new and ever-changing haptic information that counters what s/he has considered the norm before and so achieves mind-altering dimensions; the sense that is generally relied upon most – sight – is shown to be deceptive as the eyes struggle with the mirage-like quality of the surroundings: what is 'real'? What 'solid'? What is a mere refraction of the light? Where does land end and water take over? Sounds are either muffled or echo haphazardly across the vast expanse of the empty mudbanks, suggesting deceptive distances and false directions. The temptation is to counter everything the rational walker knows – stick to the path; observe the tidal schedule scrupulously – and to simply keep walking and losing oneself in the sheer endless mirror-world caught between land and sea. The body is affected in previously unknown ways. Brian Massumi explains that

> The thinking-perceiving body moves out to its outer most edge where it meets another body (materiality, force, energy) and draws it into an interaction in the course of which it locks onto that body's affects (capacities for acting and being acted upon) and translates them into a form that is functional for it . . . A set of affects . . . is drawn in, transferred into the substance of the thinking-perceiving body. (1993: 36)

A path that seems to be neither here nor there – marked on maps but only navigable at low tide; a calming presence one moment, a swirling, deadly mass of water the next – becomes, for Macfarlane, a threshold between worlds – that of *terra firma* and the sea – but also a place where time itself seems to morph and play cruel tricks: as a walker, one must never forget about tidal times; yet the path seems to be a place where past, present and future merge, where the receding waters allow glimpses of submerged worlds like Doggerbank and allow a fast-forward to the future, when stretches of contemporary East Anglia might similarly have fallen victim to coastal erosion (Macfarlane 2012: 71). Despite his disturbing experiences on the Broomway that even spilled over into the writing process, however, Macfarlane asserts that, 'for days afterwards I felt calm, level, shining, sand flat' (2012: 81). This use of emotive language clearly exemplifies just how much the affective experience of the walk has impacted on Macfarlane. Crouch convincingly argues that

> the intensities of landscape, however mundane, soft, or powerful, borne in and through representations that are imagined, felt, and observed can circulate feelings of belonging ... To 'feel' landscape ... is a way to imagine one's place in the world. The individual can feel so connected with space that s/he no longer is aware, momentarily, of being (merely) human; we may *become* ... landscape. (2010: 116)

Macfarlane's sense of panic, the feeling of disorientation are both gone. Instead, the experience has left him serene, seemingly having merged with the landscape he traversed.

Critics might see Macfarlane's preoccupation with old paths, tracks and hollow-ways as the emotionally charged effusions of a romantic dreamer, charges, incidentally, also often levelled at Affect Theorists. Gregg and Seigworth highlight that theories of affect 'have sometimes been viewed as naïvely or romantically wandering too far out into the groundlessness of a world's or a body's myriad inter-implications, letting themselves get lost in an over-abundance of swarming, sliding differences' (2010: 4), and Macfarlane himself warns of the dangers of becoming 'too full of the romance of the way' (2012: 42). But Wylie points out that it is perhaps this very 'solitary romantic inheritance ... [that] is open to reflexive questioning and re-working in contemporary travelling narratives' (2005: 237). The small-scale attention Macfarlane pays to what he sees, hears, feels, tastes or touches during his walks along hollow-ways or sea paths ultimately deviates from the larger picture that traditional, romantic travel accounts have presented. In many of those accounts, the solitary walker experienced a moment of epiphany that explained to him who he was and where he belonged in the world. By contrast, the landscapes presented in contemporary affective travelogues are seen as 'affective bloom space[s]' full of the 'promise' and 'potential' that Seigworth and Gregg (2010: 10, 2, 12) refer to. The paths and tracks Macfarlane traverses offer limitless and ever-changing experiences: changes in the weather, in the season, will immediately create different affects as the walker has to adapt to changes in the path, be more vigilant to his surroundings. So, like the paths he walks, Macfarlane's ambling and winding narrative links and connects to construct a more intimate picture of the landscape that he travels through that is far removed from the corporate image of 'the countryside' as a place of one powerful, all-pervasive and unifying meaning sold to us by the media and, by extension, those in power. Macfarlane's countryside does not hark back nostalgically, nor does it conform to populist notions of a green and pleasant land inhabited largely by a happy breed of sheep. Instead, it blends past, present and future histories and affirms that all these experiences, feelings and sensations are out there for all of us to see and experience in our own ways if only we allow ourselves to be open to them. Affectively engaging with the landscapes around him means that, for

Macfarlane, the process of walking, the journey, the space he traverses, and the active and critical engagement with them during the writing process commingle and merge.

Affect Theory thus allows for a more meaningful engagement not only with landscape but with the world around us at large. Drawn from a variety of disciplines it liberates us from overly restrictive academic jargon and enables us to focus on the subjective, the personal, the haptic. Affects are indeed, as David Crouch's epigraph to this chapter suggests, 'diverse and multiple' (2010: 132). Encountered in both the extra- and the ordinary, the everyday and the special occasion, 'affect' allows us to perceive the unlimited possibilities of life, where nothing is finite or set in stone, nothing preconceived or prescribed, and so engenders an ongoing process that changes 'being' into 'becoming'.

QUESTIONS FOR FURTHER CONSIDERATION

1. As set out at the beginning of the chapter, 'affect', at its most basic, refers to the senses and the personal, to things that move us. What is your spontaneous response to that as a new academic theory?
2. Affect Theory makes the 'ordinary' and the 'everyday' the focal point of academic work. Does that make it fundamentally different from other theories you have encountered so far?
3. How does affect shape us and our evaluation of the world around us, and how does it, in turn, affect our environment?
4. In its beginnings, 'Affect Theory' has been employed mainly by psychogeographers, urban walkers exploring their surroundings and trying to see them with new eyes. Over the past few years, though, it has developed into a cross-disciplinary theory. How relevant do you consider it for Literary Studies, and how can it be differentiated from the much earlier Romantic Movement?
5. Landscape has, traditionally, been used not only as a marker of national identity but also as an active tool in the creation of national identity. It has often been presented in an overarching metanarrative with a political agenda. How is the affective landscape writing of Macfarlane and other writers like him different from that?
6. Go on an 'affective walk': follow your usual way to work / university / college but try to pay close(r) attention to your surroundings. Walk without earphones, or without using your phone; don't hurry; listen to the sound of your footfall on the pavement; look around you, taking in the surroundings that are often ignored on a familiar route. Does this way of walking a familiar path become a different experience and can it, indeed, become 'limitless'?

BIBLIOGRAPHY

Ahmed, Sara (2010) 'Happy Objects', in Gregory J. Seigworth and Melissa Gregg, eds., *The Affect Theory Reader*, Durham NC: Duke University Press.

Anderson, Ben (2010) 'Modulating the Excess of Affect', in Gregory J. Seigworth and Melissa Gregg, eds., *The Affect Theory Reader*, Durham NC: Duke University Press.

Armitage, Simon (2012) *Walking Home: Travels with a Troubadour on the Pennine Way*, London: Faber & Faber.

Bachelard, Gaston (1994) *The Poetics of Space* [1964], trans. Maria Jolas, Boston: Beacon Press.

Barthes, Roland (2005) *The Neutral*, trans. Rosalind E. Krauss and Denis Hollier, New York: Columbia University Press.

Bennett, Jane (2001) *The Enchantment of Modern Life: Attachment, Crossings, and Ethics*, Princeton: Princeton University Press.

Berberich, Christine, Neil Campbell and Robert Hudson (2013) 'Affective Landscapes: An Introduction', *Cultural Politics* 9:3, pp. 313–22.

Berberich, Christine, Neil Campbell and Robert Hudson, eds. (forthcoming) *Affective Landscapes in Literature, Art and Everyday Life*, Aldershot: Ashgate.

Bertelsen, Lone and Andrew Murphie (2010) 'An Ethics of Everyday Infinites and Powers: Félix Guattari on Affect and the Refrain', in Gregory J. Seigworth and Melissa Gregg, eds., *The Affect Theory Reader*, Durham NC: Duke University Press.

Carroll, Charlie (2013) *No Fixed Abode: A Journey Through Homelessness from Cornwall to London*, Chichester: Summersdale Publishers Ltd.

Clough, Patricia Ticineto (2007) 'Introduction', in Patricia Ticineto Clough with Jean Halley, eds. (2007) *The Affective Turn: Theorizing the Social*, Durham NC: Duke University Press.

Crouch, David (2010) *Flirting with Space: Journeys and Creativity*, Aldershot: Ashgate.

Deleuze, Gilles and Félix Guattari (1994) *What is Philosophy?*, trans. Graham Burchell and Hugh Tomlinson, London: Verso.

Dewsbury, John D., Paul Harrison, Mitch Rose and John Wylie (2002) 'Enacting Geographies', *Geoforum* 32, pp. 437–41.

Edensor, Tim (2000) 'Walking in the British Countryside: Reflexivity, Embodied Practices and Ways to Escape', *Body and Society* 6:1, pp. 81–106.

Hardt, Michael (2007) 'Foreword: What Affects are Good for', in Patricia Ticineto Clough with Jean Halley, eds. *The Affective Turn: Theorizing the Social*, Durham NC: Duke University Press.

Ingold, Tim (2007) *Lines: A Brief History*, London: Routledge.

Macfarlane, Robert (2010) 'A Counter-Desecration Phrasebook', in Di Robson and Gareth Evans, eds., *Towards Re-Enchantment: Place and Its Meaning*, London: Art Events.

Macfarlane, Robert (2012) *The Old Ways. A Journey on Foot*, London: Hamish Hamilton.

McNaghten, Phil and John Urry (2000) 'Bodies of Nature: Introduction', *Body and Society* 6:1, pp. 1–11.

Massey, Doreen (1994) *Space, Place and Gender*, Cambridge: Polity

Massumi, Brian (1993) *A User's Guide to Capitalism and Schizophrenia: Deviations from Deleuze and Guattari*, Cambridge MA: MIT Press.

Massumi, Brian (2002) *Parables for the Virtual: Movement, Affect, Sensation*, Durham NC: Duke University Press.

Mortimer, Peter (2006) *Broke Through England: One Man's Penniless Odyssey* [1999], Edinburgh: Mainstream Publishing Company Ltd.

Seigworth, Gregory J. and Melissa Gregg (2010) 'An Inventory of Shimmers', in Gregory J. Seigworth and Melissa Gregg, eds., *The Affect Theory Reader*, Durham NC: Duke University Press.

Smith, Jos (2013) 'An Archipelagic Literature: Re-framing "The New Nature Writing"', *Green Letters: Studies in Ecocriticism* 17:1, pp. 5–15.

Solnit, Rebecca (2002) *Wanderlust: A History of Walking* [2001], London: Verso.

Stenning, Anna (2013) 'An Interview with Robert Macfarlane', *Green Letters: Studies in Ecocriticism* 17:1, pp. 77–83.

Stewart, Kathleen (2003) 'The Perfectly Ordinary Life', *The Scholar and Feminist Online* 2:1.

Stewart, Kathleen (2007) *Ordinary Affects*, Durham NC: Duke University Press.

Watkins, Megan (2010) 'Desiring Recognition, Accumulating Affect', in Gregory J. Seigworth and Melissa Gregg, eds., *The Affect Theory Reader*, Durham NC: Duke University Press.

Wylie, John (2005) 'A Single Day's Walking: Narrating Self and Landscape on the South West Coast Path', *Transactions of the Institute of British Geographers* 30:2, pp. 234–47.

SPACE AND PLACE IN CRITICAL READING

Phillip E. Wegner

All the world's a stage,
And all the men and women merely players.
They have their exits and their entrances,
And one man in his time plays many parts,
His acts being seven ages.

As You Like It (II. vii. 11.139–43)

These celebrated lines from William Shakespeare's *As You Like It* effectively illustrate some of the dominant assumptions about space and spatiality that come to prevail in the histories of Western modernity: space is understood as an empty container, of very little interest in and of itself, within which unfolds the real drama, that of history and human passions. Michel Foucault similarly notes in an often cited 1976 interview the 'devaluation of space' that had prevailed for 'generations of intellectuals': 'Space was treated as the dead, the fixed, the undialectical, the immobile. Time, on the contrary, was richness, fecundity, life, dialectic.' Foucault goes on to argue:

> For all those who confuse history with the old schemas of evolution, living continuity, organic development, the progress of consciousness or the project of existence, the use of spatial terms seems to have an air of an antihistory. If one started to talk in terms of space that meant one was hostile to time. (1980: 70)

The Australian historian Paul Carter, even more directly echoing Shakespeare's lines, describes the dominant narrative mode of what he calls modernity's 'imperial history' as one 'which reduces space to a stage, that pays attention to events unfolding in time alone . . . Rather than focus on the *intentional* world of historical individuals, the world of active, spatial choices, empirical history of this kind has as its focus facts which, in a sense, come after the event' (1987: xvi).

This privileging of temporality and history over space has its literary analogue in a critical tradition that, especially beginning in the latter part of the nineteenth century with writers like Henry James and, as we shall see below, Joseph Conrad, celebrates the portrayal of the complex psychology of characters as the highest achievement of narrative art. Characters are fundamentally temporal constructs that unfold in a space, or 'setting', which, once established, seems to remain constant. Space is thus once again treated as the 'stage' upon which the drama of character development unfolds, and setting in such a tradition is viewed as distinctly secondary in importance to character. Moreover, in the increasing interiorization that occurs in certain strands of modernist fiction – which, in turn, have a marked influence on how we read earlier literary works as well – any concern with setting or space outside that of the individual consciousness seems to vanish. This occurs in a moment that, as the geographer Edward Soja points out in his groundbreaking study, *Postmodern Geographies: The Reassertion of Space in Critical Social Theory*, also saw the subordination of the spatial problematic in social theory (1989: 31–5).

It is precisely these presuppositions that have been increasingly called into question by a growing interdisciplinary formation centred on the problematics of 'space', 'place' and 'cultural geography'. The last three decades of the twentieth century saw a dramatic increase in scholarly interest in these questions. Contributors to this vast and multiform research project might be numbered to include, among others, social theorists and historians like Arjun Appadurai, Carter, Michel de Certeau, Mike Davis, Foucault, Anthony Giddens, Henri Lefebvre and Saskia Sassen; geographers Derek Gregory, David Harvey, Doreen Massey, Neil Smith, Soja and Yi-Fu Tuan; architects Zaha Hadid, Rem Koolhaas, Daniel Libeskind, Manfredo Tafuri and Bernard Tschumi; anthropologists James Clifford, Allen Feldman and Paul Rabinow; philosophers Judith Butler, Edward S. Casey, Giles Deleuze, Jacques Derrida and Elisabeth Grosz; art critics Victor Burgin and T. J. Clark; and literary and cultural critics, Susan Stanford Friedman, Inderpal Grewhal, bell hooks, Fredric Jameson, Caren Kaplan, Lydia Liu, Louis Marin, Meaghan Morris, Kristin Ross, Edward Said and Raymond Williams. There was also in these years a return to the work of earlier thinkers who each in their own way took up what were in their time unfashionable spatial questions: this would include the discussions of embodiment, 'world', enframement and dwelling in Martin Heidegger's *Being and Time* and later essays; the explorations of the relationships between northern and southern Italy in a moment of dramatic social and cultural modernization found in Antonio Gramsci's *Prison Notebooks*; the lyrical spatial phenomenology of Gaston Bachelard's *The Poetics of Space*; the detailed analysis of an array of the novelistic 'chronotopes', 'the intrinsic connectedness of temporal and spatial relationships that are artistically expressed in literature', offered by Mikhail M. Bakhtin (1981: 84); and the stunning mappings of the spaces and cultural flows of nineteenth-century Paris found in Walter Benjamin's fragmentary and incomplete *Passagen-werk* (*Arcades Project*).

What links the diverse projects of these thinkers together is a common challenge to the Enlightenment and Cartesian notion of space as an objective homogeneous extension (*res extensa*), distinct from the subject (*res cogitans*), and the Kantian concept of space as an empty container in which human activities unfold. Against such presuppositions, the work of these thinkers show how space itself is both a *production*, shaped through a variety of social processes and human interventions, and a *force* that, in turn, influences, directs and delimits possibilities of action and ways of human being in the world. Western modernity, as Soja emphasizes, is thus to be reconceived as a historical *and* a geographical-spatial project, a continuous dissolution and reorganization of the environments, including our bodies, that we all inhabit.

This new attention to the productions of space entered into literary studies from a number of different directions: from Marxism and critical theory, space being, as Soja and Harvey effectively demonstrate, already a central concern in much of Marx's own work; from colonial and postcolonial studies, which brought into focus the effects of European domination over space and the migrations and interactions of different cultures and populations; from feminism, gender and sexuality studies, where the issues of the body, affect, sexuality and the embodiment of the subject have been of crucial importance; from popular culture and genre studies, where the specific practices of non-canonical cultural forms have been brought into sharper focus; and, as the list above suggests, from a rich and growing conversation with work being done in a broad range of other disciplines.

Two of the thinkers who contributed the most to the revival of interest in the role of space in the projects of Western modernity are the French social theorists, Henri Lefebvre and Michel Foucault. Lefebvre's major work of spatial theorization, *The Production of Space* (1974) – first translated into English in 1991 – has had a dramatic impact on work being done in a wide range of disciplines, ranging from urbanism, architecture and social theory to literary and cultural studies. In his rich and brilliant example of a spatial dialectical thinking, Lefebvre rejects the older 'representation' of space as 'a preexisting void, endowed with formal properties alone . . . a container waiting to be filled by a content – i.e. matter, or bodies' (1991: 170). Instead, he shows in great detail how the emergence and development of capitalist modernity occurs through a particular '(social) production of (social) space' – that is, a space that is fundamentally produced by and through human actions, and which is thus 'constituted neither by a collection of things or an aggregate of (sensory) data, nor by a void packed like a parcel with various contents, and . . . it is irreducible to a "form" imposed upon phenomena, upon things, upon physical materiality' (1991: 26–7). '(Social) space', Lefebvre maintains, 'is not a thing among other things, nor a product among other products: rather, it subsumes things produced, and encompasses their interrelationships in their coexistence and simultaneity – their (relative) order and/or (relative) disorder' (1991: 73). For Lefebvre, such a space is deeply historical, its moments of apparent stability short-lived and contingent at best: indeed, Lefebvre suggests that one of the great temptations produced by the Enlightenment conceptualization of space as a static construct is that we think of it as a reified thing rather than as an open-ended, conflicted and contradictory *process*, a process in which we as agents continuously intervene.

Moreover, Lefebvre argues that such a space is itself never constituted as a singularity, as other traditions of spatial thought might suggest, such as those of structuralism and phenomenology with their respective focus on the subjective and objective dimensions of space. Instead, Lefebvre develops a 'concrete abstract' tripartite model of space that attempts at once to take account of and draw into a coherent ensemble these various dimensions. Lefebvre argues that any socially produced historical space is constituted by a dialectically interwoven matrix of what he calls 'spatial practices', 'representations of space' and 'spaces of representation', each allied with a specific cognitive mode through which we 're-present' it to ourselves: respectively, the domains of the 'perceived', the 'conceived' and the 'lived' (1991: 33–46). The first of his three 'levels' of space pertains to the most abstract processes of social production, reproduction, cohesion and structuration, and hence bears a striking resemblance to the concerns of the various structuralisms whose 'perceptual' apparatus takes on the abstract conceptual systematicity of a science. The third set of terms refers, on the other hand, to the space of the embodied individual's cultural experience and the signs, images, forms and symbols that constitute it: it is this level of space that has been mapped so thoroughly by phenomenology, whose emphasis on the individual's 'lived' existential experience of space resonates with that found in this dimension of Lefebvre's work. The middle terms, those of the representations of space or the realm of the conceived, point towards what we more conventionally think as 'space' proper, mediating between and drawing all three of the levels together into a coherent ensemble. Of the social and cultural practices that constitute this middle dimension of space, Lefebvre writes, 'conceptualized space, the space of scientists, planners, urbanists, technocratic subdividers and social engineers, as of a certain type of artist with a scientific bent – all of whom identify what is lived and what is perceived with what is conceived' (1991: 38).

Thus, bringing together the very different projects of structural and phenomenological criticism, Lefebvre's work also offers a powerful rejoinder to the tangential textualization of the world, or what he calls the 'generalization of the concept of mental space', at play in certain strands of structuralist, semiotic and poststructuralist theory (1991: 3). Lefebvre links these theorizations to a growing predominance in modern times of the 'visual', which, he argues, 'has increasingly taken precedence over elements of thought and action deriving from other senses' (1991: 139). This in turn is connected to the increasingly global trend in the history of capitalism towards what Lefebvre names 'abstract space' – a homogeneity on the level of spatial practices and fragmentation and isolation on the level of representations of space, or 'lived' experience (1991: 285–91). This latter formulation also had a marked impact on the development in the 1970s and 1980s of the theorization of 'postmodernism', especially in the work of thinkers such as David Harvey and Fredric Jameson. And in another important refinement of Lefebvre's project, Neil Smith eloquently argues for the necessity, when reading any particular cultural phenomenon, of taking into account its simultaneous embeddedness in a number of different 'nested' spatial contexts: body, home, community, city, region, nation and globe. Smith notes, 'By setting boundaries, scale can be constructed as a means of constraint and exclusion, a means of imposing identity, but a politics of scale can also become a weapon of expansion and inclusion, a means of enlarging identity' (1993: 114).

While Lefebvre's work offers a powerful framework for thinking through the spatial dimensions of modern society and culture, Michel Foucault, especially in his central text of the mid-1970s, *Discipline and Punish: The Birth of the Prison* (1975), presents a meticulous genealogical history of the spatial transformations that give rise to our modern world. Foucault's text is written very much in the spirit of earlier critical histories of modernity such as those offered by Max Weber and Theodor Adorno; however, Foucault's great achievement is to give this narrative a distinctively spatial turn. Foucault opens his examination by focusing a heightened attention upon the body, and in particular 'the way in which the body itself is invested by power relations' (1977: 24). Foucault announces that 'Our society is one not of spectacle, but of surveillance', and throughout his text he meticulously reconstructs the genealogy of such a modern form of power (1977: 217).

In the moment of the Absolutist monarch, Foucault argues, the individual body becomes the subject of a highly public 'theatre' of punishment that is located in a specific ritualized space, still distant from everyday life. However, precisely because this system is such a public and spectacular one, it is deeply unstable, open to a dramatic reversal at the hands of those who are its intended subjects. (A wonderful example of such an older system of power, as well as its potential for transgressive, carnivalesque inversion, is portrayed in the opening chapters of Walter Scott's *The Heart of Mid-Lothian*.) Thus, in place of this older logic of power there gradually emerges a new system in which every body finds itself located in 'a great enclosed, complex, and hierarchical structure', and subject to a continuous regime of surveillance and manipulation (1977: 115). A whole series of operations, which Foucault names 'discipline' – instruments, techniques, procedures, levels of application, targets' (1977:

215) – arise with the aim of producing 'normal' subjects as well as marking out a whole finely graduated realm of deviancies: 'Thus discipline produces subjected and practised bodies, "docile" bodies' (1977: 138).

The model and most complete realization of this new kind of machinery of power are to be found in Jeremy Bentham's ideal of prison architecture, the panopticon. Within this structure, the individual prisoner is placed in a state of permanent 'visibility', subject to the unseen gaze of authority. Never knowing when they are under observation, these subjects come to internalize the self-policing demanded of them. Crucially, Foucault maintains that

> the Panopticon must not be understood as a dream building: it is the diagram of a mechanism of power reduced to its ideal form; its functioning, abstracted from any obstacle, resistance or friction, must be represented as a pure architectural and optical system: it is in fact a figure of political technology that may and must be detached from any particular use.
>
> It is polyvalent in its applications; it serves to reform prisoners, but also to treat patients, to instruct schoolchildren, to confine the insane, to supervise workers, to put beggars and idlers to work. It is a type of location of bodies in space, of distribution of individuals in relation to one another, of hierarchical organization, of disposition of centres and channels of power, of definition of the instruments and modes of intervention of power, which can be implemented in hospitals, workshops, schools, prisons. (1977: 205)

'Is it surprising', Foucault later asks, 'that prisons resemble factories, schools, barracks, hospitals, which all resemble prisons?' (1977: 228) As such a technology gets generalized across the social space, it generates a veritable 'carceral network' which 'in its compact or disseminated forms, with its systems of insertion, distribution, surveillance, observation, has been the greatest support, in modern society, of the normalizing power' (1977: 304).

The influence of Foucault's work across a wide range of disciplines has been profound. In terms of literary scholarship, his influence has been especially evident in work in the so-called 'New Historicism', Foucault's model of the panopticon being one of the inspirations, for example, of Stephen Greenblatt's re-reading of Thomas More's *Utopia* in his book *Renaissance Self-Fashioning From More to Shakespeare* (1980). Similarly, the questions concerning the production of the body and subjectivity raised by Foucault have been developed in fascinating and important new ways by feminist theorists. Elizabeth Grosz, to take only one example, argues that while it is important to think of questions of subjectivity in corporeal rather than disembodied conscious terms, the investigation needs to move even further: 'It is not enough to reformulate the body in non-dualist and non-essentialist terms. It must also be reconceived in specifically *sexed* terms. Bodies are never simply *human* bodies or *social* bodies' (1995: 84). Finally, one of the most interesting extensions of

Foucault's investigation of social space can be found in the US anthropologist Paul Rabinow's *French Modern: Norms and Forms of the Social Environment* (1989). This rich and wide-ranging genealogical history focuses upon how a diverse group of nineteenth-century intellectuals, working in a number of distinct fields, all came to understand the ways in which 'norms' – proper behaviours in, inhabitations of and movements through the world – are shaped by various spatial 'forms' – architectural, urbanistic, national and so forth. Emphasizing the deeply spatial nature of the revolutions of modernity, Rabinow investigates transformations in nineteenth-century architectural and urban practices, among a diverse range of linked fields, in order to trace out a developing programme, termed in English 'welfare', for using 'the planned city as a regulator of modern society' (1989: 12).

While Rabinow diverges from Foucault in his greater willingness to consider the progressive possibilities of certain productions of modern spatiality, both thinkers acknowledge that if social and cultural spaces, including the body, are indeed the product of human actions, then there is the possibility of our reconstituting human spaces, and hence human being-in-the-world as well. Space then is conceived not only as the *site* of politics, conflict and struggle, but also the very thing being fought over. This approach too suggests a link between contemporary critical examinations of space and spatiality and the great transformative architectural and urban planning programmes developed by Ebenezer Howard, Tony Ganier, the Bauhaus, Le Corbusier, Frank Lloyd Wright and others in the moment of cultural modernism – a moment that also witnessed in the visual arts a widespread challenge to the perspectivalism that had dominated both Western art and thought from the Italian Renaissance onwards.

Not surprisingly, a good deal of the contemporary projects for reconstructing social space also arise from within the discourses of architecture and urbanism: these include, for example, Rem Koolhaas's 'retroactive manifesto' for the unfulfilled project he labels Manhattanism (1994: 9–10), and Jacques Derrida's provocative collaborations with architect Peter Eisenman on spaces produced for Bernard Tschumi's innovative *Pare de La Villette* in Paris. Derrida has described the latter project as involving a deconstruction of some of the fundamental assumptions that have underwritten Western architectural discourse and practice: 'for instance, the hegemony of the aesthetic, of beauty, the hegemony of usefulness, of functionality, of living, of dwelling'. However, this is only part of the project of a deconstructive architecture, and Derrida goes on to argue that

> then you have to *reinscribe* those motifs within the work. You can't (or you shouldn't) simply dismiss those values of dwelling, functionality, beauty and so on. You have to construct, so to speak, a new space and a new form, to shape a new way of building in which those motifs or values are reinscribed, having meanwhile lost their external hegemony. (Papadakis et al. 1989: 73)

Other figures who have been influenced by Derrida's thoughts on architecture include architects such as Daniel Libeskind, Coop Himmelblau and Zaha Hadid, and critics including Kojin Karatani, Jeffrey Kipnis, Marc Wigley and Anthony Vidler. Vidler, in *Warped Space: Art, Architecture, and Anxiety in Modern Culture* (2000), extends this project in exciting new directions by exploring the ways various forms of anxiety became incorporated into the very texture of modern architectural, urban, and mass media space.

There has also been increasing attention given to the ways that diverse subaltern publics are able to 'divert and reappropriate' dominated spaces. Such lessons are to be found, for example, in Michel de Certeau's celebrated evocation of a transgressive 'walking in the city' effected by the very people who inhabit it (1984: 91–110); in Meaghan Morris's extraordinary reading of the innovative spatial project to be discovered in the Australian 'documentary' film, *A Spire* (1998: 123–57); in Judith Butler's examination of the new communal spaces figured in the film *Paris is Burning* (1993: 121–40); and in Allan Feldman's stunning analysis of the 'radical deconstruction and reassemblage of the body' that occurred in the IRA Hunger Strike of 1981 (1991: 204). Such practices are of 'great significance', Lefebvre notes, 'for they teach us much about the production of new spaces' (1991: 167). However, as Lefebvre goes on to note, and indeed as Derrida and many of these other thinkers also point out, such moves must be considered only opening gestures, 'which can call but a temporary halt to domination' (1991: 168). The real aim always remains the 'production' of new kinds of spaces.

The conceptual reorientations that Lefebvre, Foucault and these other thinkers offer also promise to transform literary and cultural analysis in a number of different ways. First, their work has helped to foster an increasing attention to the representation of space within literary and other cultural texts and to the ways that an attention to spatial questions transforms how we think about literary history. Such a dual project is already evident in Raymond Williams's classic survey of modern British literature, *The Country and the City* (1973). Williams examines the changing 'structures of feeling' concerning the relationships between the 'city' and the 'country', as well as the transformations and expansions that occur in the very definition of each of these inseparable conceptual poles, as these are negotiated in the tradition of modern British literature, a tradition he traces from the country-house poems of the sixteenth century up through the global literatures of his present. Williams argues for a special significance of the English experience in this narrative, 'in that one of the decisive transformations, in the relations between country and city, occurred there very early and with a thoroughness which is still in some ways unapproached' – he is referring here to the British industrial revolution (1973: 2). Williams is especially sensitive to the ways literary and cultural texts *reflect* changes in actual spatial practices, those initiated by these processes of modernization, and to these works' capacity to register changing sensibilities before they enter fully into explicit public discourse.

More recently, a similar kind of investigation continues in such ground-breaking works as Kristin Ross's *The Emergence of Social Space: Rimbaud and the Paris Commune* (1988), a study drawing directly upon Lefebvre's work and looking at the ways Arthur Rimbaud's poetry, as well as a host of other cultural productions, respond to and find inspiration in both the expansion of French imperial power and the revolutionary urban spatial possibilities illuminated in the short-lived 1871 Paris Commune. Edward Said's magisterial *Culture and Imperialism* (1993) argues for the importance of a careful attention to the 'geographical notation, the theoretical mapping and charting of territory that underlies Western fiction, historical writing, and philosophical discourse' (1993: 58). Franco Moretti's *Atlas of the European Novel, 1800–1900* (1998) examines the productions of fictional space that occur within European novels of the nineteenth century, and of the circulation and distribution of various novelistic productions across the 'real' space of Europe and the globe. Sharon Marcus's *Apartment Stories: City and Home in Nineteenth Century Paris and London* (1999) tackles literary representations of an often overlooked and yet central urban phenomenon, the apartment house. The author of this essay, in *Imaginary Communities: Utopia, the Nation, and the Spatial Histories of Modernity* (2002), uses the work of Lefebvre and many of the other figures discussed in this essay to read the imaginings of a new national community that takes place in utopian literature beginning with Thomas More. Cesare Casarino's *Modernity at Sea: Melville, Marx, Conrad in Crisis* (2002) interrogates the ship novels of Conrad and Herman Melville through the lens of Foucault's spatial figure of the 'heterotopia' (also see Foucault 1998: 175–85). Julian Wolfreys's three-volume *Writing London* (1998, 2004 and 2007) explores an extraordinary range of literary representations and negotiations of metropolitan space in writings from William Blake up through the late twentieth century. In a much-discussed 2006 essay, Susan Stanford Friedman makes an appeal for a 'full spatialization of modernism', which she maintains 'changes the map, the canon, and the periodization of modernism dramatically' (2006: 426). Finally, Edward Dimendberg's *Film Noir and the Spaces of Modernity* (2004) investigates the preoccupation with the urban landscape in US cinema in the decades following the Second World War.

At the same time, an attention to spatial concerns further calls into question the very constitution of the literary canon as it helps us to become more sensitive to the different kinds of work that are performed by various literary genres, modes and other forms of textuality. This kind of reorientation is perhaps nowhere more evident than in the wide-ranging intellectual project of the influential Marxist literary and cultural scholar Fredric Jameson. For example, in his landmark book, *The Political Unconscious* (1981), Jameson contrasts the different representational work performed by the modern novel and the older prose romance. The goal of the romance, Jameson shows us, is to spark in the reader a new awareness of what it means to be-in-the-world by highlighting the *'worldness' of world'*, the specific constructedness of the geographies and environments such a reader always already inhabits (1981: 112). Thus, if the novel focuses on 'character', making us aware of and even contributing to the development of a modern centred subjectivity, the romance gives expression to the 'experience' of settings, worlds or spaces. Character, Jameson maintains, thus functions in the romance in a very different way than in the novel: in this older form it serves as a formal 'registering apparatus' whose movements during the course of the narrative action produce a traveller's itinerary of both the 'local intensities' and 'horizons' of the space that the narrative itself calls into being (1981: 112). Jameson uses this rethinking of the work of the romance as the basis for reading the particular narrative operations of texts ranging from the classical chivalric cycles to Stendhal's *The Red and the Black* and Emily Brontë's *Wuthering Heights*.

Jameson has explored similar spatial mapping operations in genres and works as diverse as the *noir* detective fiction of Raymond Chandler, More's *Utopia*, James Joyce's *Ulysses*, the 'national allegory' of Third World literature, the conspiracy film and the major modern form of the prose romance, what H. G. Wells first named 'scientific romance', and today we call science fiction. In each case, Jameson maintains that we need to dispense with the grail of a singular universal set of criteria defining 'great literature', against which we can then evaluate all works, regardless of the time, place or situation of their production, and instead become more sensitive to the particular aims, practices and strategies of diverse works, genres and forms. Thus, for example, in his much discussed essay on Third World literature, Jameson argues that one of the most common contemporary critical errors is the reading of 'non-canonical forms of literature' in terms of the canon itself (by which he means here the forms and rhythms of a hegemonic European realism and modernism): not only is such an approach 'peculiarly self-defeating because it borrows the weapons of the adversary', it passes 'over in silence the radical difference' of these works (1986: 65). Similarly in one of his early essays on science fiction, now collected together in *Archaeologies of the Future: The Desire Called Utopia and Other Science Fictions* (2005), Jameson suggests that works in this genre eschew the pleasures and demands of canonical forms of literature – those of complex psychological portraits of 'realistic' characters and 'well-formed plots' – and thereby free themselves for an operation of *spatial* imagining: 'the collective adventure accordingly becomes less that of a character (individual or collective) than that of a planet, a climate, a weather and a system of landscapes – in short, a map. We need to explore the proposition that the distinctiveness of SF as a genre has less to do with time (history, past, future) than with space' (2005: 313).

This attention to the way various cultural texts 'map' space has also contributed to one of Jameson's most influential formulations, that of the political aesthetic practice he names, drawing upon the work of architectural historian Kevin Lynch, 'cognitive mapping'. Jameson first describes the practices of cognitive mapping in his widely influential 1984 essay on 'postmodernism', which he characterizes as 'the cultural logic of late capitalism'. One of the most significant aspects of the new cultural situation of postmodernism is, according to Jameson, 'the waning of our historicity, of our lived possibility of experiencing history in some active way'; conversely, our culture is one 'increasingly dominated by space and spatial logic' (1991: 21, 25). Indeed, while Jameson acknowledges, again following the lead of Lefebvre, that all social organizations are defined by distinctive productions of space, 'ours has been spatialized in a unique sense, such that space is for us an existential and cultural dominant, a thematized and foregrounded feature or structural principle standing in striking contrast to its relatively subordinate and secondary (though no doubt no less symptomatic) role in earlier modes of production' (1991: 365). Jameson's periodizing description of postmodernism thus also enables us to account for the sudden renewal in the early 1970s of interest in questions of space and spatiality (it's worth noting here that the texts of Williams, Lefebvre, Foucault and de Certeau discussed above all appear within a few years of one another): for this is the moment, Jameson argues, when postmodernism emerges as a new 'cultural dominant' within Western industrial nations. These theorizations of space then themselves become both symptomatic of and important preliminary efforts to navigate the terrain of this new cultural situation.

However, mutations in space on all its levels have created difficulties for us as individual and collective subjects. 'We do not yet possess the perceptual equipment' to navigate and position ourselves within this increasingly urbanized and global social and cultural space, our cognitive 'organs' having been developed in an earlier historical situation (1991: 38). In order to help us overcome this lag, Jameson issues a call for a new kind of 'cognitive and pedagogical' cultural practice, one which 'will necessarily have to raise spatial issues as its fundamental organizing concern' (1991: 50–1). It is this aesthetic practice which Jameson names cognitive mapping: 'a pedagogical political culture which seeks to endow the individual subject with some heightened sense of its place in the global system' (1991: 54). Thus, occupying a place similar to Lefebvre's 'conceived' space, the *practice* of cognitive mapping – which, it should be stressed, is never to be confused with some impossible total cognitive 'map' – provides a way of connecting our lived experiences of the present to the abstract systematic theorizations we have of this new global cultural and social network. On this basis, Jameson investigates the way an incredibly rich variety of cultural practices – ranging from the science fiction novels of Philip K. Dick, Hollywood films such as *Dog Day Afternoon*, *Something Wild* and *Blue Velvet*, the installation art of Robert Gober and the architecture of Frank Gehry – engage in incomplete forms of or stand as allegories for cognitive mapping. For example, in his discussion of Gehry's much-analysed home in southern California, Jameson argues that

> the very concept of space here demonstrates its supremely mediatory function, in the way in which its aesthetic formulation begins at once to

> entail cognitive consequences on the one hand and sociopolitical conse-
> quences on the other . . . The problem, then, which the Gehry house tries
> to think is the relationship between that abstract knowledge and convic-
> tion or belief about the superstate and the existential daily life of people
> in their traditional rooms and tract houses. (1991: 104, 128)

As the above descriptions suggest, Jameson's model of cognitive mapping
represents an attempt to develop the tools required to 'think' a new kind of
global cultural and social reality, as well as our place within it, a project he
then makes explicit in his film study, *The Geo-Political Aesthetic: Cinema and
Space in the World System* (1992). In this book, Jameson notes that such an
emerging global space

> may henceforth be thought to be at least one of the fundamental allego-
> rical referents or levels of all seemingly abstract philosophical thought: so
> that a fundamental hypothesis would pose the principle that all thinking
> today, is *also*, whatever else it is, an attempt to think the world system as
> such. All the more true will this be for narrative figurations, whose very
> structure encourages a soaking up of whatever ideas in the air are left and
> a fantasy-solution to all anxieties that rush to fill our current vacuum.
> (1992: 3–4)

In this way, the increased attention to questions of space and spatiality more
generally converges with the burgeoning interest in what in the 1990s begins
to be characterized as 'globalization'. The geographer David Harvey has suggested that while the attention now given to globalization does indeed put the
issues of space and cultural geography on centre stage, we need to recognize
that any concept like 'globalization' is always already a deeply ideological
one, occluding the particular agency and interests involved in such a process
of spatial 'reterritorialization' – to deploy the concept first developed in Gilles
Deleuze and Félix Guattari's great work of spatial thinking, *Capitalism and
Schizophrenia* (1983/1987) – while also potentially performing the same pedagogical role as its temporal twin, the 'end of history', teaching us to think of
it as a baleful and inexorable, almost natural, process of evolution towards
a world of universal commodification and cultural homogenization. Harvey
thus proposes that we shift our language from 'globalization' to 'uneven geographical development' (2000: 68), thereby laying emphasis on the fact that
our present moment is witness to a rearticulation on a new spatial scale of the
contradictory logics of capitalist modernization, the latest in what is in fact an
unbroken historical series of 'spatial fixes' and reterritorializations. Jameson
similarly returns to the questions of globalization in the essays collected
together in *The Ideologies of Theory* (2008), *Valences of the Dialectic* (2009)
and *Representing Capital* (2011).

One of the most significant and influential discussions of our emerging
global world is to be found in the trilogy of *Empire* (2000), *Multitude: War*

and Democracy in the Age of Empire (2004) and *Commonwealth* (2009), by Michael Hardt and Antonio Negri. The brilliance of Hardt and Negri's analysis lies in their ability at once to account for the two extremes of the contemporary global space – on the one hand, the original nature of the world order itself and, on the other, the situation of the bodies that inhabit it. Drawing extensively upon the late work of Foucault, Deleuze and others, and first developing their insights in the context of the burgeoning World Trade Organization and alter-globalization protests of the late 1990s, Hardt and Negri describe a new global mode of sovereignty that they call 'Empire', which displaces the hegemony of the older nation-state system and operates through biopolitical forms of power or 'biopower', 'a form of power that regulates social life from its interior, following it, interpreting it, absorbing it, and rearticulating it' (2000: 23–4). While the spatial system they describe seems a seamless and total one, Hardt and Negri also show how Empire calls up against itself other potential spatial relations in an emerging global 'commons' occupied by the radical transnational collective they name, following the lead of Baruch Spinoza, the 'multitude'. The spatial figures that work their way through Hardt and Negri's writings – Empire, biopower, biopolitics, commons, multitude – have had a decided impact on the work of a diverse range of literary and cultural scholars. The great social theorist, Saskia Sassen (2008), has likewise taken up the question of how the relationships between territory, authority and rights, constitutive of any historical social formation, have been transformed by the 'denationalizing' pressures of globalization. Even more recently, in *The Structure of World History: From Modes of Production to Modes of Exchange* (2014), Kojin Karatani both replaces the long dominant Marxist model of spatially distinct 'modes of production' with the notion of 'modes of exchange', and on this basis theorizes a different model of a global space dominated by what he names the Borromean knot of 'capital-nation-state'. However, like Hardt and Negri, Karatani points towards a potential new form of global space he describes, after Kant, as the 'world-republic'.

In his introduction to *The Structure of World History*, Karatani talks about how his mode of analysis was transformed by the global 'situation that emerged after 9/11 in 2001' (2014: xv); Hardt and Negri's project is similarly inflected in unexpected directions by the irruption of the global 'war on terror'. This new global context produces a number of other original and often darker analyses of contemporary cultural space. Susan Willis, for example, in her book *Portents of the Real: A Primer for Post-9/11 America*, investigates the way that the immediate aftermath of these events gave rise to 'a tremendous burden of cultural forms meant to explain and manage the crisis' (2005: 4), including flag displays, the anthrax hoaxes, the Washington DC sniper attacks, and the Abu Ghraib prison photos. Mike Davis's *Planet of Slums* (2006) explores an emerging global spatial apartheid and warehousing of the permanently unemployed, giving rise to the kinds of violence evident in the war on terror. Davis's next book, *Buda's Wagon: A Brief History of the Car Bomb*

(2007), investigates how the deployment of this particular weapon of terror has begun to transform the very space and habits of urban dwelling. Finally, Eyal Weizman describes the 'forensic architecture' and 'practice of the design of ruins', combining 'the calculation of life and death with those of structural stability' (2011: 133), that has emerged in those places on the globe where imperial state violence is most directly felt.

As evident in all of these studies, any attention to the historical spatial dimensions of globalization will similarly transform how we think about literary history and contemporary cultural practices. In many ways, this has long been the case in much of the work in postcolonial literary studies. In *Culture and Imperialism*, for example, Said critiques Williams's earlier *The Country and the City* for what he finds to be its narrowly national focus. In contrast, Said argues that there is no 'British' national culture that can be understood independent of the nation's large far-flung imperial networks and spheres of influence and investment, and this is the case from a much earlier moment than Williams and others would grant. Thus, any discussion of modern national literature must be attentive to the ways the works composing it respond to and negotiate its global spatial context, a practice Said names 'contrapunctual reading':

> In practical terms . . . it means reading a text with an understanding of what is involved when an author shows, for instance, that a colonial sugar plantation is seen as important to the process of maintaining a particular style of life in England . . . The point is that contrapunctual reading must take account of both processes, that of imperialism and that of resistance to it. (1993: 66)

A similar claim is advanced in Pascale Casanova's influential *The World Republic of Letters*, where she argues that 'appropriation of literature and literary histories by political nations' has the effect of rendering criticism 'blind to a certain number of transnational phenomena that have permitted a specifically literary world to gradually emerge' (2004: xi).

In terms of our own historical situation, Jameson points out that cultural forms such as the Hollywood film should be understood as 'not merely a name for a business that makes money but also for a fundamental late-capitalist cultural revolution, in which old ways of life are broken up and new ones set in place' (2007: 443). Meaghan Morris similarly notes that the emergence of 'theory' is itself linked to the current production of new kinds of global spaces: 'what we call "theory" does the work of fabricating an address to the topics deemed inherently interesting in a given transnational space. Within such a space, theory *is* the work of extracting a cosmopolitan point from the most parochially constructed or ephemeral "events"' (1998: 6). And finally, Franco Moretti (2013) has issued a call for a new kind of 'world literature' studies, one that eschews the demands of the canonical close reading, and instead attempts to map the intersections and connections between the trends in a wide variety of national and cultural traditions, a project greatly aided by the development of new 'big data' visualization technologies.

A number of more recent studies point towards the continued interest in what has been called the 'spatial turn' in interdisciplinary humanist scholarship (see for example Massey 2005; Hubbard and Kitchin 2010; Warf and Arias 2008; Tally 2012). Some of the innovative projects growing out of this turn include increasing numbers of studies of the cultural consequences of globalization and neoliberalism; ongoing work in queer theory, feminism, Deleuze studies, the so-called new materialisms, and other kin research areas on the body and affect (see Ahmed 2006; Coole and Frost 2010; Gregg and Seigworth 2010); the maturation of 'ecocriticism' (see Glotfelty and Fromm 1996; Medovoi 2009); and, finally, the increasing use of new digital media technologies and geographic information systems (GIS) for creative quantitative and geographical explorations of literature and cultural production and circulation (see Moretti 2013; Bodenhammer et al. 2010). All of these projects emphasize the necessity for any mapping of the global space to move beyond the canonical opposition of high and low, or the spatial one of core and periphery, and instead produce a multi-perspectival view of literature and cultural activities, exchanges and flows. Only in this way, they all suggest, can we gain a richer sense of the complexity of past spaces and the originality of those we inhabit today.

NOTES TOWARDS A READING OF JOSEPH CONRAD'S LORD JIM

For all the excitement it has generated in recent decades, an awareness of the emergence of a global cultural, social and economic space is already evident in literary works produced early in the last century. This is very much the case, for example, in the great turn-of-the-century novels written by Joseph Conrad, *Heart of Darkness* (1899), *Lord Jim* (1900) and *Nostromo* (1904). In order to give some sense of how a literary criticism oriented towards spatial concerns might enable us to read familiar texts in new ways, I would like to take a brief look at the work many now consider to be Conrad's masterpiece, *Lord Jim*. Originally published at the high point of British imperial power, this narrative represents one of the first attempts to 'think' or, to use Jameson's phrase, 'cognitively map' an emerging global reality. A good deal of the brilliance of Conrad's novel lies in the ways it accomplishes such a task on the levels of both content and literary form.

Lord Jim is divided into two distinct parts. The first centres on the story of the steamship, *Patna*, and the revelation of Jim's 'failure' while serving as first mate aboard it: when the *Patna* threatens to sink and take down with it all of its 400 passengers, Jim, along with the other crew members, 'jumps' ship. The great irony of this event (and Conrad is one of the great masters of modern irony) lies in the fact that Jim sees himself as somehow distinct from and superior to these, and indeed all other, men: 'The quality of these men did not matter; he rubbed shoulders with them, but they could not touch him; he shared the air they breathed, but he was different' (Conrad 1989: 61). Raised on a tradition of 'light holiday literature' – romantic tales not unlike those that led to the undoing of Jim's great predecessor in modern literature, Don Quixote – Jim constructs an image of himself as 'an example of devotion to duty, and as unflinching as a hero in a book' (47). Put to the test, however, his self-image collapses: Jim, we learn, is, to take one of the central repeated motifs of the novel, really 'one of us' – an imperfect and fallible human being. The central ethical question the novel raises concerns whether Jim himself ever learns this lesson: he attempts to 'escape' the truth of his experience, first wandering from port to port across the great expanse of the south seas. Then, in the second part of the novel, he apparently succeeds in leaving 'his earthly failings behind him' as he becomes the ruler of the fictional Sumatran island community of Patusan (204). In this latter place, he does seem to redeem himself, as he now willingly accepts death as the consequence of his later errors in judgment: in this way, he confirms his commitment to a 'shadowy ideal of conduct' (351).

Every reader who encounters this novel for the first time is struck by the difficulties raised by Conrad's mode of presentation and style in the work's opening section: from the book's first pages, Conrad repeatedly manipulates chronology, multiplies points of view, deploys impressionistic techniques, and uses devices such as what Ian Watt names 'delayed decoding', the presentation of an effect while withholding, sometimes for many pages, its cause. All of these strategies and devices exemplify Conrad's deeply experimental modernist sensibility: his dissatisfaction with the older 'realist' practices of representation, his critical 'estrangement' of them, to use the term developed by the Russian Formalist critic, Viktor Shklovsky, and his attempt to produce new and more 'effective' aesthetic forms.

The first question this form raises concerns why such a dissatisfaction with the older ways of doing things – a dissatisfaction clearly not limited to Conrad alone – arises when and where it does. The conventional answer is that through these means, Conrad, and writers like him, can more 'accurately' reveal the essential 'truths' of human psychology, epistemology and ethics. Of course, such an answer is deeply teleological and even anti-historical, suggesting a singular linear development of literary practice as it moves towards some ultimate perfection of form.

Moreover, and even more importantly for our concerns here, such an answer occludes the deeply spatial orientation of this particular novel. This focus is already made explicit by the novel's third paragraph. Here, Conrad describes Jim's efforts to escape the 'fact' of what he had done while a mate on board the *Patna* (while deferring the revelation of what that act in actuality was):

> When the fact broke through the incognito he would leave suddenly the seaport where he happened to be at the time and go to another – generally farther east. He kept to seaports because he was a seaman in exile from the sea, and had Ability in the abstract, which is good for no

other work but that of a water-clerk. He retreated in good order toward the rising sun, and the fact followed him casually but inevitably. Thus in the course of years he was known successively in Bombay, in Calcutta, in Rangoon, in Penang, in Batavia – and in each of these halting-places was just Jim the water-clerk. Afterwards, when his keen perception of the Intolerable drove him away for good from seaports and white men, even into the virgin forest, the Malays of the jungle village, where he had elected to conceal his deplorable faculty, added a word to the monosyllable of his incognito. They called him Tuan Jim: as one might say – Lord Jim. (46)

As this passage so beautifully indicates, the progression of the plot will involve a movement through a succession of spaces. Conrad's very choices of verbs in this passage – 'leave', 'go to', 'retreated', 'drove' – all suggest a restless dynamic motion forward. And in so doing, the plot's unfolding will generate for the reader a veritable map of the space it covers. Indeed, we might take Jim's 'story' as no more than, to use another concept of the Russian Formalists, 'the motivation of the device', the excuse to pursue this project of spatial mapping.

One of the most striking aspects of this first section for the spatially oriented reader is the immense scope of the space in which Jim's adventures unfold: 'To the common mind he became known as a rolling stone, because this was the funniest part: he did after a time become perfectly known, and even notorious, within the circle of his wanderings (which had a diameter of, say, three thousand miles), in the same way as an eccentric character is known to a whole countryside' (187). Our narrator, Marlow, also travels across an immense amount of space as he collects different elements of Jim's story. The comparison Conrad makes in this passage is instructive for another reason: it suggests Conrad's recognition of the fairly recent *expansion* of the *scale* of space that human beings inhabit, and within which their tales must now unfold. The very fact that Jim's story becomes 'known' across such a tremendous space also points towards the development of transportation and communication technologies that enable this kind of knowledge and information to circulate across such space as readily as did older tales across the local space of the countryside. Moreover, despite its immense scope, Conrad suggests that such a space is in fact a closed one. Jim cannot escape the knowledge of his actions, and at the end of Chapter 13, in a kind of internal climax, we get a tragic image of Jim as a man pursued by an implacable fate: 'He was running. Absolutely running, with nowhere to go to. And he was not yet four-and-twenty' (157).

This awareness of the tremendously expanded spatial scope of the narrative action thus offers us a way to construct an alternative account of the reasons for Conrad's difficult experimental form. Mikhail Bakhtin shows in great detail how the formal strategies and context of the modern realist novel, in the form of what he calls its 'second stylistic trend', serve as a way of bringing into focus the space of the modern nation-state: central to such a practice is the chronotope of the road, linking together diverse spaces and producing a place of encounter for the various publics making up what Benedict Anderson calls the 'imagined community' of the nation (Bakhtin 1981: 243–4). If these strategies emerge as a way of grasping a particular kind of enclosed space, then Conrad's – and indeed all of the great modernist writers' – dissatisfaction with them may now be understood as their implicit recognition of the insufficiency of these older practices for 'representing' a newly expanded and unified space. Conrad's 'experiments' thus participate in a great multinational effort aimed at developing the representational tools that might be adequate for making sense of not only the scale but also the complexity of this emerging global space – a space in which we as individuals must learn to navigate.

And yet, interestingly enough, Conrad abandons these experimental strategies in the novel's second part, wherein he describes Jim's adventures in the imaginary community of Patusan. Here the narrative becomes much more conventionally linear, and even deploys many of the plot devices associated with the 'light holiday literature', the popular prose romances, which Jim had consumed as a youth to such a deleterious effect. Conrad himself acknowledges this shift at a number of places: when Jim is provided with a talismanic ring by one of the community's inhabitants, he tells Marlow, 'It's like something you read of in books' – but really this is true only in the kinds of books that Jim himself reads (215). And later, Conrad writes, 'But do you notice how, three hundred miles *beyond* the end of telegraph cables and mail-boat lines, the haggard utilitarian lies of our civilization wither and die, to be replaced by pure exercises of imagination, that have the futility, often the charm, and sometimes the deep hidden truthfulness of works of art? *Romance* had singled Jim for its own – and that was the true part of the story, which otherwise was all wrong' (251; emphasis added).

Many critics, following the lead of F. R. Leavis, find this second section to be markedly inferior to the first. Of course, such an evaluation once again imposes a single set of criteria – criteria established in a large part by the novel's first part – against which all literary and representational practices are to be evaluated. There is a tremendous circularity in such an approach: finally, are we saying anything more than that the first part of the book does what it does better than the second part does what the first part does? As I suggested above, a spatial criticism is much more sensitive to the *differences* between specific literary practices. Thus, we need to consider the possibility that Conrad's *decision* to shift form indicates not a slackening of artistic energy, but rather signals that the very aims of the novelistic mapping have changed as well.

Interestingly in this regard, Conrad makes it clear to his readers, as evident in the passage cited above, that upon entering Patusan, Jim has also entered into a very different kind of space. Indeed, Marlow's first reference to the place takes the form of a question: 'I don't suppose any of you have ever heard of Patusan? . . . It does not matter; there's many a heavenly body in the lot crowding upon us of a night that mankind had never heard of, it being outside the sphere of its activities and of no earthly importance to anybody but to the astronomers who are paid to talk learnedly about its composition, weight, path' (203). And later, Marlow will describe the village as 'one of the lost, forgotten, unknown places of the earth' (281). Of course, to describe Patusan as 'outside the sphere' of 'mankind's' activities, and as a 'lost, forgotten, unknown' place is in fact to *locate* it very precisely in relationship to the closed world illustrated in the novel's first part: Patusan remains, for the moment at least, 'beyond the end of telegraph cables and mail-boat lines', the communication and transportation network that serves to suture together the space in which Jim's failure and subsequent wanderings take place. Such a place is, of course, the 'world' space produced by European imperial and economic expansion. The fact that Patusan has only been 'forgotten' by Europe, and is not truly 'unknown' to it, is emphasized at the beginning of Chapter 22, where we learn that 'the seventeenth-century traders went there for pepper, because the passion for pepper seemed to burn like a flame of love in the breast of Dutch and English adventurers about the time of James the First' (209). The story Conrad tells us in the rest of the novel concerns Europe's 'remembering' of this place, and the consequences that follow from such an act of recovery.

Here then we have our answer to why Conrad decided to shift his prose form in the second part of the novel: in so doing, he reinforces the sense of the exteriority of this older space to that then being produced by European economic and political power. The tenuous thread linking these two worlds is the figure of Marlow's friend, the adventurer-turned-trader, Stein. Once a figure of romance himself (tales of his youthful adventures are related to us in Chapter 20, and Marlow describes his earlier life as one rich 'in all the exalted elements of romance' [202]), and now very much ensnared in the 'haggard utilitarian lies' of European economic calculation, Stein recognizes Jim's inability to fit within the modern world – 'I understand very well. He is romantic' (199). It is Stein then who enables Jim to kick free of the 'earth', the dramatically expanded 'old world' of European power, and 'leap' into the 'new' frontier landscape of Patusan. Here, the 'rules' that order the closed world of empire no longer hold; and, in such a space, Jim-the-failure has the chance to realize his romantic image of himself as Jim-the-hero – that is, as Lord Jim.

And yet, ultimately, this heroic project fails; as Marlow succinctly puts it, 'He had retreated from one world, for a small matter of an impulsive jump, and now the other, the work of his own hands, had fallen in ruins upon his head' (345). A group of men, led by the demonic Gentleman Brown, arrive from Jim's previous 'world' – 'These were the emissaries with whom the world he had renounced was pursing his retreat' (328) – and instigate a series of events that culminate in the murder of Jim's native friend, Dain Waris, and Jim's submission of himself for summary execution at the hands of Dain's father (350–1).

However, crucially, Conrad makes it clear that it is Jim's very activities in Patusan that guarantee the eventual arrival of these kinds of men. That is,

Jim unwittingly becomes the tool of his own destruction. Dain Waris is first described by Marlow as a 'being' who possesses the gift of being able to 'open to the Western eye, so often concerned with mere surfaces, the hidden possibilities of races and lands over which hangs the mystery of unrecorded ages' (236). It will be Jim himself then who will tap into this hidden potential, as he begins a project of spatial modernization in the land:

> The ground rose gently, the few big trees had been felled, the undergrowth had been cut down and the grass fired. He had a mind to try a coffee-plantation there. The big hill, rearing its double summit coal-black in the clear yellow glow of the rising moon, seemed to cast its shadow upon the ground prepared for that experiment. He was going to try ever so many experiments. (280)

These activities have the effect of inserting Patusan at once into the space and history of European imperial power. The great irony here is that Patusan can serve as a 'retreat' for Jim only as long as it remains 'separate' from the European sphere of influence; and yet, the very activities that Jim performs guarantee that this spatial autonomy will very quickly come to an end. Indeed, the choice of a coffee-plantation for Jim's primary 'experiment' is not accidental: for coffee is a trade export crop, one whose production cannot sustain the community independent from the larger global networks of exchange (in other words, you can't eat coffee). Thus, the arrival of Gentleman Brown and his men simply accelerates a process that Jim himself had already begun.

The real brilliance of Conrad's decision to switch his prose form in the novel's second part now at long last becomes clear. In this latter part of the book, Conrad provides a devastating allegory of the process of what has been called 'informal' British imperial expansion, the ways that what appear to be local spatial transformations in fact reinscribe, often unintentionally, these spaces within a larger network of global economic circulation. The motivations behind these activities are, Conrad also suggests, similarly 'informal' – the very desire for 'adventure' and 'heroism' so much a part of Jim's make-up, and inculcated in him by the reading of popular romances. The realization of the romance plot, Conrad meticulously demonstrates, in effect destroys the world, the spaces 'outside' the stable and closed networks of European power, where romance might still seem possible. Conrad's story then is one of the closure of the imperial frontier, the apparently irrevocable process of reconstructing the entire globe in Europe's image. And it is this world, the world their own actions inadvertently produce, which has no place for Jim, or his predecessor, Stein. Conrad signals this fact in the novel's bittersweet closing lines: 'Stein has aged greatly of late. He feels it himself, and says often that he is "preparing to leave all this; preparing to leave. . ." while he waves his hands sadly at his butterflies' (352). If there will be any challenge to the terrible inevitability of this process of spatial incorporation, it is one Conrad cannot, from his location in time and space, see. We fortunately, as Said and other postcolonial scholars remind us, might be able to see differently. And seeing differently is, finally, the goal of the kinds of spatial critical reading strategies outlined above.

QUESTIONS FOR FURTHER CONSIDERATION

1. Most of what we currently value as the highest expressions of literary art are concerned with what Edward Soja calls Lefebvre's 'Thirdspace' – 'spaces of representation', or the lived. Discuss the impact of Lefebvre's tripartite schema of space on how we think about the work of different kinds of literary texts. Are there literary works that focus upon the other two *levels* of space? What do they look like? How does an attention to all three, as well as the more nuanced model of spatial scales outlined by Neil Smith, influence how we read literature and culture? What things suddenly come to our attention?

2. Mikhail Bakhtin maps out a range of traditional 'chronotopes' in the history of the novel, including the road, the parlour, the castle, the provincial town, and the threshold. In what ways have the developments of our world – globalization, digital media technologies, the war on terror – transformed these novelistic chronotopes? Have new ones emerged? For example, does the electronic informational space or what Weizman calls 'forensic architecture' and 'practice of the design of ruins' produce new chronotopes for the novel and other literary practices? Discuss some possible examples.

3. Jameson's description of cognitive mapping offers a strategy for both the production and the interpretation of various kinds of cultural practices. Discuss how a work of literature might be said to engage in forms of cognitive mapping. What are some of the criteria for its success? In what ways does this occur through form as well as explicit content? How does our attention to these operations transform how we think about literature and culture?

4. An attention to issues of space and spatiality promises to change not only how we read literature, but, as Williams, Jameson, Said, Freidman, Moretti and many others point out, also what we read. What assumptions and expectations about literary value are revealed when we shift our attention in some of the ways outlined above? How might we then read canonical texts in new ways? What are some of the marginalized forms and practices that become increasingly important? Why so?

5. A good deal of work in contemporary literary and critical theory and cultural studies brings into sharper focus questions of identity – class, race, gender, sexuality and so forth. In what ways do the questions of space supplement, intersect with and pose anew these vital concerns? What roles do space and spatial differences play in the production of identities? How does an attention to these differences shape how we

think about bodies? How does the attention to space enable a different reading of the production of identity itself?

6. A literary criticism and cultural studies attentive to questions of space is not only interested in the ways cultural productions map and illuminate already existing spaces, but also in the contributions they might make to the vital political project of imagining, and then making, space anew. This project of spatial remaking ranges from the most abstract global level to that of our individual bodies, all spaces we all inhabit all of the time. Discuss the role that literary and other cultural texts play in such a spatial politics. How do they help us to imagine new kinds of space? What forms do this kind of work most effectively? What lessons do we learn? How might we then put these lessons into practice in our activities outside of the classroom?

BIBLIOGRAPHY

Ahmed, Sara (2006) *Queer Phenomenology: Orientations, Objects, Others*, Durham NC: Duke University Press.

Anderson, Benedict (1991) *Imagined Communities: Reflections on the Origin and Spread of Capitalism*, London: Verso.

Appadurai, Arjun (1996) *Modernity at Large: Cultural Dimensions of Globalization*, Minneapolis: University of Minnesota Press.

Ashcroft, Bill (2001) *Post-Colonial Transformation*, London: Routledge.

Bachelard, Gaston (1969) *The Poetics of Space*, trans. Maria Jolas, Boston: Beacon Press.

Bakhtin, Mikhail M. (1981) *The Dialogic Imagination: Four Essays*, ed. and trans. Caryl Emerson and Michael Holquist, Austin: University of Texas Press.

Benjamin, Walter (1999) *The Arcades Project*, trans. Howard Eiland and Kevin McLaughlin, Cambridge MA: Harvard University Press.

Bodenhamer, David J., John Corrigan and Trevor M. Harris, eds. (2010) *The Spatial Humanities: GIS and the Future of Humanities Scholarship*, Bloomington: Indiana University Press.

Buck-Morss, Susan (1990) *The Dialectics of Seeing: Walter Benjamin and the Arcades Project*, Cambridge MA: MIT Press.

Burgin, Victor (1996) *In/Different Spaces: Place and Memory in Visual Culture*, Berkeley: University of California Press.

Butler, Judith (1993) 'Gender is Burning: Questions of Appropriation and Subversion', in *Bodies That Matter: On the Discursive Limits of 'Sex'*, London: Routledge.

Carter, Paul (1987) *The Road to Botany Bay: An Essay in Spatial History*, London: Faber & Faber.

Casanova, Pascale (2004) *The World Republic of Letters*, trans. M. B. Debevoise, Cambridge MA: Harvard University Press.

Casarino, Cesare (2002) *Modernity at Sea: Melville, Marx, Conrad in Crisis*, Minneapolis: University of Minnesota Press.

Casey, Edward S. (1997) *The Fate of Place: A Philosophical History*, Berkeley: University of California Press.

Clifford, James (1997) *Routes: Travel and Translation in the Late Twentieth Century*, Cambridge MA: Harvard University Press.

Colomina, Beatriz, ed. (1992) *Sexuality and Space*, Princeton: Princeton Papers on Architecture.

Conrad, Joseph (1989) *Lord Jim*, London: Penguin Books.

Coole, Diane, and Samantha Frost, eds. (2010) *New Materialisms: Ontology, Agency, and Politics*, Durham NC: Duke University Press.

Davis, Mike (1990) *City of Quartz: Excavating the Future in Los Angeles*, London: Verso.

Davis, Mike (1998) *Ecology of Fear: Los Angeles and the Imagination of Disaster*, New York: Henry Holt.

Davis, Mike (2000) *Late Victorian Holocausts: El Nino Famines and the Making of the Third World*, London: Verso.

Davis, Mike (2002) *Dead Cities and Other Tales*, New York: The New Press.

Davis, Mike (2006) *Planet of Slums*, London: Verso.

Davis, Mike (2007) *Buda's Wagon: A Brief History of the Car Bomb*, London: Verso.

de Certeau, Michel (1984) *The Practice of Everyday Life*, trans. Steven Randall, Berkeley: University of California Press.

Deleuze, Gilles (1988) *Foucault*, trans. Seán Hand, Minneapolis: University of Minnesota Press.

Deleuze, Gilles and Félix Guattari (1983) *Anti-Oedipus: Capitalism and Schizophrenia Vol. 1* [1972], trans. Robert Hurley, Mark Seem and Helen R. Lane, Minneapolis: University of Minnesota Press.

Deleuze, Gilles and Félix Guattari (1987) *A Thousand Plateaus: Capitalism and Schizophrenia Vol. 2* [1980], trans. Brian Massumi, Minneapolis: University of Minnesota Press.

Derrida, Jacques and Peter Eisenman (1997) *Chora L Works*, ed. Jeffrey Kipnis and Thomas Lesser, New York: Monacelli Press.

Dimendberg, Edward (2004) *Film Noir and the Spaces of Modernity*, Cambridge MA: Harvard University Press.

Feldman, Allen (1991) *Formations of Violence: The Narrative of the Body and Political Terror in Northern Ireland*, Chicago: University of Chicago Press.

Foucault, Michel (1977) *Discipline and Punish: The Birth of the Prison*, trans. Alan Sheridan, New York: Vintage.

Foucault, Michel (1980) 'Questions on Geography', in *Power/Knowledge: Selected Interviews and Other Writings, 1972–1977*, New York: Pantheon Books.

Foucault, Michel (1997) *Ethics, Subjectivity and Truth: Essential Works of Foucault, 1954–1984*, Vol. 1, ed. Paul Rabinow, trans. Robert Hurley and others, New York: The New Press.

Foucault, Michel (1998) *Aesthetics, Method, and Epistemology: Essential Works of Foucault, 1954–1984*, Vol. 2, ed. Paul Rabinow, trans. Robert Hurley and others, New York: The New Press.

Foucault, Michel (2000) *Power, Essential Works of Foucault, 1954–1984*, Vol. 3, ed. Paul Rabinow, trans. Robert Hurley and others, New York: The New Press.

Friedman, Susan Stanford (2006) 'Periodizing Modernism: Postcolonial Modernities and the Space/Time Borders of Modernist Studies', *Modernism/Modernity* 13:3, pp. 425–43.

Gallagher, Catherine and Stephen Greenblatt (2000) *Practicing New Historicism*, Chicago: University of Chicago Press.

Glotfelty, Cheryll and Harold Fromm (1996) *The Ecocriticism Reader: Landmarks in Literary Ecology*, Athens: University of Georgia Press.

Gramsci, Antonio (1971) *Selections from the Prison Notebooks*, ed. and trans. Quintin Hoare and Geoffrey Nowell Smith, New York: International Publishers.

Greenblatt, Stephen (1980) *Renaissance Self-Fashioning From More to Shakespeare*, Chicago: University of Chicago Press.

Gregg, Melissa and Gregory J. Seigworth, eds. (2010) *The Affect Theory Reader*, Durham NC: Duke University Press.

Gregory, Derek (1994) *Geographical Imaginations*, Oxford: Blackwell.

Grewhal, Inderpal and Caren Kaplan, eds. (1994) *Scattered Hegemonies: Postmodernity and Transnational Feminist Practices*, Minneapolis: University of Minnesota Press.

Grosz, Elizabeth (1995) *Space, Time, and Perversion: Essays on the Politics of Bodies*, London: Routledge.

Hardt, Michael and Antonio Negri (2000) *Empire*, Cambridge MA: Harvard University Press.

Hardt, Michael and Antonio Negri (2004) *Multitude: War and Democracy in the Age of Empire*, New York: Penguin.

Hardt, Michael and Antonio Negri (2009) *Commonwealth*, Cambridge MA: Harvard University Press.

Harvey, David (1989) *The Condition of Postmodernity*, Oxford: Basil Blackwell.

Harvey, David (1989) *The Urban Experience*, Baltimore: Johns Hopkins University Press.

Harvey, David (1999) *The Limits to Capital*, new edition, London: Verso.

Harvey, David (2000) *Spaces of Hope*, Berkeley: University of California Press.

Harvey, David (2003) *The New Imperialism*, Oxford: Oxford University Press.

Harvey, David (2006) *Spaces of Global Capitalism*, London: Verso.

Hubbard, Phil and Rob Kitchin, eds. (2010) *Key Thinkers on Space and Place*, London: Sage.

Jameson, Fredric (1970) 'On Raymond Chandler', *Southern Review* 6, pp. 624–50.

Jameson, Fredric (1981) *The Political Unconscious: Narrative as a Socially Symbolic Act*, Ithaca: Cornell University Press.

Jameson, Fredric (1986) 'Third World Literature in the Era of Multinational Capitalism', *Social Text* 15, pp. 65–88.

Jameson, Fredric (1991) *Postmodernism, or, The Cultural Logic of Late Capitalism*, Durham NC: Duke University Press.

Jameson, Fredric (1992) *The Geopolitical Aesthetic: Cinema and Space in the World System*, Bloomington: Indiana University Press.

Jameson, Fredric (1993) 'The Synoptic Chandler', in Joan Copjec, ed., *Shades of Noir: A Reader*, London: Verso.

Jameson, Fredric (1994) *The Seeds of Time*, New York: Columbia University Press.

Jameson, Fredric (2005) *Archaeologies of the Future: The Desire Called Utopia and Other Science Fictions*, London: Verso.

Jameson, Fredric (2007) *The Modernist Papers*, London: Verso.

Jameson, Fredric (2008) *The Ideologies of Theory*, London: Verso.

Jameson, Fredric (2009) *Valences of the Dialectic*, London: Verso.

Jameson, Fredric (2011) *Representing* Capital: *A Reading of Volume One*, London: Verso.

Karatani, Kojin (1995) *Architecture as Metaphor: Language, Number, Money*, ed. Michael Speaks, trans. Sabu Kohso, Cambridge MA: MIT Press.

Karatani, Kojin (2014) *The Structure of World History: From Modes of Production to Modes of Exchange*, trans. Michael K. Bourdaghs, Durham NC: Duke University Press.

Kipnis, Jeffrey (2013) *A Question of Qualities: Essays in Architecture*, Cambridge MA: MIT Press.

Koolhaas, Rem (1994) *Delirious New York: A Retroactive Manifesto for Manhattan*, New York: Monacelli Press.

Koolhaas, Rem and Bruce Mau (1994) *S,M,L,XL*, New York: Monacelli Press.

Lefebvre, Henri (1991) *The Production of Space*, trans. Donald Nicholson-Smith, Oxford: Blackwell.

Lefebvre, Henri (1996) *Writings on Cities*, trans. and eds. Eleonore Kofman and Elizabeth Lebas, Cambridge MA: Blackwell.

Lefebvre, Henri (2009) *State, Space, World: Selected Essays*, eds. and trans. Gerald

Moore, Neil Brenner and Stuart Elder, Minneapolis: University of Minnesota Press.

Marcus, Sharon (1999) *Apartment Stories: City and Home in Nineteenth Century Paris and London*, Berkeley: University of California Press.

Marin, Louis (1984) *Utopics: The Semiological Play of Textual Spaces,* trans. Robert A. Vollrath, Atlantic Highlands: Humanities Press International.

Massey, Doreen (1994) *Space, Place, and Gender*, Minneapolis: University of Minnesota Press.

Massey, Doreen (2005) *For Space*, London: Sage.

Medovoi, Leerom (2009) 'The Biopolitical Unconscious: Toward an Eco-Marxist Literary Theory', *Mediations* 24:2, at <http://www.mediationsjournal.org/toc/24_2> (accessed 17 September 2015).

Moretti, Franco (1996) *Modern Epic: The World System from Goethe to García Márquez*, London: Verso.

Moretti, Franco (1998) *Atlas of the European Novel, 1800–1900*, London: Verso.

Moretti, Franco (2013) *Distant Reading*, London: Verso.

Morris, Meaghan (1998) *Too Soon, Too Late: History in Popular Culture*, Bloomington: Indiana University Press.

Papadakis, Andreas, Catherine Cooke and Andrew Benjamin, eds. (1989) *Deconstruction: Omnibus Volume*, New York: Rizzoli.

Rabinow, Paul (1989) *French Modern: Norms and Forms of the Social Environment*, Cambridge MA: MIT Press.

Ross, Kristin (1988) *The Emergence of Social Space: Rimbaud and the Paris Commune*, Minneapolis: University of Minnesota Press.

Said, Edward (1993) *Culture and Imperialism*, New York: Alfred A. Knopf.

Sassen, Saskia (1998) *Globalization and Its Discontents*, New York: The New Press.

Sassen, Saskia (2008) *Territory, Authority, Rights: From Medieval to Global Assemblages*, Updated edition, Princeton: Princeton University Press.

Sennett, Richard (1994) *Flesh and Stone: The Body and the City in Western Civilization*, New York: W. W. Norton.

Smith, Neil (1993) 'Homeless/Global: Scaling Places', in Jon Bird et al., eds., *Mapping the Futures: Local Cultures, Global Change*, London: Routledge.

Smith, Neil (2008) *Uneven Development: Nature, Capital, and the Production of Space*, 3rd edition, Athens: University of Georgia Press.

Soja, Edward. W. (1989) *Postmodern Geographies: The Reassertion of Space in Critical Social Theory*, New York: Verso.

Soja, Edward (1996) *Thirdspace: Journeys to Los Angeles and Other Real-and-Imagined Places*, Oxford: Blackwell.

Soja, Edward (2000) *Postmetropolis: Critical Studies of Cities and Regions*, Oxford: Blackwell.

Tafuri, Manfredo (1976) *Architecture and Utopia: Design and Capitalist Development*, trans. Barbara Luigia Penta, Cambridge MA: MIT Press.

Tally, Jr., Robert T. (2012) *Spatiality*, London: Routledge.

Tschumi, Bernard (1996) *Architecture and Disjunction*, Cambridge MA: MIT Press.

Tuan, Yi-Fu (1977) *Space and Place: The Perspective of Experience*, Minneapolis: University of Minnesota Press.

Vidler, Anthony (2000) *Warped Space: Art, Architecture, and Anxiety in Modern Culture*, Cambridge MA: The MIT Press.

Warf, Barney and Santa Arias, eds. (2008) *The Spatial Turn: Interdisciplinary Perspectives*, London: Routledge.

Wegner, Phillip E. (2002) *Imaginary Communities: Utopia, the Nation, and the Spatial Histories of Modernity*, Berkeley: University of California Press.

Wegner, Phillip E. (2009) *Life Between Two Deaths, 1989–2001: U.S. Culture in the Long Nineties*, Durham NC: Duke University Press.

Wegner, Phillip E. (2014) *Periodizing Jameson: Dialectics, the University, and the Desire for Narrative*, Evanston: Northwestern University Press.

Wegner, Phillip E. (2014) *Shockwaves of Possibility: Essays on Science Fiction, Globalization, and Utopia*, Oxford: Peter Lang.

Weizman, Eyal (2011) *The Least of All Possible Evils: Humanitarian Violence from Arendt to Gaza*, London: Verso.

Williams, Raymond (1973) *The Country and the City*, Oxford: Oxford University Press.

Willis, Susan (2005) *Portents of the Real: A Primer for Post-9/11 America*, London: Verso.

Wolfreys, Julian (1998) *Writing London, Volume 1: The Trace of the Urban Text from Blake to Dickens*, New York: Palgrave Macmillan.

Wolfreys, Julian (2004) *Writing London, Volume 2: Materiality, Memory, Spectrality*, New York: Palgrave Macmillan.

Wolfreys, Julian (2007) *Writing London, Volume 3: Inventions of the Other City*, New York: Palgrave Macmillan.

TRAUMA, TESTIMONY, CRITICISM: WITNESSING, MEMORY AND RESPONSIBILITY

Julian Wolfreys

For history to be a history of trauma means that it is referential precisely to the extent that it is not fully perceived as it occurs; or to put it somewhat differently, that a history can be grasped only in the very inaccessibility of its occurrence.

Cathy Caruth

In order to cope with a trauma, we symbolize.

Slavoj Žižek

Although there is a significant number of critical works addressing the figure and effects of trauma, or what Ulrich Baer calls 'unresolved experience' (2000: 1) and the related role of testimony in literature, there is no single school of criticism, no one methodology as such, dealing with these issues. It is not the purpose of this chapter to read this apparent absence as a deficiency. Nor is it my intention to supply an 'introductory' discussion or objective summary of the work so far done in order to supplement that work and thereby make up for any supposed lack. On the contrary, it must be admitted from the outset that any gesture in the direction of regulating a response to trauma or establishing a methodology or mode of analysis should be resisted, if one is to do justice to trauma and the work of testimony. As Dominick LaCapra has suggested, 'a post-traumatic response . . . becomes questionable when it is routinized in a methodology or style that enacts compulsive repetition' (2001: 47). Equally, it has to be acknowledged that what is being named as an interest in critical studies and what I wish to explore in this chapter as the possibility of a critical modality could come under the headings of 'mourning', 'memory work', 'acts of bearing witness' (another possible description of testimony) or, more obliquely and generally, 'responsibility' in the acts of reading we call criticism. Perhaps that in reading which we will approach here might most appropriately be understood as 'a grammar of shock, absorption and loss', to cite Avital Ronell (1989: 89). Therefore, however one orientates oneself, the emphasis must be placed on a careful reading in response to that which marks the text, hence Ronell's apposite use of the term 'grammar', rather than any application of paradigmatic procedures or protocols.

To speak of a 'grammar' is not to deny the material horror and after-effects of a historical event such as the Holocaust; nor is such a remark the sign of some formalist retreat into language games and trivializing quibbles over truth claims, into 'hyperbolic or speculative acts' as Dominick LaCapra argues in *Writing History, Writing Trauma* (2001: 185, 195), against what he perceives to be the occasional linguistic 'excesses' of so-called poststructuralist discourse. It is, instead, to acknowledge and observe how 'absence is a structural part of witness', as Michael Bernard-Donals and Richard Glejzer put it (2001: 56). As they continue: 'the act of witness is only ever available in another place and in another time [than that of the experience of the traumatic event] . . . Witness can only be accessible to the extent that it is not fully perceived or experienced as it occurs, and it can only be grasped in the very inaccessibility of its occurrence' (2001: 58). It is this 'grammatical' register that Cathy Caruth also addresses, and to which we will return, below. However, it has to be said, concerning the figures of 'loss' and 'absence', that these are not simply figures which speak 'transhistorically to absolute foundations . . . induc[ing] either a metaphysical etherealization, even obfuscation, of historical problems or a historicist, reductive localization of transhistorical, recurrently displaced problems – or perhaps a confusingly hybridised, extremely labile discourse . . . that seems to derive from the deconstruction of metaphysics', in the words of LaCapra (2001: 195). What is 'transhistorical' is, in fact, LaCapra's own analysis here. For he reduces and generalizes, in what seems a fairly metaphysical way, the reading of loss and absence, precisely to the extent that he assumes that each figure is conceptualized in an undifferentiated manner, in the theoretical analyses he addresses. What it is important to realize, in any reading of absence or loss as that which necessitates structurally any response to trauma, is that what is absent or lost is singular, particular to the historial instant of the traumatic event and its subsequent reading or writing. As Ulrich Baer suggests, there is an 'obligation to recognize another's experience of trauma as irreducibly *other* and irreducible to generalizations'; moreover, to cite Baer again, every text, every other, attesting to the traumatic makes 'an uncompromising claim . . . to be read in its own terms. Yet at the same time . . . each . . . opens itself to iteration, understanding, and address' (2000: 11). There is thus the 'necessity of considering the poetic representation of unresolved experience [that is to say, trauma] . . . as absolutely singular' (2000: 9).

This is of course to point to the very difficult ground on which we find ourselves, hence my own caution concerning the questions of terminology and of methodological regulation. It is doubtless the case that such terms and phrases as those towards which I express an initial wariness, if not suspicion, might resonate in various ways in relation to particular protocols or programmes, or certain manifestations of institutionalized analysis, more or less obviously. You might believe on the evidence of words such as 'trauma' or phrases such as 'memory work', for example, that there is a certain 'psychoanalytic' register at work in my discourse. This is so of course, undeniably, as the discussions of Freud below indicate. It has to be said, however, that while the question of 'reading and writing trauma' is indebted in particular ways to psychoanalysis and psychoanalytic literary criticism – or, to be more precise, certain strands within these nominations – there will also be other aspects to the critique in the present chapter that are not directly accounted for in psychoanalysis, and which therefore exceed the institutional, discursive parameters of such work, while also acknowledging other epistemological models and critical discourses.

There is observable, for example, the matter of a reorientation towards reading history, of reading 'history' and its representations differently in relation to trauma, as Caruth makes plain in my first epigraph. Whether or not history can be thought as *always* or *only* a history of trauma, it is important to note two aspects of Caruth's complication of the notion of history: first, that there is the matter of referentiality, of the signs, traces or marks by which we attempt to recover or reconstruct history. History, in this account, is comprehended as textual. This is not, to stress the point once more, to suggest that historical events do not happen. Instead, as Caruth informs us, the materiality of the historical event is *only ever available* through the relay and concomitant deferral that is the condition of the materiality of signifiers. Therefore, what we call history always comes down to a matter of reading and, equally, rereading and rewriting in as responsible a manner as possible, however neutral we seek to be, or (mis)believe we can be. Second, and at the same time, the work of reading history must necessarily take place precisely because the historical occurrence is neither fully perceivable in the event nor subsequently accessible after the fact of its occurrence.

As another particular dimension to the problem of reading, there can be discerned also, and especially in the use of the word *responsibility*, an indebtedness to ethical demands and requirements and the question of ethics in general. This is also true.[1] If, as Shoshana Felman has remarked apropos of trauma and testimony, there is 'a parallel between [a] kind of teaching [and, we would add, reading] (in its reliance on the testimonial process) and psychoanalysis', then the former is not reducible to the latter. Despite this, both 'are called upon to be *performative* . . . both strive to produce, and to enable, *change*. Both . . . are interested not merely in new information, but, primarily, in the capacity . . . to *transform*' (Felman and Laub 1992: 52). It is precisely in this demand for the performative dimension[2] and the transformation it entails that responsibility is heard. What amounts to an ethical call announces itself as the possibility of exceeding analysis and, indeed, representation. So, to recap: while there are, or may be, parallels between discourses, there is neither a method nor a school. There is only the necessity, and the risk, of enabling reading as transformative critique. This being the case, it is perhaps best to begin approaching the subject in hand by offering the following provisional statement as a means of initial orientation, or, indeed, an affirmation of responsibility: all critical acts should manifest responsibility to texts being read beyond, and in excess of, the calculation of any programme of reading (within limits), methodology or school of thought, but what that responsibility might be cannot be decided ahead of the encounter.

Paradoxically, though, no reading can ever account for everything in a text. Reading, therefore, can never be completed. There will always be (and have been, always already) some trace, some haunting remainder, with which we have to live, which we must admit, and yet for which we cannot account, finally. As Gayatri Spivak has remarked, 'One cannot be mindful of a haunting, even if it fills the mind' (Spivak 2001: 221), and this is chiefly because, with regard to trauma, there is what Baer calls a 'twofold *structural* disjunction between an experience and its integration into narrative memory, understanding, and communicability . . . All such experiences . . . [are] located somewhere outside memory yet within the psyche' (Baer 2000: 10). That this paradox or impasse exists in no way lets the reader off the hook from assuming responsibility. Rather, reading, considered as precisely the response which recognizes its responsibility in the face of the impossibility that reading also entails, must continue, must respond to the other, all the while accepting and acknowledging that, in bearing witness to the other, one cannot master, control, determine or domesticate the other through some normative ontological or epistemological process. This is all the more so when it is a question of seeking to represent traumatic events, of seeking the adequate or appropriate mode of representation. As Bernard-Donals and Glejzer make clear throughout *Between Witness and Testimony: The Holocaust and the Limits of Representation*, there is that about the trauma of an event such as the Holocaust beyond representation or narrative adequation, so excessive is its horror. All responsible criticism engages in both a recognition of its own responsibility and the impossibility of such an endless demand, a call to conscience if you will. Reading trauma as a material manifestation of the other in a given text may well be asked to call on the discourses or disciplines of psychoanalysis, history and ethics (considered narrowly as one 'strand' in the discipline of philosophy), but it is irreducible to any disciplinary economy, or the calculation implied by accommodation between programmatic discourses. Reading and writing trauma, always as the response to singularity, effect its transformation, if this happens at all, not in any calculable control of critical position or the representation which any critical or historical modality may believe it can make possible, but in the production of a reiteration of the traumatic excess 'which troubles testimony and narrative and forces the reader to confront the horror of the limit' (Bernard-Donals and Glejzer 2001: 5).

At the risk of repeating myself, let me re-emphasize these issues in other words: the act of criticism as the manifestation of nothing more nor less than good reading in these terms becomes, therefore, a form of testimony, a bearing witness or being called to witness. This is good reading as such. But the radical otherness, the alterity of that to which we must respond, is understood when it comes to be recognized that testimony, as with responsibility and in order to be responsible, *in order to be testimony and not merely an account generated according to some protocol*, has to be transformative or inventive. It must take that risk. It cannot be dictated according to the prescription of certain rules operative in the same fashion every time reading takes place. On the subject of a responsibility exceeding any programme or protocol, Jacques Derrida remarks:

> I will even venture to say that ethics, politics, and responsibility, *if there are any*, will only ever have begun with the experience and experiment of the aporia. When the path is clear and given, when a certain knowledge opens up the way in advance, the decision is already made, it might as well be said that there is none to make: irresponsibly, and in good conscience, one simply applies or implements a program. Perhaps, and this would be the objection, one never escapes the program. In that case, one must acknowledge this and stop talking with authority about moral or political responsibility. The condition of possibility of this thing called responsibility is a certain *experience and experiment of the possibility of the impossible: the testing of the aporia* from which one may invent the only *possible invention, the impossible invention.* (Derrida 1992: 41)

Testimony, therefore, and 'testimonial criticism', if such a thing takes place, cannot be prepared or prepared for ahead of the event, the arrival of the other. Testimony, in order to be such, cannot be calculated, for every testimony must respond to the singular specificity of the traumatic experience. If responsibility is understood, then both the alterity and the singularity of the other have to be admitted. If, as Shoshana Felman suggests, we live 'in the age of testimony', by which name she indicates 'the era of the Holocaust, of Hiroshima, of Vietnam' (Felman and Laub 1992: 53), and to which it would be necessary to add '11 September 2001', then it has to be recognized at the same time that what is called an era or an age is marked by the registration of historical events incommensurate either with one another or with that very epochal similitude that the notion of the era or age, in the naming of an identity based on sufficient, that is to say calculable, resemblance, suggests. Testimony is irreducible to some concept or figure, some genre or species of narrative within historical narrative or literature.

The aporia of responsibility that I have sketched above demonstrates this in showing how conceptual thinking operates within limits and with the imagined horizon of some limit, as does Felman's invocation of 'age' or 'era'.[3] To speak of either 'trauma' or 'testimonial criticism' is both to assume that one knows what both trauma and testimony are, i.e. that there are stable concepts appearing in the same form, time after time, and to believe also that such a criticism is, in fact, a delineable or delimitable conceptual form. Yet, as Ulrich Baer cautions, 'in addition to historical differences [the very differences that the thinking of an 'era' occludes], "trauma" is not a stable term. An experience registers as . . . traumatic. And this remains fundamentally unresolved, not because of the event's *inherent content*, but because recourse to an external frame of reference is unavailable' (2000: 9). To risk a somewhat counter-intuitive formula at this juncture therefore, which doubtless says too little and tries to say too much, literature *just is* testimony and it is this which imposes upon the reader and the act of criticism the burden of an incalculable responsibility. (Another way to think this would be to recall Walter Benjamin's well-known comment that all documents of civilization are also documents of barbarity.) Reading is the act of bearing witness to literature's memory work, where the reader must respond, must make impossible decisions, in response to the attestation of impersonal memory. And the responsibility entailed herein truly *is* incalculable, for, in every act of witnessing, every response to the other in its singularity, I sacrifice countless others (Kronick 1999: 15).[4] Yet, it is for this reason that we cannot reductively assume similarity through the act of reading by a gesture of generalization. In a very risky gesture, Jacques Derrida identifies the dangers of such thought, precisely around what is taken by many as the name of trauma par excellence, Auschwitz. While, to quote Alexander García Düttman, it is undeniable that the singularity of Auschwitz 'is incommensurable: not only because *nothing similar* can be thought or imagined but above all because something unlike anything else compels us to think and act in such a way that *nothing similar* ever happens' (2000: 97), Derrida – as Düttman points out – 'warns us against discourses, which, taking Auschwitz as the model',

> are in danger of reconstituting a sort of centrality, a 'we' which is certainly not that of speculative dialectics but which is related to the unanimous privilege which we occidental Europeans accord to Auschwitz in the fight or the question which we oppose to speculative dialectics, to a certain type of occidental reason. The danger is that this 'we' would take from memory or sideline proper names other than Auschwitz, ones which are just as abominable, names which have names and names which have no name. (Derrida, quoted in Düttman 2000: 99)

It would be a gross misreading to see in this statement some kind of denial of either the historical event or the traumatic significance of Auschwitz. It is, though, crucially, urgently important that we comprehend how Derrida is illustrating the dangers in a certain limit-thinking with regard to certain aspects of normative historical representation and, equally, the dangers of letting the proper name do your thinking for you. In fact, the danger of the proper name is that, in letting it come to assume some privileged position in one's discourse, thinking – and, therefore, responsibility – stops. There is, then, the difficult business of thinking Auschwitz, and, indeed, any traumatic event, in all its inexpressible, irreducible singularity, a difficulty which remains with regard to any narrative of trauma. For what remains, as the trace of the traumatic figuring, the articulation of a name such as Auschwitz or the name which has no name, such as 11 September 2001, is what Düttman calls 'the possibility of survival, of another memory and another promise, [which] depends on a certain unreadability' (2000: 74).

The work of criticism that addresses trauma, testimony and memory must then necessarily explore what Cathy Caruth has described as the 'enigma of the otherness' in the revenance and articulation of trauma, which the human agent 'cannot fully know' (1996: 3). Caruth demonstrates a two-part disruptive or disjunctive structure in the nature of narrative form, of which more, in relation to trauma, below in the second section of this chapter. This structure allows for the articulation of the subject's act of witnessing and responsibility involved in acts of memory and witnessing through the other's arrival which forces on the subject a knowledge which had previously been withheld. The return of the other opens the subject's complicity to him- or herself, not necessarily as a specific guilt for a specific act, but as the culpability, and the responsibility which *that* entails, as a condition of Being, in which, as beings, we all share, and which has itself to be acknowledged (as Martin Heidegger makes plain in his analysis of Dasein in *Being and Time*).

In exploring this mode of narrative, then, I am seeking to show how criticism's function is to reiterate, and thereby bear witness itself, to the disarticulating modality already installed in various forms of fiction or 'the literary' as so many acts of witnessing and memory. The question of trauma and testimonial criticism becomes one, I will argue, of a patient tracing of that which constitutes the literary text as both a function of memory and responsibility and as a mode of technicity, a making appear, to which, in every act of reading, all readers must bear witness and for which they must take responsibility as a definition of the act of reading itself. There is implied an open series of responses, each opening itself to, and in, a potentially infinite disjunctive chain.

Such a model of reading and the understanding of the literary which it invokes has at least two effects, which it will be the function of this chapter to examine and explain: (1) The motion of the return or supplement, the revenance of testimony, implies the call of the other as intrinsic to the act of narration; as such, it inscribes an iterable circulation. In this, we may read a narrative modality which functions against the facts of history and which is suggestive of a poetics of witnessing and of the work of trauma as the work of memory irreducible to any historical model. (2) At the same time, such return, and the persistence of witnessing which it implies, is suggestive of the fact, once again, that we can never be let off the hook as regards our acts of responsible reading. In short, the function in part of testimonial criticism is to open to the reader through a recognition of the other's articulation a recognition that what Heidegger calls the 'call of conscience' is not simply always already in effect but always remains to come. Thus we will never have done with reading, and reading remains also that which is to come. The folding and unfolding of structure traced by Caruth thereby is read as the necessary ethical figure of a reading resistant on the one hand to closure and on the other hand to any simple sense of continuity or linearity in narrative motion. As Ulrich Baer puts it, trauma remains open and undecidable because there is no possible immediate recourse to 'an external frame of reference' (2000: 9). The very idea of narrative itself, or, more generally, textuality, involves the 'epistemological possibility and the moral necessity of considering the poetic representation of unresolved experience . . . as absolutely *singular*' (Baer 2000: 9), and knowable only, paradoxically, in its singularity through the open seriality which narrative makes possible.

In exploring the work of critics such as Baer and Caruth, Derrida and Felman, among others, I am therefore attempting to engage with these particular exemplary interventions by tracing, albeit briefly, the fractured intercessions between and exceeding various discourses, as these concern themselves with matters of memory and subjectivity, guilt and being. The impossibility of a representation in relation to the singularity *and* iteration of trauma ties the question of testimony both to the idea of the secret and the question of the unrepresentability of the instant of the traumatic event, as Derrida has made clear in *Demeure*. However, as I wish to argue, our inability to represent the traumatic instant is neither simply a moment of replaying the silencing of articulation by which the traumatized subject is produced, nor is it, equally simply, an acknowledgement of empathy and, therefore, an undifferentiated identification with the victim of trauma;[5] instead, the work of criticism becomes a matter of addressing the 'impossibility and necessity' of bearing witness to the 'unexperienced experience' (Derrida 2000: 47), and it is through the structural gap, in that grammar of absence and loss, that the other comes to be heard.

Trauma, then, might be said to be a ghost. Given that 'the essential character of traumatism' is best described as a 'nonsymbolizable wound' (Ronell 1994: 327), to read trauma is to register the sign of a secondary experience and recognition of the return of something spectral in the form of a trace or sign signifying, but not representing directly, that something, having occurred, has left its mark, an inscription of sorts on the subject's unconscious, and one which, moreover, can and does return repeatedly, though never as the experience as such. This is not to say that the traumatic event, that factual or historical event which one day took place, never happened or was not real. It is to register, however, that for trauma to be comprehended as trauma, as that which, in appearing, inflicts itself on the subject and thereby causes suffering, it is never experienced for the first time *as trauma*. As Dominick LaCapra rightly remarks, 'something of the past always remains, if only as a haunting presence or symptomatic revenant' (2001: 49). The traumatic is that, therefore, which is phantomatic or phantasmatic. Structural through and through, the traumatic phantasm – and, indeed, all phantasms in general – are contradictory, as Louis Althusser suggests. As he puts it, 'something occurs . . . but nothing happens . . . everything is immobile' (1996: 103). The subject of trauma is rendered immobile, unable to move beyond the haunting effects left by trauma, and can only experience in a damaging, repetitive fashion, the disjunctive spectres, remains of what is 'nonsymbolizable'. And yet, paradoxically, the phantasm is a symbol; what has to be understood, however, is that the symbol is not a mimetic representation, it is not an image of the experience itself. It belongs to the order of apperception rather than perception. As Althusser argues, Freud's notion of the phantasm is analogous with the workings of figural language:

> we are obliged to observe that in the phantasm Freud designates some-thing extremely precise, an existent – though nonmaterial – reality, concerning which no misunderstanding is possible, and a material reality that is the very existence of its object: the unconscious. But we are also obliged to observe that the name Freud gives to that reality . . . is the name of a *metaphor*: phantasm . . . the concept of the phantasm in Freud . . . can . . . be, *for us*, the concept *of the limit* . . . (1996: 104)

While I would revise Althusser's understanding by suggesting that, at least as far as the phantasm of trauma is more of the order of catachresis than meta-phor, it is clearly incontestable that the phantasm thus remarks both the other-wise unsymbolizable, and also the grammatical or structural displacement, as the necessary movement in the production of meaning; in doing so, it becomes available – it is only ever available – as the inscription of (and, indeed, *at*) the very limit of representation, rather than being or belonging to representation. The haunting trace not only attests to that which is 'outside memory yet within the psyche', to recall Ulrich Baer's words, it also reveals an irreversible and therefore structural passage between, in Dianne Sadoff's words, 'the material, physiological realm and the correlate mental realm' (1998: 45). In coming to terms with this disjunctive passage as intrinsic to the psychic incorporation of trauma, and the subsequent ghostly reiteration by which trauma came to be comprehended, Freud 'stumbled', as Sadoff continues, 'on the concept of rep-resentability . . . Mnemic symbols, reproduced scenes, and dreams . . . situated images . . . in a pictorial and verbalized space, traversed by memories, fears and desires' (1998: 50).

Interested by what Cathy Caruth describes as the 'peculiar and *uncanny* way in which catastrophic events seem to repeat themselves for those who have passed through them' (1996: 1, emphasis added), Freud sought to explain the experience of trauma through Tasso's story of Tancred and Clorinda. Tancred:

> unwittingly kills . . . Clorinda . . . when she is disguised in the armour of an enemy knight. After her burial he makes his way into a strange magic forest which strikes the Crusaders' army with terror. He slashes with his sword at a tall tree; but blood streams from the cut and the voice

of Clorinda . . . is heard complaining that he has wounded his beloved again. (Freud 1989: 24)

As Tasso's narrative, recounted by Freud, illustrates, the protagonist is led inadvertently to repeat his initial act, and it is only through the structural repetition, that unconscious re-enactment and the resulting haunting traces of Clorinda's fate – the blood, the voice – whereby she 'returns', not as herself but as a phantasm of herself, that Tancred receives the forceful shock of understanding the significance of his earlier action. Structurally, the event becomes dislocated, doubled *and* displaced in reiterative fashion in both Tasso's and Freud's accounts, its meaning *for its subject* produced through the spatio-temporal disjunctive inscription that Derrida names *différance* between the 'first' recounting of act, the historical fact, and the subsequent, supplementary textual remarking in the revenant signs. As Caruth says, 'this understanding of trauma in terms of its indirect relation to reference does not deny or eliminate the possibility of reference but insists, precisely, on the inescapability of its belated impact' (1996: 7). And it is for this reason that, in Freud's account, trauma is 'understood as a wound inflicted not upon the body but upon the mind', whereby 'knowing and not knowing are entangled in the language of trauma' (1996: 1, 4).

Cathy Caruth elucidates further the structural significance of trauma, expanding Freud's insights beyond the already undeniably significant recognition of that which haunts through the traces of its reiteration. What the critic finds powerfully moving in this scene is not only Tancred's illumination. It is also Clorinda's voice: 'a voice that is paradoxically released *through the wound*' (1996: 2). Caruth explains: 'the voice of his beloved addresses him and, in this address, bears witness to the past he has unwittingly repeated. Tancred's story thus represents traumatic experience' (1996: 3) as double. On the one hand, there is that dimension already acknowledged by Freud, where trauma is figured and read as 'the enigma of the human agent's repeated and unknowing acts'. On the other hand, the story admits for Cathy Caruth the 'enigma of the otherness of a human voice . . . that witnesses a truth' (1996: 3) not completely comprehended by the subject. It is thus a matter of giving acknowledgement to the other, of bearing witness to that alterity. In learning how to read and write in response to trauma one must therefore acknowledge the crucial problem 'of listening, of knowing, and of representing' (Caruth 1996: 5). Critical readings and literary or filmic texts concerned with such issues are obligated to bear witness by asking 'what it means to transmit and to theorize around a crisis that is marked, not by a simple knowledge [by which one might suggest a knowledge available to adequate representation, if such exists], but by the ways it simultaneously defies and demands our witness' (Caruth 1996: 5).

Such is the '"technical" difficulty', to use a phrase of Avital Ronell's, regarding any critical or literary act concerning trauma and testimony (1994: 313).

I believe that Ronell employs the word 'technical', simultaneously marking it off through the cautionary use of quotation marks, in order to emphasize the fundamental condition of technicity, that is, as remarked above, an act of making something appear. How does one verbalize or visualize where there is nothing present as such, and yet where there is a non-material reality and its material effects? The difficulty, Ronell suggests, 'consists in the fact that trauma can be experienced in at least two ways ... as a memory that one cannot integrate into one's own experience, and as a catastrophic knowledge that one cannot communicate to others' (1994: 313–14). Slavoj Žižek puts the problem another way:

> There is an inherent link between the notions of trauma and repetition, signalled in Freud's well-known motto that what one is not able to remember, one is condemned to repeat: a trauma is by definition something one is not able to remember, i.e. to recollect by way of making it part of one's symbolic narrative; as such, it repeats itself indefinitely, returning to haunt the subject – more precisely, what repeats itself is the very failure, impossibility even to repeat/recollect the trauma properly. (Žižek 2001: 36–7)

The difficulty explained by Žižek and Ronell is that of some impassable point in thinking, where what comes to be revealed, even though we cannot say what it is, is the acknowledgement of a radically discontinuous structure between self and other. As Derrida remarks, 'one needs the other to be determined, in order to relate to history, to memory, to what is kept as a nameable or nameless secret. There is some sealed memory, kept as a crypt or as an unconscious, which is encrypted here' (1997: 115).

Acknowledging that the aporia of trauma is impassable, to the extent that the experience cannot either be integrated into memory or remembered in such a fashion that one can 'overcome' trauma through a kind of mimetic reassembly of the absent experience, perhaps it remains the case that one's response and responsibility has to assume different forms, different modalities, different readings. Such possibilities, in acknowledging the limit of representation, opening themselves to other articulations, might make it possible to 'begin again' in such a way that the traces of the traumatic are comprehended in their irrecoverable condition so as to allow for what architect Daniel Libeskind describes as a 'hopeful future' (1997b: 102). Clearly, it would seem that the question of how one responds is not so much a matter of *mimesis* as it is of *poiêsis*.

Libeskind himself has confronted just such a problem as an architect asked to respond in the appropriate manner to the Holocaust, and to the relation between the violence of forgetting imposed by trauma and what he describes as the 'invisible matrix or anamnesis of connections in relationship ... between figures of Germans and Jews' (1997a: 34) on several projects. One such project is the Jewish Museum, Berlin, in which the architect has sought to address the memory of the relation between Jewish culture and tradition and German culture, not simply in dialectical terms but, instead, through the material reality offered by the memory and history of the city of Berlin, as one space wherein traumatic erasure and silencing took place. Libeskind's project was thus to be able to speak of the invisible within the visible, the unspeakable within the articulated, thereby symbolizing indirectly the unsymbolizable of the traumatic event. To this end, the museum could not be merely a memorial, imposing itself as another form of silencing by gathering so many 'representations' of absence as though these were somehow representative of all the facts that were the case of the Holocaust, and thereby allowing for the possibility of the necessary act of witnessing to slide into some form of empathic voyeurism. Instead, Libeskind chose to rethink the very space of the museum, and passage through it, in order that every 'participant', as he puts it, 'will experience [the museum] as his or her own absent present' (1997a: 34); in order that every visitor's 'role', as it were, is not defined solely as objective or constative – as a visitor, I do not simply observe and reflect on represented events to which I believe I have little or no relationship, as is the case in conventional museums – but is, also, inescapably, participatory and performative (and therefore transformative, auto-transformative) – in the act of passage I experience and thus am asked to remember, to symbolize, the invisible, the silenced, the erased, of Berlin *within* the visible, present, articulated structure of the museum, which both belongs to Berlin and yet which also traces Berlin's alterity. This is achieved by Libeskind through the very nature of the spatial and architectural experience rather than because of any single item in the museum's collection, each of which is always in danger of functioning as synecdoche for the trauma of the *Shoah* as a whole, and thereby falling into mimetic representation inappropriate to the 'anamnesis of connections in relationship'. Specifically, Libeskind has sought to rethink the museum in performative terms through the incorporation of 'roads' and 'voids' between the galleries, and between the previously existing Berlin Museum and the Jewish Museum designed by Libeskind. Libeskind's comments from his website are worth quoting at length:

> In specific terms the building measures more than 15,000 square meters. The entrance is through the Baroque Kollegienhaus and then into a dramatic entry Void by a stair which descends under the existing building foundations, crisscrosses underground and materializes itself as an independent building on the outside. The existing building is tied to the extension underground, preserving the contradictory autonomy of both the old building and the new building on the surface, while binding the two together in the depth of time and space.
>
> There are three underground 'roads' which programmatically have three separate stories. The first and longest 'road', leads to the main stair, to the continuation of Berlin's history, to the exhibition spaces in the Jewish Museum. The second road leads outdoors to the E.T.A.

Hoffmann Garden and represents the exile and emigration of Jews from Germany. The third axis leads to the dead end – the Holocaust Void.

Cutting through the form of the Jewish Museum is a Void, a straight line whose impenetrability forms the central focus around which the exhibitions are organized. In order to cross from one space of the Museum to the other, the visitors traverse sixty bridges which open into the Void space; the embodiment of absence.

The work is conceived as a museum for all Berliners, for all citizens. Not only those of the present, but those of the future who might find their heritage and hope in this particular place. With its special emphasis on the Jewish dimension of Berlin's history, this building gives voice to a common fate – to the contradictions of the ordered and disordered, the chosen and not chosen, the vocal and silent.

I believe that this project joins Architecture to questions that are now relevant to all humanity. To this end, I have sought to create a new Architecture for a time which would reflect an understanding of history, a new understanding of Museums and a new realization of the relationship between program and architectural space. Therefore this Museum is not only a response to a particular program, but an emblem of Hope. (Daniel Libeskind, http://www.daniel-libeskind.com/projects)

Libeskind's architecture responds to the singularity of historic catastrophe and its material effects. His work does this moreover in taking into account the urgent need, the responsibility once again, to make possible an event that can exceed the programming of institutional representation, and the calculability, the economy, of witnessing and memory within any mimetic paradigm. As his commentary makes clear, we can only attest to what is absent, not bring that which cannot be symbolized back. In bearing witness, however, there is always a question of a poetics of witnessing which is affirmative in that it is open, and opens itself, in radical ways in relation to an understanding to come, incommensurable with any knowledge.

On another occasion, Libeskind was asked to design an urban project for the site belonging to the SS surrounding Sachsenhausen concentration camp. The initial suggestion that the site could be used for housing, thereby effectively 'domesticating' and forgetting the experience which haunted the location, was rejected by the architect as being inadequate to, and incommensurate with, any project of 'mental rehabilitation' (Libeskind 1997b: 102), necessary in Germany. As Libeskind describes it, 'the paradoxical challenge of the work is to retain a strong memory for generations to come and at the same time to formulate a response which provides new possibilities, new activities' (1997b: 102). One of the ways in which this was achieved was through decentralizing the site of the concentration camp, originally to have been the 'monumental central' location of the proposed housing development; deregulating the order of the site provided for Libeskind a way of displacing the camp from its axial prominence, which would simply have repeated without transforming what was represented. Another transformation proposed was to use the land in such a way as to effect 'ecological intervention and invention' (1997b: 102), allied to the economic needs of the city of Oranienberg. Libeskind saw the necessity of providing training facilities for the unemployed, as well as other public services such as 'physical and mental health clinics', 'a library, archive, museum', and the accommodation of small companies, specifically those 'connected to cultural production, such as instrument makers, furniture restorers or ceramicists' (1997b: 102). Libeskind's responses to the Sachsenhausen location suggest an affirmation of responsibility in the face of one singular instance of trauma, a responsibility which manifests itself in the resistance to a predictable programming of redevelopment and which therefore situates its own affirmative singularity. Yet, while retaining the singularity of both trauma and response as the work of an act of 'reading' (in the broad sense) as discussed above, Libeskind also acknowledges a more theoretically broad comprehension of the task engendered after trauma, without reducing that to a method in itself. He writes: 'The task of urbanizing the territories formerly connected with the Sachsenhausen concentration camp raises the most fundamental political, cultural and spiritual issues of the 20th century.'

> What must be faced in any endeavour to recreate and redevelop such an area is the need to mourn an *irretrievable* destiny, in the hope that this *morning* will *affect* the connection between the political program, the area's topography and its social use. (1997b: 102, emphases added)

Libeskind's language gives full recognition to the condition of trauma, but also demonstrates how the possibility of thinking transformatively according to a poetics of mourning and memory irreducible to any simple act of representation can bring about the translation from 'mourning' to 'morning'. A new start which does not forget and yet which moves forward is signified precisely in Libeskind's erasure of the 'u', yet leaving both the letter and the erasure to remain, in order that the necessity for mourning is not abandoned, while also indicating that it not become a form of passive identification with the victims of the camp, thereby forestalling any hope of political or spiritual change.

NOTES TOWARDS READINGS OF *FRANKENSTEIN* AND *HEART OF DARKNESS*

Trauma effects an incision in the self, so that one effectively becomes two (Felman and Laub 1992: 178), by a process of what Nicolas Abraham and Maria Torok have called an 'internal psychic splitting' (1994: 100). These two selves are the one who experiences and the one who survives (King 2000: 17–19). This is the case, whether by 'self' one indicates a single subject, an individual subjected to a catastrophic experience, or a national, communal or cultural subject, such as a nation or race.

Yet this splitting, this division and doubling that produces the discontinuous subject, doomed to be haunted by the repetitive return of the spectres of trauma, is not only a form of forgetting brought on by the extremity of some original experience; it is also, as Freud's narrative example makes clear, a manifestation of incorporation. The subject incorporates into him- or herself the signs of the traumatic, thereafter being unable to comprehend them. What distinguishes such incorporation as traumatic, however, is that the signs do not become assimilated in that psychic process termed 'introjection', whereby the subject grows in a 'continual process of self-fashioning . . . introjection represents our ability to survive shock, trauma, or loss' (Rand, quoted in Abraham and Torok 1994: 14). As Abraham and Torok put it, *incorporation results from those losses that for some reason cannot be acknowledged as such . . .*'

> There can be no thought of speaking to someone else about our grief under these circumstances. The words that cannot be uttered, the scenes that cannot be recalled, the tears that cannot be shed – everything will be swallowed along with the trauma that led to the loss. Swallowed and preserved. Inexpressible mourning erects a secret tomb inside the subject . . . Sometimes . . . the ghost of the crypt comes back to haunt the cemetery guard, giving him strange and incomprehensible signals, making him perform bizarre acts, or subjecting him to unexpected sensations. (1994: 130)

Where the phantasm had been for Althusser a metaphor, for Abraham and Torok, the spectre of trauma, in its incorporation, is *antimetaphor*, as they term it, because it effectively blocks all access to figurative contiguity or correlation, and therefore to any proper or appropriate narrative or symbolic reassembly. Hence, my suggestion that we would do well to understand the trace of trauma, in its resistance to any naturalization or domestication, as a figure of catachresis, the absolutely monstrous trope without discernible or otherwise accessible relation to its source or origin.

The figural paradox of incorporation and that amnesiac mechanism belonging to trauma may be comprehended if, in following Slavoj Žižek's reading of Primo Levi on the Holocaust (2001: 37–8), we make the distinction between understanding and knowledge, which, in other terms, is also the distinction already alluded to between representation as *poiêsis* and as *mimesis*. While, rationally, we may know or be able to have access to all the historical facts (or as many of the facts as can be discovered) concerning a particular traumatic historical event, neither historical facts nor statistics, nor any historical account aiming to represent faithfully the past solely through the narrative ordering of such factual details, will ever wholly help either those witnesses who survive or those who after the event bear witness to what took place *understand*. There is always already an opening, once again, that incommensurable gap, and with it, the fateful repetition. Understanding does not belong to the rational, the logical, the mimetic; it arrives, if it arrives at all, through articulating a certain relationship to that of which the facts cannot speak, and whereof they must, therefore, keep silent. Understanding is only possible – and this is not some guarantee or promise – if one begins by comprehending the process of a certain 'translation' already discussed – where the corporeal registration of shock and horror is effectively *decorporealized* and simultaneously *incorporated*.

Thus, if, as I have already claimed, literature just names, or is understood as the name of, *for*, the work of witnessing and memory, and if it does bear witness and remember, moreover, through the symbolization of what remains unsymbolizable and unrepresentable, it has to be appreciated and grasped that reading literature, in order to be responsible, cannot merely content itself with a reading of character motivation, of plot summary, or, indeed, with an analysis the epistemological grounding for which is to be located in an assumption of literature as conforming to realist criteria of representation. Rather, as one possible hypothesis, narrative takes place through the assembly of signifying fragments moving through various flows, the intersections of which gather in moments of intensity so as to project phantasmatic symbolizations of that which otherwise cannot be articulated. In such terms, narrative or, perhaps, even literature itself is the indirect articulation of what Maurice Blanchot has described as 'a speech unheard, inexpressible, nevertheless unceasing, silently affirming that where all relation is lacking there yet subsists, there already begins, the human relation in its primacy' (1993: 135).

Take, for example, the narrative of Mary Shelley's *Frankenstein, or the Modern Prometheus* (1818). The story of a man, Victor Frankenstein, who assembles something almost human but not quite – something other than human which, in its uncanny resemblance to the human animal, constantly reminds its maker of a disturbing otherness within any notion of self or being – is, in one sense, clearly fantastic, impossible. The narrative thus represents what is, strictly speaking, unrepresentable, even though Mary Shelley is at pains to point out that there are those in the scientific community who have suggested that her narrative represents a not 'impossible occurrence' (1994: 3). The author goes on to remark, in a form of qualification, that 'however impossible as a physical fact, [the narrative event of the construction of a human being] affords a point of view to the imagination for the delineating of human passions more comprehensive and commanding than any which the ordinary relations of existing events can yield' (1994: 3). At pains to point out that *Frankenstein* is not merely some supernatural tale of spectres, Shelley clearly wishes it to be understood that the story concerns the articulation of a certain imaginative, psychological understanding – a poetics, in short – incommensurable with any strictly realistic representation or adequate knowledge.

Thus we find ourselves witness to a particular, singular narrative responding to that process of transition between physical and mental realms and, at the same time, that narrative's inability to verbalize or bear witness to epistemological crisis. Historically, *Frankenstein* is available to us as being both caught in and traversing the space between the external and internal, symbolizing, we might say, the registration of a cultural experience of trauma in the face of the epistemological shock to the self of then 'new' sciences. It moves between differing modalities of comprehension concerning self and other, or the two halves of the split self, which it remarks materially through the characters of Victor Frankenstein and his creature. The novel is suspended in its traversal between external physical world and internal psychic states, however, in that – and this is a sign of the materiality, the historiality of the narrative's attempt to respond to the traumatic reception of new knowledge, and out of which comes the narrative's imaginative understanding – it still finds it necessary to apprehend its concerns through the ostensible depiction of creator and creature as essentially separate, and yet inseparable, characters.

Yet, what is really fascinating in Shelley's narrative, despite the corporeal externalization – and thus as a manifestation of anthropomorphic representation signalling the inability to move beyond the otherwise inaccessible, inexpressible experience of trauma – is the movement of structural repetition. Victor Frankenstein's creation pursues his creator relentlessly, returning and haunting both Victor and the narrative itself. Significantly, apropos of the question of traumatic revenance, we should read such returns and reiterations not as the arrival of a significant character so much as we should comprehend how the narrative is itself marked and interrupted, traumatized, by this iterable interruption. And while Victor Frankenstein may have scientific knowledge, he has no understanding of what he has done; its meaning is inaccessible to him, and so he is pursued by this monstrous phantasm of his own making. Similarly, the narrative can only function through its various doublings and repetitions, and its material, uncloseable fissure between externality and internality, its constant reminders of the divisions of the subject announcing, in a quite singular manner, the trauma of modernity. The reciprocal shuttling of its various 'voices' render the text as a weaving machine, the sovereign narrator dismembered through a technology of witnessing. And the reader is confronted, perhaps traumatized, by an image of a possibly traumatized creator unable to take responsibility for the other, a figure of abjection, trauma and alterity, not-quite-human enough and yet all-too-human in a particularly modern sense: technologically reproduced, grafted, re-marked, commodified and made monstrous. And yet, to conclude this brief sketch by reiterating what is, for me, the key issue here, this is not only to describe Frankenstein's creature, or even Victor Frankenstein's non-recognition; it is also to say something, albeit indirectly, about *Frankenstein*, the text:[6] for, arguably, it bears all the hallmarks of traumatic narrative unable to escape its own condition, doomed to fold onto itself that otherness which haunts it throughout.

It might be said that it took less than a hundred years for literature to respond to the processes of internalization which trauma simultaneously names and encrypts.[7] That wholesale internalization finds itself remarked in Joseph Conrad's *Heart of Darkness* (1902). While *Frankenstein's* registration of the traumatic is fundamentally epistemological in nature, Conrad's narrative strives to address the trauma of the colonial enterprise, and to bear witness to that. Were we simply interested in reading characters as traumatized, we could, doubtless, focus on Kurtz. (And, indeed, I do wish to turn, if not to Kurtz entirely, then, at least, to his final words.) However, I want to stress that *Heart of Darkness* records trauma at its most basic lexical levels, through the very choice of words by which the attempt at representation takes place. (Again, given that Conrad's novel offers its readers a first-person narrative, it would be easy enough to domesticate the reading of trauma by seeing its articulation as, simply, only, the articulation of the narrator, Marlowe's, psychological condition.) The narratorial voice (which, it has to be stressed, cannot be equated simply with Marlowe's, if only because Marlowe's account is both marked by the voices of others, as well as being a response to, and therefore framed by, an anonymous, invisible narrator who begins *Heart of Darkness*) is traced by a poetics of the limit, a materiality of the letter attesting to both the limit and inadequacy of representation in the face of catastrophe and horror, and the importance of bearing witness to the fact, and in the face, of the inexpressible.

This 'limit-language' occurs throughout the novel through the use of several hundred words, all sharing prefixes the work of which is either to say that determinate knowledge or representation cannot take place or that knowledge and representation are only this admission that one cannot know, one cannot represent trauma. These are words such as *interminable, immensity, imperceptible, untitled, inscrutable, incomprehensible, inconclusive, uncanny, unknown, insoluble, impossible, unfamiliar, incredible, impenetrable, unspeakable, inconceivable, inexorable, unforeseen, invisible, indistinct.* Their frequency both maintains the narrative and yet interrupts, disables the narrative at every point. Such words speak to the obligation to read and to the impossibility of a reading.

Thus, one aspect of Conrad's writing situates the responsible act *in* the materiality of the letter in order to respond *to* the materiality of history, and in order to acknowledge how, on the one hand, it is impossible to record historical events in any direct representation, while, on the other, to show indirectly, how any such mimetic act is inadequate to the intensity, the immensity, of traumatism. Rather, Conrad's poetics of indirection attest to history as a history of trauma, to recall Cathy Caruth's words. In its deployment of a limit-language, Conrad's novel attests to the technical difficulty concerning trauma spoken of by Avital Ronell, for it undeniably inscribes the trauma of colonialism as (in Ronell's words) 'a memory that one cannot integrate into one's own experience, and as a catastrophic knowledge that one cannot communicate to others'. What such language also gives us to understand is how 'repetition [is] at the heart of catastrophe' (Caruth 1996: 2). Nowhere is this, along with Ronell's traumatic double bind, articulated more clearly, than in Kurtz's final moments:

Did he live his life again in every detail of desire, temptation, and surrender during that supreme moment of complete knowledge? He cried in a whisper at some image, some vision, – he cried out twice, a cry that was no more than a breath –

'"the horror, the horror!"'
(Conrad 1995: 112)

If repetition is at the heart of catastrophe, it is also at the heart of darkness, a darkness naming the absolute inaccessibility of the traumatic event. Kurtz's words clearly repeat themselves in the rhythm of trauma's return and which iteration 'splits the mark [in this example, Kurtz's doubling, dividing articulation] into a past that can never be fully rendered present and a future which is always about to arrive' (Weber 1996: 149). Structurally, what has to be acknowledged here is that not only is Kurtz not experiencing the traumatic as such, but is only responding to its inaccessibility, while expressing the mark it has indelibly inscribed upon him; also, his articulation – one which, in its reiteration, has the possibility of echoing and remarking itself endlessly – is itself doubled by Marlowe's memory of it (a memory which haunts Marlowe, and which returns on Marlowe's visit to Kurtz's fiancée [Conrad 1995: 118]). It is to be noticed that Marlowe cannot say for certain what Kurtz is witness to, he can only pose an unanswerable question. Furthermore, that repetition is worked out in Marlowe's own words. He says twice of Kurtz that 'he cried', 'he cried out twice', and that, whatever Kurtz bears witness to, it is both an image and a vision. There is a splitting and duplication at work here, once again, both of which are the signs of traumatic incorporation; these effects do not merely 'belong' to a particular character's psyche, but are inscribed at the heart of the language. Moreover, the extent to which trauma is both witnessed and replayed is to be comprehended in the way in which, in the iterable movement of Marlowe's response, constative description appears to fall into performative speech act. What this suggests, *what it imposes*, is an open structure of witnessing. Marlowe does not know how to assimilate Kurtz's words, but bears witness to them and to the trauma they appear to signal, thereby enacting otherwise, transformatively, the act of attestation, and, in the process, opening an ethical relay. The structure of *Heart of Darkness* is thus mobilized by what J. Hillis Miller has called a 'proliferating relay of witnesses . . . The relay of witness behind witness behind witness, voice behind voice behind voice . . .' (1990: 188). That we as readers comprehend this means that we are only the latest, not the last, in the relay of witnesses to the unspeakable in every singular traumatic event. This is the impossible responsibility we bear. For, to recall the words of Maurice Blanchot, what is encrypted in those words, 'the horror, the horror', and in the relay they interrupt and maintain, is 'a speech unheard, inexpressible, nevertheless unceasing, silently affirming that where all relation is lacking there yet subsists, there already begins, the human relation in its primacy'. And what is important, as Blanchot reminds us, and as we come to understand from *Heart of Darkness*, 'is not to tell, but to tell once again, and, in the retelling, to tell again each time a first time' (1993: 314).

QUESTIONS FOR FURTHER CONSIDERATION

1. Consider how trauma is structured like a language.
2. If trauma is unsymbolizable as such, what in narratives such as *Frankenstein* and *Heart of Darkness* make the effects of trauma readable (if they are)?
3. In what ways might *Heart of Darkness* be said to 'tell again each time for the first time'?
4. In what ways does the psychological concept of trauma challenge conventional understandings of historical event and representation?
5. If conventional, particularly mimetic, acts of representation are inadequate in their response to catastrophic historical events, what other modalities of representation do literature and film make available to us?
6. To what extent does the narrative inability to articulate an adequate or final response to 'the horror, the horror' in *Heart of Darkness*, while showing how it can only say that it cannot say, address the condition of trauma while making the reader aware of her/his own responsibility?

BIBLIOGRAPHY

Abraham, Nicolas and Maria Torok (1994) *The Shell and the Kernel, Vol. I* [1987], ed., trans. and intro. Nicholas Rand, Chicago: University of Chicago Press.

Althusser, Louis (1996) *Writing on Psychoanalysis: Freud and Lacan* [1993], trans. Jeffrey Mehlman, New York: Columbia University Press.

Baer, Ulrich (2000) *Remnants of Song: Trauma and the Experience of Modernity in Charles Baudelaire and Paul Celan*, Stanford: Stanford University Press.

Bernard-Donals, Michael and Richard Glejzer (2001) *Between Witness and Testimony: The Holocaust and the Limits of Representation*, Albany: State University of New York Press.

Blanchot, Maurice (1993) *The Infinite Conversation* [1969], trans. and Foreword Susan Hanson, Minneapolis: University of Minnesota Press.

Blanchot, Maurice/Jacques Derrida (2000) *The Instant of My Death/Demeure: Fiction and Testimony*, Stanford: Stanford University Press.

Caruth, Cathy (1996) *Unclaimed Experience: Trauma, Narrative and History*, Baltimore: Johns Hopkins University Press.

Castle, Terry (1995) *The Female Thermometer: Eighteenth-Century Culture and the Invention of the Uncanny*, Oxford: Oxford University Press.

Conrad, Joseph (1995) *Heart of Darkness* [1902], in *Heart of Darkness with The Congo Diary*, ed. and intro. Robert Hampson, London: Penguin.

Derrida, Jacques (1992) *The Other Heading: Reflections on Today's Europe* [1991], trans. Pascale-Anne Brault and Michael Naas, Chicago: University of Chicago Press.

Derrida, Jacques (1995) *The Gift of Death* [1992], trans. David Wills, Chicago: University of Chicago Press.

Derrida, Jacques (1997) 'Response to Daniel Libeskind', in Daniel Libeskind, *Radix-Matrix: Architecture and Writings*, Munich: Prestel.

Derrida, Jacques (2000) *Demeure: Fiction and Testimony*, in Maurice Blanchot / Jacques Derrida, *The Instant of My Death / Demeure: Fiction and Testimony*, trans. Elizabeth Rottenberg, Stanford: Stanford University Press.

Düttman, Alexander García (2000) *The Gift of Language: Memory and Promise in Adorno, Benjamin, Heidegger, and Rosenzweig*, London: Athlone.

Felman, Shoshana and Dori Laub (1992) *Testimony: Crises of Witnessing in Literature, Psychoanalysis, and History*, London: Routledge.

Freud, Sigmund (1989) *Beyond the Pleasure Principle* [1920], trans. and ed. James Strachey, intro. Gregory Zilboorg, biographical intro. Peter Gay, New York: W. W. Norton.

Germain, Sylvie (1993) *The Weeping Woman on the Streets of Prague* [1992], trans. Judith Landry, intro. Emma Wilson, London: Dedalus.

Keenan, Thomas (1997) *Fables of Responsibility: Aberrations and Predicaments in Ethics and Politics*, Stanford: Stanford University Press.

King, Nicola (2000) *Memory, Narrative, Identity*, Edinburgh: Edinburgh University Press.

Kronick, Joseph G. (1999) *Derrida and the Future of Literature*, Albany: State University of New York Press.

LaCapra, Dominick (2001) *Writing History, Writing Trauma*, Baltimore: Johns Hopkins University Press.

Libeskind, Daniel (1997a) 'Between the Lines', in *Radix-Matrix: Architecture and Writings*, Munich: Prestel.

Libeskind, Daniel (1997b) 'Morning: Sachsenhausen, Oranienberg', in *Radix-Matrix: Architecture and Writings*, Munich: Prestel.

Miller, J. Hillis (1990) 'Heart of Darkness Revisited', in *Tropes, Parables, Performatives: Essays on Twentieth-Century Literature*, Hemel Hempstead: Harvester Wheatsheaf.

Ronell, Avital (1989) *The Telephone Book: Technology-Schizophrenia-Electric Speech*, Lincoln: University of Nebraska Press.

Ronell, Avital (1994) *Finitude's Score: Essays for the End of the Millennium*, Lincoln: University of Nebraska Press.

Sadoff, Dianne (1998) *Sciences of the Flesh: Representing Body and Subject in Psychoanalysis*, Stanford: Stanford University Press.

Shelley, Mary (1994) *Frankenstein, or the Modern Prometheus* [1818], ed. and intro. Marilyn Butler, Oxford: Oxford University Press.

Spivak, Gayatri Chakravorty (2001) 'A Moral Dilemma', in Howard Marchitello, ed., *What Happens to History: The Renewal of Ethics in Contemporary Thought*, New York: Routledge.

Weber, Samuel (1996) *Mass Mediauras: Form Technics Media*, Stanford: Stanford University Press.

Žižek, Slavoj (2001) *On Belief*, London: Routledge.

NOTES

1. In pointing to a 'psychoanalytic' or an 'ethical' criticism, I am merely alluding to two of the more obvious 'contexts' or frameworks, conceptual languages or institutionally recognized discourses, which someone reading this might highlight in order to 'explain' the origins of the present critical act. Thus there is the possibility for recognizing a degree of overlap or resemblance between this chapter and, say, that on the subject of 'ethical criticism' by Kenneth Womack, or the specific project of the work of Emmanuel Levinas, as explored by Frederick Young, both in the present volume.

   The psychoanalytic and ethical registers are not the only ones at work here, however. Equally, the question of history is announced. One might also suggest that, within the current volume, there are aspects of my chapter touching on those raised by Tom Cohen's in his consideration of materiality. Another way of commandeering the chapter in terms of a master discourse might be to see it as an articulation of particular aspects of Jacques Derrida's later work, and therefore, by the usual, wholly predictable extension, to apprehend this chapter as an example of so-called deconstruction. Such assumptions or, to be more accurate, calculations, exemplify the ways in which conceptualization proceeds, and which the introduction of this chapter seeks to unpack in relation to the motifs of 'testimony', 'trauma', 'witnessing' and 'responsibility'.

2. On the subject of performativity, see Sarah Gamble, Frederick Young and Tom Cohen's chapters in this collection.

3. I am borrowing the contours of this commentary from the work of Jacques Derrida, who, in *The Gift of Death*, commented that 'the simple concepts of alterity and singularity constitute the concept of duty as much as that of responsibility. As a result, the concepts of responsibility, of decision, or of duty, are condemned a priori to paradox, scandal, and aporia. Paradox, scandal, and aporia are themselves nothing other than sacrifice, the revelation of conceptual thinking at its limit, its death and finitude' (1995: 68). See the following note.

4. Kronick elaborates this point from a discussion of Derrida's in the third chapter of *The Gift of Death*: 'I can respond only to the one (or to the One), that is, to the other, by sacrificing that one to the other. I am responsible to any one (that is to say to any other) only by failing in my responsibility to all the others, to the ethical or political generality. And I can never justify this sacrifice, I must always hold my peace about it. Whether I want to or not, I can never justify the fact that I prefer or sacrifice any one (any other) to the other ... What binds me to singularities, to this one or that one ... remains finally undecidable ... as unjustifiable as the infinite sacrifice I make at each moment. These singularities represent others, a wholly other form of alterity: one other or some other persons, but also places, animals, languages. How would you ever justify the fact that you sacrifice all the cats in the world to the cat that you feed at home every morning for years, whereas other cats die of hunger at every instant' (Derrida 1995: 70–1).

5. It has to be acknowledged, of course, that the act of 'secondary witnessing', a kind of working-through the trauma of others, is a problem fraught with the dangers of identification. As LaCapra remarks, 'a difficulty arises when the virtual experience involved in empathy gives way to vicarious victimhood, and empathy with the victim seems to become an identity' (2001: 47).

6. In a possible development of this sketch of a reading of Shelley's novel, it can be argued that Shelley's comprehension of the aberrant, the traumatic and the monstrous that inform modernity figures cultural experience in a proleptic, if not prosthetic manner, as that comes to be analysed by Karl Marx at the beginning of *Capital*. As Thomas Keenan's persuasive analysis of Marx's opening rhetorical gestures makes plain, Marx addresses the ways in which the economic 'shows itself by hiding itself, by announcing itself as something else or in another form'; wealth is figured as something monstrous, 'compounded of elements from different forms ... grown beyond the control of its creators'. This monster cannot be domesticated; neither can it be rendered as an organic unity, being 'nothing but parts, unnatural and uncommon ... [a]berrant, deviant ... This figure of monstrosity, living and dead (the *Wahrig* [*Deutsches Wörterbuch*] links *ungeheuer* [*enormous, immense, monstrous*] to *unheimlich*, [*uncanny*, lit. *unhomely*] unhomely monstrosity to ghostly recurrence), haunts the chapter' (Keenan 1997: 104). Marx even quotes himself, thereby engaging in an act of mechanical grafting, according to Keenan, where this monstrous or ghostly act serves only to point further for the critic to the ways in which words themselves are 'nothing but commodities, to be accumulated, moved and removed ... transferred like (*als*) property or the mechanical limb ... on a monster' (1997: 105). It is arguable that, while Keenan does not speak directly of trauma in the context of reading the opening passages from Marx, he does mobilize, through his analysis of the monstrous and spectral rhetoric that Marx engages

around the subject of the commodity, a transformative critique of the essentially traumatic effect on cultural identity (including Marx's own, given his choice of words) of capitalist economics.

7. Terry Castle provides a compelling account of the nineteenth century as a century of incorporation and internalization, through an analysis of the figure of 'phantas-magoria' and its transformation from the literal meaning, pertaining to the technological production and representation of ghosts in exhibitions and other public entertainments to the wholly internal 'successions of . . . phantasms . . . as called up by the imagination, or as created by literary description' (Castle 1995: 141).

MEMORY AND MEMORY WORK

Torsten Caeners

Where does one begin with memory? With memory work? Involuntarily, with the past, my past, our past, a past the pastness of which is always already effaced, effaces itself constantly into the present, presents its absence, inscribes itself in the endless succession of the now, the temporality of the Cartesian *cogito*, the Freudian consciousness, the Platonic thought, the *logos*. Laboriously, working past layers of recollection and repression, past darkening and darkened images, past the edges of forgettings that punctuate the tissue of identity, the narrative of the self . . . and in the end, again, past pastness, beyond memory, again, into the present, arriving, never finally, at the presence of the absence of the past. The 'again' of recollection, the p*r*esence of the 're', is never pure, repetition recalls nothing, repeats an absence, the other of the past. The 're' has 'the general sense of "back" or "again"' (*OED*), it is

> prefixed to ordinary verbs of action (chiefly transitive) and to derivatives from these, sometimes denoting that the action itself is performed a second time, and sometimes that its result is to reverse a previous action or process, or to restore a previous state of things. With nouns of action the force of the prefix may frequently be rendered by 'second' or 'new'. (*OED*)

The 're', the 'again', expresses action, movement, process and progress. At the same time the 're' figures repetition, reversal and restoration. It is the action and movement, the process and progress of repetition and restoration of a 'previous state of things'. It is thus no mere again, but a return, second and new. Its transitive nature organizes more than one relationship simultaneously.

Memory is therefore, first and foremost, multi-relational, a process of forming dynamic relations between the present and a previous. 'But memory relates to the past' (Aristotle 1941: 449b15). It is the setting up of relations to the past that defines memory not as the past, nor as a reproduction of the past and, even less, a re-presentation of the past. The return of the past through memory is second, secondary, supplementary, a restoration which is at the same time a reversal, a change into the new, temporally and with regard to identity. Memory emerges as a function of relations rather than as a fixed and firmly delineated concept used to describe mental or psychic states of consciousness. In facilitating relations to the past, by means of this activity, memory becomes the very condition of those actions of consciousness termed recollection and remembering. Consequently, rather than presenting and counter-positioning varying and differing definitions and concepts of 'memory', I will circumscribe, primarily, the reciprocal relations of memory to time and to identity. I will not primarily engage with memory by means of its conceptual differentiations (individual and collective memory, repressed and voluntary memory, and so forth) for the simple reason that little can be gained from comparing within such a widely differentiated conceptual space. I believe that more can be gained via a re-focusing on those dynamic relations that generate the major functions and functionalizations of memory. This gesture of de-differentiation can, of course, only be relative as it constitutes in itself another mode of differentiation. In any case, some conceptual frameworks about memory necessarily have to be brought forth. Memory pertains to so many different and varying discourses, intersects with all aspects of existence and is appropriated by such a vast array of methods, epistemological perspectives and approaches that each necessarily resorts to its own notion of 'memory' in the manner of *bricolage*. *Bricolage*, Derrida notes, is 'the necessity of borrowing one's concept from the text of a heritage which is more or less coherent or ruined' (1978a: 285). The gesture of *bricolage* tends towards catachresis in that meaning relations are re-fashioned to organize different contexts. 'Memory' must, as all concepts, be put under erasure by the catachrestic process of *bricolage*.

Currently, Memory has become a master word that, like all words that have attained power over discourses, remains essentially hollow, oblivious of its own identity. Andreas Huyssen speaks of 'a hypertrophy of memory' (2003: 3). In order to function as a master word, Memory necessarily had to become hypertrophic, had to insert itself everywhere and, by being everywhere, memory has, in fact, been displaced elsewhere. Memory and catachresis are thus further linked: memory's relational iteration is one of transgression, openness, transfiguration. I will engage with memory by means of its relation to identity, time and writing as the inscription of the trace, a web of signification that layers its own open, iterable structurality into a potentiality facilitating a re-integrating of past experiences into the present by means of a ceaseless process of catachresis. This ceaseless process of transformation, transgression and (re-)integration is one that calls forth the notion of the palimpsest. The palimpsest as a figure of memory, recollection and forgetting opens itself cat-achrestically to this iteration. Sarah Dillon contends that

> the 'present' of the palimpsest is only constituted in and by the 'presence' of texts from the 'past', as well as remaining open to further inscription by texts of the 'future'. The presence of texts from the past, present (and possibly future) in the palimpsest does not elide temporality but evidences the spectrality of any 'present' moment which always already contains within it 'past', 'present', and 'future' moments. (2007: 37)

The palimpsest figures the dynamics of memory at the intersections or thresholds of forgetting and recollecting by taking seriously its nature as inscription and re-inscription, i.e. as textual traces that are simultaneously immaterial and non-relational in that they only relate to themselves. Casey notes that 'the probable range of indefiniteness is established by recourse to material not contained in the memory itself – most typically, to *other memories* from the same general period' (1987: 22, emphasis original). Memory relates to the other in relating to itself and to itself as other ('to *other memories*'). In this sense, it layers itself into an open textuality that gestures, poetically, narratively and critically, towards other texts, towards palimpsestuousness. This is, again, a catachrestic process. The texts that inhabit the palimpsest can never be restored in their original, isolated form. They will always be and, indeed, have always been in a relationship to the other texts that make up the textuality of the palimpsest, their meaning is inevitably influenced by all other texts: 'the palimpsest is only constituted in and by the "presence" of texts from the "past", as well as remaining open to further inscription by texts of the "future"' (Dillon 2007: 37). Textual boundaries do not exist within the palimpsest except in that they are always already transgressed, kept in suspension. Palimpsestuous textuality of memory is thus essentially catachrestic in its multi-relational existence. In the same manner in which the texts of a palimpsest are never pure, do not exist as individual texts, memory allows access to previous states of consciousness and experiences, but these are not accessible as 'the past'. Consciousness only ever perceives pastness as integrated into the presence, as always already re-shaped, re-done, by the demands of the moment. The pastness perceived in recollection is one of catachrestic palimpsestuousness.

If remembering is the appearance of relations, the apparition of links, a resurgence of connections to the past in a present moment, memory is the bridge that facilitates the connections between these two temporalities. Ricoeur notes that remembering is

> the return to awakened consciousness of an event recognized as having occurred before the moment when consciousness declares having experienced, perceived, learned it. The temporal mark of the before thus constitutes the distinctive mark of the before that constitutes the distinctive feature of remembering, under the double form of simple evocation and of the recognition that concludes the process of recall. (2006: 58)

Ricoeur suggests that for the process of remembering to arrive at a memory-image, that is, to facilitate a manifestation of an absent thing in the present, there has to be the recognition of an evocation as past. The 'distinctive mark' of the past is thus a 'temporal mark' which marks difference. The recognition of this temporal distinction is the moment that memory becomes active in that it relates between differences. The past, once evoked or evoking itself, has then to be recognized as past, recognized as 'again', its otherness faced and welcomed, before memory can transform the radical otherness of the past, the death of the present, which is lost to perception forever, into a presence in the 'awakened consciousness' again. For Henri Bergson, memory 'must constantly mingle with our perception of the present and may even take its place' (1991: 66). Memories enrich present perceptions constantly. According to Bergson, 'perceptions are undoubtedly interlaced with memories, and, inversely, memory . . . only becomes actual by borrowing the body of some perception into which it slips' (1991: 67). What characterizes the process of perception and remembering according to Bergson is thus a temporal interlacing of past and present, a borrowing, *bricolage*, catachresis. Remembering is hence not to 're-member', to put together, again, the 'members' of a body or form that was previously dis-membered. Neither is it, taking into consideration the phal-logocentric implications condensed in the word 'member', a re-empowering or de-emasculating of the past as past. 'Remembering' is the return of the past in the presence as a relational function of perception. The remembered past is thus not a re-membered body of the past; memory 'borrow[s] the body of some perception' and by relating it to the past, by marking it with the temporal mark of the before, interlaces present perception with perceptions marked as past. Memory thus always relates in the service of the present. In this context, Bergson differentiates between memory as habit and memory as recollection. The first denotes the involuntary repetition of learned or automatized actions and habits. The second involves an active search for memory-images of the past. Both types of memory relate to the past (as they must). The difference is that, in the case of habit memory, the past involves itself in the present in the form of action that is preformed bodily; in the case of memory as recollection, memory is constituted via a virtual movement back in time that yields a rep-resentation of the past transformed by present necessities and desires. I follow Ricoeur (2006: 24–36) when I now link Bergson's twofold notion of memory with Plato and Aristotle. The ancient Greeks termed the involuntary appear-ance of memory *mnēmē* and the work involved in recollection *anamnēsis*. The first term can be roughly compared to habit memory or evocation and the second may come to represent the labour of a conscious search for recollection. For Plato, birth is the inaugural moment of forgetting. When the soul enters into corporeal form, it loses all knowledge of the world of ideas (cf. Plato's *Meno* and *Phaedo*). The didactics employed by Socrates thus in fact constitute a mode of *anamnēsis*, a search for lost knowledge, a knowledge that takes the form of ideal memory, pure memory, the origin. The pastness of the past, however, makes sure that the past is always past and beyond *anamnēsis*. 'The past itself cannot be preserved by [memory], and thus it is continually subject to the process of reorganization according to the changes taking place in the frame of reference of each successive present' (Assmann 2011: 27). The aporia of the pastness of the past is supplemented by relations that result in memory-images. The becoming conscious of memories is oriented towards the present moment and present circumstances. Memories emerge according to a certain more or less overt teleology that is determined by a presence that is itself oriented teleologically towards a non-existent future. Even Bergson's habit memory is not pure repetition, pure re-enactment of the past; it is a habitual action which is adopted to serve the moment in light of influencing the future. Hence, memory always 'operates simultaneously in two directions: backwards and forward. It not only reconstructs the past but also organizes the experience of the present and the future' (Assmann 2011: 28). One of memory's main characteristics is therefore the simultaneous threefold relation to time which effectively results in a conflation of the past, the present and the future.

The indefiniteness of time in the context of memory manifests itself, for instance, in Husserl's concepts of primary and secondary memory. 'Secondary memory' denotes the retrieval and revival of past experiences. This can be involuntary or consciously desired. The term 'primary memory' denotes the persistence of moments that have just passed. Husserl calls it a 'comet's trail' (1964: 52) that trails away from the ever moving now. In this sense, it is also an involuntary form of memory, but one in which time is always in flux. The persistence or retention of primary memory cannot be located in either past, present or future. Primary memory is past, because it is no longer lived, no longer actively part of perception. But it is simultaneously still present as it persists in the comet's trail, part of a present that is itself moving towards the future, becoming the future by making it the present and becoming the past itself. In primary memory, the three temporalities of past, present and future merge inextricably. What Ricoeur states with reference to Heidegger's *Being and Time* in the context of the relation between time and narrative is true for the relation between time and memory, namely that

> there is not a future time, a past time, and a present time, but a threefold present, a present of future things, a present of past things, and a present of present things ... The words 'future,' 'past,' and 'present' disappear, and time itself figures as the exploded unit of the three temporal extases ... Yet it is always preoccupation that determines the meaning of this time. (1988: 60–1)

Memory figures the 'preoccupation that determines the meaning' of this 'exploded' temporality; memory makes present the absence of both the past and the future in that it inserts the otherness of the past into the present in order to deal with the dialectic of the desire for and anxiety about the otherness of the future. The presence thus stands between two opposing absences of past and future, and memory offers the presence of an absence to the active consciousness. It is this double absence that memory seeks to remedy and control in order to provide a foundation, a basis, for the actions of remembering and recollecting that are performed in the present and motivated towards the future. In this sense, memory functions as an antidote to chaos and indefiniteness. Although memory is itself in essence indefinite and ungrounded, it is marked by the previous, by completion which is the nature of the past. In the act of recollection, both as *mnēmē* and *anamnēsis*, notions of fixity, completion and fulfilment that the past evokes lodge themselves into consciousness, inscribing themselves into the 'exploded unity' of the threefold temporality. In this manner, memory orients and structures the present moment, providing an identity to the no-ness of the present. Identity is thus negotiated in the present by memory-relations to the past.

To base identity and, consequently, the self on the ability of recollecting memories rather than on the sameness of one's outward actions and appearance can be traced from Augustine via Hume and Locke to Husserl. Ricoeur calls this discourse the 'school of inwardness' (2006: 97). Hume, for instance, states that 'as a memory alone acquaints us with the continuance and extent of this succession of perceptions, 'tis to be considered, upon that account chiefly, as the source of personal identity' (2000: 168). Locke, in particular, binds memory to the self; the *tabula rasa* has to be filled with experiences which define the self in the form of recollect-able memories. Locke's *tabula rasa* recalls Plato's metaphor for memory introduced in the *Theaetetus*. Here Socrates proposes the following theory of memory:

> Now I want you to suppose, for the sake of argument, that we have in our souls a block of wax, larger in one person, smaller in another, and of purer wax in one case, dirtier in another; in some men rather hard, in others rather soft, while in some it is of the proper consistency ... We may look upon it then as a gift of Memory, the mother of the Muses. We make impressions upon this of everything we wish to remember among the things we have seen or heard or thought of ourselves; we hold the wax under our perception and thoughts and take a stamp from them, in the way we take the imprints of signet rings. Whatever is impressed upon the wax we remember and know so long as the image remains in the wax; whatever is obliterated or cannot be impressed, we forget and do not know. (Plato 1997d: 191c7–191e2)

The contents of memory are imprinted on the waxen surface where they remain ready to be held again 'under our perception and thoughts'. Since the substance of the wax varies from person to person, so does the capacity for memory and, conversely, the tendency to forget. Plato's concept is a simple one of storage and retrieval.[1] For Plato, memory and Being only intersect intermittently for memory is only present, actually, when it is re-called into consciousness in the service of knowledge, of the *logos*. The 'school of inwardness', on the other hand, in its desire for memory, proposes, in various ways, a constant interaction between memory and consciousness. Consciousness is experiencing, the past is the experienced; both are constantly adapted and adapting in the unceasing negotiations of memory between the past and the present consciousness which is experience:

> in being remembered, an experience becomes a different kind of experience. It becomes 'a memory' with all that this entails, not merely the consistent, the enduring, the reliable, but also the fragile, the errant, the confabulated. Each memory is unique, none is simple repetition or revival. The way that the past is relived in memory assures that it will be transfigured in subtle and significant ways. (Casey 1987: xii)

The question of the identity of memory is opened here. Memory only becomes memory, Casey argues, when it is remembered, when it, again, becomes experience, when it is re-experienced in a second and new context. Thus, at the moment when memory's identity as memory dissolves, when it becomes, again, experience, this is the moment that memory comes into itself. Memory relates to the past precisely by not being of the past. Memory becomes memory when it is no longer memory and only then is it truly memory, again. Memory that is purely of the past is silence and death, it is non-relational, the idle repetition of nothingness, a loss rather than a gain of recollection. The identity of memory is one of unfixity and iteration; its nature is 'the fragile, the errant, the confabulated', necessarily so for otherwise it could not take on the characteristics of 'the consistent, the endurable, the reliable'.

The tension between memory as retrieval and memory as experience, between death and life, can be traced in what is called 'episodic memory' and 'semantic memory', both, in their different ways, essential for the constructions of identities (cf. Tulving 1972; Gennaro 1996; and Parkin 1997). The differentiation memory experiences in these two concepts provides an opening that illuminates the positings that 'relate memory to specific horizons of time and identity' (Assmann 2010: 113). Semantic memory provides identity with facts that form the basis of identity but which are either not self-experienced or not tied to a specific spatio-temporal event. For instance, the fact – the place and time – of my birth is highly relevant for my identity, but I possess no memory of the event. The statement 'I am a teacher' is a statement of identity, but it is not tied to a single episode of my life. Semantic memory thus entails a double otherness: the otherness of the pastness of the past and, additionally and simultaneously, the fact that its content is not self-experienced, but given by the other, acquired and learned. Episodic memory, on the other hand, is defined by its self-referentiality. As the term implies, this type of memory stages lived experiences from the past to be re-experienced in the form of an integration into a person's life story, the narrative containing those past experiences that, by means of constant reiteration, guarantee the continuity of one's diachronic identity. Narrative memory is inherently episodic.[2] The events organized by episodic memory constitute the building blocks of life narratives. Within this narrative, episodes are but traces of a past continuity that blend with and co-determine the expression – the narrative speech act – of a present continuity. This latter continuity bends back upon itself for it is always only continuous with itself and must enter discontinuity with every new 'now', every new moment of presence. The sequentiality of narrative trying to construct identity constitutes a structure that incorporates episodic memory in what is, ultimately, a catachrestic fashion:

> In contrast to narratives, which unfold a (temporal) sequence of events, metaphors or the ekphrastic descriptions of images freeze or arrest the chronological flow and – due to their visual quality – evoke manifold associations, which are not reducible to narrative representation. They embody a sort of amalgam, in which past, present, and future intermingle in manifold ways. (Neumann and Nünning 2008: 11)[3]

The quotation recalls Ricoeur's notion of time as an 'exploded unity'; here, the pastness of which memory is the link becomes effaced or 'exploded' with the integration into the life narrative. The passive mode of the word 'exploded' suggests involuntariness, coercion, violence, catachresis. Hence, the relation between memory, narrative and identity is not simply one of integration. It is predominantly a process of textualization, of violent recontextualisation, translation and transformation that occurs when memory inscribes itself into the present. The relation to the past that memory enacts is one of textuality, of writing. Only as a text, as a continuous iteration of traces, can memory return, re-appear, exist and transgress simultaneously and again in the exploded unity of time. Memory *is* this simultaneous and reiterated inscription.

As with memory's relation to time where it is desired as a remedy for chaos and indefiniteness, so memory is also conceived of as medicine for the soul, the organizing medium of identity:

> Individuals possess various identities ... and equally multifarious are their communicative and cultural, in short: collective memories. On all levels, memory is an open system. Still, it is not totally open and diffuse; there are always frames that relate memory to specific horizons of time and identity on the individual, generational, political and cultural levels. Where this relation is absent, we are not dealing with memory but with knowledge. Memory is knowledge with an identity-index, it is knowledge about oneself, that is, one's own diachronic identity. (Assmann 2010: 113–14)

Memory's relational character is not only re-emphasized again here, but postulated as the *conditio sine qua non* for memory. Where there is no relation, 'we are not dealing with memory'. Memory is an 'open system', open on 'all levels', always ready to relate. Simultaneously, it is 'not totally open and diffuse'. Memory relates to language here. Like language, which is based on the arbitrariness of relations, memory is a web of supplementing traces, an unstructured structure. The open system of memory is always welcoming, always waiting to be called, calling to be re-called, conjured and conjuring itself by closing itself, de-diffusing itself, positing itself as *a* memory into the presence of consciousness. It is by closing up, by abandoning the endless potential of its boundless totality, that memory relates to the states of unexploded time, consolidating its 'own diachronic identity' which inscribes itself into the identity of presence and consciousness. When it becomes relational, memory frames its openness into 'specific horizons of time and identity'. The dialectic between openness and closure within which memory functions, and which grants a cautious stability to its consciously apprehensible representations, corresponds to the process of signification delineated by Julia Kristeva. She

> designate[s] *two modalities* of what is . . . the same signifying process. We shall call the first '*the semiotic*' and the second '*the symbolic.*' These two modalities are inseparable within the signifying process that constitutes language, and the dialectic between them determines that type of discourse (narrative, metalanguage, theory, poetry, etc.) involved; in other words, so-called 'natural' language allows for different modes of articulation of the semiotic and the symbolic . . . Because the subject is always *both* semiotic *and* symbolic, no signifying system he produces can be either 'exclusively' semiotic or 'exclusively' symbolic, and is instead necessarily marked by an indebtedness of both. (1984: 23–4, emphasis original)

The signifying process that moves in the dialectic between the semiotic and the symbolic that constitutes language and, more importantly, constitutes the *subject-in-language*, is identical to the process of recollection which moves in the dialectic of the past that, like Kristeva's *chora*, is a 'non-expressive totality' (Kristeva 1984: 25) as long as it remains non-relational and the present that lives in and through expression. Memory without relations is pre-memorial, it articulates 'a non-expressive totality' as an 'essentially mobile and extremely provisional articulation' (Kristeva 1984: 25). Non-relational memory as a non-expressive totality is the potentiality of the past, the 'movement which produces difference . . . It does not depend on any sensible plenitude, audible or visible, phonic or graphic. It is, on the contrary, the condition of such a plenitude. Although it *does not exist*, although it is never a *being-present* outside of all plenitude, its possibility is by right anterior to all that one calls sign' (Derrida 1976: 62, emphasis original). Memory thus emerges as a dynamic 'signifying system', a web of writings, a textuality from the incessant play between 'exploded' temporalities.

Memories are carriers of the supplementary trace of the uncommunicable. Baer notes that all traumatic experiences 'share the ambiguous and adverse position of being located somewhat outside memories yet within the psyche' (2000: 10). For trauma to be outside memory means for it to be outside and beyond expression. Conceptually, Baer creates a rupture here because he separates the psyche, the locus of the (perceiving) self, from memory. This is only seemingly so, however, because for traumatic experiences to be 'outside memories' does not necessarily mean they are also outside memory. If memory is the memoricity of memories, the negativity[4] from which the inscription of the past into the present that remembering is proceeds, traumatic memories, repressed past experiences, are always potentially (or hauntingly) present in the psyche. One way to conceptualize this is via the notion of the 'crypt' as envisioned by Abraham and Torok. Ellmann explains:

> [Abraham and Torok] distinguish between two modes of psychic internalization, 'introjection' and 'incorporation', the first of which augments the ego while the second splits it apart. Introjection . . . overcomes the repression of the drives awakened by the object and reabsorbs them into an expanded ego. This labour is accomplished by means of language . . . Incorporation, on the other hand, occurs when 'words fail to fill the subject's void and hence an imaginary thing is inserted into the mouth in their place'. . . . Incorporation creates a 'crypt' within the ego in which the object and the passions it aroused are held in quarantine. (2000: 230–1; Ellmann's reference is to Abraham and Torok 1994: 111–15, 127–9)

The passions and memories held in the 'crypt' are still within the psyche, but remain 'outside memories'. Since the 'crypt' partakes in the process of incorporation it shies representation and symbolization in language, it cannot enter narrative memory and remains non-functional for the individual's constructions of identity. In this sense, memory, when it is non-relational, is *choric* and as such always remains incorporated. It is only when relations are set up that the crypt is opened and memory becomes mediating. This is also why the past can never be incorporated into memories and, hence, be present in consciousness *as* past. The semiotic, to continue the parallel with Kristeva's concepts, cannot be incorporated into the symbolic *as* the semiotic. The signification process would cease to be, signification would stop, difference would be erased: the 'non-expressive' would make an appearance in the realm of symbolization, the non-symbol would present itself to be re-presented by itself and thus re-present nothing. For the same reason, the past cannot appear as itself in the present. Memory is therefore no 'incorporation' of the past in the present; rather, it is a mode of introjection where it never appears as anything but a relational trace of the pastness of the past.

It is time to recall Huyssen's phrase 'hypertrophy of memory' again. The *OED* defines 'hypertrophy' as the 'enlargement of a part or organ of an animal or plant, produced by excessive nutrition; excessive growth or development'. While Huyssen does not directly state that memory is an illness, he does imply that too much exposure to memory is harmful. At the same time, as was shown above, memory, or better: the capacity to re-call memories, is understood to be essential to the construction of personal and collective identities. A life without memory 'is without aim or direction; it spins in the void of the forgotten, a void in which one cannot even be sure of one's identity' (Casey 1987: ix). To live in forgetfulness is to be without identity; conversely, to remember is to be a self. For memory understood as the fountain of identity there is no hypertrophy, no 'incessant growth'; the excess of memory is the desired state in this context. Rather than hypertrophic, it is cornucopious in nature. The desire for cornucopious memory that is associated with the self and identity appears to stand in bipolar opposition to Huyssen's hypertrophy which comes down to a desire for forgetting. Memory, however, is both cornucopious and hypertrophic at the same time. If hypertrophy results from 'excessive nutrition', then it emerges on the basis of cornucopia. Along the same lines, the 'excessive' that defines hypertrophy is the essential characteristic of cornucopia. Memory here recalls to itself the notion of Plato's *pharmakon*. We are faced with a notion of memory which is split by its double signification as both illness and remedy, a redoubling that is itself the mark of its catachrestic nature, its continuous overflowing of its own boundaries. It is both poison and medicine, hypertrophy and cornucopia, past and present, symbolic and semiotic, all notions of memory supplementing the others. Memory is a slippery thing. Huyssen is well aware that 'as soon as we try to define it, it starts slipping and sliding, eluding attempts to grasp it either culturally, sociologically, or scientifically' (2003: 3). Derrida notes that

> when a word inscribes itself as the citation of another sense of the same word, when the textual centre-stage of the word *pharmakon*, even while it means *remedy*, cites, re-cites, and makes legible that which *in the same word* signifies, in another spot and on a different level of the stage (*poison* for example, for this is not the only thing *pharmakon* means), the choice of only one of these renditions by the translator has as its first effect the neutralization of the citational play, of the 'anagram', and, in the end, quite simply of the very textuality of the translated text. (1981: 100–1)

Memory, one can argue, is the citational play of the past in the (non-)form of un-encrypted traces of the past. These consolidate into memory-images which neutralize the very play from which they emerge. In the end, the integration, the inscription of these memory-images into the narrative life story, also consolidates – albeit only seemingly and never completely, never without fully erasing the peripheral presence of the negativity of supplementary traces encroaching on or haunting these established boundaries – the signification of said story and, through this, identity. Memory's signified is never what it is; it is but another signifier in an endless chain of potentially signifying traces. Memory is the signifier of the signifier. If, as Derrida notes, the 'advent of writing is the advent of this play' (1976: 7) of supplementation, *différance*, and memory exists in the logic of the *pharmakon*, then memory as writing, as the inscription of the trace, pays tribute to its catachrestic nature, its openness, its transgression, its enfolding and unfolding of the past, by becoming subject to a catachrestic process of curbing and containment within the frame of narrative identity. Memory memorizes the present, makes the present memorial, mnemonic, explodes consciousness into a space welcoming the absence of the past as the presence of memory. 'It adds only to replace. It intervenes or insinuates itself *in-the-place-of*; if it fills, it is as one fills a void. If it represents and makes an image, it is by the anterior default of a presence' (Derrida 1976: 145).[5] Memory adds what it brings with it, the play of traces, to replace the absence, the lack of the irrevocable past, the non-expressive, that it has brought into consciousness in the first place. 'As substitute, it is not simply added to the positivity of a presence, it produces no relief, its place is assigned in the structure by the mark of an emptiness' (Derrida 1976: 145). What has to be filled is precisely the unfillable pastness of the past and it is only ever filled with a supplementary sign. The sign of memory takes the place of the past. [6]

It is at this point that the palimpsest re-asserts or introjects itself into the present discussion on memory. In his *Suspiria de Profundis*, Thomas De Quincey establishes a connection between the power of the human brain for storing as well as recollecting the past and the notion of the palimpsest. He states:

> What else than a natural and mighty palimpsest is the human brain? Such a palimpsest is my brain; such a palimpsest, O reader! is yours. Everlasting layers of ideas, images, feelings, have fallen upon your brain softly as light. Each succession has seemed to bury all that went before. And yet in reality not one has been extinguished. (1998: 144)

De Quincey conceives of the brain as an entity which is capable of housing diverse forms and sources of knowledge ranging from purely mental ones ('ideas') to external sense impressions ('images') as well as internal 'feelings'. The 'human brain' holds on to every piece of information it has ever processed. Even though it might appear to the individual as if certain pieces of information have been lost, i.e. forgotten, De Quincey puts particular emphasis on the fact that in truth 'not one has been extinguished'. The fact that information might not be readily available to the brain or may have receded into the back of the mind, that memories may have faded or have become superimposed by some more recent impressions does not mean that these and other forms of knowledge are no longer there and impossible to resurrect. They exist in encrypted form, non-relational, but open to form relations. It is only a question of the ever-changing present circumstances and contexts for an idea to insert itself into consciousness, attaching itself, inscribing itself into the present again. In this sense, the human psyche as envisioned by De Quincey exhibits the fundamental properties of a palimpsest.[7] Before delving deeper it is best to base the discussion on a definition. The *OED* has the following entries for 'palimpsest' relevant in the current context:

1. Paper, parchment, or other writing material designed to be reusable after any writing on it has been erased. *Obs.*
2. A parchment or other writing surface on which the original text has been effaced or partially erased, and then overwritten by another; a manuscript in which later writing has been superimposed on earlier (effaced) writing.

As can be seen from these definitions, the essential quality of palimpsests is that they are textual spaces the particular nature of which is their housing of multiple empirical texts, either side by side (as glosses or marginal writings) or by means of 'overwrit[ings]' and new markings 'superimposed on earlier (effaced) writing'. By proposing the link between the brain and the inherently textual notion of (material) palimpsests, De Quincey initiates a metaphorical use of the palimpsest. Dillon explains that 'coupling "palimpsest" with the definite article "the" (for the first time in a non-specific sense), De Quincey's essay *inaugurated* . . . the substantive concept of the palimpsest' (2007: 1, emphasis original).

Memory calls simultaneously for openness as well as fixity; for an unfolding of possibilities, an 'openness on all levels', and an enfolding of these possibilities in the confines of the construction of identity and, more precisely, identity that takes the form of language in the emplotment of narrative. The logic of the palimpsest presents itself here as particularly akin to memory by virtue of its being inherently textual; its textuality is defined by containing various texts interlaced with each other, some hidden, some beyond deciphering, beyond decryption, some totally incorporated, unknown, totally other. The palimpsest

> carries within itself the trace of a perennial alterity: the structure of the psyche, the structure of the sign. To this structure Derrida gives the name 'writing.' The sign cannot be taken as a homogeneous unit bridging an origin (referent) and an end (meaning), as 'semiology,' the study of signs, would have it. The sign must be studied 'under erasure,' always already inhabited by the trace of another sign which never appears as such. (Spivak 1976: xxxix)

The palimpsest is writing. Its upper layer is always necessarily cut through by the traces of all the other writings contained within it, of 'the traces of a perennial alterity', in the same manner that consciousness is always introjected with memory-relations. Both the experiencing consciousness and the palimpsest are spaces that are inhabited by multiple writings. In 'Civilization and its Discontents', Freud states that 'if we want to represent historical sequence in spatial terms we can only do it by juxtaposition in space: the same space cannot have two different contents' (1962a: 70–1). Huyssen clearly disagrees, noting with regard to urban buildings and monuments, that 'an urban imaginary in its temporal reach may well put different things in one place: memories of what was before, imagined alternatives to what is . . . The strong marks of the present merge in the imaginary with traces of the past, erasures, losses and heterotopias' (2003: 7). In short, Huyssen ascribes to memory the ability to inscribe itself, again and again, simultaneously and differently, into the present of one and the same space. This multiple inscription of memory, super-imposed, super-inscribed onto a single scene, existing simultaneously in the exploded unity of past, present and future, denotes palimpsestuous textuality. The instant where memory and palimpsest become conjoined is in the recognition of indifferent difference. In the representation of memory, when memory has inscribed itself into the present as text, as an emplotted narrative, difference is annulled. The version of the past represented by the memory-image can no longer be anything else; it is impossible to extract from it the movements, cancellations, repressions, metonymic displacements and metaphorical condensations that were traversed in order to arrive at the expression of memory that finds its way into the narrative memory-image. Still, these movements and all their alternatives are present as absences in the final image, otherly, spectrally, palimpsestuously:

> The 'present' of the palimpsest is only constituted in and by the 'presence' of texts from the 'past', as well as remaining open to further inscription by texts of the 'future'. The presence of texts from the past, present (and possibly future) in the palimpsest does not elide temporality but evidences the spectrality of any 'present' moment which always already contains within it 'past', 'present', and 'future' moments. (Dillon 2007: 37)[8]

The iteration of traces, the play of differences, is annulled in the memory-image, but another difference is born, namely the recognition of the difference between the past and the present. The 'distinctive mark of the before' asserts itself (Ricoeur 2006: 58). By consolidating into one memory-image, the past can be recognized as past and can be differentiated from the present. Both the past and the pastness of the past exist as textualities, and both exist negatively, as potentialities, absences and presences, within a palimpsest the exploded temporalities of which are open to all levels of meaning. 'Textuality being constituted by differences and by differences from differences, it is by nature absolutely heterogeneous and composing with the forces that tend to annihilate it. One must therefore accept, follow, analyze the composition of these two forces or these two gestures' (Derrida 1981: 101). The two simultaneous gestures of difference and of the annihilation of difference that mark both textuality and the 'before' are also at the heart of both memory and the palimpsest. As Dillon notes: '"Palimpsestuousness" – a simultaneous relation of intimacy and separation – provides a model for this form, preserving as it does the distinctness of its texts, while at the same time allowing for all their essential contamination and interdependence' (2007: 3). Dillon contends that 'just as the underlying layers of palimpsests are susceptible to resurrection by the atmosphere and chemical or digital reagents, the layers of the palimpsest of the mind are ever-ready for revival and resurrection' (2007: 28). Dillon paraphrases De Quincey here, but she might also have paraphrased Freud. In 'A Note upon "The Mystic Writing Pad"' Freud compares the psychic apparatus to the 'Mystic Writing Pad', a children's toy which

> is a slab of dark brown resin or wax with a paper edging; over the slab is laid a thin transparent sheet, the top end of which is firmly secured to the slab while its bottom end rests on it without being fixed to it . . . To make use of the Mystic Pad, one writes upon the celluloid portion of the covering-sheet which rests on the wax slab. For this purpose no pencil or chalk is necessary, since the writing does not depend on material being deposited on the receptive surface . . . If we lift the entire covering-sheet – both the celluloid and the waxed paper – off the wax slab, the writing vanishes and, as I have already remarked, does not re-appear again. The surface of the Mystic Pad is clear of writing and once more capable of receiving impressions. But it is easy to discover that the permanent trace of what was written is retained upon the wax slab itself and is legible in suitable lights. Thus the Pad provides not only a receptive surface that can be used over and over again, like a slate, but also permanent traces of what has been written, like an ordinary paper pad: it solves the problem of combining the two functions *by dividing them between two separate but interrelated component parts or systems*. But this is precisely the way in which, according to the hypothesis which I mentioned just now, our mental apparatus performs its perceptual function. (1962b: 228–30, emphasis original)

Essentially, the 'Writing Pad' is a surface upon which one can write again and again. By applying pressure, marks – words – are inscribed into the surface. These marks can be erased again by lifting off the covering sheet. However, the 'permanent trace of what was written' remains imprinted upon the lower wax surface. For Derrida, Freud's use of the 'Writing Pad' as a metaphor for the psychic apparatus signifies arche-writing or the trace.[9] When the traces of the past consolidate into an emplotted memory-image, the text thus produced becomes itself a trace that becomes itinerant and may potentially be called upon, re-called again at a later time to re-inscribe itself into another presence. This process is palimpsestuous in nature; it is a process of palimpsesting, because 'any new text about the palimpsest erases, superimposes itself upon, and yet is still haunted by, other texts in the palimpsest's history. Writing about the palimpsest is a process of writing *on* the palimpsest' (Dillon 2007: 9, emphasis original). All in all, both the process of introjecting memory as well as 'the process of palimpsest production [are processes] of layering – of erasure and superimposition . . . The palimpsest is a space in which two or more texts, often different and incongruous, coexist in a state of both collision and collusion . . . the space that marks their difference' (Dillon 2007: 47). Furthermore, 'there is no necessary relationship between the texts that co-inhabit the space of a palimpsest – one text is not derived from the other, one does not serve as the origin of the other – the palimpsest does not *properly* figure the relationship between a text and its sources, including its own earlier drafts' (Dillon 2007: 47, emphasis original). The texts inhabiting a palimpsest do not necessarily relate to each other except in inhabiting the same space. They are related to each other because they reciprocally bear the mark of the other by means of their belonging to the palimpsest. Their relation is not one of origin or source, nor of cause and effect, but solely one of difference. Along the same lines, the past and the present do not necessarily share a direct link, but their boundaries are annulled through memory work. In this context, the nature of the palimpsest and of the palimpsestuous textuality which is memory, recalls, again, the notion of the crypt:

> This so-called 'underlying' layer of the palimpsest is, in fact, like the crypt: . . . The palimpsest does not conform structurally to a psychoanalysis of surface and depth, latent and manifest. The palimpsest of the mind is not structurally akin to Freud's first stratified topography of the unconscious, preconscious and conscious systems. Rather, the palimpsest presents a complex structure of cryptic incorporation . . . the palimpsest of the mind has more in common figuratively with Freud's second topography, in which the mind is haunted by the ghostly figures of the Id, the Ego and Superego. (Dillon 2007: 29)

Traces of the past that are the midwives of memory constitute a potentially endless palimpsestuous textuality that remains encrypted, in the state of incorporation as non-relational memory. Such memory in play among the cryptic layers of the palimpsest is always itinerant and ready to become introjected again into the presence, the outer, symbolized layer of palimpsestuous textuality; this latter layer takes the form of a manifest text, the emplotted memories of narrative memory. It is the recognition of difference, of heterotopias in sameness and discovery of sameness in difference that makes memory apprehensible. This is precisely the nature of the palimpsest: here, it is the recognition of the simultaneous presence of multiple texts by means of marking their individual differences. It is this movement which actually facilitates and circumscribes the palimpsest, textuality and memory, which brings these three modalities of writing together in a catachrestic fashion *as* memory, text and palimpsest. Essentially, the palimpsest constitutes an alternative way of approaching and critically engaging with memory and memory work which takes into account the nature of memory as iterant, introjecting trace.

NOTES TOWARDS A PALIMPSESTUOUS READING OF SEAMUS HEANEY'S BOG POEMS

If memory is the introjected re-fashioning of past traces as displaced memory-images in the present, the iterability of the past of memory and the spectrality associated with it retain their essences, their openness, their catachrestic palimpsestuousness in the expressions of those memory-images. Seamus

Heaney's poetry, and here particularly, I argue, those poems known as 'the bog poems',[10] lend themselves as an exemplary case of how a palimpsestuous reading of literature in the context of memory can proceed. Heaney's poetry has from the very beginning been intimately concerned with memory and relations of the past with the present such as family history, traditions, personal memories, national trauma and history. The process of introjection delineated above is, for Heaney, the poetological *raison d'être* of his writing. He sees

> poetry as divination, poetry as revelation of the self to the self, as restoration of the culture to itself; poems are elements of continuity, with the aura and authenticity of archaeological finds, where the buried shard has an importance that is not diminished by the importance of the buried city; poetry as a dig, a dig for finds that end up being plants. (1980: 41)

Poems become 'elements of continuity' via a process of 'dig[ging] for finds that end up being plants'.[11] The idea is that of an archaeological dig, of *anamnēsis*, which does not end up with a dead artifact, but a 'plant'. The metaphors of digging and of archaeology are in themselves already palimpsestuous, evoking the removal of level after level of earth, discovering heterogeneous and unrelated traces that occupy the same space. The metaphorical image of the plant gestures towards the present, a living, growing and active thing which is nevertheless not simply there, but has to be unearthed, dug out, something which is precisely not what one set out to find. Like memory, poetry, for Heaney, must elide temporalities, but its traces must in the end become subject to a *telos* that centres on the present and is facing towards the future. Poetry must simultaneously evoke 'a sensation both of arrival and of prospect, so that one does indeed seem to "recover a past" and "prefigure a future", and thereby to complete the circle of one's being. When this happens, we have a distinct sensation that . . . poetry is "strong enough to help"; it is then that its redress grows palpable' (Heaney 1996a: 9). The processes of recovering the past and prefiguring the future in the present which, for Heaney, become expressed in the poetic text, supplement the aporia of the past and the future in the present in the same way that memory does. 'As long as the coordinates of the imagined thing correspond to those of the world that we live in and endure, poetry is fulfilling its counterweighting function. It becomes another truth to which we can have recourse, before which we can know ourselves in a more fully empowered way' (Heaney 1996a: 8). This introjection of the past in the form of poetry, offers 'consciousness a chance to recognize its predicaments, foreknow its capacities and rehearse its comebacks in all kinds of venturesome ways, it does constitute a beneficent event, for poet and audience alike. It offers a response to reality which has a liberating and verifying effect upon the individual spirit' (Heaney 1996a: 2). Poetry opens consciousness up to alternatives, allows it to make iterable the fixed, discovers its nature as a palimpsest of layered textuality, de-crypts the otherwise encrypted, unmoors its supplementary traces to catachresis, to transgression, to introjection into a present writing. 'This redressing effect of poetry comes from its being a glimpsed alternative, a revelation of potential that is denied or constantly threatened by circumstances' (Heaney 1996a: 3–4).

The poem 'Tollund' expresses the palimpsestuous nature of memory, the desire for pure recollection in the face of the impossibility of that desire. The poem begins with these lines:

> That Sunday morning we had travelled far.
> We stood a long time out in Tollund Moss:
> The low ground, the swart water, the thick grass
> Hallucinatory and familiar. (1–4)

The poem fulfils the promise made in Heaney's poem 'The Tollund Man', namely that 'One day I will go to Arhus' (1). 'Tollund''s beginning thus is no beginning at all, it is not untainted presence; rather it contains within it a promise of a past promise, a promise that is absent but not unexpressed, it is expressed at another layer, in another poem, encrypted elsewhere where it hovers 'hallucinatory and familiar'. The beginning is thus no beginning, it is a response to a specific desire that has already found expression and finds expression here again, though silently: to visit the museum in Arhus to see the Tollund Man[12] who lies exposed there. However, this is precisely what the speaker of 'Tollund' does not do. Rather than to visit the Tollund Man's petrified remains in the museum, the speaker has chosen to visit the Tollund Man's actual burial place. Tollund Moss is the name of a bog near Arhus where the body of the Tollund Man was found and unearthed. Tollund Moss is a place of memory as opposed to the museum which is a place of exhibition. In visiting the bog, the speaker thus intends to visit the past. The speaker is looking for a place that expresses the past, but what he finds expressed is only the present. This is no longer a burial place. The burial place the speaker desires exists only as a semantic memory, as an otherness of and in memory. The past as past is unexpressed, non-expressive; the pastness of the past that is sought has been irrevocably lost. The desire is not to see, in the museum, the past exposed in the present, the past incorporated, traumatically, into an exhibition. Rather, the desire is to experience the past through memory, through imagination, through the mind. In the case of Tollund Moss this desire is futile as Tollund Moss exists only semantically for the speaker and, hence, as doubly other. Consequently, the experience at Tollund Moss is described as 'hallucinatory and familiar'. This vision consists of generic images of bogland: 'the low ground, the swart water, the thick grass' ('Tollund', 3), images that call forth the 'flat country nearby' ('The Tollund Man', 5), of 'The Tollund Man' which itself recalls the metaphor of digging, so insistently repeated and refashioned in 'Digging', in the line 'Where they dug him out' ('The Tollund Man', 6). The spectre of bogland and/or the poem 'Bogland' is also present in the poem. Bogland is the land of palimpsestuous memory where

> Our pioneers keep striking
> Inwards and downwards,
> Every layer they strip
> Seems camped on before.
>
> The bogholes might be Atlantic seepage.
> The wet centre is bottomless. ('Bogland', 23–8)

'Tollund' is an inherently catachrestic poem, it stages and effects a palimpsestuous textuality in which memory relates to and recalls other poems as well
as traces beyond the poems which become part of, supplement introjectively,
its itinerant palimpsestuousness. The poem's language evokes this by means
of the word 'hallucinatory'. 'To hallucinate' stems from the Latin *alucinari*
which means to 'wander in the mind'. The locus of memory where the poem is
set, Tollund Moss, is itself itinerant, based on wanderings of the mind rather
than consistency and permanence, because, for the speaker, it is a place of an
imagined past. The land itself is indeed bogland, memory land, layered and
heterogeneous. But it does not correspond, in the present, to the semantic
memory created by the speaker's desire. In fact, there is 'light traffic sound'
('Tollund', 5), 'gated farmyards' (7), a scarecrow and a satellite dish. 'It could
have been Mulhollandstown or Scribe' (17), the poet contends. It is, to use the
poem's word, a 'landscaped' countryside. The non-rural has invaded the rural
and effaces its being as bogland; it is bogland, 'camped at before' and camped
at anew, constantly and continuously. The Tollund Moss of the present, the
uppermost layer of this 'bottomless' bogland, is the only one available to the
speaker as a present experience. The past the speaker came here to experience is absent, encrypted elsewhere, buried and unexcavated. Nonetheless,
it is a familiar place, 'home beyond the tribe' (20). Home is here established
elsewhere on the basis of absence, of the non-presence of home. The difference can only be established by recalling 'home' and noting the differences.
Thus, homeliness is experienced by means of the wanderings of the mind, hal-
lucinatorily. The 'low ground, the swart water, the thick grass'; these generic,
non-descript images of bogland are so indifferent that Tollund Moss becomes
a non-locus that is set against the 'landscaped' truth of perception, a perception, of course, which only masquerades as present perception, but which is,
again, at best, re-inscribed recollection. The hallucinatory traces that surface
here culminate in the final stanza, where the speaker himself becomes a ghost,
that is, he hallucinates his own hallucinatory self: 'More scouts than strangers,
ghosts who'd walked abroad / Unfazed by light' (21–2). The speaker becomes
a self-reflexive ghostly recollection. A future past of the speaker's death and
post-mortem ghostly existence is imaginatively introjected here as a memorial
image in the poem.

The spectrality that is only alluded to at the end of this poem is given
central emphasis in Heaney's sonnet cycle 'The Tollund Man in Springtime'.
The ghostliness of the signifier 'Tollund' becomes spectral here as the Tollund

Man awakens from his exhibition case in the Arhus museum and ponders on his hallucinatory relationship with the surrounding landscape. This is the process of memory, of introjecting the present with the past, of holding in abeyance multiple text in the manner of the palimpsest. In 'The Tollund Man in Springtime' the figure of the Tollund Man becomes a metaphor for memory and its relational function, a figure of all the traces that the palimpsest of 'Tollund' organizes. Tollund is bogland, bogland is memory, and the Tollund Man is part of bogland. The experience of memory which is focalized through the spectre of the Tollund Man introjects itself into the present thus exploding sequential time. At the very beginning of the sonnet cycle the Tollund Man already speaks in the future past, saying 'Into your virtual city I'll have passed / Unregistered by scans' (Sonnet I, 1–2). His time is an unreal one, a hallucinatory, palimpsestuous one. The *OED*'s entry for 'virtual' states: 'possessed of certain physical virtues or capacities; effective in respect of inherent natural qualities or powers; capable of exerting influence by means of such qualities'. We are dealing with an entirely 'virtual' world in which the Tollund Man is a spectral presence, a virtual entity that is associated with memory linked with bogland. In the third sonnet, the world of bogland is described as a present experience rather than a recollection:

> Scone of peat, composite bog-dough
> They trampled like a muddy vintage, then
> Slabbed and spead and turned to dry in the sun –
> Though never kindling-dry the whole way through –
> A dead-weight, slow-burn lukewarmth in the flue,
> Ashless, flameless, its every smoke a sullen
> Waft of swamp-breath (1–7)

The Tollund Man, however, no longer fully belongs to this type of land. He represents the paradox of fragmentary unity in that he is both a mummified, fragmented corpse but also a resurrected, living entity. He is both artifact and plant. The Tollund Man anthropomorphizes this relationship and in doing so represents the inter-dependent relationships of the past and the present, and, simultaneously, the need of the non-expressive to take on an expressible form.

> . . . And me, so long unrisen,
> I knew the same dead weight in joint and sinew
> Until a spate-plate slid and soughed and plied
> At my buried ear, and the levered sod
> Got lifted up; then once I felt the air
> I was like turned turf in the breath of God,
> Bog-bodied on the sixth day, brown and bare,
> And on the last, all told, unatrophied. (Sonnet III, 7–14)

The Tollund Man figures the impossibility of full recollection, of completely resurrecting the past. This is expressed by the prefix 'un-' that is attached to 'risen' and 'atrophied', which is related to the 're' in that it expresses 'reversal or deprivation' (*OED*). As a bog mummy The Tollund Man is a fragment, an artifact, an iterant trace that has, literally, been catachrestically raised from the lower layers of the memorial palimpsest to emerge in the present. Once risen, on the seventh day, he is 'all told, unatrophied'. The Tollund Man has become a museum piece and it is from within these limits that his resurrection occurs, it is from and in the present that the past has to be resurrected as *a* past:

> In the end I gathered
> From the display-case peat my staying powers,
> Told my webbed wrists to be like silver birches,
> My old uncallused hands to be young sward,
> The spade-cut skin to heal, and got restored
> By telling myself this. (Sonnet IV, 3–8)

The Tollund Man, though he has physically transgressed the temporal boundaries between past and present, remains lifeless in the present, remains a dead mummified body. He remains dead, other, until he begins to re-write his identity textually, via language. In a poetic act, he is resurrected by the word, by telling himself so. Still, he emphasizes that he is 'neither god nor ghost / Not at odds or at one, but simply lost' (Sonnet I, 4–5). He is neither dead nor alive, neither past nor present. He is even beyond fragmentation and exists as what is lost, what is other. He is the other and finds the other everywhere, specifically in the 'landscaped' space encountered already in 'Tollund'. Upon re-calling himself into existence, he notes:

> I smelled the air, exhaust fumes, silage reek,
> Heard from my heather bed the thickened traffic
> Swarm at a roundabout five fields away
> And transatlantic flights stacked in the blue. (Sonnet IV, 3–8)

Upon reawakening, The Tollund Man can immediately smell and hear the other of modernity firmly and irresistibly calling him. These are fragmentary sense impressions, but they relate him to and into the present. They lead to the final lines of the cycle where the Tollund Man, having carried himself into the virtual city, 'spirited [him]self into the street', becoming the other in the other, erasing difference and going beyond the desire for pure memory.

The textual matrix that organizes and is organized by the signifier 'Tollund', the memoricity of its textuality and the textuality of its memory, can be circumscribed by the figure of the palimpsest. As Dillon notes: 'The plurality of . . . palimpsestuous textuality, constantly operates in, disrupts, and yet engenders the meaning of any text – this is the specificity of the text' (2007: 87). 'Tollund' becomes a metaphor for the relationship between desire and loss, desire for the past and loss of the past where the latter is joined with the knowledge of the impossibility of fully recovering the past. The relationship staged in these poems manifests the paradoxical nature of this relationship in a palimpsestuous manner. The spectrality of Tollund's textuality contains reflections of the past, fragments of memory that reflect the introjection of past traces into the present.

CONCLUSION

The figure of the palimpsest constitutes an alternative way of approaching and critically engaging with memory work. It is precisely the movement of catachresis which is inscribed in the figure of the palimpsest that gives it a dynamic particularly suitable for a critical engagement with memory, recollection and forgetting. Like the palimpsest, memory is catachrestic, it is the past brought into the present, displaced and other. Recollection is consequently not a simple matter of storage and retrieval, it is a dynamic process of negotiation in which temporality is elided and the past becomes itinerant. The catachrestic palimpsest is always already inscribed by the other it retains within it, the danger of misapplication, of partial being. A palimpsest is never fully there, its being is caught in-between, always becoming. Like memory, it never speaks fully, is never completely recollected. Something unspoken or unspeakable exists as a lack in memory and recollection thus always calls for the supplement to fill the lack. The whole is therefore always deferred, always in the future, constantly awaited and always arriving. While I do not presume that the palimpsest facilitates a full escape from the existing structural and historical frameworks, it de-centres established perspectives, prohibits simplified hierarchies and bipolarities, and emphasizes the iterability and spectrality of memory.

QUESTIONS FOR FURTHER CONSIDERATION

1. With reference to the notion of the *pharmakon*, consider possible multiple significations of Heaney's figure of the 'Tollund Man'.
2. Like the supplement, the 'Tollund Man in Springtime' 'insinuates itself *in-the-place-of*' into the modern world. Consider what possible absences his presence could mark.
3. Memory understood as a palimpsestuous process always contains 'traces of a perennial alterity'. In which way does Heaney's 'Tollund Man' reflect this?
4. The prefix 'un' is ubiquitous in 'The Tollund Man in Springtime' (e.g. 'unregistered', 'unrisen', 'uncallused', 'unatrophied'). How can the repeated use of this prefix be explained in the context of palimpsestuous memory?
5. How far does 'springtime' mentioned in the title of Heaney's sonnet cycle already implicitly evoke memory and the processes of palimpsesting?
6. In Heaney's poetry, the 'Tollund Man' is traditionally seen as a metaphor for a pre-historical unified European culture not yet divided by religious, specifically Christian, troubles. In "The Tollund Man in

Springtime" (Sonnet III), however, there are obvious Christian references. How would you account for this apparent contradiction?

BIBLIOGRAPHY

Abraham, Nicholas and Maria Torok (1994) 'Mourning *or* Melancholia: Introjection *versus* Incorporation', in *The Shell and the Kernel*, trans. Nicholas Rand, Chicago: University of Chicago Press.

Aristotle (1941) 'De Memoria et Reminiscentia' in *The Basic Works of Aristotle*, ed. Richard McKeon, New York: Random.

Assmann, Jan (2011) *Cultural Memory and Early Civilization*, Cambridge: Cambridge University Press.

Assmann, Jan (2010) 'Communicative and Cultural Memory', in Astrid Erll and Ansgar Nünning, eds., *Cultural Memory Studies*, Berlin and New York: de Gruyter.

Baer, Ulrich (2000) *Remnants of Song: Trauma and the Experience of Modernity in Charles Baudelaire and Paul Celan*, Stanford: Stanford University Press.

Bergson, Henri (1991) *Matter and Memory*, trans. M. N. Paul and W. S. Palmer, New York: Zone Books.

Casey, Edward S. (1987) *Remembering: A Phenomenological Study*, Bloomington: Indiana University Press.

De Quincey, Thomas (1998) 'Suspiria de Profundis', in *Confessions of an English Opium-Eater and Other Writings*, ed. Grevel Lindop, Oxford: Oxford University Press.

Derrida, Jacques (1976) *Of Grammatology*, trans. Gayatri Chakravorty Spivak, Baltimore: Johns Hopkins University Press.

Derrida, Jacques (1978a) 'Structure, Sign and Play in the Discourse of the Human Sciences', in *Writing and Difference*, trans. Alan Bass, Chicago: University of Chicago Press.

Derrida, Jacques (1978b) 'Freud and the Scene of Writing', in *Writing and Difference*, trans. Alan Bass, Chicago: University of Chicago Press.

Derrida, Jacques (1981) 'Plato's Pharmacy', in *Dissemination*, trans. Barbara Johnson, London and New York: Continuum.

Dillon, Sarah (2007) *The Palimpsest: Literature, Criticism, Theory*, London: Continuum.

Ellmann, Maud (2000) 'Deconstruction and Psychoanalysis', in Nicholas Royle, ed., *Deconstructions: A User's Guide*, Basingstoke: Palgrave.

Fauconnier, Giles (1997) *Mappings of Thought and Language*, Cambridge: Cambridge University Press.

Fluck, Winfried (2002) 'The Role of the Reader and the Changing Functions of Literature: Reception Aesthetics, Literary Anthropology, *Funktionsgeschichte*', *European Journal of English Studies* 6:3, 253–71.

Freud, Sigmund (1962a) 'Civilization and its Discontents', in *The Standard Edition of the Complete Psychological Works*, Vol. XXI, trans. and ed. James Strachey et. al., London: Hogarth.

Freud, Sigmund (1962b) 'A Note on the "Mystic Writing Pad"', in *The Standard Edition of the Complete Psychological Works*, Vol. XXI, trans. and ed. James Strachey et. al., London: Hogarth.

Gennaro, Rocco (1996) *Consciousness and Self-Consciousness*, Philadelphia: John Benjamins Publishing Co.

Heaney, Seamus (1966) *Death of a Naturalist*, London: Faber and Faber.

Heaney, Seamus (1969) *Door into the Dark*, London: Faber and Faber.

Heaney, Seamus (1972) *Wintering Out*, London: Faber and Faber.

Heaney, Seamus (1975) *North*, London: Faber and Faber.

Heaney, Seamus (1980) *Preoccupations: Selected Prose 1968–1978*, London: Faber and Faber.

Heaney, Seamus (1996a) *The Redress of Poetry*, New York; Farrar Straus Giroux.

Heaney, Seamus (1996b) *The Spirit Level*, London: Faber and Faber.

Heaney, Seamus (2006) *District and Circle*, New York: Farrar, Straus and Giroux.

Heidegger, Martin (2008) *Being and Time*, trans. John MacQuarrie and Edward Robinson, New York: Harper Perennial.

Hume, David (2000) *A Treatise of Human Nature*, ed. David Fate Norton and Mary J. Norton, Oxford: Oxford University Press.

Husserl, Edmund (1964) *The Phenomenology of Internal Time-Consciousness*, trans. J. S. Churchill, Bloomington: Indiana University Press.

Huyssen, Andreas (2003) *Present Pasts: Urban Palimpsests and the Politics of Memory*, Stanford: Stanford University Press.

Iser, Wolfgang (1980) *The Act of Reading*, Baltimore: Johns Hopkins University Press.

Kristeva, Julia (1984) *Revolution in Poetic Language*, trans. Margaret Waller, New York: Columbia University Press.

Lakoff, George and Mark Johnson (1980) *Metaphors We Live By*, Chicago: University of Chicago Press.

Lakoff, George and Mark Johnson (1999) *Philosophy in the Flesh: The Embodied Mind and Its Challenges in Western Thought*. New York: Basic Books.

Locke, John (1975) *An Essay Concerning Human Understanding*, ed. Peter H. Nidditch, Oxford: Clarendon.

Neumann, Birgit and Ansgar Nünning (2008) 'Ways of Self-Making in (Fictional) Narrative: Interdisciplinary Perspectives on Narrative and Identity', in Birgit Neuman, Ansgar Nünning and Bo Petterson, eds., *Narrative and Identity: Theoretical Approaches and Critical Analyses*, Trier: WVT.

The Oxford English Dictionary, Online Version, www.oed.com.

Plato (1997a) *Phaedrus*, in *Plato: Complete Works*, ed. John M. Cooper, Indianapolis: Cambridge: Hackett.

Plato (1997b) *Meno*, in *Plato: Complete Works*, ed. John M. Cooper, Indianapolis: Cambridge: Hackett.

Plato (1997c) *Phaedo*, in *Plato: Complete Works*, ed. John M. Cooper, Indianapolis: Cambridge: Hackett.

Plato (1997d) *Theaetetus*, in *Plato: Complete Works*, ed. John M. Cooper, Indianapolis: Cambridge: Hackett.

Parkin, Alan. J. (1997) *Memory and Amnesia*, 2nd edition, New York: Basil Blackwell.

Ricoeur, Paul (2006) *Memory, History, Forgetting*, trans. Kathleen Blamey and David Pellauer, Chicago: University of Chicago Press.

Ricoeur, Paul (1988) *Time and Narrative*, Vol. 3, trans. Kathleen Blamey and David Pellauer, Chicago: University of Chicago Press.

Spivak, Gayatri Chakravorty (1976) 'Preface', in Jacques Derrida, *Of Grammatology*, trans. Gayatri Chakravorty Spivak, Baltimore: Johns Hopkins University Press.

Strawson, Galen (1990) 'A Fallacy of our Age', *Times Literary Supplement*, 15 October 2004.

Tomm, Karl (1990) 'Foreword', in Michael White and David Epston, *Narrative Means to Therapeutic Ends*, New York: W. W. Norton.

Tulving, Endel (1972) 'Episodic and Semantic Memory', in Endel Tulving and Wayne Donaldson, eds., *Organization of Memory*, New York: Academic Press.

Turner, Mark (1998) *The Literary Mind: The Origins of Thought and Language*, Oxford: Oxford University Press.

White, Michael and David Epston (1990) *Narrative Means to Therapeutic Ends*, New York: W. W. Norton.

NOTES

1. This concept of memory as storage and retrieval has also become the common understanding of memory today thanks to the rise of computer and tele-technologies.

Casey tackles this, indeed, hypertrophic understanding of memory stating: 'If the past can be reduced to a dead weight, then it can be deposited in machines as just one more item of information. Our most commonly employed metaphors for memory betray this action of consignment along with a scarcely concealed denigration: "memory machine," "machine memory," "photographic memory," "memory bank," "storage system," "save to disk," "computer memory," "memory file" and so on. What is most noticeable in any such list of descriptive terms is the way in which memory is constructed by reference to an apparatus or procedure that is strictly mechanical and nonhuman in nature' (1987: 4–5). In such a context, memory is reduced to the retaining and restoration of dead information, information that remains dead even when restored to consciousness. Memory is no longer relational here; it is simply retrievable.

2. Cf., for instance, Neumann and Nünning: 'Through narrativization, heterogeneous and potentially ever-fluctuating experiences are transformed into a more or less coherent form, suggesting closure of one's life and relative stability of one's (diachronic) identity. Self-narratives bridge the temporal and cognitive gap between the former, experiencing I and the present, narrating I . . . Identity, thus seen, is not rooted in any kind of psychological continuity, it rather emerges from the relative unity of character and action imposed by the unity of narrative' (2008: 6). Cf. also Ricoeur: 'psychoanalysis constitutes a particular instructive laboratory for a properly philosophical inquiry into the notion of narrative identity. In it, we can see how the story of a life comes to be constituted through a series of rectifications applied to previous narratives, just as the history of a people, or a collectivity, or an institution proceeds from a series of corrections that new historians bring to their predecessor's descriptions and explanations . . . The same thing applies to the work of correction and rectification constitutive of analytic working-through. Subjects recognize themselves in the stories they tell about themselves' (1988: 247).

3. Cf. also: Lakoff and Johnson 1980 and 1999; Turner 1998; Fauconnier 1997; and Strawson 1990.

4. I use the concept of 'negativity' here in the sense of Iser and Fluck: 'Negativity as unformulated constituent of the text makes it possible to experience something which is not literally presented. Because it is absent, it has an unlimited negating potential. In this sense, it is the negation of negation. It is negation in principle, because it is not restricted to those norms, meanings, and forms of organization we would like to negate' (Fluck 2002: 259). 'In this way, negativity not only shows that it is not negative, since it constantly lures absence into presence: While continually subverting the presence, negativity, in fact, changes it into a carrier of absence of which we would not otherwise know anything' (Iser 1980: 230).

5. Cf. here also Casey who, in the context of commemoration, wonders whether the presence of textual elements in commemorative practices might 'supplement ritual . . . in Derrida's more radical sense of being the very condition for that which it is supplementing' (1987: 232).

6. On the nature of memory as sign, cf. Assmann: 'Just as thinking is abstract, remembering is concrete. Ideas must take on a form that is imaginable before they can find their way into memory, and so we have an indissoluble merging of idea and image' (2011: 23–4).

7. De Quincey's palimpsest of the mind finds itself in a palimpsestuous relationship with Plato's wax tablet, Locke's *tabula rasa*, and Freud's 'Mystic Writing Pad'.

8. Cf. also the following explanation by Dillon: 'the palimpsest . . . has a double import. It contains within its structure and its definition both the wearing away of "original" meaning . . . and the productive creativity that results from that erasure. Literal palimpsests were created by process [*sic*] of erasure that enabled a subsequent productivity; the concept of the palimpsest – which is at play in literary, critical and theoretical discourse subsequent to De Quincey – is a philosophical concept

that has emerged from an erasure of it "literal" or "proper" meaning. At the same time, the concept of the palimpsest, by its very meaning, constantly draws one's attention to the partiality of that erasure and to the persistent presence within the concept of the palimpsest of its "original" meaning, the palaeographic palimpsest. Moreover, as a metaphor for metaphor, the palimpsest embodies a reminder that metaphor itself is a metaphorical concept' (2007: 54).

9. Derrida sees Freud as a precursor of his own understanding of the trace: 'The irreducibility of the "effect of deferral" – such, no doubt, is Freud's discovery. Freud exploits this discovery in its ultimate consequences, beyond the psychoanalysis of the individual, and he thought that the history of culture ought to confirm it' (1978b: 203).

10. Originally, the following poems: 'The Tollund Man' (Heaney 1972), 'Nerthus' (Heaney 1972), 'Come to the Bower' (Heaney 1972), 'The Grauballe Man' (Heaney 1975), 'Bog Queen' (Heaney 1975), 'Punishment' (Heaney 1975), 'Strange Fruit' (Heaney 1975) and 'Kinship' (Heaney 1975). To these have to be added 'Tollund' (Heaney 1996) as well as 'The Tollund Man in Springtime' (Heaney 2006) and, thematically, 'Bogland' (Heaney 1969).

11. Cf, also: 'I had been vaguely wishing to write a poem about bogland, chiefly because it is a landscape that has a strange assuaging effect on me, one with associations reaching back into early childhood . . . So I began to get an idea of bog as the memory of the landscape, or as a landscape that remembered everything that happened in and to it . . . Moreover, since memory was the faculty that supplied me with the first quickening of my own poetry, I had a tentative unrealized need to make a congruence between memory and bogland and, for the want of a better word, our national consciousness' (Heaney 1980: 54–5).

12. 'Tollund Man' is the name given to a mummified body from Iron Age times found in the bogs of Jutland. The Tollund Man appears for the first time in the poem of the same name in Seamus Heaney's 1972 volume *Wintering Out*, which, together with the subsequent volume *North*, contains the majority of the bog poems.

NOTES ON CONTRIBUTORS

Christine Berberich is Senior Lecturer in English Literature at the University of Portsmouth. Her research has two distinct specialisms. For the past decade she has worked on literary and cultural representations of English national identity. Apart from her book on *The Image of the English Gentleman in Twentieth-Century Literature* (2007), she has published widely on Englishness in contemporary literature, as well as co-edited a book on *These Englands: A Conversation on National Identity* (2011). She is now focusing more specifically on the relation between 'Englishness' and 'landscape', here in particular the 'affective' nature of landscape in the formation of a specific national identity. She recently co-edited the book *Land & Identity: Theory, Memory, and Practice* (2012) and is currently co-editing *Affective Landscapes in Literature, Art and Everyday Life* (forthcoming 2015). Her new monograph project looks at the current craze for the 'Home Tour', traveling around England in order to find the self. More recently, she has also begun to work on Holocaust Studies. Her interest in particular is in contemporary fictional representations of the Holocaust and their ensuing problematics.

Torsten Caeners studied English and American Literature and Culture as well as Computational Linguistics at the University of Duisburg, Germany, from 1998 to 2004. He finished his studies with an MA thesis on the shorter poetry of the Augustan poet Dr. William King. Since then he has been teaching at the Department for Anglophone Studies at the University of Duisburg-Essen. In 2010 he finished his PhD with a thesis investigating the application of poetic writing for psychoanalytical treatment in the context of poststructuralist literary theory. Since the beginning of 2007, he additionally holds the position of Programme Coordinator for the BA/MA Anglophone Studies and the BA/MA Business Administration and Culture within the Department of Humanities. His research is focused on literary and cultural theory and contemporary poetry, and he is also interested in contemporary (science fiction) TV series as a means of social and cultural commentary.

Tom Cohen is Professor in Literary, Cultural and Media Studies at the State University of New York. His work began in literary theory and cultural politics and traverses a number of disciplines – including critical theory, cinema studies, digital media, American studies, and more recently the contemporary shift of twenty-first-century studies in the era of climate change. He has published broadly on American authors and ideology (Poe, Whitman, Melville, Faulkner, pragmatism, Morrison, among them) as well as on Greek and continental philosophy. His *Anti-Mimesis: From Plato to Hitchcock* (1994) explored the relations between close reading techniques alter the paradigms of historical representation, while *Ideology and Inscription: 'Cultural Studies' after Benjamin, de Man, and Bakhtin* (1998) examined modes of thinking cultural and interpretive politics in relation to scriptive memory. His two-volume work on *Hitchcock's Cryptonymies* explored cinema's hyperbolic links to writing, perceptual memory and representational politics. His current interests focus on how the dawning 'era of climate change' resets the protocols of twentieth-century theoretical concepts. Cohen has lectured and taught widely internationally, including assignments in China and Fulbright-sponsored work in Thailand. He has essays in forthcoming volumes or special journal issues on Nietzsche and Media, War, Digital Theory, the Materialist Spirit, The Technologies of 'The Book', Deconstruction and 'Life', among others. Book projects that are in progress include a study of Faulkner, 'race' and technics (titled *Catafalque*); a monograph on the Brazilian director Jorge Padilha's *Bus 174* and cinema 'after' biopolitics; and a book on the *Aporia of Travel*, a counter-narrative inquiry into temporalities and contemporary 'travel'. He is also working on a monograph on *Oil and the Image*. For 2013–15, he has been awarded a Distinguished Visiting Professorship by Shanghai Municipality.

Claire Colebrook is Edwin Erle Sparks Professor of English at Penn State University. She has published books on philosophy, poetry and literary theory. Her most recent book is *Death of the Posthuman: Essays on Extinction* (2014).

Jennifer Cooke is Senior Lecturer in English at Loughborough University. She is the editor of the book of essays *Scenes of Intimacy: Reading, Writing and Theorizing Contemporary Literature* (2013), and a special issue of *Textual Practice* entitled *Challenging Intimacies: Legacies of Psychoanalysis* (September 2013). She is the author of *Legacies of Plague in Literature, Theory, and Film* (2009) and has published articles and book chapters on contemporary poetics, modernist female writers, psychoanalysis, affect theory, life-writing and Hélène Cixous. She is also a published poet.

Sarah Gamble is a specialist in contemporary women's writing and gender theory. She has a particular interest in the work and career of Angela Carter: she is the author of *Angela Carter: Writing from the Front Line* (1997) and *Angela Carter: A Literary Life* (2005), and the editor of *The Fiction of Angela Carter: A Reader's Guide to Essential Criticism* (2001). She is also the editor of *The Routledge Companion to Feminism and Postfeminism* (2001), an extensively revised and updated edition of which is forthcoming. Current projects include a monograph on Angela Carter and the Gothic, and a study of twenty-first-century women writers, to be co-written with Professor Lucie Armitt of the University of Salford.

Kate Rigby is Professor of Environmental Humanities in the School of Languages, Literatures, Cultures and Linguistics at Monash University and a Fellow of the Australian Humanities Academy and of the Alexander von Humboldt Foundation. Her research ranges across German Studies, European philosophy, literature and religion, and culture and ecology. She is a Senior Editor of the journal *Philosophy Activism Nature*, and her books include *Topographies of the Sacred: The Poetics of Place in European Romanticism* (2004), *Ecocritical Theory: New European Approaches* (co-edited, 2011) and *Dancing with Disaster: Histories, Narratives, and Ethics for Perilous Times* (2015). Kate was a founding member of the Australian Ecological Humanities (www.ecologicalhumanities.org), the inaugural President of the Association for the Study of Literature and Environment (Australia-New Zealand) (www.aslec-anz.asn.au), and the founding Director of the Forum on Religion and Ecology@Monash.

Lynn Turner is Senior Lecturer in Visual Cultures at Goldsmiths, University of London. She publishes on deconstruction and animals, sexuality, feminism, film and science fiction. She is the editor of *The Animal Question in Deconstruction* (2013), co-author of *Visual Cultures As . . . Recollection* (2013, with Astrid Schmetterling), and co-editor of *The Edinburgh Companion to Animal Studies* (2016, with Undine Sellbach and Ron Broglio).

Phillip E. Wegner is the Marston-Milbauer Eminent Scholar in English at the University of Florida. His most recent books include *Life Between Two Deaths, 1989–2001: US Culture in the Long Nineties* (2009), *Shockwaves of Possibility: Essays on Science Fiction, Globalization, and Utopia* (2014), and *Periodizing Jameson: Dialectics, the University, and the Desire for Narrative* (2014).

Roger Whitson is Assistant Professor of English at Washington State University. He is co-author (with Jason Whittaker) of *William Blake and the Digital Humanities: Collaboration, Participation, and Social Media* (2012), along with several articles on Blake, steampunk, maker culture and media archaeology. He is currently working on a second book project called *Steampunk and Alternate History: Nineteenth-Century Digital Humanities*, which explores steampunk as a literary and design practice to theorize materialist and anachronistic histories of computing.

Julian Wolfreys is Professor of English and Director of the Centre for Studies in Literature at the University of Portsmouth. Most recently, he has co-authored, with Maria-Daniella Dick, *The Derrida Wordbook* (2012), and has completed a novel, *Silent Music* (2014). He is currently working on a collection of essays focusing on a phenomenology of loss, and another on memory, loss, and the idea of place in English literature.

Kenneth Womack is Professor of English and Senior Associate Dean for Academic Affairs at Penn State University's Altoona College. He is the author or editor of numerous books, including *Long and Winding Roads: The Evolving Artistry of the Beatles* (2007) and the *Cambridge Companion to the Beatles* (2009). He is also the author of three award-winning novels, including *John Doe No. 2 and the Dreamland Motel* (2010), *The Restaurant at the End of the World* (2012), and *Playing the Angel* (2013). He serves as the editor of *Interdisciplinary Literary Studies: A Journal of Criticism and Theory* and as co-editor of Oxford University Press's *Year's Work in English Studies*.

Frederick Young received his PhD in Critical Theory from the University of Florida. Before joining the faculty at the University of California, Merced, he taught at Georgia Tech and was a visiting scholar in Sweden. He has published many articles in philosophy, critical theory and art practice. He is co-editing a book of essays on animality and technics, *We Have Never Been Human*, forthcoming from Routledge. His current manuscript is on Walter Benjamin and Deleuze, exploring the intersections and interventions between philosophy and art practice.

INDEX